Research Methods in the
Social and Behavioral Sciences

Research Methods in the Social and Behavioral Sciences

Second Edition

Russell A. Jones
University of North Florida

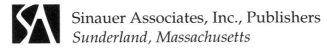

Sinauer Associates, Inc., Publishers
Sunderland, Massachusetts

Cover Art

Physicist by Ben Shahn, 1961, private collection.
Copyright © 1996 Estate of Ben Shahn.
Licensed by VAGA, New York, NY.

Research Methods in the Social and Behavioral Sciences
Second Edition

Sinauer Associates, Inc.
23 Plumtree Road
Sunderland, MA 01375 U.S.A.

FAX: 413-549-1118
Internet: publish@sinauer.com

LIBRARY OF CONGRESS CATALOGING-IN-PUBLICATION DATA
Jones, Russell A.
   Research methods in the social and behavioral sciences / Russell A.
Jones. — 2nd ed.
    p. cm.
   Includes bibliographical references and index.
   ISBN 0-87893-372-7 (pbk.)
   1. Social sciences—Research—Methodology.   2. Social psychology—
Research—Methodology.   I. Title.
H62.J62 1995
300'.72—dc20

                                                95-37162
                                                  CIP

Printed in Canada
5 4 3 2 1

To Karen

Contents

Preface

Chapter 1. Investigating Social Behavior   1

The Nature of Research   2
    BOX 1. PERSONAL EXPERIENCE IS SUGGESTIVE,
        NOT CONCLUSIVE   4
Meaning, Intentions, and Behavior   5
    The Complex Nature of Behavior   5
    The Goal of Research   7
Creativity and Mental Blocks   8
    BOX 2. BLOCKS TO CREATIVE THINKING   10
    Curiosity and Sources of Ideas   11
    BOX 3. IGNORING BASE RATES   14
    Observation   15
Reliability and Validity   19
Research Strategy   21
    Multiple Hypotheses   21
    Triangulation and Replication   24
    Building and Testing Theories   28
The Ethics of Research   32
Summary   36
Recommended Readings   37

Chapter 2. Observing Social Behavior   41

Participant Observation   42
    An Example: Preserving the Self   44
    BOX 1. LEARNING THE TRICKS OF THE TRADE   45
    Where the Action Is   49

The Initial Stages   50
Field Notes and Filing   53
   BOX 2. IS A PICTURE REALLY WORTH A THOUSAND WORDS?   54
Reliability and Validity   58
Pitfalls for the Unwary   60
Psychological Pitfalls   60
Interpersonal Problems   64
Ethical Issues   65
   BOX 3. ETHICAL DILEMMAS: OBSERVING ILLEGAL AND IMMORAL
     ACTIVITY   67
When Observation Is Appropriate   68
Summary   69
Recommended Readings   71

Chapter 3. Using Observation to Test Ideas   73

People Watching   74
   BOX 1. EXPERIENCE SAMPLING: A METHOD FOR
     SELF-OBSERVATION   76
Varieties of Behavior for Observation   77
Validity   79
Avoiding Reactivity   80
Some Ethical Considerations   83
   BOX 2. COMPUTERIZED OBSERVATION IN THE WORKPLACE   83
Observational Systems   86
*An Illustration: Interaction in Mutual Help
  Groups*   86
   BOX 3. HALOS AT THE OLYMPICS?   87
Category Construction   90
   BOX 4. HOW TO SCORE INTERACTION CATEGORY 10   93
Observer Training   94
Observer Reliability   95
Summary   98
Recommended Readings   99

Chapter 4. Archival Research and Content Analysis   103

Archival Research   104
   BOX 1. ORAL HISTORIES   105
An Illustration: Threat and Authoritarianism   106
Operationalizing Concepts   110
   BOX 2. SEARCHING FOR THAT NEEDLE   112
   BOX 3. CHOOSING THE RIGHT DENOMINATOR   115
Factors Affecting Validity   116
The Ethics of Access and Use   118

BOX 4. DATA SHARING? 120
Content Analysis 121
  *Sexist Ads, Robert E. Lee, and Significant Life
    Events* 122
  Categories, Coding, and Reliability 127
  Sampling and Generalization 130
  Uses and Abuses of Content Analysis 133
Summary 134
Recommended Readings 136

Chapter 5. The Interview 139

Qualitative Interviewing 140
  Developing the Interview Guide 141
    BOX 1. NECESSARY BACKGROUND KNOWLEDGE 142
  Questions, Language, and Meaning 144
  Making Sense of It All 147
Standardized Interviewing 150
  Questions, Answers, and How People Think 151
    BOX 2. ONE PERSON'S CONSTANTLY IS ANOTHER'S HARDLY
      EVER 153
  Sequence and Context 158
  Constructing the Interview Schedule 161
  Pretesting and Interviewer Training 165
The Interview as a Social Occasion 170
Summary 170
Recommended Readings 172

Chapter 6. Survey Research 175

Why Do a Survey? 175
Sources of Error and Survey Design 177
  The Overall Plan 177
    BOX 1. THE TIP OF THE ICEBERG 178
  Sampling 180
    BOX 2. SELF-SELECTION AND BIASED SAMPLES 182
  Outlining the Research Questions 184
  Mode of Presentation 188
  Cross-Sectional versus Longitudinal Surveys 196
  Mixing Modes 198
Revise, Revise, Revise 200
Summary 201
Recommended Readings 203

Chapter 7. Quasi-Experiments and Field Experiments 205

Interventions and Naturally Occurring Changes 206

Nonequivalent Groups   207

BOX 1. THINGS ARE DIFFERENT IN THE DIELD   208

Problems in Making Causal Inferences   211

BOX 2. GETTING THE RESULTS YOU EXPECT IS NOT ENOUGH   212

Ruling Out Alternative Explanations by Design   216

BOX 3. THE HAWTHORNE EFFECT   222

Interrupted Time Series   223

An Illustration: The North Carolina Seat Belt Law   226

Some Ethical Considerations   230

Summary   232

Recommended Readings   234

Chapter 8. The Experiment   237

The Essence of the Experiment   239

Manipulation   239

BOX 1. DID IT REALLY MAKE THAT MUCH DIFFERENCE?   240

Assigning Subjects to Conditions   243

An Illustration: Stereotypes as Energy Savers   248

BOX 2. REPLICATE, REPLICATE, REPLICATE!   254

Designing What You Need   255

Some Standard and Not-So-Standard Designs   255

Setting the Stage   259

Chance and Other Alternative Explanations   263

What Experiments Can and Cannot Do for You   267

Summary   269

Recommended Readings   270

Chapter 9. Evaluation Research   273

What Is Evaluation Research?   274

*Policies, Programs, and the Need for
Evaluation*   274

BOX 1. A METAPHOR FOR EVALUATION RESEARCH?   275

What is Supposed to Be Accomplished?   277

Implementation in Complex Environments   280

Using All the Tools You Have   283

BOX 2. THE OVERSIGHT BIAS   284

Is it Really Worth It?   287

Politics in Real-World Settings   288

Multiple Constituencies   289

BOX 3. METHODOLOGY AS AN ETHICAL ISSUE   290

Mixed Motives   292

An Illustration: Respite for Caregivers   293

Summary   297

Recommended Readings   299

Chapter 10. Simulation   303

Scientific Metaphors   304
   Role-Playing   305
      BOX 1. ROLE-PLAYING AND THE MEDICAL INTERVIEW   307
   Analogue Experiments   308
   Games as Research Settings   313
      BOX 2. COORDINATING THE FLIGHT TEAM   317
Evaluating Simulations   317
   When to Simulate   318
   Validity   320
Summary   322
Recommended Readings   323

Appendix: Table of Random Numbers   325

Glossary   329

References   341

Name Index   359

Subject Index   363

Preface

For many years I worked in an unusual academic department. It was atypical in that it was made up of faculty members from a variety of different social science disciplines. To complicate things further, the major teaching responsibility of the staff was to students enrolled in a college of medicine. The research interests of department members ranged from longitudinal field studies of aging to laboratory research on xenophobia. One thing that you quickly learn to appreciate in such an environment is the diversity of the perspectives and methodologies that guide research in the social and behavioral sciences. Social behavior is complex and multidetermined, and it soon became clear to me, as I listened to my erstwhile colleagues rhapsodize about their latest research, that no one methodological approach was, by itself, adequate.

Thus, when I started work on the first edition of this book, I wanted to capture some of the excitement I had felt when I began to truly appreciate the variety of methodological approaches that can be used to study social behavior. In the methodology courses I had taken as an undergraduate and as a graduate student, there was none of that. There was, we were told, one path to truth, and its name was the laboratory experiment. Not so, of course, but if you understand that from the start, it seems to me, it will make research and its possibilities much more exciting. Introducing you to methodological diversity is what this book is all about. But the fact that there are so many methods available doesn't mean that you can just pick one at random. The best method is a function of what you are interested in finding out, and I hope to help you to develop an appreciation for the sorts of hypotheses and questions that can be most profitably investigated with each.

We shall begin with a general discussion of the cultural, situational, and personal determinants of behavior, a discussion that underlines its complex nature. That very complexity can be a fertile source of hypotheses, however, and hypothesis generation can be one of the most exciting parts of research. It is not necessary to be a genius to come up with interesting ideas for investigation. One of the major goals of the first chapter, in fact, is to demystify the whole research process. Research methods are simply procedures and techniques that will help you to obtain evidence, in as unbiased a manner as possible, on the questions of interest. The general research strategy described in

Chapter 1 (and recommended wholeheartedly) is this: When some phenomenon occurs that needs explaining, think up as many plausible explanations as possible to account for it, then devise the necessary methods for gathering evidence on the validity of those explanations. The ideal to be pursued is triangulation of measurement—obtaining evidence for the hypothesis or explanation using several different methods. Chapter 1 will try to make clear why that is a good thing to do.

Following the introductory chapter, the body of the book consists of a series of chapters each devoted to a particular research method. The basic format of all these chapters is the same. The method is defined and then illustrated with a detailed description of one or more research applications. In each case, examples have been selected that not only illustrate important methodological points but are also of interest from a substantive point of view. (There is some fascinating research being carried out on social and behavioral processes). Along with the illustrative research in each chapter, the advantages and disadvantages of each method are discussed. Thorough familiarity with the positive and negative aspects of each method is essential, for it will enable you to make intelligent choices among available methods for specific research purposes.

Individual chapters are devoted to the following methods: participant observation; nonparticipant observation; content analysis and archival research; survey research; quasi-experimentation; experimentation; evaluation research; and simulation. This ordering of the methods was intentional: we shall begin with what appears, superficially at least, to be the simplest and progress to the most complicated. This arrangement is slightly different from that in the first edition, in which the chapter on evaluation research preceded that on experimentation. Several readers pointed out that evaluation research can, and often does, make use of experimentation. Therefore, it makes sense to understand the experiment before learning about evaluation research.

About halfway through the above sequence is a general methodological chapter on the interview. This chapter follows the chapter on archival research and content analysis because some components of interviewing are basic tools of nearly all the methods discussed subsequently—including survey research, evaluation research, and, yes, even experimentation. How questions are worded, the manner of the interviewer, the setting, the respondent's motivation, and a host of other factors can affect the validity of the information obtained in any interview. Both art and science are involved, and with a little effort, both components can be mastered.

The chapter arrangement should also make clear how each method controls for some of the sources of bias that were uncontrolled in those preceding it. Unfortunately, there is no perfect method, none that is completely free of bias. That, of course, is one of the main reasons why it is important to have a variety of methods at your disposal—but more about that later.

Acknowledgments

This text has benefited greatly from the combined wisdom of several reviewers who took the time to read and comment on earlier drafts of the chapters. These include Chet Ballard of Valdosta State College, Ann Baker Cottrell of San Diego State University, Nicholas DiFonzo of Rochester Institute of Technology, Herbert Fink of SUNY College at Brockport, Robert Groves of the University of Michigan, Melvin Mark of Pennsylvania State University, and Bruce Rind of Temple University. The text has also been enhanced by the copyediting skills of Norma Roche and her work is greatly appreciated. But most of all I would like to thank the staff of Sinauer Associates. Peter Farley, my editor, has the patience of Job. He and Carol Wigg, project editor, have deftly guided this book through publication from beginning to end.

1

Investigating Social Behavior

Judging from the daily papers, research in the social and behavioral sciences appears to excite a great deal of interest. Hardly a day goes by without the results of a new survey appearing, and the commentaries of learned academicians fill the pages. We can read about everything from what's bad about our spending habits to why the divorce rate is up and SAT scores are down. Further, social scientific controversies appear to make especially good copy. Just a couple of years ago, for example, a Berkeley professor named Neil Gilbert made headlines (and talk shows) by denouncing the methodology and conclusions of an earlier survey that reported a high prevalence of date rape on college campuses (Collison, 1992). He and his conclusion—specifically, that the reported rate was greatly inflated—were, in turn, roundly castigated in the media, and such controversies about surveys of sexual behavior show no signs of disappearing (e.g., Pollitt, 1993; Lewontin, 1995). They come on the heels of a similar controversy ignited in 1987 by the publication of Shere Hite's book *Women and Love*. Based on a survey she had conducted, Hite claimed to have found that many American women were extremely unhappy with their current relationships. The problem was that within weeks of the publication of Hite's book, other polls were published (Parker, 1987) indicating that just the opposite was true. Eighty-five percent of American women were said to be so happy with their relationships that they would marry their current husbands all over again.

The reason for the interest in such topics is fairly obvious. The social and behavioral sciences deal with things that are familiar and important to us all, things that are part of our daily lives: interpersonal relations, achievement, growth and development, social structure, politics, conflict. It would be surprising if people were not interested in these things. People also have strongly held beliefs and values about many of the topics of social and behavioral research (e.g., Faludi, 1992). The very familiarity of these topics also gives a clue as to why controversies in the social and behavioral sciences appear to interest the public so much. As Judd, Kidder, and Smith (1991, p. 6) have pointed out, to the average person, social science methods seem quite ordinary. They seem similar to things that most of us do every day. After all, don't survey researchers simply ask people to answer a few questions? Don't anthropologists just hang around exotic places and write about what they see there? It may be that it is precisely because social science methods do seem so familiar that people enjoy reading about the controversies they raise. They are understandable—usually—and, what's even more important, everybody can form their own opinion about what's "right."

As we shall see in the following pages, there are indeed similarities between research in the social and behavioral sciences and our ordinary, commonsense ways of learning about the world. But there are differences as well. When it is done well, research in the social and behavioral sciences adds a new element to our naive attempts at understanding the world. It is not that it differs in kind from ordinary knowing. It differs in being more systematic about reducing the errors in our observations and in helping us control for the effects of potential biases in the ways we evaluate evidence (Ross and Nisbett, 1991). When we can show that the evidence on a topic is clear and unbiased, all opinions on that topic are not equal.

It also seems to be true that many people have an unrealistic view of "real research." You are probably well aware of the stereotype. It is perpetuated by numerous television series and old movies in which bright, attractive, but unusually intense men and women dressed in white lab coats and carrying clipboards are seen conducting crucial experiments. After carefully scrutinizing the results and discussing the serious implications of their findings in hushed tones, they reveal the new discovery to a thankful world. Thereupon, with modest smiles, they retreat to the lab to continue their quest for truth.

There are several interesting components to this fictional version of science. First, there is usually the implication that elaborate equipment is essential: banks of flashing lights, electronic paraphernalia, and five or six microcomputers. Further, the whole process is depicted as being quite formal, rather cut-and-dried. You stick the data into the magnificent machine, which analyzes and interprets them, and the truth is revealed in the form of a printout or (more dramatically) an electronic display.

The Nature of Research

In fact, nothing could be further from the truth. Research is simply not like that. It is an informal, messy-looking process. It is so different from the stereotype that it has even been suggested—somewhat facetiously—that the history of science be rated "X" (Brush, 1974) and kept from impressionable young students because it does such violence to the image of scientists as careful weighers of evidence pro and con, concerned only with being objective. As Marks (1993, p. 380) points out: "The most significant challenge to an old and entrenched view that science is the aloof, objective collection of facts involves recognizing that *people* are the ones doing science—with their own motivations, ambitions, viewpoints, prejudices and personalities."

The most important parts of research are, in fact, subjective and have little to do with elaborate quantitative analyses or expensive laboratory equipment. The essential components of research—where it begins and where it leads—have to do with observations of phenomena and the development of hunches, ideas, and questions about the hows and whys of things. Why do females generally excel in verbal skills and males in mathematics? Is it all a function of social learning? Is there a genetic component? Why do people contribute to charities? In answer to this last question, Cialdini (1993) explains that it is not all altruism. Some organizations have perfected influence tactics that elicit contributions even from those who would prefer not to give.

Once an idea, or a potential explanation, is developed for some phenomenon, the scientific approach requires that it be tested. Is it accurate? Does it account for the phenomena of interest? Research methods are the tools for finding out. They are simply techniques and skills that help you find answers to your questions, that help you check on your hypotheses. And, as we shall see in the chapters that follow, the method that you use depends to a very great extent on exactly what question you are trying to answer. But first I want to make it very clear that there is nothing mysterious about scientific research. It is simply a broad term that refers to any of a number of ways of taking a systematic approach to finding out about things. But it is important to note how the scientific approach differs from other, nonscientific endeavors. The sciences focus on relationships among empirical phenomena of the real world. The attempt is, first, to *describe* and second, to *explain* those phenomena. The social and behavioral sciences, then, focus on accurate and precise description of how and why people behave as they do. But there is more. Taking a scientific approach also requires *objectivity*. Opinions alone are not acceptable. There has to be some objective evidence.

As a process, science usually begins with a question. All of the research methods and all of the fancy equipment are simply aids for finding out answers to questions. As Pirsig (1974) put it, a mechanic who blows the horn to check on the battery is informally conducting true research. He assumes that if the battery is okay, the horn will blow. He is testing a hypothesis by putting the question to nature: Does the horn blow? The danger is that you may conclude more from your findings than is warranted. If, for example, the horn fails to blow and the mechanic thus concludes that a new battery is needed, then there is the very real possibility of money being wasted. There may simply be a loose connection between the battery and the horn. As you will see, the major value of research methods is that they help you clarify, *and be objective about*, the conditions under which you seek answers to your questions. Thus, they help you avoid concluding more than is justified from the answers you receive (Gilovich, 1991). In everyday life, the problem is that there are often many different things varying at once. Thus, when something occurs, it is difficult to know exactly what produced it. For some well-known examples of this kind of ambiguity, see Box 1.

Research on human behavior is important because it helps us to understand ourselves and others. It can also be fun, and anybody who is interested can do it. You do not have to be a genius. In fact, above a certain optimum

Box 1

Personal Experience Is Suggestive, Not Conclusive

In the last few years, a spate of advice books has appeared with detailed instructions on everything from how to lose 100 pounds to how to run a megabusiness. Most are based on the successful personal experiences of the author, who—in fact—has lost 150 pounds or run several Fortune 500 companies. One of the most popular in the latter category has been Al Neuharth's (1992) exposition of how he managed to climb to the top of the Gannett Company and launch the first general-interest national newspaper, *USA Today*, getting the best of the competition and the naysayers in his own company in the process. Neuharth's advice, of course, boils down to "Do what I did, it worked for me—it'll work for you." Maybe. An earlier version of this same story was Robert Townsend's (1984) account of how he managed to improve profits and employee satisfaction at Avis, American Express, and several other corporations. The key, according to Townsend, is a hands-on, people-oriented, participative management style. He has advice on everything from the parking lot (no reserved spaces for *anybody*) to written job descriptions (avoid them). Similarly, David Thomas (1992), the founder of Wendy's Restaurants, offers six steps for bringing back a dying business— step two is "Paint the Place"—and, again, they seemed to work for Dave, so maybe they'll work for you.

The thing to remember when reading books like these is that there is no way of knowing the extent to which *any* of the suggestions the authors make actually made a difference in their success stories, much less whether they will make a difference for you. For example, when Neuharth launched *USA Today*, there was nothing similar, that is, no nationally circulated daily paper of its type. *USA Today* filled a niche in the marketplace, and Neuharth's management strategies for getting it going may have had nothing to do with its subsequent success. Similarly, at Avis, when Townsend hired the advertising firm that eventually came up with a very successful campaign for the company ("We're #2, We try harder"), he made an agreement with the head of the firm that Avis would run whatever ads the agency recommended. And what they recommended worked. As a result, Townsend's advice about advertising firms is this: Hire a good one and then do whatever they suggest. After all, it worked at Avis.

The idea makes sense, of course. But note that Townsend really has no evidence for the conclusion that it was the advertising campaign that turned Avis's fortunes around. Simultaneously with the new advertising campaign, many other changes were being made at Avis to streamline operations, improve productivity, and hence increase profits. Therefore, advice about how to run a business based on success stories such as those of Neuharth, Thomas, and Townsend should be treated as possible hypotheses, not established conclusions. And remember, if your circumstances differ from those in which they were operating, their recommendations may not work for you. They may not have even worked for them, even though they think they did.

level—such as that of the average college student—intelligence may be less important in conducting good research than curiosity, nonconformity, and a tendency to question authority. Further, research on human behavior and social processes can be thought of as an extension and refinement of the sort of informal research that you have been doing all your life. From observing and reading, asking your friends, and conducting informal experiments, you have already learned a great deal about human behavior, and in the process you have learned a great deal about how to learn about human behavior. If you had not, you probably would not have been able to function well enough to get out of the first grade, much less into college. Thus, rather than an introduction to research methods in the social and behavioral sciences, you might want to think of this text as a guide to continuing education, or even advanced study.

Meaning, Intentions, and Behavior

The study of human behavior and social processes is, by definition, focused on people. And, as you are well aware, unless they are suffering from a major depression or have somehow been rendered temporarily unconscious, people are all too animate. They have plans, purposes, and goals. They argue and disagree. They interpret and give meanings to aspects of their worlds. Consider almost any social exchange between two people—for example, a smile or a pat on the back. What is really important is the *interpretation* of the act—what it is taken to mean—and that cannot be determined by the physical characteristics of the act alone. Whether a smile is taken as an expression of friendliness, of condescension, or of evil intent is partly a function of what Gergen (1980) referred to as the **retrospective context,** that is, those events believed to have led up to a smile. But the meaning attached to a smile is also subject to infinite revision, and those revisions are a function of the **emergent context,** that is, the events that follow the smile. What was taken for friendliness may later be seen as having been an expression of condescension. Thus, the problem of meaning, or interpretation, makes the study of human behavior both more complex and more interesting than the study of inanimate matter (Scarr, 1985).

It is also true that if you could ignore what people were trying to accomplish by behaving in particular ways—that is, if you could ignore their purposes, their plans, their motives—then research on human behavior might be quite simple. But, as any good detective will tell you, motives cannot be ignored. Quite the contrary: Discovering a motive is often the key to solving a case. Sherlock Holmes once was puzzled by a man chasing around London trying to find a Christmas goose—not just any goose, but one particular goose. Inquiry revealed that (1) the man worked in a hotel in which a large diamond had recently been stolen from a guest; (2) the man's sister ran a small goose farm not far from the hotel; and (3) several days after the theft, the man's sister had sold all her geese. Holmes began to suspect that the man was a thief who had chosen an unusual hiding place for his booty. By attributing a motive to the man, his behavior was made meaningful; needless to say, Holmes was correct. Individual purposes are important in the interpretations and explanations we generate about behavior. But there is more.

The Complex Nature of Behavior

As Ross and Nisbett (1991) point out, in trying to understand and explain behavior we need to consider not only individual goals and preferences, but also the nature of the situation to which a person is responding and how they understand or construe that situation. We must also attend to the background social and cultural context out of which the behavior emerges. On a general level, then, it seems to be the case that most explanations of human behavior have at least three components: Behavior is seen as being a function of the person, the specific situation in which the person is immersed, and the cultural context (Cronbach, 1957; Bowers, 1973; Wheeler, 1988).

It is a truism that very few situations influence everybody in the same way. Consider a restaurant or a movie. Ask 10 people what they think of a particular restaurant and you will get 10 different opinions—often with little overlap. Some people will base their evaluation on the prices, some on the quality of the food, some on the service, some on the range of selections, some on the atmosphere, some on the noise level. People react to situations differently, of course, because of who and what they are, because of what they bring to the situation in terms of past experiences, genetic endowment, expectations, preferences, and even such fleeting phenomena as whether they are having a good day or a bad day.

But people are basically rational beings, and you need to keep that in mind. They are not simply automatons that respond to situations. Typically, even apparently odd behavior has functional significance for the person; that is, it accomplishes something useful, important, or desired. It is not always easy to discover what that "something" is, but you must begin with the assumption that it can be done.

Take an example. To an outsider, the Hindu refusal to eat beef seems very odd. How can it be that those millions of cows wander around the countryside in India while famine is endemic there? Why don't the people just eat some of those cows? It comes as something of a surprise that those sacred cows have to be kept alive, at all costs, or India's rather shaky economy would collapse. According to Harris (1974, 1985), in the early 1970s India had 60 million farms. Each needed at least one pair of oxen or water buffalo as draft animals. There were only 80 million draft animals available, however—a shortage of 40 million. This shortage of draft animals was a serious threat to the Indian peasant farmer because, had he lost an ox, he would have been unable to plow and would have lost his farm. Oxen, of course, come from those sacred zebu cows, and even a skinny cow can breed.

Further, Harris pointed out that India's cattle produced 700 million tons of recoverable manure each year, about half of which was used as fertilizer and the rest as fuel for cooking. The annual thermal equivalent of the cow dung used for cooking would have been 27 million tons of kerosene, 35 million tons of coal, or 68 million tons of wood—resources that India simply did not have. Also, the cows are effective scavengers, and what they eat is usually not fit for human consumption. There is more to the story, but the point is simply that even apparently nonfunctional aspects of human behavior often have reasonable explanations. And, a "reasonable explanation" may have to take into account not only individual motives, but situational and cultural factors as well.

The Goal of Research

What, then, is the goal of research in the social and behavioral sciences? Stated very broadly, it is the development of explanatory concepts that help you understand individual behavior and social processes, concepts that help make life intelligible. As Greenberg et al. (1988) put it:

> The primary goal of basic scientific inquiry is to provide an *understanding* of the phenomena under consideration. Theories are the basis of such understanding in that they are explanations for how and why particular phenomena occur and for how they are related to other phenomena. (p. 566)

Another way of saying this is to note that good science—whether it is social, physical, or biological—is more than just piling up documented instances of empirical relationships. The census bureau does that and does it quite well. It can tell you how many people in the United States under the age of 16 live in homes with only one parent present, how many people over 65 live alone, how many households with 8 people have only one bathroom, and so on, ad infinitum. It is important information and it can indeed be useful to some social scientists, but it is not science.

The thing that distinguishes science from the mere collection of facts, then, is the search for explanations of those facts, the search for understanding. The terms *understanding, explanation,* and *theory* imply more than prediction. People could predict that the sun would rise in the east long before they understood why. The development of theoretical explanations that can integrate and make intelligible large bodies of isolated facts is the major way in which science advances.

Consider this example. For most of the twentieth century, one of the problems that has interested social scientists is the effect of the presence of others on an individual's performance. For many years, the data were very unclear. Sometimes the presence of others appeared to facilitate performance and sometimes it appeared to inhibit it. It began to seem that the only generalization one could draw was that the presence of others had an effect, even when no competition was involved. Often it was found that within the same setting, the presence of others facilitated performance on some tasks and inhibited performance on others.

However, in reviewing the pertinent research, a psychologist named Robert Zajonc (1965) discovered a single thread of consistency in the results. The learning of new responses always seemed to be inhibited by the presence of others, whereas the performance of familiar responses seemed to be facilitated by the presence of others. Zajonc argued that there is a general class of psychological processes known to increase the likelihood of dominant (or well-learned) responses. This class consists of drive, arousal, and related processes. If it could be shown that the presence of others is physiologically arousing (and it was), that would account for the findings on social facilitation of performance because arousal is known to facilitate dominant responses. But what about social inhibition? Zajonc reasoned that in ambiguous situations, or in learning situations in which the individual has not yet mastered the task, the dominant responses will usually be incorrect ones. If performance accuracy is used as the criterion, the presence of others will inhibit correct responding because their presence facilitates dominant—and in this case, incorrect—responses. Zajonc's initial formulation has been extended and refined by others (e.g., Baron, 1986), but it remains an excellent example of how an insightful theoretical development can bring order to apparent chaos. And that is what the scientific approach is all about.

So, if the goal of research is to create theories and develop explanations that help us understand human behavior and social processes, how exactly are we supposed to go about it? It is obviously one thing to be admonished to "Go Forth and Be Creative" and quite another to do it. What's involved, and why aren't we more creative than we are?

Creativity and Mental Blocks

Science is indeed a creative enterprise in which progress often consists, as in the above example, of looking at some old data in a new way. It sounds simple, and it can be. But it can also be quite difficult—particularly in the social and behavioral sciences, where much of the subject matter is at least somewhat familiar to everyone. It is as if we "know" too much sometimes and, believing that we understand, don't push ourselves to see things in a different light or at a more meaningful, theoretical level.

To be creative, of course, means to do something new, to bring something original into being, to have a different thought about the way things work. The major problem in our attempts at creativity, as VanGundy (1992) and others have pointed out, is that we often hobble our own thinking with implicit assumptions about what is and is not permissible. That is, based on our past experiences, most of us make certain assumptions about the way things are and about what sorts of explanations and answers are permissible. Typically, these assumptions serve us well, but when it comes to dreaming up hypotheses for research, or trying to be creative, they get in the way. Consider a couple of examples that VanGundy (1992, p. 64) uses to illustrate this:

1. A car is parked on a straight road facing west. A man gets into the car and begins driving. After traveling for a while, he finds that he is east of his starting point. How can this be?
2. Consider the figure below. How many squares does it contain?

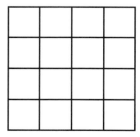

When confronted with the first problem, most people *assume* that the man will drive forward. He could just as easily have put the car in reverse and backed away, in which case the answer is simple. Also, he may have made a U-turn and struck out for the sunrise—there is nothing in the problem statement to prevent him from doing so—but, again, most people *assume* that the problem statement does not permit that solution. It does. Also, he might have just driven around the world. With the second problem, the assumption to be overcome is that the squares to be counted are non-overlapping. Then, there are sixteen small squares, plus the large outer square. There are also four 3×3 squares and nine 2×2 squares.

One particularly bothersome assumption is the idea that problems have only one right answer. Maybe they do in math, but not in the social and behavioral sciences. The difficulty is that if we assume that problems have only one right answer, then we stop looking for a better solution as soon as we find one that is at least minimally satisfactory. If we are afraid of making a mistake, we are unlikely to try anything novel. If we are convinced that we are not creative, we are indeed unlikely to be creative. For some other blocks to creativity, see Box 2.

Our ability to think creatively also suffers when we oversimplify the multidimensional and multidisciplinary nature of reality. Do not misunderstand. Simplification is important, even essential, for day-to-day existence. We do not have the time or energy to react to every person or object in all their glorious uniqueness. If we did take the time, we might never get past breakfast each morning—inspecting and tasting each cornflake, evaluating each for crispness, flavor, similarity to other cornflakes, dissimilarity to Cheerios, to oatmeal, to Rice Krispies. We would go crazy. A cornflake is a cornflake, and we have better ways to spend our time.

But simplification, while generally beneficial, can inhibit creativity. Consider the way in which your **expectations** can keep you from seeing a person or a thing in more than one way. Once you have categorized an object as a chair, say, it is hard to think of any use for it other than to sit on—or, possibly, to stand on to reach something on a shelf. With people, expectations are even worse because they often become self-fulfilling prophecies (Jones, 1977; Jussim, 1986). The way in which you categorize someone influences your behavior toward that person, which, in turn, influences their behavior—often in such a way as to validate the label that started the whole vicious circle.

As Schur (1984) notes, this process is particularly visible in our reactions to others whom we have labeled as "deviant." Their deviancy becomes for us a master status, overriding all other ways of viewing them and influencing all our reactions to them. Whether the particular deviancy is that of being a paraplegic, a psychiatric patient, or a criminal, the person is often responded to as nothing more than an "example" of the label, and his or her individual characteristics are ignored. The typical result is discomfort on both sides and a strained interaction that is taken to confirm that "they" are indeed different. Thus, you need to be doubly watchful about the biasing effects of expec-

---

Box 2

Blocks to Creative Thinking

Many people seem to assume that being creative is like having red hair: Either it's in your genes or it isn't. But, as Norins (1990) and others have pointed out, creative thinking is actually more of a skill, a skill that can be developed and improved. The way to do that, as with any skill, is to focus on your performance and consciously try to improve it.

According to Adams (1980), when you do focus on being creative, you are likely to find that there are a number of relatively subtle blocks that will impede your progress. Consider these examples:

- *Saturation:* Some objects and items of information are so familiar and commonplace that we do not pay attention to them. So, when we need to recall and use the relevant information, we cannot. For example, can you draw the face of a touch-tone phone with the letters and numbers in their proper places?
- *Inability to see other viewpoints:* Once we have defined a problem in a particular way, it becomes very difficult to see it in any other way. For example, many therapists claim that progress in marital counseling often begins with simply getting the partners to see how the other person views the situation.
- *Follow the rules:* We become so accustomed to following rules in our everyday life that we may fail to act on ideas that require breaking old rules. As an illustration, Adams describes a puzzle in which a dollar bill was to be removed from beneath a precariously balanced object without tipping the object over. The only way to succeed was to tear the dollar bill in half, but no one was willing to do that.
- *Nonsupportive environments:* New, creative ideas are often fragile, delicate things at the outset, and they can be squelched all too easily by ridicule and criticism. According to Adams, an atmosphere of honesty, trust, and support is absolutely essential if people are to make the best of their conceptual abilities and take the risk of revealing their far-out ideas to others.

There are other impediments to creative thinking, both personal and cultural. According to Adams (1980), von Oech (1983), and Norins (1990), the key to overcoming them and to being creative is to develop an attitude of playing with ideas, of being willing to try new things, and of not being afraid of looking foolish just because your idea is a little different from everyone else's.

---

tations on your thinking. They may, under some conditions (Copeland, 1993), partially induce the very reality you think you perceive.

Unfortunately, there are not just individual perceptual blocks to a clear-eyed appreciation of the world out there, but institutional ones as well. Consider the typical university or college. There are departments of psychology, sociology, political science, anthropology, education, philosophy, history, and physiology, each with a separate body of knowledge, each with a different tradition of research and theory, and each rarely looking at what the others are doing.

It is important to remember, then, that the disciplines most departments represent are arbitrary subdivisions of knowledge. Pick a topic you find interesting (sex roles, memory, group interaction). Each of these topics has been the subject of research by psychologists, anthropologists, historians, educators, physiologists, and philosophers. To assume that one of these disciplines has a better, or more valid, perspective on any of these topics is simply unjustified. And, imagine the potential for fresh new approaches if you were to cultivate the habit of looking at any topic from a variety of perspectives!

It is, of course, possible to stumble onto a creative solution to a problem, or a creative explanation for some apparently problematic behavior. But history suggests that most scientific discoveries and advances—whether in the social sciences or in the natural sciences—are not, repeat not, accidental. Somebody was looking for an answer to a question. Somebody was curious!

Curiosity and Sources of Ideas

It helps, of course, to be able to look at topics from different vantage points. It will also help if you can cultivate an open-mindedness that will allow you to take surprises seriously. But, as Beveridge (1980) points out, knowing what is "odd" or "surprising" often requires a detailed working knowledge of the field of interest. For example, for years prior to his discovery of penicillin, Sir Alexander Fleming had been looking for something to kill bacteria. Thus, when in 1927 he "happened" to pick up a petri dish containing colonies of staphylococcus bacteria that had been contaminated by a mold, he immediately understood what he saw. Something from the mold had inhibited the growth of the bacteria. Fleming made a subculture of the mold and, eventually, became the father of what many believe was the greatest single medical advance in this century.

Even when you are unable to immediately follow up observations of interest, you need to store them in question form so that later observations can be screened for their pertinence to the question. Some people make it a point to jot down things that pique their interest; they keep a notebook of things they are curious about. Charles Darwin was a master of this technique. While he was sailing toward South America on HMS *Beagle*, he noticed a large number of spiders in the rigging of the ship one day and was curious about how they could have gotten so far from land. Some weeks later at Santa Fe, he was watching a spider on top of a post when it suddenly sent out a number of threads from its spinners. These threads diverged upward from the spider's body like ribbons blown by the wind. When the spider released its grip on the post, it sailed away, borne by the wind. Darwin was not idly watching a spider on a post. He had been curious about how spiders could arrive on board the *Beagle* when it was in mid-ocean. He was seeking an answer to a specific question.

Curiosity about things is the source of all research. Darwin himself was often exasperated by people who did not share his enormous curiosity. He could not understand why many people never seemed to wonder why some springs were hot and others were cold, why there were earthquakes and volcanoes, why mountains existed in one area but not in others.

Curiosity alone may be too diffuse to be of much use; it needs to be given focus and direction. One of the best ways to do that is to make a list of possible explanations for the thing you are curious about and look for evidence on the validity of your explanations. Looking for evidence will be discussed more fully in a later section, but first, a word about generating possible explanations is in order. It is a very important part of the process because the potential explanations you begin with will determine what sort of evidence you seek, which, in turn, will very likely determine what you find. Also, as McGuire (1973) has noted, it is hardly worth developing a great methodological arsenal if the explanations you want to examine are trivial. What is not worth doing is not worth doing well.

In the following pages the terms "proposed explanation" and "hypothesis" will be used interchangeably; again, be sure to note that a simple prediction is neither. You may be able to predict many things that you do not understand. Many people find their curiosity engaged by just such phenomena, and the creative process begins when they start trying to explain them. Often curiosity is piqued, given focus, and articulated into hypotheses only as a result of confrontations with data of various sorts. Concreteness and familiarity with the thing to be explained are essential. It is very difficult to come up with good hypotheses about drug addiction if you know nothing about the life situations and styles of drug addicts, if you know nothing about the functions that drugs can serve for people, or if you know nothing of the physiological effects of drugs.

Suppose you find yourself in a situation in which something unusual occurs, something you do not understand. A careful analysis of the elements of the situation may be a fruitful source of hypotheses about the event. Such an analysis, of course, is a way of becoming intimate with the problem, a way of forcing yourself to be very precise and concrete about what actually happened. Consider this example. While eating dinner at a large New York restaurant, one of Freud's colleagues, A. A. Brill, developed the hypothesis that what appears to be telepathic communication between two people in the same setting may be explained by their simultaneously seeing something in the environment that independently triggers the same thought in each (Freud, 1938). It happened like this. As he and his wife were eating, Brill casually remarked that he wondered how a friend of theirs was liking Pittsburgh. His wife was quite surprised and claimed that she had just been thinking the same thing. For a while Brill was mystified, but careful inspection of the setting revealed a man, seated toward the rear of the restaurant, who bore a remarkable resemblance to their friend in Pittsburgh. Apparently, busy with eating and talking, Brill and his wife had not noticed the man consciously, but his visual image had triggered the same association for both of them.

Careful analysis of the components of a specific situation is conceptually very similar to the sort of intensive case study carried out by many psychiatrists and clinical psychologists during the course of psychotherapy with an individual patient. Such long-term, in-depth studies of individual lives can be fertile sources of hypotheses—potential explanations—about the forces that shape behavior.

Another important source of hypothesis formation is the use of analogy, borrowing some principle from one area of knowledge and seeing if it can be applied in another. One of the best examples of this is McGuire's (1964) work on inducing resistance to persuasion. McGuire noted that people can be immunized against many diseases by actually being given a very weak case of the disease—the principle of vaccination. Vaccination works by stimulating the body's defenses against the particular disease so that if the individual is later exposed to that disease, the defenses will be better able to combat infection. It occurred to McGuire that, by analogy, a similar principle might operate in the area of persuasion and attitude change. That is, one might use the vaccination analogy to derive hypotheses about producing resistance to persuasion. To adhere to the analogy, however, it was necessary to use beliefs that subjects had seldom, if ever, heard being attacked, because vaccination acts against diseases to which the person has not previously been exposed. McGuire found an appropriate category of beliefs to fit the analogy: cultural truisms, such as "It's a good thing to brush your teeth." Without going into all the details of McGuire's research, it should be noted that the analogy proved quite useful. One finding, for example, was that people were more resistant to changing their beliefs following a mild attack on those beliefs (vaccination) than they were following receipt of a message supporting their beliefs. The mild attack seemed to stimulate their defense of the belief. Analogies can be an excellent source of hypotheses. Original, creative research often begins with the perception of an analogy between two things previously thought to be unrelated.

A particularly intriguing source of hypotheses about human behavior is the careful dissection of some bit of folk wisdom or rule of thumb. This is a somewhat ticklish area for many social scientists. They, apparently, do not want to be contaminated by dealing with what everybody already knows. If they do deal with such things, it may be only to dredge up examples of instances in which common sense is mistaken. The motivation seems to be nothing more than a need to prove that social science is really scientific. Their hesitancy seems a little silly, however, because in the study of human behavior and interpersonal relationships, the greatest body of knowledge available is contained in the day-to-day experience of people. Hence, rules of thumb and folk wisdom are not only important, they are crucial sources of hypotheses (e.g., Fletcher, 1984). The task is to try to make such folk wisdom more precise, to try to understand its limits, to dissect it, to analyze it. There is little to be gained by merely scoffing at it.

One of the forms in which folk wisdom comes down to us is the **aphorism,** a pithy saying that is assumed to express an important truth or principle. Interesting hypotheses about behavior can often be extracted from such sayings. What, for example, is the hypothesis contained in this quotation from John Stuart Mill? "One can, to an almost laughable degree, infer what a man's wife is like from his opinions about women in general." Stated formally, the implicit hypothesis has nothing to do with husbands and wives or even with males and females. It has to do with one's perspective, and might be phrased, "Everyone assumes that their own experience is typical"—an idea that has some interesting implications (see Box 3). As an exercise, see if you can formulate the general hypotheses contained in the aphorisms listed below, all of which come from the 16th edition of *Bartlett's Familiar Quotations* (1992).

- In this world there are only two tragedies. One is not getting what you want, and the other is getting it. (Oscar Wilde)

- Beauty is in the eye of the beholder. (Margaret Hungerford)
- Thinking is a momentary dismissal of irrelevancies. (Buckminster Fuller)
- No one can make you feel inferior without your consent. (Anna Eleanor Roosevelt)

The hypotheses implicit in these aphorisms have led to some very interesting research. For example, the idea that beauty is in the eye of the beholder

---

Box 3

Ignoring Base Rates

One of the things that appears very difficult for many people to understand is that their particular experiences may not be typical of the experiences of others. That is, we often fail to recognize that the data we are exposed to, the things we see with our own eyes or hear with our own ears, may be unusual, biased, or even unique. For example, Robert Zajonc (1989) notes that several years ago he was giving a talk at Bell Telephone Laboratories—a place, as he put it, "with more Ph.D.s per square inch than any other I know" (p. 358). His talk was about some data he had collected over the years, comprising "over one million observations," that demonstrated a negative relationship between family size and intelligence: the larger the family, the lower the intelligence of the later-born siblings. After the talk, a member of his audience suggested that this simply couldn't be true because he himself came from a family of eight children, all of whom had gone on to important professional and scientific achievements. The point, as Zajonc notes, is that quite often we simply cannot trust our own observations and intuitions. Or, as Fiske and Taylor (1991) put it:

> The problem is the tendency of people to ignore general, broadly based information about population characteristics (i.e., base-rate information) in favor of more concrete anecdotal but usually less valid and reliable information. (p. 359)

There is some controversy as to why this occurs. Nisbett and Ross (1980) suggest that it may be the greater vividness and memorability of personal experience, in contrast to dry statistical summaries, that produces the effect. Or, as Fiske and Taylor (1991) suggest, it may be that people simply do not see the relevance of base rates to the judgments they make.

But relevant they are. Yet people apparently give vivid, concrete information from their own experience more weight than it deserves. When confronted with summary statistics such as those found in *Consumer Reports* or the *Surgeon General's Report on Smoking*, people often respond with:

- Yes, but I know *someone who* bought a Honda and the transmission fell out before it was a year old.
- Yes, but I know *someone who* smokes a pack a day and is 74 years old.
- Yes, but I know *someone who* dropped out of school in the ninth grade and is now making $200,000 a year.
- Yes, but I know *someone who* . . .

When someone tries to convince you with such arguments, you should ask yourself how representative their example is. Do *most people* who drop out of school in the ninth grade end up making that much?

---

stimulated some of Snyder's (e.g., 1992) work on behavioral confirmation. That is, when we have certain beliefs about others—that they are friendly, say—we tend to behave toward them in ways—warmly and generously, for example—that induce them to confirm our initial beliefs. The point here, however, is that folk wisdom remains a vast, and largely untapped, reservoir of hypotheses for those curious about human behavior.

There are many other sources of hypotheses. Conflicting and apparently contradictory research results are another. When one investigator finds that television violence does not instigate or legitimize aggression among viewers and another investigator finds that it does, a genuine intellectual puzzle is posed. What accounts for the discrepancy? Maybe the levels of violence differed in the studies. Maybe there were differences between the viewers questioned in the two studies. Maybe . . . and so it goes. Many of the possible explanations may be testable, and strategies may be devised for obtaining evidence on their plausibility.

Observation

The first step in obtaining and evaluating evidence about the hows and whys of behavior is simply to pay attention. The necessity for careful observation can hardly be overemphasized. Particularly when dealing with human behavior, we are likely to get caught in the trap of thinking we know more than we really do because so much that goes on around us is unnecessary for us to attend to during our usual day-to-day routines. We learn to ignore whole chunks of the behavior of those around us. That is typically a useful habit, but it is one you need to be able to suspend at will so that you can attend to the details of behavior when you need to. Well-trained habits of observation can be more important in research than a great store of academic knowledge.

One might argue that, in fact, all research methods are simply ways of helping you increase the precision of your observations. Slovenly habits of observation are not only unscientific, they can lead to embarrassing consequences, as illustrated in the following anecdote (Beveridge, 1957):

> A Manchester physician, while teaching a ward class of students took a sample of diabetic urine and dipped a finger in it to taste it. He then asked all the students to repeat his action. This they reluctantly did, making grimaces, but agreeing that it tasted sweet. 'I did this,' said the physician, … 'to teach you the importance of observing detail. If you had watched me carefully you would have noticed that I put my first finger in the urine but I licked my second finger.'

A serious obstacle to accurate observation is the influence of preexisting beliefs, such as the expectations discussed earlier. And, there is evidence that under certain conditions, people see and remember only what they expect to see. Madey and Gilovich (1993) make a distinction between one-sided and two-sided events that is important here. A two-sided event is one that we are likely to notice regardless of how it comes out—that is, whether the outcome is consistent or inconsistent with our expectations. The Super Bowl, for example, is a two-sided event, and we are likely to remember who won, even if we expected the other team to win. In contrast, a one-sided event is one that we are likely to attend to only if it comes out in a certain way, a way consistent with our expectations about how it will turn out. Have you developed the expectation that no matter which line you get in at the bank (or the ticket office, or the grocery checkout), it will be the slowest-moving line? If so, then if the line you pick actually moves at about the same speed as the others, you are less likely to remember that than if it takes you forever to get up to the window—which is what you expected would happen. In a series of four experiments, Madey and Gilovich were able to demonstrate that, indeed, with one-sided events, people are much better at recalling evidence consistent with their previously existing expectations than they are at recalling evidence inconsistent with those expectations. With two-sided events, expectations make much less of a difference in the recall of consistent and inconsistent evidence.

The line between errors of observation and errors of inference is a very unclear one. It is often difficult to tell where observation ends and inference begins. Seeing what we expect to see, for example, might just as well be termed an error of inference as of observation—that is, we infer that what we expected to see was really there. Whichever way you classify it, there is a very real tendency to fill in gaps in your observations based on how things normally occur or how they have occurred in your past experience. The danger, of course, is that things may change. They do not always continue on their normal course, and your past experience with the thing you are observing may not be typical.

In addition, your desires may interfere with accurate observation and inference. Consider the task of judging the logical validity of a syllogism such as this:

- Tighter gun control laws will lead to a lower murder rate.
- A lower murder rate is desirable.
- Therefore, tighter gun control laws are desirable.

It has been found that people who agree with the conclusion of such a syllogism are more likely to accept invalid arguments as logical. On the other hand, people who disagree with the conclusion are more likely to err by rejecting valid arguments. A syllogism, of course, may be perfectly logical, even if you disagree with its conclusion.

It will probably come as no surprise to you that the desires, emotions, and ambitions of people engaged in research can cloud their vision and bias their interpretations. One of the things that separates good researchers from bad ones, however, is that the good ones devise ways of checking themselves. In his autobiography, Darwin (1887/1969) noted that he had one golden rule:

> whenever a published fact, a new observation or thought came across me which was opposed to my general results, to make a memorandum of it without fail and at once; for I had found by experience that such facts and thoughts were far more apt to escape from the memory than favorable ones. (p. 123)

There are many other kinds of observation errors. You may, for example, simply miss some detail because it blends so well with its surroundings—

that is, it does not stand out sufficiently to be noticed. Trying to find a penny that has been dropped in dirt the same color as the penny is an example. This observational bugaboo is termed the inability to distinguish figure from ground, a name that comes from the fact that objects we perceive are always seen against a contrasting background. Optical illusions, such as those illustrated in Figure 1, are another source of inaccurate observations.

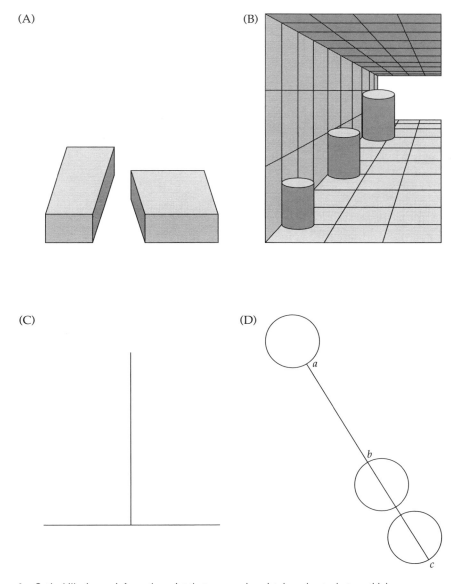

1 Optical illusions reinforce the point that we may be mistaken about what we think we see, even when the evidence is right in front of us. (A) The tops of the two boxes are identical in size and shape. (B) The three cylinders are all the same size. (C) The horizontal and vertical lines are the same length. (D) Line *ab* is the same length as the line *bc*. If you have never seen these illusions before, you might want to check them with a ruler.

Observation and inference are the bases for a pair of important concepts having to do with the development and testing of ideas: induction and deduction. **Induction** involves going from the specific to the general. For example, you might notice that most of your friends have tastes very similar to your own, that most of your father's friends appear to be about the same age, and that most college professors seem to hang around with other college professors. From these isolated observations you might formulate a general proposition something like, "People seem to be attracted to similar others." You would have exemplified the process of induction. **Deduction,** on the other hand, involves applying a general principle to a specific instance. If you have already developed the principle that similarity leads to attraction, you might predict that travel groups composed of alumni from a single university will like each other better—and, hence, have a better time on their trip—than will randomly composed groups. Induction and deduction are intricately woven into everyday life, and you use them all the time. Horse race fans who do not know much about horses typically use an inductive approach when placing their bets. They may, for example, look at how many races a horse has already won—"he's won five races so he'll win this one." Bettors who know more about horses (or like to think they do) will usually use a deductive approach. They want to know about things like the horse's bloodlines. How fast was the sire when he was racing?

Neither induction nor deduction is infallible, of course, a fact that racetrack owners will gleefully confirm. With induction, you may find that the specific instances you have examined are a peculiar, unrepresentative sample of those you could have examined. Thus, the general principle you have induced from them may not be very general after all. This difficulty will be examined in more detail in Chapter 6. With deduction, on the other hand, the general principle (fast horses sire fast horses) that you attempt to apply to a particular situation may be wrong. Even such a master of deduction as Sherlock Holmes sometimes operated with false premises. He once deduced that a man he was looking for was a man of exceptional intelligence. The basis for this deduction was his belief that a large head was a sure sign of high intelligence, and he had the man's hat, which was enormous. It is now known, of course, that head size and intelligence are not necessarily related.

Interest, curiosity, and observation are important—they are indeed the starting points for research. But they are not enough. One of the ways in which social and behavioral research goes beyond ordinary knowing is in its explicit concern for the quality of the observations we make. In everyday life, we do learn from observing, but our observations are often casual, and, because of who and what we are, they are often biased and idiosyncratic. But when we can establish that our observations are repeatable by others and that what we have inferred from them is accurate, we are well on the way to true science. Another way of saying this is that scientific understanding requires that we establish the reliability and validity of our observations.

Reliability and Validity

To say that our observations must be reliable means that, given similar circumstances, they must be repeatable. Others must be able to verify that what we claim to have seen is not a figment of an overactive imagination. Further, when our observations cannot be duplicated, they do not qualify as "evidence" for or against anything. For example, in the late 1700s, a flamboyant Viennese physician named Franz Anton Mesmer claimed to have cured blindness in a young girl by simply passing his hands over her face. A medical miracle indeed! A wave or two of the hand is even cheaper than aspirin. The only problem was that the girl was unable to see when anyone other than Mesmer was present. Needless to say, the Viennese medical society took a dim view of such hokum and decided that Mesmer might find life more pleasant in another locale. There have been many cases of what, today, we would term scientific fraud that were discovered because others were unable to repeat, or duplicate, what someone claimed to have done. But intentional scientific fraud is relatively rare, while the more general problem of ensuring that our observations are reliable is a constant one.

How do we find out whether our observations are reliable? By definition, observations are reliable if we can duplicate them. So, to establish reliability, we try to repeat whatever it is that we have observed. This is where social scientific knowledge begins to diverge from everyday knowing: with the self-conscious effort to establish the reliability of what we think we have seen. It sounds simple, but it can be a little tricky. The reason is that it is often quite difficult to specify precisely the conditions under which we have observed something. And that is what is required for an assessment of the reliability of an observation, or a test score, or a response to a survey question: precise specification of the conditions under which it was obtained.

Consider this example. Suppose that you had made an appointment to take the written, eye, and road tests necessary in order to obtain your driver's license. On the appointed day, you show up and score 90 on the written exam and 100 on the road test, but fail the eye exam miserably. Three weeks later, after having visited the optometrist and gotten your vision corrected to 20/20 with glasses, you take the three exams again. This time you score 90 on the written exam, squeak by with a 70 on the road test, and score 100 on the eye exam. What would we say about the reliability of the three tests?

First, the written examination appears to give a very *reliable* indication of your knowledge of the rules of the road—that is, you made precisely the same score on both occasions. The written exam, then, appears to have good test-retest reliability. But not necessarily! That would be true only if you actually knew the same amount both times you took the test. If you had really studied the rules during the 3-week interval, you may have known more on the second test. Then the written exam would actually be unreliable, even though you made the same score both times you took it. Superficially, the eye examination appears to be completely *unreliable*. You failed it the first time and made a perfect score the second time. But note that the rule for assessing reliability has been violated: The conditions under which the test was taken have changed. The second time you took the exam, but not the first, you were wearing glasses. Therefore we can't really say anything about the reliability of the eye exam. That leaves the road test. The first time you scored 100, the second time 70. Assuming that your driving ability had not really deteriorated in three short weeks, why the change? There are several possibilities. First, you may have inadvertently changed the conditions of the test by taking the first test in the middle of the afternoon, when traffic was light, and the second test during rush hour. Another possibility is that you had a stricter examiner the second time around, one who took off points for every maneuver that was not executed with perfect style and grace. There are other possibilities, but the point here is simply that in any given situation there may be many subtle factors that can influence the apparent reliability of our observations. Some things may make our observations appear more reliable than they really are, while other things may contribute to an appearance of unreliability. A self-conscious effort to identify both sets of factors and mitigate their effects is one of the things that separates social scientific research from the casual observations of everyday life. Establishing reliability is a first step in research, and we shall have much more to say about it in the following chapters.

The second thing that separates social scientific research from everyday knowing is an explicit concern with the validity of our observations and inferences. In everyday usage, the term *valid* means correct, or well-grounded, or sound. Thus, a valid opinion would be one that is supportable, one based on what appear to be the "facts." The use of the concept of validity in social and behavioral science research is an extension and elaboration of this common language meaning. Basically, a measure is said to be valid to the extent that it really measures what it is supposed to—nothing more and nothing less. A valid indicator of self-esteem, for example, would be one on which only those people with high self-esteem scored high and only those people who thought poorly of themselves scored low. If that occurred, we would say the measure of self-esteem had high **construct validity.**

As we shall see, however, there is more to it than this. In fact, there are several different types of validity, each of which helps us to focus on potential sources of bias in our efforts to accurately describe and explain social and behavioral events. For example, when we want to use scores on a test, such as the Scholastic Aptitude Test, to estimate how well someone will do in college, we are concerned with **predictive validity.** Performance on the SAT is compared with subsequent college grades. College grade point average in this case is the criterion—that is, the direct indicator of that which the test is designed to predict (Anastasi and Urbina, in press). The assumption is that smarter people will do better on the test and that those same people will make better grades in college. But are such assumptions accurate? The concept of predictive validity calls attention to biases in both our choice of predictors and our selection of criteria. As another example, the issue in the Hite

(1987) survey mentioned earlier is what is referred to as **external validity**. To what extent are the results obtained from the people who took the time and effort to reply to Hite's questionnaire representative of adult females in the United States? That is, can those results be generalized, or are they biased because of something odd about the people who chose to answer the questionnaire? The concept of external validity in this case calls attention to the nature of the people who responded and how they might differ from others.

There are several other forms of validity that we shall define and illustrate in the chapters that follow. Rather than asking you to memorize their names now, we shall introduce each in connection with the particular research method in which it is most problematic. That way you should be able to see more clearly how concern for each form of validity can help you to refine and improve your use of the method in question. Before moving on to the fine points of specific methods, however, we need to discuss a general research strategy that will be applicable to all.

Research Strategy

When you become curious about some aspect of human behavior, how do you proceed? There is a great deal of information about behavior and social processes already available, of course, so there are many things that you might be able to just look up in some reference book. Suppose, for example, you were interested in the frequency of abortions. Are abortions rare occurrences or not? How does the number of abortions compare with the number of live births in various parts of the country? Answers to questions like these are easily available. The Centers for Disease Control, a branch of the U.S. Public Health Service, publishes an annual summary of morbidity and mortality statistics for the United States. In 1988, there were 401 reported legal abortions for every 1000 live births in the country, but there was tremendous variation in this ratio from state to state—from 81 to 1248 abortions for every 1000 live births (U.S. Bureau of the Census, 1992).

The answers to most questions about behavior, however, are not quite so easily found. Usually what you want to know is a little more involved than a simple rate of occurrence, although that can be quite important. The more interesting questions concern the hows and whys of behavior. Why do some women and not others get abortions? Why was George Bush defeated in his bid for reelection? How can I improve my study skills? How does racial prejudice originate and how is it maintained? To answer questions like these, you may have to do some original research. The answers to these questions are likely to be quite complex, and even though some things are already known about each of them, much remains to be learned. But where do you begin?

Multiple Hypotheses

When you are curious about some aspect of behavior, whether it is your own behavior or that of someone else, one of the best ways to begin your effort to understand it is simply to sit down and write out as many plausible explanations for the behavior as you can. Make a list. It is worth forcing yourself to spend some time on this, because many people have a tendency to take the first reasonably coherent explanation that comes to mind and run with it—that is, they assume that it must be *the* explanation. The technique of listing possible explanations is not new. Over a hundred years ago, Chamberlain (1890/1965) strongly advocated the self-conscious development of every rational explanation of the phenomenon of interest, calling this strategy the **method of multiple working hypotheses**.

In addition to keeping you from jumping too quickly into some ill-advised data-chasing expedition (the scientific equivalent of the wild goose chase), taking the time to list all the plausible explanations you can think of for some behavior has other advantages. Perhaps most important is that it is likely to make clear to you that the behavior or social process in question does not have a single, simple cause. Adequate explanations of behavior usually involve several factors, and the relative contributions of these causal factors may vary depending on the circumstances. The explanation for behavior, in short, is likely to be complex (Figure 2). Such a concern for the multiple causes of behavior makes research both more interesting and more difficult. You will find that you become less concerned with isolating the cause of the behavior in question and more interested in understanding the conditions under which one cause predominates and how those conditions differ from the ones under which a second cause predominates. In other words, the same behavior may be produced by a number of different means. For example,

2 Explaining the relationship between events is essential to the advancement of understanding. (Cartoon © Sidney Harris.)

"I think you should be more explicit here in step two."

Berkowitz (1989), Dabbs and Morris (1990), and others have shown that interpersonal aggression may have many sources. Interpersonal violence may be triggered by drugs, frustration, imitation, and even certain characteristics of the victims themselves. To assume that any behavior has a single, prime cause is, usually, just plain silly.

Before you go any further, try it. Suppose that last October, the police department in your town began a home-cruiser program. Off-duty police officers were allowed to drive their patrol cars home and, as long as they paid for the gas used, could use the cars as they would their own—to go shopping, to the movies, to buy groceries, and so on. The idea was that this would make the police much more visible, with cruisers parked in residential areas and at shopping centers and, generally, on the streets. The hoped-for consequence of this increase in visibility, of course, was a decrease in crime. In January, after a 3-month evaluation of the program, the mayor called a press conference, at which it was announced that the program was a smashing success. Between October and January there had been a sizable decrease in burglaries, car thefts, muggings, and vandalism throughout the city. You read this in the newspaper the next day and it arouses your interest. Was the home-cruiser program a success? How many explanations can you think of that might account for the decrease in crime referred to by the mayor?

There are some obvious possibilities. One is that crime generally decreases in cold weather, especially outdoor crime like car thefts, muggings, and vandalism. Thus, the late fall and winter weather between October and January may deserve the credit. You also should not rule out the possibility that the mayor was right, that the ubiquitous police cars made some would-be criminals think twice about the wages of sin and forgo the crime they had contemplated. Another potential explanation is that crime had been steadily decreasing in the city, even prior to October, because of stepped-up patrols by on-duty police officers. Perhaps several new industries had opened up, providing jobs for the unemployed.

Whether you are interested in the evaluation of the home-cruiser program or the question of why you do not seem to have many friends, once you have generated a number of possible explanations the next step is the same. You use all the ingenuity you can muster to devise methods for gathering evidence on the validity of your various hypotheses—one, all, some, or none of which may turn out to be adequate. The task of the chapters that follow is to acquaint you with the variety of methods that are available. As you will see, each method has certain advantages and certain disadvantages. The purpose of acquainting you with this wealth of ways of answering questions about behavior is to help you make intelligent choices about which method or methods would be appropriate for answering a given question.

First, however, a few words about **criticism** are in order. When you are trying to develop explanations, being too critical of your ideas may hinder progress. If you stifle an idea just because it appears to be a little far-out, you may be ensuring that you will not come up with any new perspectives on the question of interest. At the stage of hypothesis generation or theoretical analysis, then, you need to encourage the free flow of ideas. A little bone-cracking, audacious thought is needed. Many people (e.g., VanGundy, 1992) have suggested strategies that might help to improve the quality of your hypotheses. Consciously try looking at the question from several points of view; consider the assumptions behind the question and extend them to the borders of absurdity; try fitting the question into some new analogies. Save your critical powers until later, because you will need them.

Specifically, you will need them when you are selecting or constructing a method to evaluate your explanations. That is the time to be critical, to look for loopholes, to play the skeptic—actually, not to play, but to be the skeptic. Will the method you select really provide an answer to your question, or will it simply help you to amass ambiguous information? Samelson (1980) has argued that at this point most people engaged in research on human behavior are not sufficiently critical. They are often too ready to accept the evidence in favor of a particular explanation if they find it congenial. That, of course, is one of the main reasons for entertaining several explanations simultaneously: It helps you to avoid the trap of becoming unduly attached to any one.

As you can probably guess, it is a difficult balance to maintain: nurturing and encouraging ideas, hypotheses, theories, but demanding rigor and precision in their evaluation. But the real purpose of all the research methods to be discussed, all the fancy equipment and paraphernalia of logic and design and sampling and measurement, is simply to make sure that we have not been led into "knowing" something that is not so (Gilovich, 1991). The following chapters will help you to hone your critical skills with respect to particular methods and learn what questions you should ask in trying to design a technique for evaluating your ideas. There are, however, a couple of general research strategies that need to be introduced before we look at specific methods, strategies that will help you to ensure that you are not misled into thinking you know something that you do not.

Triangulation and Replication

Suppose you have come up with a hypothesis that you would like to check out, one that you would like to gather some evidence on to see whether it is accurate. For example, you might be curious about the relationship between intelligence and creativity, which was mentioned at the beginning of this chapter. Specifically, you might question the implications of some of those earlier comments and hypothesize that the highly intelligent are generally more observant, less constrained by social norms, more inclined to question authority, and, thus, more creative. The problem you would immediately have to face is referred to as **operationalization.** That is, when you want to measure a concept such as "high intelligence" or "inclined to question authority" or "creativity," you must be able to point to something and say, "I am willing to take this as an indicator of that concept." To operationalize a concept, then, is to specify instances of that concept in the world around you.

There are three things to note about operationalization. First, it is imperative that you be as clear and as precise as possible about how a particular concept is being operationalized. To say that high intelligence is indicated by someone's doing well on an IQ test would not be acceptable. What does "doing well" mean, and which test are you talking about? Second, even after you have chosen a test and a score to use as an index of high intelligence, people may argue with you about the particular index you have chosen. Or the evidence may indicate that what you have chosen as an operationalization of the concept is flawed in some way. If you were to choose grade point average (GPA) as an index of intelligence, you would probably catch a lot of flak about GPA being more a function of motivation than of intelligence. Third, it should be noted, if it is not already clear, that it is possible to operationalize a concept in more than one way. How many different behaviors can you think of, for example, that might be taken as indications of a disposition to question authority?

Fortunately, the fact that such concepts can usually be operationalized in several different ways has led to a general research strategy for checking on our observations and holding our biases at least partly in check. That strategy is called **triangulation of measurement** or **multiple operationism** (Webb et al., 1981). Although the names are forbiddingly polysyllabic, the technique is really quite simple: Operationalize your concepts in several different ways and seek evidence on your hypothesis with several different methods. That is all that is involved. This is an important strategy because there is no research method without bias—as you will see in the chapters that follow—and different methods have different biases. Thus, when you can obtain evidence for your hypothesis using two or more different methods, you can rightfully have more confidence in its accuracy than when only one method is employed.

Another way of saying this is to pose it as a problem of **replication.** Suppose you were to observe some phenomenon—say, a group of people in conversation—and conclude that friends tend to be similar to one another. If, the following day, you were to observe the same people in the same situation and conclude that friends tend to be similar to one another, you would be conducting an **exact replication** of your observation. Exact replications are not very informative. If your observation of the relationship between similarity and friendly behavior was due to some peculiarity of the situation, then observing the same situation again will not eliminate the peculiarity. Perhaps the people you saw were rehearsing their parts in a play. If you can observe a relationship between similarity and friendship in several different situations, among several different kinds of people, at several different times of the year, you can be more positive that the relationship really exists. It is unlikely that all those groups of people were rehearsing for that same play. Looking for a relationship in different situations, with different subjects, under different circumstances, and using different techniques of measurement is known as **conceptual replication,** as opposed to exact replication (Jones, 1966).

For example, suppose you had developed the idea that in forming an impression of another person we often pay too much attention to the person's overt behavior and not enough attention to how that behavior has been forced by the situation, by the role that the person has been put in. The issue of interest, then, might be phrased as the extent to which the social roles we play in our day-to-day existence make us appear to have qualities and characteristics that we do not really possess. What are some of the ways in which you might investigate this question?

You might select participant observation, a method to be discussed in the following chapter. In one of the best-known and most provocative examples of participant observation, a sociologist named Erving Goffman (1961) became the assistant athletic director of St. Elizabeth's, a large psychiatric hospital in Washington, D.C. During the year that he spent there, observing and taking notes on all facets of the role of psychiatric patients, Goffman focused most of his attention on the manner in which both the institution and the staff stripped away all supports that could have enabled patients to maintain or regain a normal self-concept. He found that the hospital disrupted nearly all the activities that allow people to think of themselves as normal, responsible adults with some degree of self-determination and freedom of action. Further, this disruption begins even before the patients are fully admitted. The admission process is often what Goffman refers to as a betrayal funnel, in which the soon-to-be patients find themselves odd person out in a triad consisting of a psychiatrist, the patient's next of kin, and the patient. The next of kin, who may have suggested hospitalization, is not likely to be able to provide a realistic picture of what life in the hospital will be like and the extent to which the patient's personal freedom will be curtailed. Hence, one side effect of the admission process is that the patient is likely to become embittered about and distrustful of this person.

At each stage of the admission process, there is a further loss of adult status: Personal possessions are taken away, institutional clothes are issued, and often the patients must even request permission to go to the bathroom. Patients soon learn that they must defer to all staff members, and nearly all aspects of life on the wards are regimented and performed in the company of others. Thus, the patients are denied control over their own time and energy. Those who had been work-oriented on the outside become demoralized because there is nothing to do but sit around or engage in petty activities, such as playing cards or watching television, and these only at specified times.

To an observer, it appears that these people belong just where they are. Judging only from their behavior, they appear to be irresponsible and childlike. They have to be told what to do, they never take the initiative, and most of their activities are trivial ways of wasting time. Goffman's major point, of course, is that the patients he observed were, in effect, forced to behave as they did by the nature of the institution in which they found themselves.

There are ways other than participant observation, however, to investigate this question of whether we really fail to consider the impact of the situation in which we observe another's behavior. For example, Humphrey (1985) designed a laboratory simulation of a work environment to determine whether occupational roles influence the way in which we are perceived. Groups of five college students participated in 2-hour work sessions, with two of the subjects assigned to be managers and three assigned to be clerks. It was made clear to the subjects in each group at the outset that their individual assignments—as clerks or managers—had been determined by chance. Detailed job descriptions and necessary materials were given to each participant. During the work sessions, the clerks performed a series of "relatively low-skilled, repetitive jobs," including filing, sorting cards, filling in forms, and taking dictation from the managers. Managers, on the other hand, responded to letters from customers, made sales estimates, conferred with each other, and directed some of the work of the clerks. After the work session was over, the subjects were separated and asked to fill out a questionnaire. On the questionnaire, they were required to rate themselves and the other four people in their group on a variety of personality characteristics. In comparison to how they rated the managers in their group, subjects who had been clerks rated the other clerks in their group as lower in leadership, less intelligent, less assertive, less supportive, and likely to be less successful in the future. A very similar pattern was found in the managers' ratings; that is, managers rated the other manager in their group as a harder worker and as higher in leadership, intelligence, assertiveness, and supportiveness than the clerks in their group. As an illustration, the ratings for leadership ability and intelligence are depicted in Figure 3. The thing to remember is that the assignments of manager and clerk were determined by chance. Had the roles of manager and clerk been reversed, the new managers could easily have performed the "higher-level" tasks just as well as the ones who actually got the job. As it

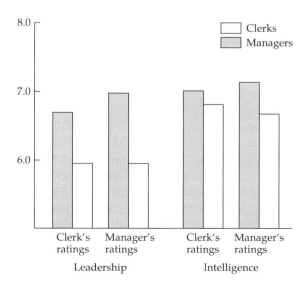

3 The influence of occupational roles: Mean ratings of the leadership ability and intelligence of clerks and managers by other clerks and managers. (Data from Humphrey, 1985.)

was, both the managers and the clerks failed to consider the self-presentational advantages offered by the managerial role.

This is not to imply that triangulation of measurement necessarily involves the use of two research methods as different as the approaches of Goffman and Humphrey. That would be ideal because the greater the difference in the methods, the less the chance that they share the same biases. It is much more common, however, for an investigator to employ variations on a single methodological theme in the attempt to operationalize a concept in different ways. For example, Langer (1983, 1989) was interested in what is referred to as the **illusion of control.** Her idea was that people often confuse situations in which the outcomes are determined by sheer chance with those in which they can exert some control over the outcome. As a result, they often behave in a chance situation as if skills and other such performance-relevant phenomena make a difference. They do not, of course. In a series of experiments, Langer operationalized this idea in several different ways. Consider two examples: In one experiment subjects drew for high card (a chance-determined event) against an opponent who was either neatly attired and apparently competent or sloppily dressed, awkward, and apparently incompetent. In a chance situation, the apparent competence of one's opponent should make no difference, but it did. Subjects were unwilling to bet as much on the draw when facing a competent opponent as they bet when facing an incompetent opponent. In a second experiment Langer found that subjects allowed to select their own tickets from a box of lottery tickets were significantly more reluctant to part with their chosen tickets than were subjects who had simply been handed a ticket from the box. All tickets had precisely the same chance of winning, but apparently the act of selecting the ticket gave subjects a feeling of greater control over the outcome—just as having an incompetent opponent did.

Thus, concepts may be operationalized in different ways, and it is good research strategy to do so. Whether you are interested in the similarity of friends, or situations that appear to coerce certain behaviors, or confusion between skill-determined and chance-determined outcomes, if you can think of a couple of different ways in which the concept could manifest itself, your research will have a firmer foundation than if you operationalized the concept in only one way.

Building and Testing Theories

The purpose of research in the social and behavioral sciences is essentially the same as the purpose of the research on your own and others' behavior that you have been doing most of your life. Both are concerned primarily with the development of concepts, explanations, hypotheses, and theories that will help to make life intelligible, that will help us to understand behavior. You know what a concept is, and in this book the terms *explanation* and *hypothesis* are used interchangeably. That leaves theories. One of the things that scares people off when someone starts discussing theory is that they envision an elaborate, hard-to-understand superstructure made up of varying amounts of hot air and gas, which—perhaps because of such a composition— rarely touches ground. Such a preconception is unfortunate and, usually, just plain wrong. A **theory** is nothing more than a possible explanation for some phenomenon. Theories can vary enormously in scope—that is, in the range of facts they seek to explain—but at bottom, a theory is purely and simply a proposed explanation. A detective who is investigating a murder and suggests that it was committed in the course of a robbery is putting forward a theory; it may or may not be accurate, but it is a theory nonetheless. Such a theory usually directs the search for evidence. If the murder was committed in the course of a robbery, it was probably not premeditated and probably not committed by the victim's spouse.

Within the broad purpose of theory development, however, there are several different aspects of the research process that will engage your attention and effort to varying degrees in various stages of research. Be forewarned that separation of these three aspects is to some extent artificial; they usually fade into each other almost imperceptibly. But definitions are in order. For convenience, these different emphases of the research process are referred to as description, theoretical elaboration, and verification. **Description** is often thought of as being the first stage of research: a careful chronicle of some situation or event, with meticulous attention to detail. In anthropology, for example, a researcher might go to live in a different culture or subculture, such as that of the fishing villages on Chesapeake Bay (Ellis, 1986), and write a detailed, descriptive account—termed an **ethnography**—of what life is like there. Ethnographies and other descriptive data, anecdotes, observations, personal experiences, readings, and any other kinds of information you may have—including the results of your own previous research —are used to begin the process of **theoretical elaboration,** which is the generation of proposed explanations to account for what has been observed (or read about, or heard). Finally, **verification** is simply the process of seeking evidence that indicates that your hunch or guess or proposed explanation is indeed correct. An illustration or two should enhance these definitions.

Some of the best examples of description are to be found in the writings of reporters and journalists such as Jan Morris (1992) and John McPhee (1990, 1993) and in biographies and autobiographies of both the famous and the infamous. A good description is very concrete and, if successful, makes the reader feel that they can almost see the scene being described. Consider how much you learn in this brief description of a bank in New York City:

> From the outside, the bank on Seventy-third Street between Amsterdam Avenue and Broadway looks like a Florentine palazzo. From the inside, it looks like the New Haven railway station, only bigger. It's an Apple Savings Bank now and there are little red apples adorning the banners inside. But the name it shows to the world, carved in stone on its outside walls, is Central Savings Bank, and only Roman numerals will do for the birth dates: Chartered MDCCCLIX Erected MCMXXVIII. Inside, the list of trustees, in carved columns, like the tablets of the

Decalogue, begins with August Belmont. The tellers work behind a foot-thick, stomach-high wall of marble, dark green with white chunks scattered through like nuts." ("Temples of thrift," 1989)

The key to good description, then, is precise and accurate detail. Careful observation of numbers, names, expressions, colors, positions, sounds, and—most difficult of all—the absence of each of these is the stuff from which descriptions are made.

Quite often the description of some social phenomenon will raise a question in your mind; when that happens, the process of theory building is likely to begin. All you have to do is speculate a little about the answer to your question and you are on your way. For example, during a year spent at the Chinese University of Hong Kong, an American social psychologist named Ladd Wheeler noticed a number of differences between Chinese and American societies. He was struck by the fact that even though in Hong Kong there are many educated, professional Chinese women, there is no feminist movement at all. Why is that? What differences between American and Chinese societies might explain the existence of a vigorous feminist movement in the former and the complete lack of one in the latter? Maybe there is a "critical mass" needed before such a movement can take hold. That is, even though Wheeler noticed many educated women, maybe there were still too few of them in Hong Kong, compared with the population as a whole. Wheeler (1988) suggests, instead, that professional women in Hong Kong did not face the same difficulties that their American counterparts do. There was, so he says, less sexual harassment in Hong Kong. That is an impression, of course, but it is a potential explanation for his observation, and, most important, it could be tested.

But what if Wheeler's observation about the lack of a feminist movement in Hong Kong was biased or inaccurate? We could develop an elaborate set of hypotheses to explain a difference between American and Chinese cultures that does not exist. And, according to Lam and Yang (1989), that difference, indeed, does not exist. That is, Lam and Yang claim that Wheeler was, quite simply, mistaken. Specifically, they note that there has been a vigorous feminist movement in Hong Kong dating back to the 1970s. The point here is not to adjudicate this dispute, but to make clear that the first step in theory building is to establish that the phenomenon we want to theorize about is real. As Merton (1987) put it:

> In the abstract, it need hardly be said that before one proceeds to explain or to interpret a phenomenon, it is advisable to establish that the phenomenon actually exists, that it is enough of a regularity to require and to allow explanation. Yet, sometimes in science as often in everyday life, explanations are provided of matters that are not and never were. (p. 2)

That is why accurate description and observation are so crucial in research.

Theory, then, must be firmly anchored in the data of the real world. If the description that piques your curiosity and gets you started spinning out possible explanations is itself a misrepresentation of reality, chances are your explanations will be totally worthless. No one needs an explanation of why males live longer than females, because females live longer than males. Also, when building theories, it is good to remember that explanations have several qualities, some of which are unnecessary but nice, and others of which are both nice and necessary. Simplicity is one of the former, and testability one of the latter. Simpler explanations are always preferable to complex ones, provided they can account for the data equally well. The simpler the explanation, the easier it is to understand and test. To test a complex, many-faceted explanation, one would have to obtain evidence on all of its components, and that, by definition, would be more difficult than gathering evidence on only one. In the early part of this century, a cartoonist named Rube Goldberg became famous for designing elaborate, intricate devices that were intended to achieve relatively simple results. His name, in fact, became a pejorative term for unnecessarily complex explanations and apparatus (Figure 4). "Less is best," then, as far as hypotheses go. It should be kept in mind, however, that

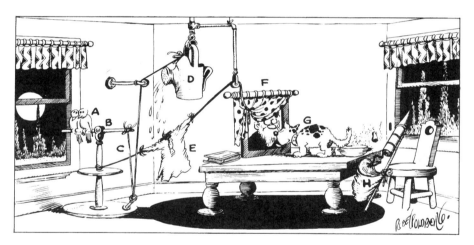

Self-Emptying Ashtray of the Future

Bright romantic moon brings love birds (A) together on perch (B), causing string (C) to upset sprinkling can (D) and wet shirt (E). Shirt shrinks, unveiling portrait (F). Dog (G), seeing portrait of his master, wags tail, brushing ashes from tray into asbestos bag (H). Smoldering butts ignite rocket (I) which carries bag of ashes out the window into the far reaches of the sky.

This should encourage young couples to start families, because the children can wear the shrunken shirts.

4　A Rube Goldberg invention. As with many overly elaborate explanations, such inventions work (if at all) only under a very precise set of circumstances. This ashtray would not work, for example, if there were no love birds in the area, if the shirt were Sanforized, if the dog did not like his master, or if the butts in the ashtray had already gone out. Similarly, overly complex explanations often do not generalize well to situations different from those that suggested them. (Cartoon by Rube Goldberg © King Features Syndicate.)

human behavior is itself complex, so you should not shy away from complex explanations when they appear warranted.

In contrast to simplicity, testability is not optional. It is a must. Hypotheses must be testable, and that is where the third aspect of the research process comes in: verification. The goal of research is to increase our understanding of behavior and social processes, and until proposed explanations are tested, they remain mere possibilities. Until they are verified, we have no way of knowing whether they add to our understanding or detract from it. The latter is, unfortunately, a real danger.

Untested explanations, especially plausible ones, may actively detract from our understanding by inducing us to believe that we know more than we really do and lulling us into complacency. After all, if we know why something occurs, it is a waste of time, energy, and money to try to demonstrate what we already know. Plausible, untested explanations about behavior do more than dampen our motivation for research, however. They may induce us to behave in ways that distort social situations and change them from what they would have been had we bothered to try to check our beliefs. Neuharth (1992, p. 274) gives an illustration of how this can work. As the head of the Gannett Company, he was inspecting a newspaper plant in Rochester, New York, when he noticed that all the women taking want ad telephone calls were white. When he asked the local manager about this, he was told: "We hired a black once. But purses started disappearing, so we never hired another." By expecting blacks to steal, the manager defined the employment situation in such a way—never hiring another black—that his stereotyped belief could go untested.

Untested assumptions and explanations for behavior, then, may so distort reality that they appear to be correct even when they are not. The research methods described in the chapters that follow will provide you with a useful bag of tools to test your hypotheses, verify your impressions, check on your hunches, and be very precise about separating what you know from what you do not know. As you will see, the best method depends on many things—including the circumstances, what you are interested in, and how much time and energy you are willing to invest. One of the characteristics that distinguishes a good researcher from a poor one is the ability to select, or, more often, design a method appropriate to the question or hypothesis of interest. This book will help you learn how to do that. Before proceeding, however, you should be alerted to a topic of considerable importance in the conduct of research. It is a topic that will be returned to again and again in the context of each of the methods.

The Ethics of Research

The need for knowledge about human behavior and social processes can hardly be overestimated. Pick up any newspaper and the acuteness of that need is likely to overwhelm you: Reports of violence, drug addiction, discrimination, poverty, international conflict, and the consequences of poor decision making and individual psychopathology fill the pages. Even the classified ads bear testimony to the consequences of divorce, social disorganization, and endemic loneliness. Further, many of the major health problems of today are caused by factors that are, or could be, under the control of individuals. For example, the National Center for Health Statistics (1988) reported that in 1986, the four leading causes of death in the United States were diseases of the heart, cancer, stroke, and accidents. Behavioral factors, from cigarette smoking to dietary choices, are known to influence each of these (Taylor, 1991).

No one would argue with the statement that we need to understand much more than we do about behavior. Research on decision making that identifies the types of errors we are most likely to make may help to improve the quality of the decisions we make tomorrow. Research on drug addiction that identifies the functions addiction serves and how it occurs may help to prevent it or, at least, help others to understand the phenomenon and react appropriately. The problem is that although we may agree that knowledge and understanding are ideals worthy of pursuit, there are other ideals that we may, at times, value even more highly. When such a conflict of ideals occurs, the issue of whether or not one should conduct the research in question may be said to pose an ethical dilemma. Quite literally, you must ask yourself, "Can this research be ethically justified?" As Kimmel (1988) has pointed out, the field of **ethics** is simply the study of our values and how they can best be realized.

On a general level, the two values most likely to conflict with the value we place on increasing our knowledge and understanding of behavior are the following: (1) you should never harm another person and (2) each individual has a right to privacy. As examples of research that highlight these conflicts, consider the two following synopses.

1. In the late 1950s and early 1960s, Berkun et al. (1962) conducted some research on psychological stress among new Army recruits at a large, undeveloped, mountainous military reservation in California. Within days after reporting for duty and prior to any training whatsoever, the men were loaded onto buses and taken to the isolated reservation. They were told merely that they were to be used to test some new "concepts of atomic-age warfare and that they would be called upon to perform individually rather than as units." In one situation, the men were taken individually to a lonely outpost and told that their job was to spot passing aircraft, identify them with the aid of a booklet provided, and relay the information via radio to the command post. While a subject was in this position he "inadvertently" became the target of artillery fire. The subject was led to believe that transmissions from his radio were not being heard, but he could hear frantic conversations between the command post and others about the idiots in artillery, conversations reinforced by a series of increasingly close dynamite explosions (incoming ar-

tillery) that went off near the subject's outpost. Numerous measures of physiological and cognitive functioning were taken as soon as the "shelling" stopped.

2. In a book called *Tearoom Trade: Impersonal Sex in Public Places*, Humphrey (1975) reported on his observations of homosexual activity in public restrooms. For a period of some months he became a watchqueen, one who stands near the doors and/or windows and warns the participants when a stranger approaches. Watchqueens are generally voyeurs, people who obtain sexual gratification by observing the sexual organs or actions of others, so Humphrey was able to witness hundreds of acts of fellatio without being expected to participate. His major interest, however, was in identifying the social characteristics of the people who did take part in such activities. Consequently, he made notes of license numbers and other identifying characteristics and traced these men so that he could find out where they lived. Later he disguised himself, and under the ruse of conducting an innocuous door-to-door survey, he interviewed the men.

When they were published, both of the above studies aroused a great deal of critical comment. Subjects in the Berkun et al. (1962) research had been alarmed, even terrified, by what they thought was happening to them. Did the researchers have the right to do that? Was the knowledge gained about the effects of acute psychological stress on cognitive and physiological functioning sufficiently important to justify the overpowering fear experienced by the subjects? In the study by Humphrey (1975), subjects did not, in fact, experience any harm as a result of the research. Their identities were never revealed, although the potential for harm in the form of blackmail and its consequences was quite real had Humphrey misplaced his notes. The issue that critics have raised with respect to Humphrey's research is invasion of privacy (von Hoffman, 1970). Was the knowledge gained about the otherwise normal, law-abiding lifestyles of many of the participants in the tearoom trade sufficiently important to justify the manner in which it was obtained?

Many people did not think so. In fact, during the 1960s and 1970s there was a growing consensus that some sort of formal mechanism was needed to protect the rights of research subjects: the right to privacy, the right not to be harmed by research, and the right to refuse to participate. Many professional societies, such as the American Psychological Association and the American Sociological Association, had already developed codes of ethics to govern the research activities of their members, but these were not sufficient. Many people doing research simply do not belong to these associations, and a professional society with a small full-time staff in, for example, Washington, D.C., could not possibly oversee all the research going on at all the colleges, universities, and research institutions around the country in any case. What was needed was "on-site" ethical expertise to examine research proposals and ensure, before the research began, that it would not be harmful to subjects. Thus, under pressure from Congress, the federal government began requiring that any institution receiving federal funds in any form—and that includes almost all schools, colleges, universities, hospitals, and research institutions—establish an Institutional Review Board (IRB) to examine all research to be conducted at the institution, or by anyone affiliated with the institution. Members of IRBs are appointed by the administration of the institution and, typically, include people with a variety of different points of view—including representatives of the population from which subjects for the research are to be recruited. It is the responsibility of anyone doing research to submit a description of that research to their local IRB. The charge of the IRB is to review such proposals before the research begins to see if there are any aspects that might be harmful and/or inappropriate. If it finds something amiss, it has the power to require the researcher to redesign the research to remove the problem. If that is not possible, it can prevent the research from being done.

The dilemmas posed by the studies of Berkun et al. and Humphrey described above can in many instances be avoided by the use of informed consent, a procedure that is typically required by IRBs. **Informed consent** is a process in which people are given an explicit choice about whether or not they would like to participate in the research prior to their participation but after they have been fully informed of any potential harmful effects of the research and made aware that they are completely free to withdraw from the research at any time. For a great deal of research on behavior and social processes, informed consent is ideal because it enlists the cooperation of participants while at the same time alleviating any anxieties about what they are letting themselves in for. If you are interested in short-term memory, for example, and want to find out whether caffeine has any effect on the ability to recall numbers, you can tell potential participants that the research would require that they drink a cup of coffee, wait 15 minutes (for it to take effect), then try to repeat backward some groups of numbers that you will read to them. If they do not like coffee (or you), have not got an hour to spare, or cannot stand number games, they can say, "No, thanks."

On the other hand, there are instances in which informed consent may be impossible, undesirable, or unnecessary. Informed consent may be impossible because the researcher does not know all the potential harmful effects of the research, or because the participants are incapable of understanding what is involved, or because the atmosphere in which the research takes place is not really conducive to a free choice to participate or not. If you contemplate doing research in which any of these three things is true, you should ponder whether or not the research can be ethically justified. Informed consent may be undesirable in certain contexts because it would change the behavior of interest. Knowing that you are interested in how aging affects memory may cause many older people to become apprehensive and not do as well as they could on memory-related tasks. It is this category of research—research in which distortions may be introduced into the results by knowledge of what the researcher is interested in—that causes the most difficulty. We shall return to it repeatedly in the chapters that follow as we examine the ethical and methodological complications that it introduces into the various ways of doing research.

Finally, informed consent may simply be unnecessary for research that investigates public behavior, involves no harm or inconvenience to subjects, and in which all subjects remain anonymous. No one would object, for example, if you wanted to look at the effects of cable television on reading habits by examining book sales and library withdrawals before and after the introduction of cable television into your town. But it would probably be a good idea to run the proposal by the local IRB, just in case.

Summary

There is a discrepancy between the stereotype and the reality of scientific research. The dividing line between scientific research on human behavior and the sort of informal research you have been doing all your life is unclear. Both begin with questions, curiosity about the hows and whys of behavior, and proposed explanations. The research methods to be discussed in the following chapters, however, help you to be very precise about the conditions under which you have found answers to your questions. They also focus your attention on the questions of reliability and validity: Are your observations repeatable? Do they really mean what you think they do? Thus, a thorough knowledge of research methods will help you avoid concluding more than is justified.

It is necessary to be precise about the conditions surrounding behavior because it is the functional significance, or meaning, of behavior that is important. The reasons why something was done, the motives behind the action, are crucial, and that is what makes research on human behavior both difficult and exciting. On a general level, behavior is usually seen as being a function of the person, the specific situation in which the person is immersed, and the cultural background. The goal of research in the social and behavioral sciences is the development of explanatory concepts that will help you to understand the complex interrelationships of individuals influencing and being influenced by a constant stream of social situations. Testable explanations are the objective.

Developing explanations for behavior is a creative process, and your own creativity can be improved by overcoming a few common blocks. The first step is to realize that reality is multidisciplinary; nobody has a monopoly on the best way to explain behavior. The second step in nurturing your creativity is to learn how to observe closely and well. Pay attention to what is going on around you. Your expectations about what is going to occur will often prevent you from seeing what does occur. That is a habit you have to kick. Close observation of a number of isolated instances of behavior and the formulation of an underlying general principle that is inherent in them all is referred to as induction. Deduction is the opposite: applying a general principle to a specific instance. Neither process is infallible, but careful observation and accurate inference are important to both.

Observation and accurate description of behavior are important, and they are usually the first steps in research, but they are definitely not enough. Understanding seems to be advanced primarily by purposeful observation, by curiosity about answers to specific questions. Thus, the general research strategy advocated here involves two additional steps: (1) when you are curious about some aspect of behavior, make a list of as many plausible explanations for it as you can; and (2) when you begin gathering evidence on a proposed explanation, operationalize your concepts in more than one way. The research process, then, involves three phases: description or observation, theory building, and verification.

A great deal remains to be learned about human behavior, but the value we place on knowledge may conflict with other ideals. Such conflicts are the sources of ethical dilemmas. Informed consent can resolve many, but not all, of these dilemmas. In the chapters that follow we shall pay particular attention to situations in which informed consent is impossible or undesirable.

Recommended Readings

Boorstin, D. A. (1983). *The discoverers: A history of man's search to know his world and himself*. New York: Vintage Books.

Boorstin's book is filled with detailed, illuminating accounts of the great discoveries of the past. But, more important, he shows how "knowledge"—the received common sense and facts of an age—can inhibit discovery. Even the great discoverers themselves were occasionally blinded by their expectations (and desires). Columbus, for example, had a vested interest in believing that he had really found the Indies. But, on his second trip to the New World, he was forced to turn back while still not having found the wealth of the Orient nor seen the Great Khan. To protect himself from accusations of cowardice and timidity, he threatened to cut out the tongue of any crew member who refused to sign a document testifying that they had indeed reached the coast of Asia. In fact, they had been sailing the southern coast of Cuba. Had they gone only 50 more miles, they would have discovered that it was an island and not the great Asian landmass. Boorstin's accounts are filled with insight about the processes and forces that both inhibit and promote discovery. It is well worth reading.

Gilovich, T. (1991). *How we know what isn't so: The fallibility of human reason in everyday life*. New York: The Free Press.

Research methods are intended to help us sort out fact from fancy, to separate what is really the case from what only seems to be so. Without a little help, our (usually) magnificent perceptual capabilities and thought processes can get us into trouble. Gilovich documents many of our erroneous beliefs and analyzes how they arise and why they persist—in the face of good evidence to the contrary! Ever heard of a phenomenon called the "hot hand"? Also known as "streak shooting," it refers to the belief that basketball players can "get hot" and, after making two or three shots in a row, become more likely to ring each subsequent shot. Or, conversely, they can "go cold," and after missing two or three shots, they become even less likely to ring the next one. By analyzing data from professional and college teams, Gilovich is able to show that there is no evidence that the "hot hand" exists, but that there is evidence that basketball fans—as well as you and I—often misperceive and misinterpret random events. Take another example. Like any good scientists, if we want to find out whether our beliefs are accurate, we should seek whatever evidence we can find, whether it confirms or—horrors—disconfirms our belief. Right? Right. Unfortunately, all too often we do not behave like good scientists. As Gilovich shows, we often place undue faith in evidence that appears to confirm our beliefs and, alas, sometimes even fail to seek out disconfirming evidence. There is a great deal more—from why some of us place so much faith in questionable health practices to the unreasonable persistence of beliefs in ESP. But read the book. It will help you think more clearly.

Memering, D. (1989). *The Prentice Hall guide to research writing* (2nd ed.). Englewood Cliffs, NJ: Prentice Hall.

Memering's text provides an excellent introduction to some of the basics of writing about research. From how to use the library, to taking notes, to evaluating evidence, to the format for citations—it's all there in clear, easily understandable English. One of the more interesting sections has to do with the fallacies that we fall prey to in evaluating evidence. The genetic fallacy, for example, is the tendency to evaluate evidence based on its source. Is the *New York Times* always more reliable than the *National Enquirer*? The slippery slope argument is based on the assumption that one thing inevitably leads to another—and it's all downhill after the first puff on that cigarette. There are a number of other fallacies that you need to be alert to, and Memering's text and examples will help you recognize them when you see them.

Ross, L. and Nisbett, R. E. (1991). *The person and the situation: Perspectives of social psychology.* Philadelphia: Temple University Press.

It has been argued in Chapter 1 that, in some respects, research in the social and behavioral sciences is quite similar to normal, everyday processes involved in trying to understand the world. But under some circumstances, those "normal, everyday processes" can lead us astray. Ross and Nisbett document many of the ways in which this happens. Leading the list is what they refer to as the "Principle of Situationism." Evidence suggests that situations exert powerful, but often relatively unnoticed, influences on behavior. Asked to account for why another person behaved in a certain way, we appear all too ready to assume that their behavior reflects the type of person they are. But, in many instances, their behavior may reflect nothing more than what appeared to be called for by the situation in which they found themselves, and anyone in that situation would have done the same. Ross and Nisbett employ the "Principle of Construal" as their second organizing theme. Simply stated, the principle calls attention to the fact that we cannot interpret someone's behavior unless we understand how they perceived, or "construed," the situation to which they were responding. We often fail to recognize that everyone does not see things the way we do—silly them—and that confounds our efforts to understand why they act the way they do. It is an excellent book, with important, wide-ranging implications.

von Oech, R. (1983). *A whack on the side of the head: How to unlock your mind for innovation.* New York: Warner.

Roger von Oech, a consultant for industry, has identified 10 implicit beliefs that keep us from being more creative. He refers to these beliefs as "mental locks," since they tend to lock us into predictable, unimaginative modes of thought. One of these "locks" is a tendency to assume that problems have one, and only one, correct answer. Many problems have multiple answers, of course. But if we tend to believe that only one exists, we are likely to settle for the first one that occurs to us, and it may not be the best. One way to overcome the deleterious effects of these locks is to be aware of them and force yourself to ignore them. When you have one answer, for example, make yourself find another that works just as well (or better). von Oech gives a number of tips for "whacking" your thinking into new and more creative paths: Generate a metaphor for your situation; ask "what if?"; try using humor; invert the rules; pose the problem as ambiguously as possible. He also provides a variety of entertaining exercises to help you unlock your creativity.

2

Observing Social Behavior

The research method we shall discuss in this chapter has its roots in cultural anthropology, urban sociology, and journalism. It is called **participant observation**. It is also referred to as **fieldwork** or **field research,** as in "going out into the field," that is, away from civilization, or away from the laboratory. It is the most holistic of the methods we shall discuss, and the basic requirement for using it is a willingness to immerse yourself in the day-to-day activities of the people, or setting, of interest. The point is to learn as much as possible about the social and behavioral processes occurring in the culture in order to both (1) describe the setting and (2) generate some theoretical notions that will explain what you have seen and heard. Goffman's study of St. Elizabeth's Hospital, briefly described in the last chapter, is an example.

The detailed description and interpretation that results from participant observation, and which underscores the method's kinship with journalism, is referred to as an ethnography. In fact, participant observation itself is sometimes called ethnographic research. According to Van Maanen (1988), this type of research, with its focus on understanding the culture of groups, emerged first in anthropology and somewhat later—in a slightly altered form—in sociology. It all began in the 19th century with the reports of explorers, missionaries, and sailors who brought back news and descriptions of exotic, faraway places. In the 1800s the published diaries and letters of missionaries who had spent time in Africa, of sailors who had seen the Sandwich Islands, and of explorers who had steamed up the Amazon were best sellers. Everyone wanted to know what those places were like. How did people live there? What did they do?

As we gradually found out about the existence of other peoples and places and ways of life around the world, we simultaneously realized that we knew very little about them, and that much of what we thought we knew was myth. While even superficial contacts with other cultures could be interesting and informative, it was clear that we needed to know more than could be learned from brief visits by merchants and missionaries and explorers. Dissatisfied with this state of affairs, a few brave souls began self-consciously trying to fill the knowledge gap by going to live in some of those exotic places, seeing what life there was like, and coming back to describe it, explain it, and contrast it with our own ways of doing things. The realization that there were areas of our own society about which very little was known and within which fieldwork might be useful developed somewhat later.

But, think about it for a moment. There are many parts of society about which outsiders know very little. Take the world of those who deal in illicit drugs, for example. We hear about them almost every day. Our newspapers are filled with stories of their exploits: shoot-outs and arrests and smuggling. But what is their world like to them? How do they spend their time? What kind of people are they? And, most important, how would we find out? One possibility is to interview some of those who have been arrested, assuming that we could get permission from the local police to talk to them. But, even if we are lucky enough to reach a few articulate and insightful informants this way, what we hear is likely to be biased and self-serving, especially if charges are pending. Another approach might be to go to the library to see if there are any memoirs or autobiographies that would shed some light. There are a few, but the pickings are slim and of dubious value for learning about the actual, day-to-day lifestyles of dealers and addicts.

Participant Observation

There is a better way, and for six years, while she was a graduate student at the University of California at San Diego, it was tried by Patricia Adler (1985) and her husband. Living in a small, informal beach town in an area she refers to as Southwest County, she participated in the daily activities of a community of high-level drug dealers and smugglers. She formed close friendships with many of them, traveled with them, attended social functions and parties with them, watched and listened while they planned and conducted their deals, interviewed them, and, in short, became a trusted member of the community. To obtain the kind of information she was after, she had to. As Adler (1985) put it:

> By studying criminals in their natural habitat I was able to see them in the full variability and complexity of their surrounding subculture, rather than within the artificial environment of a prison. I was thus able to learn about otherwise inaccessible dimensions of their lives, observing and analyzing firsthand the nature of their social organization, social stratification, lifestyle, and motivation. (p.28)

Hazardous duty, indeed. But Adler's description of life in Southwest County informed us about a segment of society about which there was no other way to learn.

Take another example. Loseke (1992) was interested in the social processes by which some women come to be defined as "battered" and, hence, provided a variety of social services—while others, who may have been subjected to equivalent violence, are not. She focused her study on a shelter for battered women, named "South Coast," which was located near a medium-sized city on the West Coast. At first, her participation in the shelter was as an evaluator, a person hired by the organization providing funding for the shelter to tabulate data on costs and clients served as well as to conduct interviews with clients, workers, and supervisors. Later, she became a volunteer worker at the shelter and ended up spending several years, off and on, hanging around, talking to clients and other workers, answering the telephone, reading the shelter logbook, and sitting in on house meetings. One of the things she discovered was that the daily workers at the shelter, who were not social service professionals and who typically had only a high school education, wielded a tremendous amount of power in deciding who would and would not be admitted to the shelter. The problem, from the point of view of the shelter administrators, was that the pay and working conditions of the workers were so unattractive that administrators did not have the luxury of hiring only those who shared their vision of what the shelter should be and who it should serve. And, it was usually only the workers who were there in the middle of the night when a potential new client showed up on the doorstep. Thus, decisions were often made about admitting clients on the basis of whether or not they matched the workers' stereotypes about battered women and whether or not they looked like they would be a lot of trouble.

Or, consider the world of doomsday cults. Specifically, suppose you were curious about what happens when the predicted disaster—usually the end of the world—does not occur on schedule. Again, you could do some reading. Or, you might try to find people who once belonged to such a cult and interview them. But again, it would be better to join such a group and see for yourself. One October, a number of years ago, a team of social scientists did just that (Festinger, Riecken, and Schachter, 1956). They became participant observers in a group predicting that a cataclysmic flood would occur on December 21 of that year, a flood that would inundate most of the western part of the United States. This prophecy had been revealed to the group's leader, Mrs. Marian Keech, through automatic writing. Festinger and his colleagues were interested in what would happen when Mrs. Keech's prediction proved false, and to find out, they joined the group. They were there, observing and sneaking out to the back porch to make notes, when the night of December 21 came and went with everybody dry as a bone.

"Aha!" you say. The task of the participant observer really is like that of a reporter. You hang around where something interesting is happening, ask questions, make a few notes, and then write up what went on. Well, yes and no. There is more involved, but there are definite parallels. Participant observation does require that you enter into the routine of the people or situation under study, usually for a rather extended period of time. The point is to develop an understanding of the participants' view of reality, the *meanings* underlying their own and others' actions (Lofland and Lofland, 1984). How do they see things, what is important to them, how do they spend their time? Observing and systematically recording things that happen, informally or formally interviewing all those who might have information pertinent to the events under study, and gathering relevant auxiliary information are all important. Note that the emphasis is on discovery, on finding out what life is like for people in the setting of interest—on learning, not on testing preconceived ideas. These things are also a part of the way good reporters operate. Similarly, both participant observers and reporters can choose from a variety of roles (Adler and Adler, 1987). That is, the modus operandi can range from complete openness about who they are and why they are there to complete secrecy and, perhaps, the assumption of a disguise.

What separates participant observation as a research method from reporting is that a reporter's work is usually complete when a story or narrative of events has been constructed. The participant observer's work is only about half done at that point. The participant observer uses that narrative and the raw materials on which it is based to develop interpretative theoretical statements, called **disciplined abstractions,** that help in understanding the processes observed in the setting (Jorgensen, 1989). This interpretative framework consists of analytic concepts derived from the firsthand observation of specific episodes and events. (For an example that touches everyday life, see Box 1.) The theoretical ideas that spring from participant observation are "disciplined" in that they must be tied to, or grounded in, specific events. You must be able to point to something that occurred, something that is recorded in the narrative, and say, "Here, this is an example of what I'm talking about." The scientific goal, then, is to use what you have seen and heard and experienced to generate explicit and articulate abstractions. Perhaps a more detailed illustration will help to make this clear.

An Example: Preserving the Self

In the last few years there has been a continuing debate about the best way to motivate employees, especially employees of large corporations. For a long time, it was assumed that money was all that was required. Better pay would automatically translate into harder work and greater loyalty to the company. But by the late 1980s, that answer no longer seemed sufficient. Surveys indicated that fewer than one out of five Americans said "good pay" was the most important thing for them in selecting—or staying in—a job (Harris, 1987). And the experience of many managers and corporate executives seemed to point to the importance of something different, something less tangible. What was needed, so they said, was the development of a strong corporate culture—a clear set of beliefs and values that the company stood for, beliefs and values that employees could be induced to identify with and share. The benefit, from the company's point of view, would be that employees who incorporated the company's beliefs and values would be likely to put the company's good above their own and to do better work—and more of it—in the absence of strict external supervision.

Of course, the company would have to find ways to "induce" employees to accept its culture and continuously reinforce them for doing so. According to Kunda (1992), the list of techniques and practices utilized by corporations to win the hearts and minds of workers is a long one. They include, but are

---

Box 1

Learning the Tricks of the Trade

Participant observation involves a great deal more than simply describing what you see and hear. The crucial component, which separates participant observation from simple descriptive reporting, is that your observations are used to arrive at some hypotheses about the social and behavioral processes operating in the setting you observe. For example, Robert Cialdini (1993), a psychologist interested in compliance, decided that he could probably learn something about the topic by studying salespeople, fund-raisers, and people employed in advertising agencies. After all, they are professionals who make their living inducing others to comply—to buy, to give, to volunteer. So, off and on for three years, he immersed himself in their day-to-day worlds. How? He answered newspaper ads for sales trainees and learned how to sell everything from vacuum cleaners to encyclopedias to dance lessons. He was taught by the pros. He worked in public relations and fund-raising organizations, and even sold Chevrolets for a while.

During this period he observed literally thousands of sales pitches and solicitations being made and hundreds of different tactics being employed to complete the transactions successfully. In contemplating this variety of persuasive approaches, he was able to conceptualize the vast majority of them as being variations on one or more of six general principles. One of these is what he refers to as reciprocation. We typically feel obligated to return favors, to do something for those who have done things for us. Hence, the person who wants you to buy something, or donate to charity, may try to induce a feeling of obligation by giving you a free sample, or doing you a favor of some kind. Members of the Hare Krishna Society approach strangers and press a small gift upon them—a flower, a book—refusing to take it back, but then asking for a donation. Charitable organizations send out unsolicited small packs of greeting cards, or address labels, or stickers, to potential donors. New car salesmen make price "concessions" and throw in "extra" accessories in their efforts to close a deal. According to Cialdini, these and similar tactics are designed to induce feelings of obligation and, hence, increase the likelihood of a donation or a sale.

There is more to Cialdini's argument. He suggests that the power of the reciprocation principle, and of each of the other five principles he identifies, lies in its ability to induce an immediate, unthinking compliance. The point here, however, is simply that he has used participant observation as it should be used: to abstract hypotheses about the social and behavioral processes underlying what he saw.

---

not limited to, participative decision making, explicit training in company policies, graded careers, job security, decentralization of authority, overt uses of rituals and ceremonies, management of symbols and meanings, stock ownership plans, and various and sundry benefits and bonuses. The basic idea, the goal of all this, is really quite simple: to induce workers to identify so closely with the good of the company—what's good for the company is good for me—that they become their own taskmasters. The result? Less supervision required, less internal conflict, more work, longer hours, better products.

What effect does this have on the worker? Clearly a company with a strong corporate culture is attempting to get more than just a day's work for a day's pay. It wants commitment, involvement, and emotional attachment. But how do employees, even those who are committed to the company, keep it from taking over their lives? How do they preserve their sense of self and autonomy in the face of an overwhelmingly strong corporate culture? Or, do they? In an effort to find out, Gideon Kunda (1992) spent a year as a participant observer in the engineering division of a sophisticated technological design and development company that he refers to as High Tech Corporation (Tech). Tech was selected because it had a reputation in the industry for treating its workers almost like family, offering its employees the closest thing to a caring total community that they were likely to find in the workplace.

Initially approached by a staff organization of Tech seeking consulting help, Kunda was eventually accepted as a "passive observer" in both the engineering division of Tech and at corporate headquarters, a few miles away. He was provided office space, a computer terminal, and permission to talk to whomever he wanted to. During the course of the year he spent at Tech, he interviewed people, sat in on workshops, went to sporting events with Techies, got invited to staff meetings, design meetings, and product review meetings, ate lunch with engineers and managers, and generally just hung out and wandered the halls, talking to people and reading everything there was to read about the company—from notices on bulletin boards, to official documents, to messages on the Internet.

One of the first things that became clear was that Tech's reputation as having a strong corporate culture was well deserved. It began in the parking lot, where I LOVE TECH bumper stickers abounded, and continued as one approached the main entrance, where large video monitors were often playing motivational speeches ("We Are One") by the company founder and president. Bulletin boards were covered with statements of the company philosophy and highlighted clippings from newspapers and magazines in which Tech and/or its products were mentioned. New employees were required to attend "Bootcamp," an orientation session at which they were given explicit instruction in the company's culture. From the president down to this week's motivational consultant, there was a continual barrage of messages—in pamphlets, speeches, videos, workshops—framing the corporate goals in moral tones (honesty, quality, success), calling attention to the desired balance between freedom and discipline, and pointing out the importance of self-discipline and "the right attitude."

Employees were indeed given considerable freedom. There were no set hours. The workspaces of the engineers and computer specialists were designed to foster interaction and teamwork—not private offices, but cubicles separated by low dividers. New products were developed by teams, even if the idea originated with an individual. So there was pressure to be available and to have your part done when it was needed—which was usually yesterday. Employees were provided with home computers hooked to Tech's mainframe so that they could work at night. As Kunda (1992) put it, at Tech:

> ...discipline is not based on explicit supervision and reward, but rather on peer pressure and, more crucially, internalized standards for performance. There is little mention of the economic structure, and the importance of economic re-

wards is underplayed, even frowned upon. It is a fact of life, but not one to be emphasized; instead, rewards are seen as arising from the experience of communion, of belonging, of participation in the community as organizationally defined. (p. 90)

To underscore that community feeling, Tech had a no-layoff policy, so that even in times of economic downturn, employees all knew that Tech would "take care of its own."

It sounds great, and the atmosphere at Tech does indeed appear to have been one of an open, informal, creative, and, yes, successful company. At the time of Kunda's observations, Tech had been in business for three decades and was considered a leader in its field. But as Kunda became more and more familiar with the day-to-day operation of the engineering division, he began to see that all was not well in paradise. For many employees, the very openness and flexibility of the company created problems. Imagine yourself in the situation. You are an engineer, being well paid by a company that doesn't care whether you get to work at 8:00 A.M. or noon. The work is in pleasant surroundings with congenial colleagues and is focused on something you love doing: designing and developing the technical aspects of new products to be marketed by other divisions of the company. The company has even furnished you the equipment necessary to work at home if you like. On the other hand, the team you are working with is in competition with other teams developing other new products for the company, and not all of the projects will be funded; there are deadlines to be met; and your contribution has to be coordinated with those of all the other members of your team. What would happen?

What many Techies found happening to them under these conditions was that they were gradually drawn into working more and more and more—day and night, home and office, weekends and weekdays. The work, after all, was never done. As soon as one project was complete, another was assigned, and the schedules and pressures to produce started all over. Thus, Kunda found that successful Techies—those who avoided burnout and stayed with the company for the long haul—developed one of two general techniques for limiting the company's claim on them and preserving the non-Tech aspects of their lives.

First, some employees devoted considerable energy to establishing clear boundaries between work and nonwork. Many explicitly made a choice to adhere to very rigid work hours—to always arrive at 8:30 A.M. and to always leave at 5:30 P.M., no matter what. Others made it a point never to turn on the home computer that the company had furnished them. Still others refused to eat lunch in the company cafeteria. They always left the building for lunch to avoid having to talk shop while they ate. Others used the lunch hour for a variety of recreational and athletic activities. As one engineer put it to Kunda (p. 165): "Without my daily bridge game I'm a wreck. Look at all those runners. What do you think they're running from?" This boundary maintenance also extended to social relationships. People at Tech were quite careful in keeping their work and leisure relationships with people separate. As Kunda (p. 170) put it: "Drawing boundaries is experienced as a struggle to limit self-involvement in the face of organizational and internal pressures to merge work and nonwork aspects of life and thus to expand organizational influence over private experience."

But Tech was, after all, an attractive place to work, and in spite of the all-enveloping tendencies of the corporate culture, many felt pulled to become "Techies." Thus, somewhat paradoxically, the second strategy for keeping the organization at arm's length was to embrace the company, but to preserve one's self by employing a variety of techniques for maintaining a degree of cognitive and emotional distance. These were the employees who appeared to lose themselves in the company and accept its values almost as one might accept a religion, through and through. They defended the company when it was maligned by outsiders; they criticized other employees who only wanted to know "what's in it for them"; they valued the security offered by Tech. But, at the same time, these people often appeared to be watching themselves play the role of a super-loyal employee and were, by turns, cynical—"Do what's right really means 'make your manager visible'"—or detached —"Tech culture is just a way to control people, to rationalize a mess"—observers of the company. This detached observer mode was often accompanied by a suppression of spontaneous personal reactions to the work environment, a sort of emotional depersonalization as a way of not letting things get to you. Others among this group simply downplayed the idea that what Tech was doing was any different from what every other company tried to do—"I don't buy all that 'we are unique' song and dance." As Kunda (p. 187) put it, embracing the company for these Techies was accompanied by a calculated stance toward managing their own thoughts and feelings, and they often appeared to be watching themselves play a game.

Note that Kunda's research resulted in more than a history of Tech or a reporting of what was said and done in a variety of specific instances, although both of those things were included. In addition, Kunda used his intimate knowledge of the engineering division, its personnel, and their interrelations to develop a series of concepts that would give meaning to what he had seen and heard. These concepts serve to place his research within a more general framework. The strong corporate culture led to unusual performance pressures and threatened to erase the division between work and nonwork in the lives of the employees. To cope with this and maintain their sense of self as separate from their work, the employees of the engineering division developed techniques for creating boundaries around their work and separating their work and nonwork social relationships. Others achieved the same end via a different route: They appeared to embrace the company culture—to be gung-ho Techies—but, at the same time, utilized a variety of cognitive and emotional distancing techniques to maintain a critical self-awareness. These derived concepts of "boundary drawing" and "cognitive and emotional distancing" serve to place the observations at Tech within a broader theoretical context. The development of such explanatory abstractions is the scientific goal of the whole operation. It is what takes participant observation beyond reporting. The hope, of course, is that those higher-level concepts may help investigators to understand what goes on in other situations that have a similar structure. For example, although their situations superficially appear quite different, one might expect that those who make a career in the military would be faced with the same problem as the engineers at Tech: How can you keep the organization from dominating your entire life (e.g., Zurcher, 1988)?

With the why clearly in mind, then, let us take a look at the how of participant observation. What is involved in getting it done?

Where the Action Is

Several years ago, the actor George C. Scott (1980) said that fame had deprived him of what he considered to be one of the most important tools of actors. Having become so well known that he was recognized almost everywhere he went, he could no longer develop his feeling for how a scene should be played, for example, by unobtrusively observing similar real-life scenes. He could no longer tune his ear for dialogue by sitting in a bar and listening to strangers talk. The point, of course, is that when you want to learn how people behave at bar mitzvahs, or Quaker weddings, or New Year's Eve parties, you have to go to a few. If you want to discover what life is like on the graveyard shift, you have to be there from midnight to 8 A.M. (and one night is not enough). The first rule of participant observation, then, is that you have to go where the action is in order to learn about it. It is not going to come to you.

It seems obvious that the social setting you choose to observe will be determined by your interest. Hafferty (1991), for example, wanted to find out how medical students coped with their initial exposures to the dead. So, he spent some time in the anatomy labs of several medical schools, observing and talking to students dissecting their first cadavers. Vesperi (1985) was interested in how society's view of old age affected the low-income elderly. So, she moved to St. Petersburg, Florida, a city with a very high proportion of people over 70. Peshkin (1986) wanted to find out how religious doctrine influenced educational practice in fundamentalist schools. So, for 18 months, he sat in on classes, attended ball games and pep rallies, interviewed teachers, parents, and students, and generally immersed himself in the life of a Christian school he refers to as "Bethany Baptist Academy." Hafferty, Vesperi, and Peshkin each defined the issues that interested them and purposefully sought out settings in which events promised to be relevant to those issues.

It does not always work that way, however. Sometimes you may find yourself in a setting that piques your interest in certain processes. Ronai (1992), for example, was working as an exotic dancer when she started graduate school. She decided to use her job as a setting for participant observation to explore the emotional world and role conflicts of strippers, herself included. Molstad (1986) worked in several beer bottling plants in the Los

Angeles area while he was a student. He took the jobs, initially, simply as a way to support himself while attending school, but became intrigued by the ways in which his fellow workers coped with monotonous, repetitive work. Adler's (1985) interest in the drug dealing and smuggling scene of "Southwest County" came about simply because she happened to rent a townhouse next door to a major dealer. There is a potential disadvantage to the approach of Ronai, Molstad, and Adler, however, especially if you are already thoroughly familiar with a setting before deciding to use it as a site for participant observation: You may have gotten so caught up in, or used to, the "routine" of the place that it may difficult to "see" what is really going on—that is, the social and psychological processes underlying the day-to-day activities.

The Initial Stages

Although their order may vary depending on whether you find yourself in a setting that piques your interest or seek out a relevant setting after defining your interest, there are three initial stages in fieldwork: doing your homework, gaining entry, and immersion in the setting.

In some respects, doing your homework is like planning a vacation. Once you have decided that you would like to spend a couple of weeks in England, say, it would probably be a good idea to buy one of Fodor's, or Frommer's, famous travel guides and do a little reading: sights to see, places to stay, prices, how to get around. It would be a mistake to wait until you stepped off the plane at Heathrow or Gatwick to decide whether you are going to spend the first night in London or Dover. The importance of these kinds of practical decisions should not be underestimated. A little bit of planning, such as sketching out a rough itinerary, can make the difference between a pleasant vacation and a real hassle. But if you really want to get something out of your vacation, then a more thorough preparation is called for. A good book or two on English history would help. If you are an architecture buff, you might read up on Sir Christopher Wren and then plan your itinerary to see a few of his buildings. If you are a literature fan, you might reread some Shakespeare and plan to spend a day or two in Stratford. The point, of course, is that such preparation will help you appreciate more fully the things you see and do. You will have some pegs to hang impressions on. You will know what to look for.

In participant observation, the danger of doing too much homework ahead of time is hinted at in that last sentence: You will know what to look for. If you are looking for something specific within the ambiguities of human interaction, chances are that you will find it. You probably will not even have to look very hard. Chances are also pretty good that you will miss a lot of more interesting and important things. For that reason, many fieldworkers are somewhat apprehensive about the biases introduced by carrying too many preconceptions into the field with them. As Jorgensen (1989) noted, for the participant observer, reviewing the relevant literature is important, but it is only a small part of preparing yourself. As you become familiar with the setting, your focus may shift to new and different concepts. Theory should emerge from the observations themselves. But the theory that you hope will emerge from participant observation will generally have to do with the *how* of social behavior. How does a teacher control a classroom? How do people end conversations? How do psychiatric patients get around institutional rules? How do the employees at Tech keep the company from taking over their lives? So, it is okay to learn as much as you can about the context and history of the setting you are going to observe ahead of time. But try to make no assumptions about what will actually be going on within the setting. That is what you are there to find out. Think about it this way: If possible, learn about the what and why ahead of time. Then use participant observation to learn how—how whatever it is that is supposed to get done really gets done.

If you are lucky enough to find yourself in a setting that piques your interest, the problem of gaining entry has been solved for you. Molstad (1986), for example, did not have to request permission to observe his fellow brewery workers. All he had to do was show up for work each day in order to see how they structured their time. As he became interested in the topic of handling boredom, however, he did have to go back and look at some of the literature on job satisfaction. In his and similar instances, gaining entry and immersion in the setting occurred prior to doing any background reading.

If you are not already in the setting you want to observe, gaining entry can be a tricky business. Nearly all veteran fieldworkers have horror stories about mistakes made in the process. Wax (1971), for example, accepted the hospitality of an Indian family, the Goodhorses, during the initial stages of her stay on the Thrashing Buffalo Reservation. Things began to go wrong almost immediately. The community seemed to turn a cold shoulder to her inquiries and no progress was made for weeks on end. Eventually, Wax discovered that the good Goodhorses "were notorious not only for cheating and defrauding white people but for cheating and defrauding the more unfortunate and helpless of their fellow Indians." Moving off the Goodhorse land and into an abandoned schoolhouse brought a dramatic change in the community's attitude toward Wax and her research. The point, of course, is that there are internal conflicts in many settings, and it is a mistake to align yourself with either side when you want to study the community or setting as a whole. Of course, when you are interested in observing only one side, say, the Democratic campaign machine, that is a different story.

The major problem of gaining entry is often one of personal acceptance. Peshkin (1986), for example, was turned down in his initial attempts to gain entry to fundamentalist schools because he was not a "born-again" Christian. One pastor told him he should become one before pursuing his study, lest he misrepresent what he saw. At the school in which he was finally allowed to observe, he obtained the endorsement and consent of both the headmaster of the school and the pastor of the church that supported the school. Such backing by key people, relatively high status members of the community who will vouch for you and whose support conveys to others that it is okay to talk to you, is often crucial for gaining entry and for continued acceptance. A related tactic for gaining acceptance is to use preexisting relationships of trust as a route into the setting. For example, in the study described earlier, the relationships that Loseke (1992) had established as an evaluator of the South Coast shelter for battered women were instrumental in her subsequent acceptance as a volunteer in the shelter, allowing her to continue her research.

Once you are in the setting, things may be difficult at first, especially if the setting is at all unusual, or is different from settings in which you have some experience. Jorgensen (1989) has suggested that at the outset it is helpful to become self-conscious and disciplined about forcing yourself to focus on various aspects of the setting. One way to do this is to ask yourself questions about the setting and then try to answer them explicitly. What kind of building is this? How are these people dressed? Is this a typical day? What are these people doing? Is anything unusual happening? Observing at first will be something like listening to someone speak a language you do not understand. In that case, it is hard to tell where one word (or sentence) ends and another begins, let alone follow the topic being discussed. With participant observation, the connections among the intersecting streams of behavior that you observe are not likely to be immediately apparent. They will emerge only as you become thoroughly familiar with the setting and the people in it. The challenge, from your point of view as an observer, is to recognize the meanings behind the behavior that you are seeing and hearing. And, note well, you must assume that there is an underlying order, even though at first it all appears to be utter chaos. The more closely you look, the more patterns you are likely to see.

In identifying meanings, Lofland and Lofland (1984) have suggested that it may help to attend to the following ten types of things:

1. *Practices:* recurring categories of talk and/or action that the participants regard as normal and unremarkable. Driving on the right side of the road is an example.

2. *Episodes:* remarkable and unusual events, such as getting a divorce or experiencing a heart attack.

3. *Encounters:* direct interpersonal interactions among two or more people. A committee meeting would qualify as an encounter, as would a casual conversation in the hall.

4. *Roles:* specific "types of people" in the setting being observed, such as a self-appointed moral guardian, a busybody, or a nerd.

5. *Relationships:* two people who interact with some regularity over extended periods of time. A mother and daughter pair would usually form a relationship, as would a store clerk and a regular customer.

6. *Groups:* from three to a dozen or so people who interact on a regular basis and who think of themselves as a social entity. An example might be a family, or the members of a street gang.

7. *Organizations:* consciously formed collectivities with formal goals and plans for achieving those goals, such as an adult education school or a business.

8. *Settlements:* intricately interrelated sets of organizations, groups, roles, and encounters that perform a variety of life-sustaining functions and exist in a socially defined territory. A village or a residential school might be an example.

9. *Social worlds:* large, amorphous entities with vague boundaries, but shared interest among the members. Football fans might be an example, or members of the American Civil Liberties Union.

10. *Lifestyles:* global adjustments to life made by large numbers of similarly situated people. The "hippies" of the 1960s or the "yuppies" of the 1980s might be an example.

Most of these will become obvious, of course, as you spend time in the setting, talk to people, and ask questions. But remember, these are just the elements, the building materials from which you must construct those theoretical abstractions mentioned earlier. Two things are involved in converting these raw materials into something useful: taking field notes and developing an analytic filing system.

Field Notes and Filing

Quick now. What did you have for lunch the first Tuesday of last month? What did you do that afternoon? What programs did you look at on TV that night? If you are like most of us, chances are you cannot answer any of those questions. You might be able to if you are a creature of habit: You never eat lunch, you have a class every Tuesday from one o'clock to three o'clock, and you always watch the CBS news on Tuesday night. But even if those things are true for you, you probably would not be able to recall what was on the news that day. However, the odds are a little better that you might indeed be able to reconstruct what was said in class that afternoon—that is, assuming that you took notes. It is amazing what a few notes can do for your memory.

In fact, it is precisely because memory is so fallible that taking **field notes** is such a crucial skill for participant observers. According to Lofland and Lofland (1984), "Aside from getting along in the setting, *the fundamental concrete task* of the observer is the taking of field notes. If you are not doing so, you might as well not be in the setting" (emphasis added). This is one of the few points on which all field researchers agree. Jorgensen (1989), for example, has said that the importance of regularly making notes *cannot be overemphasized*. But be aware that what we are talking about here involves more than the sorts of notes you are probably used to taking in class. For example, your class notes for that Tuesday last month probably contain no information on what you were wearing, what the instructor was wearing, who sat next to whom, which students asked questions, which students were late, whether or not anyone laughed at the instructor's jokes, what color the walls of the room were, and whether the room was dirty or clean. The field notes of a participant observer who sat in on that same class would contain all that information and more. They also might be supplemented by pictures, slides, or videotapes and audio recordings of the setting and events, by formal and informal interviews with other participants in the setting, by digging through records relevant to the setting—anything that gives information about the events and/or people of interest. Photographs are particularly helpful for preserving certain kinds of information about a setting. Just be sure to note that they, too, can sometimes misrepresent a scene (see Box 2). Field notes,

---

Box 2

Is a Picture Really Worth a Thousand Words?

Most people consider a photograph of an event to be more reliable evidence that the event really occurred—and of how it appeared when it did—than the testimony of several eyewitnesses. Photographs, in fact, enjoy a special, privileged status as evidence, and have for a long time. Tagg (1988) points out that as far back as 1840, the police realized the value of photographs for identification purposes. By the 1850s, psychiatrists were using photos of "lunatics" to record and convey their characteristics. By the late 1800s, those interested in social welfare were using photos to portray the squalid living and working conditions of the underprivileged in the hope of igniting reform. Many credit the graphic, explicit television coverage of the early 1970s with hastening the end of the war in Vietnam. We tend not to doubt photographs. After all, they seem to present the event itself, right there before our eyes. For this reason, there has been an increasing use of photographs by historians, participant observers, and other social and behavioral scientists in the last few years.

There are, however, a number of limitations in the use of photographs as evidence (Courtwright, 1989). Photographs can be subjected to a variety of manipulations, both intentionally and unintentionally, that change the messages they convey. Prior to the actual taking of a photo, the scene and/or people in it can be composed, or arranged, to convey a particular message. Props, apparent action, background, and details can all be supplied as needed. Probably the most famous example of this is those hauntingly beautiful "authentic" photographs of American Indians taken by Edward Curtis. Generations of admirers have been surprised and disappointed to learn that the very clothes and headpieces worn by those depicted were provided by Curtis. Manipulations are also possible with the prints and negatives themselves. A photomontage can be created by superimposing the images from two or more negatives in a single print. During the McCarthy era of the early 1950s, for example, a U.S. senator lost his seat in Congress because of the bad publicity resulting from a photomontage showing him in earnest conversation with a leading American communist. There are also techniques (airbrushing and cropping) for deleting portions of pictures, which, again, can distort the message that would have been conveyed had the entire image been presented. Once the final print is in hand, there are still ways in which the messages of photos can be, and are, manipulated. The captions given, the manner in which prints are displayed, and the very selection of prints to be displayed all have the potential for altering the message they convey.

In evaluating photographs for scientific purposes, then, you need to treat them just as any other bit of evidence. You need to ask about the conditions under which they were taken, processed, selected, and presented.

---

then, are running descriptions of events, people, and things seen and heard and felt and tasted and smelled. Put simply, they should be concrete, exhaustive descriptions. Everything has to go in, whether or not you think any particular item is important.

That is a tall order, and the taking of good field notes is indeed a demanding task. How are you to do it? If you are busy writing away in your notebook, or focusing your camera, or adjusting your tape recorder, you are going to miss a great deal of what you should be observing. Note-taking and cameras can also be disruptive in many situations. Imagine the consequences of whipping out your pad and pencil just as someone is starting to sound off about what a creep the boss is. Thus, most experienced fieldworkers recommend that during the course of a day, say, while you are observing, you only jot down occasional notes, phrases, and key words. Or, if you are taking pictures, do it as unobtrusively as possible. But pay careful attention. Observe closely. Ask questions when you need to. Then, at the end of the day—and certainly no later than the following morning—find a private place, get out your pen, your notebook, your jottings, and let it flow. That is when you write it all down, in exquisite, descriptive detail from beginning to end. Obviously, the ratio of field notes to hours of observation will vary depending on what you are observing, how many people there are, and how much action is taking place. But, just to give you a rough guideline, the Loflands (1984) say that you should plan to spend as much time writing as you do observing. Earlier, Lofland (1971) recommended a *minimum* of two single-spaced typewritten pages for every hour of observation. Jorgensen (1989, p. 97) says that after a day of observing he would typically spend several hours typing up his notes.

Fieldworkers differ among themselves on whether it is better to type, dictate, or write out the notes in longhand. Their recommendations appear to be, in part, a function of the latest technology that was available when they first began doing fieldwork. Nowadays, dictaphones, box cameras, and typewriters have been replaced by microcassette recorders, 35mm autofocus SLRs, and portable laptop computers with advanced word processing programs. But even if you do use a tape recorder to dictate your notes to yourself, they will still have to be transcribed. And for that, a computer with a word processing program is hard to beat. The advantages of the computer stem from ease of revision and the ability to move blocks of text from place to place in your notes without retyping.

Whichever technique you choose, you will find that as you are observing, or examining pictures you have made of the setting, or working on your field notes, ideas about processes will occur to you. Questions will come up that you may or may not be able to answer. Hypotheses and hunches will be suggested. Put them all in your notes, but separate them by brackets from the descriptive material, or put them neatly in the margins at appropriate places. These ideas, questions, and hunches will form the basis from which you will construct your analytic files.

To keep this from getting too abstract, let me illustrate some of what is involved with the help of Figure 1. First, look at panel A. You will see that you are going to need multiple copies of each day's notes. That should not be too difficult to arrange, given the proliferation of copying machines. And, of course, keeping your notes in a computer file will enable you to print out multiple copies quite easily. One copy of the notes must be kept intact, in chronological order. That means you need to be sure to put the date and approximate time of your observations on each day's notes. We shall get to what you do with the other copies in a moment. Before we do, read through the brief excerpt of notes depicted in Figure 1A. You will notice typographical errors, ungrammatical expressions, and, yes, even incomplete sentences. That does not mean you need to develop that style. The point is that field notes are for your eyes only. You do not need to waste time going back and correcting typographical errors or searching for the most felicitous way of expressing yourself. Nobody is ever going to see the field notes but you, so just get the facts down. You will also note that there is a rather tedious quality to the notes. That is perfectly all right. Much of everyday life has a tedious quality to it, and the purpose of field notes is to help you capture what life is really like in the setting you are observing.

Now look at Figure 1B. There you see two general categories of files: mundane files and analytic files. **Mundane files** are geared to the specifics of what you are observing: people, settings, organizations. They help you keep track of all the information you have about certain key features and people. Of course, if there were a large number of people in the setting, you probably would not have a file on each one, only the more important, central characters. The others you might lump into categories—Clowns, Complainers, Idealists—and keep a file on each category. **Analytic files** are those in which you keep track of instances from your notes that document and support your developing ideas about the interpersonal processes, tactics, and strategies that operate within the setting and make it work (or keep it from working). (See Chapter 5 for some suggestions on the physical handling of this filing process.) The set of analytic files will gradually expand as you become familiar with the setting and ideas occur to you about what is going on. You must keep asking yourself for explanations of what you see happening. In the example discussed earlier, Kunda was able to make sense of some of his observations at Tech with two key analytic concepts: (1) drawing boundaries and (2) cognitive and emotional distancing. Many of the responses of Tech employees to the corporation's grip on their lives could be accounted for quite well with the help of these two abstract, analytic notions.

As another example, Eder and Parker (1987) conducted an in-depth observational study of informal and organized peer activities in a working-class middle school. They observed extracurricular activities several times a week for an entire academic year. They went to picnics, dances, choir and band practices, ball games, concerts, cheerleading tryouts, and school plays. They observed informal gatherings before and after school, ate lunch with the kids, talked to them, sat in on classes, and even hung around the halls between

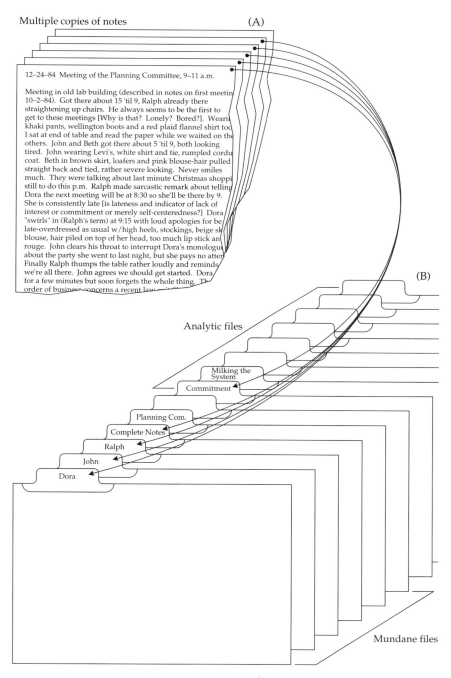

Multiple copies of notes (A)

12–24–84 Meeting of the Planning Committee, 9–11 a.m.

Meeting in old lab building (described in notes on first meeting 10–2–84). Got there about 15 'til 9, Ralph already there straightening up chairs. He always seems to be the first to get to these meetings [Why is that? Lonely? Bored?]. Wearing khaki pants, wellington boots and a red plaid flannel shirt too. I sat at end of table and read the paper while we waited on the others. John and Beth got there about 5 'til 9, both looking tired. John wearing Levi's, white shirt and tie, rumpled corduroy coat. Beth in brown skirt, loafers and pink blouse-hair pulled straight back and tied, rather severe looking. Never smiles much. They were talking about last minute Christmas shopping still to do this p.m. Ralph made sarcastic remark about telling Dora the next meeting will be at 8:30 so she'll be there by 9. She is consistently late [is lateness and indicator of lack of interest or commitment or merely self-centeredness?] Dora "swirls" in (Ralph's term) at 9:15 with loud apologies for being late-overdressed as usual w/high heels, stockings, beige skirt blouse, hair piled on top of her head, too much lip stick and rouge. John clears his throat to interrupt Dora's monologue about the party she went to last night, but she pays no attention. Finally Ralph thumps the table rather loudly and reminds we're all there. John agrees we should get started. Dora for a few minutes but soon forgets the whole thing. The order of business concerns a recent lawsuit

(B)

Analytic files

Milking the System
Commitment
Planning Com.
Complete Notes
Ralph
John
Dora

Mundane files

1 Field notes and file organization. In the example, multiple copies of each day's field notes (A) are needed so that a copy can be filed under each relevant category (B). One copy must be added to the ongoing complete set of field notes, which are crucial for establishing context. The mundane files are valuable for keeping observations on specific people (Dora, Ralph, John), places, and organizations (planning committee). Copies must also be placed in the analytic files, which are based on your own emerging ideas about important processes, strategies, and concepts (commitment, milking the system) that occur within the setting. The set of analytic files is likely to expand as new ideas and concepts emerge.

classes. They found that the visibility and prestige of two activities—athletics for boys and cheerleading for girls—served to reinforce and promote traditional gender roles and values. As they put it:

> Since male athletic events were the main social events of the school, both male athletes and female cheerleaders had considerable visibility. And since being well known was an important aspect of peer status, participants in these activities were likely to be members of the elite group. Consequently, the values they learned through these activities played a central role in the student culture. … Male athletes were encouraged to be achievement oriented, competitive, and aggressive; cheerleading candidates were encouraged to smile and be concerned about their appearance. (p. 209)

The requirements of the most visible, prestigious activities at the school, in other words, helped to perpetuate stereotypic sex roles.

There are no guarantees, however. After immersing yourself in the setting, observing carefully, asking appropriate questions, and learning to take good field notes, you may still draw a blank. You may end up without the foggiest notion of how to explain what is going on. That is not very likely, but it is possible. Just remember, do not take anything for granted. Do not be afraid to ask yourself, and others, naive questions. You are there to learn.

For a variety of reasons, what you learn in a particular setting might be different from what someone else might learn there. And what you think you have learned might not accurately reflect what was really going on. In other words, in fieldwork, as in every other form of research, you need to concern yourself about both the reliability and the validity of your observations and inferences.

Reliability and Validity

A few years ago, an Australian anthropologist named Derek Freeman made the front page of the *New York Times* by questioning Margaret Mead's famous findings about adolescent life in Samoa. Freeman claimed that back in the 1920s, when she did her fieldwork, Mead had gotten it all wrong. Far from being the peaceful, stressless society that Mead claimed it to be, Samoa—so Freeman said—was a violent, rigid, unpleasant place. The charges, countercharges, and letters to the editor continued for months. Ostensibly, the issue was the nature of Samoan society. Actually, the controversy concerned the reliability and validity of participant observation.

Margaret Mead (1928/1949) had gone to the South Pacific in the 1920s to study Samoan adolescents. She wanted to see whether the teen years were as stressful there as they appeared to be in the United States. Her method, of course, was participant observation. She spent several months immersed in village life, talking with a group of young girls, and finding out all she could about their lives. Her basic conclusion was that Samoan adolescents were remarkably happy and well-adjusted, and they also seemed to engage in playful and guilt-free sex. She attributed all of this, in large part, to what she perceived to be the permissive and pressure-free nature of their society. After years of participant observation of his own in Samoa, Freeman (1984) reached the conclusion that Mead had completely misunderstood Samoan society. Far from being the idyllic setting that Mead described, Freeman argued that Samoa was an unusually violent, aggressive, and puritanical place—not only not a nice place to live, but one you probably would not even want to visit.

Unfortunately, many people took this disagreement to be an indictment of the method that both Mead and Freeman had employed. Here were two professionals, both employing participant observation in the same place, who arrived at diametrically opposed conclusions about Samoa. How can that be? Does it mean that participant observation does not produce reliable results? And, if results are not reliable, how can they be valid?

Think back to the definition of reliability that was given in Chapter 1. To say that one's observations are reliable means that *given similar circumstances*, they can be duplicated, or repeated. Others must be able to verify what we claim to have seen. Freeman was, in fact, unable to verify what Mead claimed to have seen. But the Samoa that Mead described in the 1920s was not the same Samoa that Freeman came to know years later. Just as an example of the differences, consider this. In 1925, when she set sail for the South Pacific, Margaret Mead was a young woman, very small and girlish in appearance. She used as her informants girls who themselves were only 13 or 14 years of age. Derek Freeman gathered his information about Samoa over a number of years, first as a mature, then as an older man. His informants were Samoan chiefs and mature men like himself. It is no wonder that they came away with different pictures. As Scheper-Hughes (1984, p. 90) has pointed out, "Freeman could never have asked Samoan girls of 13 and 14 the kinds of questions that Mead had asked without being run off the island as a 'dirty old man.'"

Thus, the discrepancies between Mead's and Freeman's images of Samoa do not mean that either is, necessarily, inaccurate. The circumstances of their observations were dissimilar. They brought different backgrounds to bear on Samoa, they observed different people, with different kinds of knowledge about Samoan society, at different points in time. But the discrepancies between Mead's and Freeman's images of Samoa do point up the fact that in some cases, the reliability of participant observation will be indeterminate. Only if you could document that the setting was substantially the same from one observation period to another could the reliability of participant observation be assessed. The reliability of Molstad's (1986) observations about how brewery workers cope with repetitious and boring work could, presumably, be assessed as long as the bottling operations within breweries and the characteristics of the workers remained the same.

But there will be many instances of participant observation for which we are simply unable to assess reliability in any systematic way. Does that mean that they are automatically suspect, that we can have no faith in the findings? Not necessarily. The point of participant observation, you will recall, is to develop disciplined abstractions—theoretical concepts that will help us to explain and interpret what went on in the setting (Lofland and Lofland, 1984). As implied by the word "disciplined," and as noted earlier, it is incumbent upon the observer to ground these abstractions in observed instances of behavior. That means that the descriptions of occurrences in the setting should be as objective and concrete as possible, and that the abstractions derived from them should be closely tied to and illustrated with specific examples of actual events.

The issue of the validity of participant observation, then, becomes the issue of the extent to which the derived theoretical concepts provide an accurate explanation of what was seen in the setting itself. Does Kunda's (1992) notion of "drawing boundaries" provide a reasonable explanation of the behaviors he observed among the engineers at Tech? Do Loseke's (1992) ideas about the discretion of untrained day workers at the South Coast shelter for battered women account for why only certain "types" of women were admitted to the shelter? The major obligation of the participant observer with respect to validity is to provide sufficient objective evidence in the description of events in the setting to render the proposed interpretations plausible. In other words, as Kirk and Miller (1986) have pointed out, the validity of concern in participant observation is whether phenomena have been given proper theoretical labels. In Chapter 1, this was referred to as construct validity.

Participant observation, then, is a method for generating explanations and interpretations of the social and behavioral processes that occur in particular settings. The reliability and validity of these interpretations are assessed qualitatively, primarily with reference to the detailed description of the setting in question. The existence of the hypothesized processes is supported by appeal to particular aspects of the setting. Note that two observers witnessing the same events might generate different explanations and suggest different interpretations. That does not mean that either is invalid. It simply means that participant observation is not to be used for the testing of hypotheses. It is most appropriately used in the exploratory, descriptive, hypothesis-generating stage of research.

Another way of summing up is to say that the participant observer's job is to learn, to attempt to understand, and to generate ideas. There are, of course, some things that we know will interfere with learning. Alerting you to them now may help prevent your ending up empty-handed, or empty-headed.

Pitfalls for the Unwary

Francis Bacon once said that it is easier to evolve truth from error than from confusion. Keep that in mind. It may provide some consolation in your first efforts at fieldwork because, as you will see, there are ample opportunities for error. For convenience, I have grouped the more serious pitfalls into three broad categories: psychological, interpersonal, and ethical.

Psychological Pitfalls

The taking in of information by observation is referred to as **perception**. There are actually a number of different processes involved in perception: attention, encoding or interpretation, short-term memory, and rehearsal of what has been stored in short-term memory (e.g., Reed, 1988). Unfortunately, each of these processes is subject to bias.

Take **attention,** the process of concentrating on some aspect of your surroundings. In most situations there is simply more information available than we can handle. We are overwhelmed with sights, sounds, and smells and have to select small portions of what is available to attend to and encode. The aspects of a situation that we choose to attend to are a function of many things, such as our interests and our experience. There is some evidence, however, that in many situations we do not choose at all. Sometimes it seems as if situations choose for us by drawing our attention to certain of their features. All too often, we unthinkingly devote the lion's share of our attention to whatever or whomever happens to be the most salient stimulus in our environment, to whatever or whomever seems to stand out relative to other aspects of the situation.

Fiske and Taylor (1991, p. 248) point out that there are a variety of things that might make a particular person salient. For example, a person might be salient because they are somehow novel, or different from others in the situation. A black member of a group in which all others are white would be salient, as would a solo male in a group in which all others were female. A person might be salient because they dress in a way that is different from the others around them—wearing brighter clothes, for example, or formal clothes when everyone else is in jeans and T-shirts. People also capture the attention of others when they behave in unusual, unexpected ways. And if a person is somehow relevant to your goals (i.e., a prospective date), or if they occupy a prominent position in the setting, you may end up paying more attention to them than they really merit. These sources of salience are summarized in Table 1. The problem is that perceptually salient information may subsequently be more accessible to memory when you later try to make sense of what you have seen. You may infer, erroneously, that that person or thing had more of an influence on what occurred than they or it really did. Therefore, you must be very careful not to fall into the trap of paying too much attention to the salient people, or features, of the setting. Make a conscious effort to distribute your attention to all aspects of the situation.

The second component of the perceptual process, the encoding or interpretation of what you observe, is also subject to distortion. It is impossible to go into any situation with your mind a complete blank. Because of who you are and the events that you have experienced recently and/or frequently, certain concepts and certain ways of looking at things will be more accessible to you than others. The technical name for this is *priming*—that is, you will be primed to activate some ideas more readily than others. As Fiske and Taylor (1991, p. 257) put it: "Social perception is heavily influenced by the *accessibility* of relevant categories, that is, categories that are easily activated, given the perceiver's current goals, needs, and expectations." For example, some research by McKenzie-Mohr and Zanna (1990) demonstrated that among males

Table 1 The Causes of Social Salience

A PERSON CAN BE SALIENT RELATIVE TO THE PERCEIVER'S:

Immediate context

By being novel (sole person of that race, sex, hair color)

By being figural (bright, complex, moving)

Prior knowledge or expectations

By being unusual for that person (e.g., behaving in unexpected ways)

By being unusual for that person's social category (e.g., behaving in out-of-role ways)

By being unusual for people in general (e.g., behaving negatively or in some extreme way)

Other attentional tasks

By being goal-relevant (e.g., being a boss, or a date)

By dominating the visual field (e.g., sitting at the head of the table, being on camera more than others)

By the perceiver being instructed to observe the person

Source: Fiske and Taylor, 1991, p. 248.

who tended to think in stereotypic terms about male-female differences, those who had recently viewed a pornographic movie were more likely to respond in a stereotypic manner to a woman they subsequently encountered in an apparently unrelated context. That is, their behavior was rated as being more sexually suggestive and, later, they mainly recalled the woman's physical features rather than what she had said. Males who had similar beliefs, but who had not been primed by the movie, did not react in this way.

There is a related way in which expectations may blind us to what is really out there to be observed. On the basis of one or two items of information about a person, we may categorize them as being a certain type. We then expect them to behave in certain ways, and those expectations may interfere with our ability to see and utilize new information about the person, especially information that would contradict the initial categorization. For example, Phillips and Dipboye (1989) studied a number of district managers of a large corporation, as well as job applicants who had been interviewed by those managers. This corporation required that applicants first submit written materials, such as a résumé and an application form. Subsequently, they were contacted and asked to come in for an interview. Phillips and Dipboye found that on the basis of the initial written application materials, the managers were forming definite expectations about what each applicant would be like. These preinterview expectations influenced the nature of the interviews themselves. The more positive the managers' expectations about a given applicant, the more likely the managers were to use the interview to try to "recruit" rather than "evaluate" that applicant, and the more likely the applicant was to receive a job offer. The point, of course, is that it is important not to fall victim to the **primacy effect:** that is, do not let the first things you learn about a setting or the people in it have undue influence on your impressions. First impressions may be seriously distorted.

Reconstructing a day's events from a few jotted notes taken at odd moments during the day can also be a hazardous enterprise as far as accuracy is concerned. Shweder (1975) provided some important evidence on this point, using data originally collected by Newcomb (1929) in a summer camp for boys. The camp lasted for about 3½ weeks and, during that time, the day-to-day behaviors of each camper were recorded by six observers. The observers noted every occurrence of each of 26 separate behaviors exhibited by the boys. Some examples of the behaviors recorded are the following:

- Speaks with confidence of his own abilities
- Spends more than an hour of the day alone
- Painstaking in making up his bed
- Talks more than his share of the time
- Gets into scraps with other boys

These observations, noted as soon as possible after they occurred, constitute a record of the actual behavior of the boys. At the end of the entire camp session, each of the six observers was asked to give an overall rating to each boy on each of the 26 behaviors. The latter ratings constitute what Shweder termed the rated behavior of the boys, and these ratings were made purely on the basis of memory, that is, without looking at the earlier recordings of actual behavior. Finally, Shweder asked some graduate students to look at the 26 behaviors and, for each possible pair of those behaviors, rate the conceptual similarity of the behaviors themselves. These ratings constituted what Shweder referred to as the **preexisting conceptual scheme,** that is, the expectations about which behaviors are similar, or related, or likely to be exhibited by the same person. The major results of interest are the following. First, the actual behavior of the boys did not correspond very closely to what the observers remembered 3 weeks later. In other words, memory is unreliable. Second, the preexisting conceptual scheme *did* correspond fairly closely to the rated behavior. Thus, not only is memory unreliable, but there is also a systematic, predictable distortion in memory in the direction of our expectations about what is likely to be related to what. Therefore, you must devise ways of checking on yourself. Writing up field notes promptly, as soon after observation as possible, will help, but it will not completely solve the problem.

Similarly, you should be aware that informants are subject to memory distortions just as you are. Just because they were "there" when the events of interest took place does not mean that they will remember those events accurately. For example, in a historical study of the development of a public service corporation, Simmons (1985) had occasion to interview many of the people who, years earlier, had helped to plan the corporation. She found that in their recollections, the participants tended to exaggerate and expand those periods of time when things had been going well and to shrink and minimize those periods when things were not. She also found that informants who thought they knew the whole story often had only a small fragment of it. When events occurred for which they did not have an explanation, they often invented seemingly plausible explanations, which were then remembered as having been what actually occurred.

The potential observer biases we have been discussing are internal ones. They all stem from normal psychological processes, imperfections in the ways we take in, manipulate, and try to make sense of the information available to us. The other major category of potential observer bias is more external in nature. The problems here stem from the nature of the observer's relations with other people in the setting being observed.

Interpersonal Problems

Moving into a strange setting and trying to learn its nuances and subtleties can be a frightening experience. The more different the setting is from what you are used to, the more frightening it is likely to be. Nothing can be taken for granted. Everything has to be learned from scratch. In fact, it is not at all unusual for beginning fieldworkers to feel overwhelmed by the task. Commenting on her own first experience in the field, Margaret Mead (1928/1949) once said: "For my first two months in Samoa, as I learned to speak the language, eat the food, and interpret the postures and the gestures of the people, I found myself often saying under my breath, 'I can't do it. I can't do it.'" Similarly, Buford (1992, p. 20) notes that in his first attempts to make contact with some of the violent football hooligans in England, he felt extraordinarily out of place: "…after a while, I became convinced that my manner was starting to make everyone around me uncomfortable … that they thought I was a strange, creepy little moron, and that I should disappear."

Such feelings seem to be the rule, although there are, as always, exceptions. The culprit seems to be a complete lack of any meaningful social relationships during the initial stages of research. Even when people have agreed to allow you to be present, you are initially only in, but not of, the setting. According to Wax (1971), it is only with the establishment of a few genuine personal relationships that those feelings of incompetence and lack of progress are likely to pass. That makes sense, of course, because what you are there to learn are the nuances and subtleties of social life, which means you must participate in and observe that life up close. If the others in the setting merely tolerate your presence at public events and are polite to you, you will not learn what you need to know. You must win the confidence and friendship of at least a few people in the setting so that they will explain things to you, share confidences, help you meet others who can assist you, and tell you when you blunder.

There is a potential problem, however, that you need to be aware of. Given your marginal, in but not of, status in the setting, you may attract some of the more peripheral characters. That is, there is a real danger that the people most likely to gravitate toward you will be those who are themselves marginal for one reason or another. You would not want to disregard what those people have to say, of course, but you would need to keep it in perspective. You would need to take into account, for example, their status, or lack of status, in the setting. You would also not want to be perceived as attending only to those who are malcontent. People might begin to question your motives for being there.

But even in building relationships with the more central, well-integrated members of the setting, there is the potential for bias. There is ample evidence (e.g., Myers, 1993) that we are most attracted to those who are similar to us in any of a variety of ways. Thus, it is quite likely that there will be some people in the setting with whom you more easily and naturally establish a good rapport. There will be others whom you find it somewhat more difficult to talk to. The danger, of course, is that you will rely too heavily on what the former have to say and not give equal time, or credibility, to the latter.

As you become known and accepted within the setting, a new problem arises. Ideally, the setting and the interactions within it should be unaffected by your presence. That may be an impossible ideal. People who treat you in a relatively normal manner will expect you to reciprocate. Having helped you by telling you about the setting, showing you around, answering your questions, and introducing you to others, they have a right to expect that you will help them should the occasion arise. There is probably no way to avoid performing some service for others within the setting, assuming you want to maintain your acceptability. Look at it as an opportunity to learn more about what is going on. Wax (1971), for example, let Indian children wait in her house for the school bus on cold winter mornings. She took the opportunity to talk to them about school and a variety of other topics. Loseke (1992) notes that she was drawn into greater involvement at the South Coast shelter for battered women by starting to answer the telephone when none of the regular workers was around. Whyte (1951) was elected secretary of a club he was observing. He was reluctant to accept, but did so because it gave him an excuse for openly taking copious notes while meetings were in progress.

Ethical Issues

People behave differently around strangers, particularly strangers doing research. That is one reason why you should not expect to go into a setting and learn all about it in a week or two. It will take time, but after a few months, you will no longer be a stranger. One option for participant observers is **concealed identity**—that is, concealing the fact that you are doing research. There is ample precedent for that, and sometimes it is necessary. In a well-known example, Rosenhan (1973) and his colleagues concealed the fact that they were doing research when they gained admittance to the wards of psychiatric hospitals. If they had not, if the nurses and doctors and ward attendants had been told that they were being observed, chances are that they would not have behaved normally. Concealing your identity, then, can have advantages (Adler and Adler, 1987). It enables you to observe certain settings that you would not be able to otherwise. It can also hasten your acceptance into settings, and people are more likely to behave "naturally" during the initial stages of your observation.

Unless it is absolutely necessary, however, the ethical problems created by such undercover research seem to outweigh the advantages. It is clearly a form of deception, and some people feel that deception cannot be justified in research. As Kimmel (1988) has pointed out, however, others argue that deception such as this is justifiable when no alternative means of investigation is possible and when the risks to those being observed are minimal. The deception involved in concealing your identity as an observer also violates the principle of informed consent. Most formulations of ethical principles governing research, such as those of the American Psychological Association (1992), strongly advocate obtaining informed consent from research participants. People have a right to choose whether or not they want to participate in research *after* having been fully informed about any possible adverse consequences and *after* having been informed that they can terminate their participation in the research at any time. Of course, if you are observing only public behavior and individual people are not identified, informed consent is not necessary. For example, seeking out different types of saloons and cocktail bars in order to sit and observe the drinking patterns of the (anonymous) patrons (Maugh, 1989) would not require informed consent.

When you contemplate long-term immersion in a particular setting, where you will get to know the individuals involved, being open about who you are and why you are there can forestall some ethical dilemmas. Unless you are really an odd bird, for example, you are bound to make a few friends while doing your observing. Those people are likely to feel used or betrayed when they find out you were just doing research, as they probably will when you leave. Also, suppose they reveal something to you that is immoral or criminal. How would you handle that? (For some possible answers, see Box 3.) As long as people know you are doing research, they will not necessarily expect you to do everything they do, although they will—and have a right to—expect you to accept them on their own terms. However, if you have chosen to conceal your identity, things can get pretty sticky. If the group or any of its members engage in any illegal or immoral activities, you may be expected to do so as well, or, at least, not to reveal the behavior. If they find out later that you were not really one of them after all, they are likely to feel betrayed—even if you never violated their trust and they never did anything wrong.

My advice? Avoid concealing your identity. Let people know who you are and why you are there. It will forestall all sorts of problems. It will also give you greater freedom to move around, ask questions, and be pleasantly, naively, nosy. You will still have to demonstrate to people that you can be trusted to be discreet, as Adler (1985) had to do in her observations of drug dealers and smugglers and as Buford (1992) had to do in his observations of violent football supporters. You will also have to demonstrate to people that you are sincerely interested in them and their activities. That should be easy, however, because if you are not sincerely interested in them, you should not

---

Box 3

Ethical Dilemmas: Observing Illegal and Immoral Activity

Participant observation requires an intimate familiarity with the everyday routine of the people and setting being observed. One of the dangers inherent in this requirement is that, on occasion, the observer may witness activities that are illegal and/or immoral. For example, Taylor (1987) spent a year as an observer in a large state hospital on a ward with 73 severely retarded males, aged 14 to 44. As he became a familiar figure on the ward, the attendants "tested" him by drawing him into activities that were prohibited by the rules of the institution, such as drinking beer and smoking on the night shift. Once these "membership tests" had been passed, the attendants relaxed, accepting him as someone who would not blow the whistle. Subsequently, Taylor witnessed numerous acts of verbal and physical abuse. Attendants swore at patients, called them names, hit them, teased them, threw water on them, and even had them swallow burning cigarettes (repeatedly).

What should the participant observer do in a situation like this? Taylor identifies four choices: (1) intervene, that is, attempt to stop instances of abuse as they occur; (2) leave the setting completely; (3) inform appropriate authorities, including the police, about anything illegal and/or immoral; and (4) continue to observe what happens in the setting. Taylor chose the latter; that is, he continued to observe what happened on the ward, without informing anyone or attempting to intervene.

Some people may find that choice unacceptable and even, perhaps, unethical. But there are considerations that may justify it. The first is the potential impact of the research. Had Taylor reprimanded a particular attendant, or forcibly intervened to stop a specific act of abuse, he may well have been successful—at that time. But the abuse would not have stopped. As soon as Taylor was out of sight, it would have continued. On the other hand, the systematic documentation of the abuse, as revealed in Taylor's published work and testimony before the U.S. Senate, may have helped to stop the abuse permanently, both in the institution he observed and at other similar institutions. However, degree of harm must also be considered. That is, witnessing a murder or rape that one could prevent, obviously, demands intervention and blowing the whistle. In such situations, continuing to observe is not an option. But where do you draw the line between intervention and nonintervention? Another consideration is that participant observers are ethically obligated to protect the privacy of those they observe. How can that be done if you blow the whistle?

There are no easy answers to these questions. If you contemplate doing any participant observation, however, you should give them some thought.

---

be there. And remember, your task is to observe and to learn, not to pass judgment.

Having it known that you are an observer keeps everything aboveboard. You will no doubt still make friends, but there will be no sense of being duplicitous on your part or, later, of having been used on theirs. It will also make it easier for everyone when you choose to draw the line and say thanks just the same, but you would just as soon not participate in a particular activity. Asking dumb questions, taking notes, and generally being nosy are also more acceptable behaviors if everybody knows what you are doing. However, you should be aware that such openness may create another problem. Suppose your interpretations of the setting are not very flattering, that they imply something negative about the people and/or traditions in the setting. If people know why you are in the setting and that you plan to write about it, it is likely that some of them, at least, will want to see what you have written. And if what you have written makes them look bad, you may be in for some unpleasantness.

But it is still true that in participant observation, letting people know why you are there allows them to protect their right to privacy. They can decide for themselves when and how much they are willing to let you know about themselves. They can tell you some things, or let you witness some things, and not others. It is usually assumed that the information that is revealed to you will be treated confidentially. What that typically means for the participant observer is that no one else should be allowed to have access to the data (or field notes) in a form that would identify the individuals and/or the setting that was observed. One way to do this, of course, is to give fictitious names to people and settings when writing about them. Ellis (1986), for example, gave the pseudonyms "Fishneck" and "Crab Reef Island" to the two Chesapeake Bay communities she observed in order to prevent their locations becoming known. Some of the things she had said about the residents, especially the residents of Fishneck, would have caused them embarrassment had they been identified.

When Observation Is Appropriate

The major attraction of participant observation for many people is that it gives you a meaningful, coherent picture of a setting. You get to see the whole, in all its complex, dynamic reality, and not just bits and pieces. As Kirk and Miller (1986) have pointed out, it is the long-term personal interaction of participant observation that provides an understanding of a setting that cannot be attained with any other research method. Not all questions of interest can be studied with participant observation, however. Suppose you were interested in suicide rates in different groups, or the relationship between economic cycles and mob violence. Suppose you wanted to learn how Democrats feel about birth control. Participant observation is simply not an appropriate technique for finding answers to such questions.

Perhaps one way to define when participant observation is appropriate, then, is to be clear about when it is not. As Jorgensen (1989) has pointed out, participant observation is not suited for testing specific hypotheses about causal relations. Experiments, which we shall cover in detail in Chapter 8, are much better suited for that. Participant observation is, also, not the method of choice when we want to assess the opinions and/or beliefs of large groups of people. That is what surveys (Chapter 6) are for. And, unless you have incredible patience, it is inappropriate for events of long duration and very infrequent events. There are also some activities that are simply inaccessible to observers.

With groups that are small enough so that you could really get to know the people involved in a reasonable period of time and that are willing to put up with your presence, participant observation may be feasible. Some examples? Margaret Mead's fieldwork in Samoa took 9 months, and her detailed observations were confined to a group of girls living in three contiguous villages. Sato's (1991) observations of Japanese motorcycle gangs extended over a 15-month period, during which time he had contact with about 70 gang members. But, depending on the issue, time in the field may be relatively brief. The doomsday cult mentioned earlier (Festinger, Riecken, and Schachter, 1956) was observed over a 2-month period from October to December, and most of the observations were done in the prophet's household. In his examination of how time is structured in restaurant kitchens, Fine (1990) spent a month in each of four restaurants in the Minneapolis-St. Paul area. Clearly, the groups observed in these studies tended to be fairly small and the time periods fairly limited. There is sometimes the possibility of part-time observation carried out over more extended time periods. Ellis (1986), for example, carried out her observations of the two fishing villages mentioned earlier over a 10-year period. Her occasional visits ranged from a few days to a few months in length. Buford (1992) spent several years, off and on, attending soccer matches and drinking and running with "the lads" he wanted to observe. In other words, it all depends on you, what you are interested in, and how much time you can devote to it.

There is another consideration in deciding whether participant observation is an appropriate procedure in a particular situation: Do you have an ax to grind? Do you want to prove something about the situation? If you do, participant observation is definitely not for you! Because of the multiple opportunities for bias in participant observation, it should be used only when you genuinely want to learn what is going on in a setting, only when you can approach the setting with an open mind. Given the tremendous amounts of information available in dynamic social settings, the ambiguities inherent in most interactions, and the limited perspective and biases of a single observer, you could find evidence to fit almost any preconception if you looked hard enough. Thus, if you already know what is going on and you just want to gather a little evidence to prove it, don't bother. You will waste your time, and everybody else's as well.

On the other hand, if you really are curious, if you really would like to know what is going on in the particular setting and how it gets done, then participant observation may be just the thing for you. Try it.

Summary

Participant observation emerged as an extension of the descriptive narratives brought back by explorers of faraway places. There are also a number of parallels between participant observation and reporting; both involve the development of intimate familiarity with a setting, the systematic recording of observations, and the gathering of auxiliary information. What distinguishes the two is the scientific goal of the participant observer: the development of disciplined abstractions.

Kunda's fieldwork in the engineering division at Tech provides an example of the development of disciplined abstractions. Tech engineers and computer specialists had what appeared at first glance to be ideal working conditions: good pay, freedom from set hours, congenial and like-minded colleagues, and state-of-the-art facilities. But Tech had such a strong corporate culture and demanded such a commitment to the company that employees were forced into finding ways to preserve their private lives. They did so by drawing boundaries between work and nonwork or by finding ways to create cognitive and emotional distance from the all-embracing corporation.

The key to participant observation is developing intimate familiarity with some specific social setting. Three steps are involved: doing your homework, gaining entry, and immersion in the setting. The point is to learn how whatever it is that is supposed to get done in the setting really gets done. To do that, you have to be personally accepted, not just administratively accepted. Gaining acceptance is therefore your most important task.

So that you do not forget what you are learning, your second most important task is the systematic taking of field notes—every day, without fail. Multiple copies of your field notes are necessary for sorting and cross-classifying into your mundane and analytic files. The mundane files are used to deposit information on specific aspects of the people and setting. The analytic files are the basis for the development of disciplined abstractions. As ideas begin to occur to you about processes operating within the setting, you create files in which to deposit copies of notes pertinent to each idea.

There are three general classes of pitfalls that can create problems for the unwary participant observer: (1) those stemming from imperfections in the way you take in and process information; (2) those stemming from relations, or lack of relations, with other people in the setting; and (3) those stemming from ethical considerations. The first class of pitfalls includes the dangers of devoting too much attention to the most salient aspects of a setting, of letting your expectations bias what you think you see, and of trusting your memory. The interpersonal pitfalls include the initial marginal status of the observer and the observer's lack of social relations, both of which can seriously impede progress. You also need to recognize varying perspectives within a setting, but you should not give undue weight to the views of those with whom you most quickly and/or most easily establish rapport. The major ethical issues revolve around the deception involved should you choose to conceal your identity and purpose. If at all possible, being open and honest about who you are and why you are there is best.

Participant observation is not appropriate for use with large populations, events of great duration, infrequent events, and activities inaccessible to observers. It is also not appropriate when you have something to prove.

Recommended Readings

Ellis, C. (1986). *Fisher folk: Two communities on Chesapeake Bay*. Lexington, KY: University of Kentucky Press.

Carolyn Ellis began her study of two small communities on Chesapeake Bay when she was an undergraduate at William and Mary. Subsequently, over a 12-year period, she visited and lived in each of the communities on many occasions, staying from a few days to a few months each time. Fishneck and Crab Reef Island, as she calls the two, were similar in many ways. Economically, both relied on individual fishermen, mining the riches of the bay. Geographically, the two were only 60 miles apart. Racially, the residents of both were 100% Caucasian. But in other ways, the two communities were as different as day and night. In Fishneck, the illiteracy rate was extremely high, houses were crowded and run-down, yards were muddy and strewn with paper, bottles, and broken glass. On Crab Reef Island, the lawns were neat, hedges clipped, houses well tended, and inside, the rooms were tidy. Telephones, electricity, and bathrooms with modern plumbing were the rule on Crab Reef. In Fishneck, bathtubs were used mainly to hold piles of clothes. Why the differences? Ellis suggests a number of possible explanations. For example, both communities were "religious," but in Fishneck, church was an individual, expressive experience—you went to sing and be saved. The rest of the week, you could forget about it. On Crab Reef Island, the church was a central moral force in the community, organizing committees, taking part in political action, and permeating all aspects of daily life. Ellis provides an interesting analysis of how two communities that were so similar could become so different. It is well worth reading.

Freeman, D. (1984). *Margaret Mead and Samoa: The making and unmaking of an anthropological myth*. New York: Viking Penguin.

Although we have discussed this book in the text, it is worth reading in its entirety. It ignited what turned out to be one of the major social science controversies of the 1980s. You will recall that the roots of the controversy began in 1925, when Margaret Mead set out for the South Seas. Her intent was to examine the adolescent experience in a culture as different from that of the United States as possible. She wanted to see whether the conflict and stress that appeared to characterize the teen years in America was typical of teens everywhere. If they were not, then maybe there was something about American culture that produced the problems. On the island of Ta'u, in American Samoa, she found a small group of teenagers who seemed unusually happy and well-adjusted. Here, or so it seemed, was proof that culture, and not biology, was all-important. Her description of this group, which was published in 1928 as *Coming of Age in Samoa*, created a sensation, and Margaret Mead went on to become America's most famous anthropologist. Based on his own experience in Samoa, Derek Freeman has claimed that Mead got it all wrong. He attacks almost everything about her work there and paints a much darker, violent picture of Samoan society. Having denounced a patron saint of anthropology, Freeman's book has been both lauded and reviled. Just remember, as you are reading, that both he and Mead had something to "prove."

Jorgensen, D. L. (1989). *Participant observation: A methodology for human studies*. Newbury Park, CA: Sage.

One of the things that veteran participant observers recommend is that you read a number of reports of fieldwork as a way of preparing yourself for your own observations. Jorgensen's slim (132 pages) introduction to participant observation should be helpful in this respect because it is an excellent source of references to both classic and recent examples of the method in use. The book is also worth reading for itself, however. Jorgensen not only discusses the parts and pieces of participant observation, in more detail than we have been able to do here, but also provides a clear defense of how and why fieldwork must differ from other types of research. He argues, as has been suggested in the text, that in participant observation, reliability is a somewhat secondary consideration to validity. But does it really make sense to talk about valid, but unreliable, findings? Sometimes it does.

Richard, M. P. (1986). Goffman revisited: Relatives vs. administrators in nursing homes. *Qualitative Sociology, 9,* 321–338.

Participant observation requires close, firsthand involvement in a specific setting. It is the most intimate and personal of research methods, because if you are really participating in a setting, part of what you are observing consists of reactions to you. Reporting what was seen and heard, then, requires that the presence and potential influence of the observer be continually acknowledged. Not doing so is a subtle form of deception, apparently motivated by the desire to make the report appear unbiased, that is, as if it had been recorded by a hidden camera. Michel Richard uses an episode from his own life to show that such detachment from the setting being observed is not necessary and may, in fact, be detrimental. In 1982, Richard's mother, who had been diagnosed as having Alzheimer's disease, was admitted to a nursing home. His unhappiness with the care she was receiving and his efforts to change it resulted in a running 2-year battle with various physicians, administrators, and other nursing home personnel. From his experiences during that period, Richard was able to extract a number of "gatekeeping tactics," strategies used by the home staff to keep relatives of inmates at arm's length and to thwart attempts at change. The article is well worth reading as an example of how one's personal experiences can be used in theory development.

3

Using Observation to Test Ideas

Ethology is the field of study concerned with the behavior of animals in their natural settings. Through careful, painstaking observation, ethologists have contributed a great deal of information to our knowledge of the diets, activities, sleep cycles, temperature preferences, and habitats of a variety of animal species. For many animals, such data are almost impossible to obtain and, as a consequence, very little is known about them. But, think about it for a moment. How could you find out about social relationships among free-roaming chimpanzees (Goodall, 1990)? You would have to observe them in their natural settings, and that can be extremely difficult (Tuttle, 1990). In fact, our knowledge of the habits of gorillas, whales, and hundreds of other animals is so limited that any new tidbit of information is valuable.

The reason for mentioning ethology here is that it forms a bridge between participant observation (Chapter 2) and our current concern with the use of observation to test specific ideas. In ethology, the observer is usually not a participant, but the goal is still one of trying to understand how the animal lives in and adapts to its natural habitat, one that is usually different from the ethologist's. Similarly, participant observation with humans is often most useful in settings that are unfamiliar to the observer. The approach of both the ethologist and the participant observer, then, is initially an **empirical approach.** They are there simply to observe, to learn all there is to learn, even if that means they have to live among gorillas (Fossey, 1983). And there is a lot to learn. Jane Goodall (1989, 1990) has noted that even after 30 years of observing chimpanzees in Africa, she and her associates are still learning basic things about their behavior.

Because of the difficulty of observing naturally occurring animal behavior, ethologists often contrive special techniques of observation. For example, suppose you wanted to know how herring gulls find their way back to the same place year after year. Griffin (1985) reports that when he first became interested in the homing behavior of birds, all that was really known was that birds taken to a distant location and released *sometimes* found their way back home. Even those that made it home, however, often did not show up for days or weeks. No one knew whether they flew a direct, but leisurely, route home or simply scattered randomly until they happened across a familiar landmark—like the seacoast or a river—and then followed that until they arrived. If they flew *directly* home, that would have meant that they possessed a sense of direction, whether learned or innate. But if they just flew randomly about until they came across something familiar, no "homing ability" had to be posited to explain their return. Somehow Griffin had to observe the birds' entire flight, from release to return. To do so, he obtained a private pilot's license, bought a used two-seater plane, and circled overhead while herring gulls taken into unfamiliar territory inland and released tried to find their way home. He found that they apparently had no ability to head directly home. They flew about in random directions, and only those who chanced across a familiar landmark made it back.

Similarly, there are many areas in the study of everyday human life in which what is needed is some way of sorting things out, of separating fact from fancy. The approach called for here is the **rational approach.** It involves formulating a specific question, just as Griffin did about the homing of gulls, and deciding which behaviors you need to observe in order to answer that question. Thus, our continued discussion of observation in research needs a couple of changes in emphasis. The focus will be on situations in which the observer (1) is not, or is only minimally, a participant and (2) has narrowed his or her interest down to a specific question for which an answer is sought via watching what people do. It is important to note that the kind of observation being discussed here is nothing very esoteric. It is simply the systematic application of a skill that you already have. The "systematic" qualifier does imply that you are going to have to be a little more rigorous, a little more demanding of yourself (and others) in using it. But, as Weick (1985) has said, with a little instruction and effort, anyone can become a more patient observer and a more careful methodologist. There is no new, or occult, skill to be developed.

People Watching

The source of the specific question to be investigated can vary. What piques your curiosity may leave someone else bored, and vice versa. What strikes you as peculiar and in need of explanation, others may take completely for granted. But, generally speaking, there are two starting points for research—that is, two major categories of questions.

The first category consists of those questions or hypotheses that are raised by, or derived from, a theory. The goal of your observation in this case will be to clarify or test the theory. For example, Eisenberger (1992) has proposed a theory to explain why some people are more industrious than others—that is, why there are such tremendous differences among people in how long and hard they are willing to work in pursuit of their goals. Eisenberger's idea is that when people reach a goal—or are rewarded—after great exertion, the physical and mental sensations of the effort itself become associated with the reward and thus are perceived to be more pleasurable, or at least somewhat less aversive. You can probably think of several situations in which observations bearing on this theory might be made. One possible prediction is that the greater the *variety* of tasks for which a person has been rewarded after exerting effort, the more likely the person is to be willing to work hard in the future. Thus, the theory suggests, a person who letters in three sports in high school would be more likely to continue their athletic training well into adulthood than a person who trains equally hard in high school, but at only one sport. Presumably, for the three-letter person, more *different* physical and mental sensations have been associated with reward and, hence, have become pleasurable in themselves. Note that if your prediction comes from a theory, as with this example, and your intent is to test or clarify the theory, you will be engaged in what is referred to as **basic research.**

The second starting point for research, the second category of questions about how and why people do the things they do, consists of those questions arising from the need to make an intelligent decision in a specific situation. For example, suppose you were working for an appliance manufacturer and you were trying to design a stovetop with four burners and a control for each. There are an infinite number of arrangements, but you would need to select one that appears natural to people and one that does not require labels, because they detract from the appearance of the product. You might want to draw, or build, a few mock-ups and ask people to identify which controls went with which burners (Figure 1). The idea, of course, is to find a label-free layout that people can use without error and without having to memorize the connections between burners and controls. In gathering information about the optimal layout of burners and controls, you would be conducting **applied research,** research intended to help you make the best decision possible about what to do in a particular situation.

Note, again, that it is the source of your question, not the methodology employed to answer it, that determines whether you are doing basic or ap-

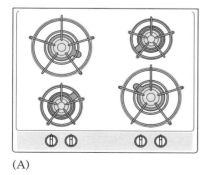 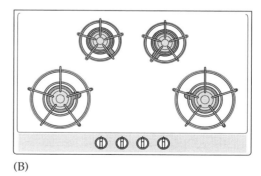

(A)   (B)

1   An example of an applied design problem: How can the burners and controls be arranged so as not to require labels and, at the same time, not force users to memorize the correspondence between burners and controls? Note that in (A), you have no way of knowing which control goes with which burner, unless the controls are labeled. In (B), there is a clear relationship between burners and controls and there is no need for labels. (From Norman, 1988, p. 76.)

plied research. Unfortunately, there has been a great deal of silliness propagated about basic versus applied research—with the pure basic research people tending to look down their noses at those mucking about with applied research problems. Ideally, of course, there should be a continuous interplay between the two (Jones, 1989). Findings from applied research should help to generate theoretical ideas, which are tested and clarified in basic research, then extended to practical settings to further the understanding of processes there and suggest directions for further applied research. As Lewin (1951) once put it, such cooperation is possible only "if the theorist does not look toward applied problems with highbrow aversion or with a fear of social

---

<u>Box 1</u>

Experience Sampling: A Method for Self-Observation

Mihaly Csikszentmihalyi suggests that under certain conditions people become totally absorbed in what they are doing. When that happens, it seems to be accompanied by the following subjective experiences: (1) a sense of being in control emerges; (2) attention becomes focused on the task at hand; (3) awareness of time disappears; (4) self-consciousness dissipates; and (5) cares are forgotten (Csikszentmihalyi, 1990). Csikszentmihalyi has named this combination of subjective experiences "flow." In attempting to study the characteristics of flow, he found that questionnaires and interviews were of limited usefulness. True, you could ask people about such experiences and try to get them to recall exactly what they were doing and how they felt, but memory is capricious and people are not very accurate in recalling what they were thinking, or how they were feeling, at a particular point in time.

To overcome these limitations, Csikszentmihalyi invented a technique called the experience sampling method. Subjects participating in the research are given a beeper and a small booklet of self-report forms. Carrying the beeper and the booklet with them, they go about their normal daily activities. At seven or eight randomly selected times each day, the beeper is signaled. When that occurs, the subjects are supposed to fill out one of the experience sampling forms about what they are doing at that moment. In addition to asking the subjects to rate their mood, feelings, and level of concentration on a series of scales, the form asks them to note the time, what they were thinking about, who they were with, and the characteristics of the activity they were engaged in.

Data from a variety of people engaged in a variety of different tasks indicate that flow is most likely to occur when one's skills pertinent to the task at hand and the perceived demands of the situation are both above average. When skills are above average, but challenges are below average, boredom sets in. You are in control, but likely to lose interest. When challenges are above average, but your skills are not up to par, concentration is high—the task has your attention—but you are likely to get anxious about it and self-conscious about your performance. The evidence also indicates that for many work and leisure situations, high demands matched by high skills not only result in absorption in the task, but also produce greater satisfaction, happiness, and motivation.

Csikszentmihalyi's use of a beeper to signal people when to attend to and note what they are doing is an attempt to circumvent the problem of memory loss in self-observation. In the self-observation of experience sampling, as in other observational schemes, the behavior of interest must be noted as soon as it occurs.

problems, and if the applied [researcher] realizes that there is nothing so practical as a good theory."

Regardless of whether the question that has captured your attention is a basic, theoretical one or a practical, applied one, there is always a common goal: valid information with which to answer the question. Considerable creative ingenuity may be required to obtain that information. (For an example of a creative solution to an observational problem, see Box 1.) It may stimulate your creativity to consider the different types of behavior that can, in fact, be observed and used to answer your questions.

Varieties of Behavior for Observation

It should come as no surprise that a great deal of observational research has focused on language, that is, on what people say. For example, Yarnold and Grimm (1988) found that subjects identified as having a "type A" personality—hard-driving, competitive, hasty, impatient—tend to dominate the more relaxed and easy-going "type B's" in discussion groups. The type A's do this by generating more and longer arguments in support of their own position and, similarly, generating more and longer arguments against their opponent's position.

Verbal behavior is, indeed, the single most important category of behavior to observe, and we shall discuss it in detail in the second half of this chapter. But people also express themselves in a variety of other ways, and each of these alternative modes of expression can serve as the basis for observational measures, depending, of course, on what it is you are interested in. The three categories of behavior that we shall consider here, all of which can be systematically observed in testing your ideas, are (1) extralinguistic, (2) nonverbal, and (3) spatial.

Extralinguistic behaviors are the noncontent aspects of speech. As you are probably well aware, it is not just what you say but also how you say it that conveys information to a listener. For example, in the study of type As mentioned above, Yarnold and Grimm (1988) found that by focusing just on what was said, a great deal of what actually went on during the discussions was missed. Tone of voice, loudness, rate of speaking, dialect, tendencies to interrupt, pronunciation, and a variety of other such markers convey information. If you were interested in the extent to which people are emotionally involved in an issue, for example, you might want to note how often they interrupt others. Or, if you were interested in the factors that contribute to first impressions, you might want to record accents. Giles (1990) has pointed out that listeners infer many things from accents, only some of which are accurate. That, in fact, raises an important question: How do you know that the behavior you are observing really means what you think it does? Is it a valid indicator of the concept of interest? Since this issue also pertains to the other kinds of behavior that can be observed, let's examine them first.

Logically, **nonverbal behavior** is all behavior other than verbal, so both extralinguistic and spatial behaviors are really special categories of nonverbal behavior. Nonverbal behavior includes everything from semiconscious gestures and cues, like fingering your beard, to specific overt action sequences, like fastening your seat belt. Any identifiable behavior can serve as the object to be observed. Kendrick and MacFarlane (1986), for example, were interested in the relation between temperature and aggression. As their index of aggression they decided to use horn honking. Hidden observers stationed by the side of the road simply counted the number of honks when one of their confederates blocked traffic with her car by sitting through a green light. The study was done in Phoenix, Arizona, in temperatures ranging up to 116°. They found that the higher the temperature, the more honking. This was especially true for drivers with their windows rolled down, drivers who presumably did not have air conditioning.

Consider a few more examples. Geller and Kalsher (1990) observed the number of beers and mixed drinks consumed at a fraternity party under two different conditions: self-service or bartender service. They found that beer drinkers drank more, and faster, when they could get their own. In contrast, those drinking mixed drinks had more to drink when they were being served by a bartender. Geller et al. (1989) used observers to document an increase in seat belt use following a "fasten your seat belt" campaign. Two observers, positioned some distance from each other, independently verbalized relevant information about passing cars into tape recorders: license plate number, shoulder belt being used, male or female driver. The license plate numbers were recorded so that the reliability of the observations could be checked—that is, when the two observers saw the same car, did they agree on whether or not the seat belt was, in fact, being used? Durdan, Reeder, and Hecht (1985) were interested in the effectiveness of antilittering prompts in inducing cafeteria patrons to clear away their trash when they had finished eating. Observation revealed that positively worded signs placed on tables—"Please be helpful! Clear your own table!"—were more effective than negatively worded ones—"Please don't litter! Clear your own table!"

There is also the possibility of focusing on **spatial behavior.** People structure their use of space with surprising regularity. It is surprising because, like many other nonverbal behaviors, it is usually done without conscious awareness. For example, individuals appear to maintain varying distances from others depending on the nature of their relationship with the others. The study of interaction distance and the variables that affect it is termed **proxemics.** The name was coined by Edward Hall (1966) and comes from the word "proximity," which means the state or quality of being near. According to Hall, there are four different spatial zones surrounding people, and only certain types of interactions occur within each of these zones: intimate (less than 18 inches from the other person), personal (18 inches to 4 feet), social (4 to 12 feet), and public (12 to 25 feet). It is highly unlikely, for example, that you would carry on an intimate conversation with someone who was 20 feet away. There are several thriving areas of research related to spatial behavior, including research on crowding (Evans and Lepore, 1993), on reactions to invasions of one's personal space (Worchel, 1986), and on territoriality (Altman, 1975). The point here is simply to alert you to the possibility of using such behaviors as indicators of social and psychological processes.

There are, of course, literally thousands of behaviors that could be made the focus of your observations. Again, the ones you choose to observe will be a function of the question of interest. But there are some additional considerations.

Validity

Many years ago, in a book called *The Psychopathology of Everyday Life*, Sigmund Freud suggested that some seemingly innocent behaviors, both verbal and nonverbal, were actually symptomatic of unconscious desires. Leaving the lights on when going out, for example, might indicate a desire to stay home. Forgetting to wind your watch might suggest a desire not to have to face tomorrow. Misreading "stocks and bonds" as "storks and bonds" may reveal a desire not to have children. Mistakenly telling someone that you will be unable to keep an appointment due to "foreseen," rather than "unforeseen," circumstances, could suggest that you never intended to keep the appointment in the first place.

Freud's hypothesis about the hidden meaning of such slips is an intriguing one, but there are problems with it. As Friedman (1982) has noted, there is much room for disagreement about what particular behaviors really mean. Leaving the lights on when you go out may mean that you would prefer to stay home, but it may also mean that you were so anxious to get away that you did not want to take the time to turn them off, or simply that you were thinking about something else as you went out the door. If you want to argue that an observed behavior is an indicator of some unseen process or state, you have to have some evidence. The process of obtaining that evidence is referred to as establishing the validity of the behavior as an indicator of whatever it is you are taking it to indicate.

Take body position, for example. What does it mean if someone leans forward rather than backward when interacting with others? It could mean that they like the person they are interacting with, but it could also mean about 50 other things: they are nervous; they have a sore back; the chair is uncomfortable; they cannot hear well. You see the problem. Unfortunately, many people doing observational research act as if they do not see the problem. They offer seemingly plausible analyses of what a specific behavior means and let it go at that. But that will not do. Even though it seems reasonable that leaning toward rather than away from someone indicates liking, you must establish that as a fact if you want to use leaning forward as your index of liking. One way to do that would be to observe interactions between people known to like each other and people known to dislike each other. If more leaning forward occurred among the former, you would have some evidence to support your use of leaning forward as a measure of liking. This point applies to all behaviors you plan to observe—nonverbal, verbal, overt body movement, extralinguistic. You must document that the behavior is a valid indicator of whatever it is you are taking it to indicate.

It also helps in your efforts to establish validity if the behavior of interest is easy to observe and clearly discriminable from other behaviors. As Cone and Foster (1982) put it, the behaviors of interest should be accessible to the observer. Some extralinguistic behaviors that are of interest for a variety of reasons, such as accents, require observers to make fine discriminations. Needless to say, the finer the discriminations required, the greater the likelihood of errors. This fact may partially explain why people have been hesitant to use extralinguistic behaviors in observational research. Such behaviors are generally more subtle than, say, gross body movements or verbal behaviors, such as asking a question or giving an opinion.

One solution to the problem of observing subtle behaviors, of course, is to record them, either with audio or video equipment. Then you can replay the recordings as many times as necessary to make sure that you are seeing, or hearing, what you think you are. For example, in an investigation of the behavior patterns of coronary-prone people, Swan, Carmelli, and Rosenman (1990) administered a structured interview to subjects and tape-recorded their answers. The tapes were later replayed—repeatedly—and scored for:

- loudness of speech
- explosiveness of speech
- rapid accelerated speech
- latency of responses to questions
- competition for control with the interviewer

As you can see, it would have been almost impossible for an observer to make these ratings with any degree of accuracy while listening to a live interview. Too many different things would have had to be attended to simultaneously. Thus, videotapes and audio recordings can be quite helpful. We shall mention them again in connection with observer training, assessment of reliability (below), and content analysis (in the next chapter). But whether we are simply observing directly or using some sort of equipment to record behavior, there is always a danger that the process of observation itself will have an influence on what we observe.

Avoiding Reactivity

One of the major concerns about the use of direct, firsthand observation in research is that, in most settings, the presence of an observer is **obtrusive.** The word itself means "tending to push self assertively forward; brash; intrusive; undesirably noticeable." And, as Foster, Bell-Dolan, and Burge (1988) have noted, awareness of being observed can create changes in the behavior of those observed. If it does, then any conclusions based on those observations will be at best suspect and probably completely invalid (Repp et al., 1988). Obtrusive assessment or observation, then, may create a reaction in those observed. Research, or measurement, that produces a change in the process or object of interest that would not have occurred otherwise is said to be **reactive.**

Such reactive effects show up in a variety of places, even in supposedly unconscious nonverbal gestures and nuances. The problem is that most people are aware that others read significance into such behaviors (Buck, 1993). Hence, they may attempt to control the nonverbal aspects of their behavior in order to project a certain image. They may make a special effort to smile and appear calm, for example, when in fact they are tense and irritable. If their efforts at control are successful, any observational measure based on recording the occurrence of gestures and expressions would be of questionable validity. Thus, whatever behaviors you plan to focus on in an observational study, you need to worry a little about whether those behaviors are likely to be a part of an act put on for your, or others', benefit. In particular, you cannot assume, because many nonverbal behaviors are performed unconsciously, that all of them are.

But, like the interpersonal effects produced by expectancies (Harris, 1993), reactive effects are not well understood. Although it is plausible that the presence of an observer and the awareness of being observed will alter the behavior of those observed, such alterations do not always occur. Thus, the issues really are (1) what kinds of behaviors are most likely to be affected by observation; (2) how reactive effects can be detected when they are present; and (3) how they can be prevented. Let us consider these one at a time.

One of the major reasons reactive effects occur is that people generally are concerned about the impressions they make on others. They are concerned about how others will judge them. In Rosenberg's (1965) phrase, they suffer from **evaluation apprehension.** It follows that the presence of an observer is likely to increase the occurrence of socially desirable behaviors and decrease the occurrence of socially undesirable behaviors. **Socially desirable behaviors** are just what the name implies: those behaviors that are socially sanctioned and approved, such as coming to a full stop at stop signs, being polite, dressing appropriately. Most state police officers appear well aware of the evaluation apprehension-social desirability link. Parking a patrol car beside the highway is usually sufficient to slow traffic down for a mile or two in both directions. Similarly, diet centers and weight reduction spas apparently owe part of their success to their clients' knowledge that each week they are going to have to weigh in in front of other people. The threatened embarrassment of having put on a few pounds instead of taking them off helps to motivate adherence to the weight reduction plan.

That last example suggests another possible mechanism underlying reactive effects, an attention-feedback-regulation cycle. Conceptually, at least, this mechanism is independent of evaluation apprehension, although the two would often lead to the same prediction if the behaviors being observed were socially desirable or undesirable. The **attention-feedback-regulation cycle** is simply that the presence of an observer calls attention to certain behaviors, that is, those being observed. The person being observed begins to notice (self-feedback) what he or she is doing and, as a result, changes (self-regulates) how it is done, or even what is done. Another possible explanation for the reactive effect of observation involves a phenomenon described briefly in

Chapter 1: that is, hundreds of studies have documented (e.g., Guerin, 1993) that the presence of an observer is arousing. Unfortunately, that alone can be sufficient to produce changes in the observed behavior. Physiological arousal is known to facilitate the performance of dominant, well-learned responses and to inhibit efforts to learn new tasks or perform less well mastered tasks.

Whatever the explanation for reactivity in a particular situation, it is your responsibility as a researcher to demonstrate that your observations are not contaminated by its subversive influence. The easiest way to detect the presence of reactivity effects involves a little deception: You place observers in the setting for a while and then withdraw them, but you continue to observe the behavior of interest surreptitiously. For example, suppose you were interested in the effects of a drug such as Ritalin on the classroom behavior of hyperactive children, but you were worried that such children might be particularly sensitive to the presence of a stranger in the classroom. To check on that, you might arrange to be present in the back of the classroom observing on alternate days. On the other days, you might observe from a remote location via a television camera mounted unobtrusively in the classroom. If the behavior of the hyperactive children was essentially the same on the days you were present and the days you were not, you could feel confident that your presence was not affecting their behavior. Of course, to avoid reactive effects being produced by the camera, it would be best for it to be a permanent fixture in the classroom and for no one to know (except you) when it would be turned on. In a study patterned along these lines, Roberts and Renzaglia (1965) tape-recorded counseling sessions under several different conditions. In one, both client and counselor knew that the recording was being made. In another, neither client nor counselor was aware that the session was being recorded. The nature of the interaction did vary in several respects when the results from these two conditions were compared, a finding indicating that knowledge of being recorded did indeed produce reactive effects.

A number of people have suggested ways to avoid, or at least minimize, reactive effects. Foster, Bell-Dolan, and Burge (1988) suggest allowing subjects to get used to being observed by extending the observation period until the behavior(s) of interest appear to stabilize. They also suggest that making efforts to reduce the conspicuousness of observers in the setting may help. Such efforts might include having observers dress so as not to call attention to themselves and placing observers so that they can see and hear what goes on, but are not in the way. In a classroom setting, for example, observing from the rear is preferable to observing from the front. It may also help to choose behaviors for observation that are not intrinsically socially desirable or undesirable.

There is also, of course, the possibility of concealment, of simply not letting people know that what they are doing is being observed. Teubner and Vaske (1988), for example, have described a system for monitoring computer usage in an office environment. A program installed in the computers themselves simply records such details as when the computer is turned on and off, which programs are used and for how long, and even how fast the computer

---

Box 2

Computerized Observation in the Workplace

In addition to facilitating work, computers in the workplace can function as mute, but all-seeing, observers of work habits and productivity. For office workers engaged in word processing, computers can easily be programmed to record when they turn the machine on in the morning, how long the machine stands idle during the day, the rate of typing, and, yes, even spelling errors. For those who use telephones, computer-based call-accounting systems are often used to record numbers called and time on the line. As Shaiken (1987) points out, not even long-haul truckers are immune from computer surveillance. Many of those big 18-wheelers carry an on-board computer under the hood that records the gas mileage, the average speed of the truck, and the number, time, and length of stops.

If you are interested in work habits and productivity under different conditions, such data can be a gold mine. But from the workers' point of view, the belief that their every move is being monitored can create problems (e.g., Kunda, 1992). Typically, even workers who have routine, repetitive jobs find ways to retain some degree of control and autonomy. They can, for example, work faster just prior to taking a break or to make up for time spent talking on the phone. With continuous computer monitoring, however, there is perceived pressure to work constantly. The computer not only "knows" when you're goofing off, it makes a record of it for the boss to see. In fact, the Office of Technology Assessment (1987) reports that workers whose work was monitored by computers reported significantly more stress-related symptoms than those whose work was not so closely tracked.

Like other observational techniques, then, computer monitoring needs to be used with caution. While appearing to be almost completely unobtrusive, it is, in fact, quite reactive—that is, it often appears to create changes in the behavior of interest.

---

user types. Such workplace surveillance, of course, can be done with or without the knowledge and consent of workers. (See Box 2 for some unintended consequences.) Dykman and Reis (1979) simply noted the seats chosen in a classroom by students on whom they had previously collected personality data. The students with the most positive self-concepts tended to pick seats near the front of the room, but the point here is simply that the students did not know that anyone was paying attention to where they sat.

The idea of surreptitious observation is distasteful to many people. But before you reject that option entirely, let us examine it a little more closely. Observation also raises some other ethical issues that need to be discussed.

Some Ethical Considerations

The major ethical question about the kinds of observations being discussed in this chapter is whether the observations will constitute an invasion of privacy. One possible answer, of course, is to let the people being observed decide—that is, ask them if they mind being observed doing whatever it is you want to watch them do. This approach has a couple of pitfalls. We have just discussed one: the potential reactive effects produced by the knowledge that one is being observed. If you can demonstrate that such effects are minimal or nonexistent, then getting the informed consent of the people you want to observe may indeed be the way to go. As noted in Chapter 1, obtaining informed consent simply means giving people an explicit choice, prior to participation, of whether or not they would like to participate in the research. You also need to tell them of any potential harmful effects and let them know that they are free to withdraw from the research at any time. If you decide to do that, however, you need to be especially sensitive to another ethical consideration: that is, do the people of whom you are making this request really have the freedom to say no? If they do not, then do not ask.

People should not be coerced, even subtly, into participating in research. Noncoercion is an important principle and it is one that has been much abused. Prisoners being asked by prison administration officials to take part in research, military personnel volunteering for research projects, and, yes, even students fulfilling course requirements by taking part in research are all being coerced. In each of these and similar situations, the request cannot really be turned down. After collecting information on a number of incidents in which people had been coerced into research participation, the Committee on Ethical Practices in Research of the American Psychological Association (APA, 1992) formulated the following principle:

> Using language that is reasonably understandable to participants, psychologists inform participants of the nature of the research; they inform participants that they are free to participate or to decline to participate or to withdraw from the research. … When psychologists conduct research with individuals such as students or subordinates, psychologists take special care to protect the prospective participants from adverse consequences of declining or withdrawing from participation.

This and the other principles formulated by the committee were all hotly debated. They are not cast in stone, but are the result of compromises between conflicting values: need for knowledge, freedom of inquiry, self-determination, right to privacy.

But sometimes informed consent does seem unnecessary. Surely there are behaviors you can observe without obtaining informed consent. You do it every day. Obviously there are limits, both ethical and legal. Wiretapping, for example, is clearly out of bounds. It is legally beyond the pale. You might be interested in knowing that some legal limits on research, such as the prohibition against recording jury deliberations, were in fact enacted in reaction to specific social science research projects (Strodtbeck, James, and Hawkins, 1957; Burchard, 1958). But where is the ethical boundary?

For most people, the location of that boundary has to do with the notion of privacy, which Webster's (1993) defines as "the quality or state of being apart from company or observation; freedom from unauthorized intrusion." The word "unauthorized" is the key. The idea is that each person should be able to *control* what, and how much, others find out about them. If you were to stand up in class and start reading from your diary, people might be embarrassed or think you were behaving inappropriately, but they would not think your privacy had been invaded. On the other hand, if someone else were to stand up in class and start reading from your diary (without your permission), your privacy would indeed have been invaded. The key to privacy, then, is that individuals must be able to choose how much or how little to reveal about themselves. As Inness (1992) put it, privacy means control over access to intimate areas of the individual's self and intimate information about the individual and his or her actions. "Intimate" is defined by the motivations of the individual in terms of those things he or she loves, values, and/or cares about.

What that means for research is that public behaviors are usually considered to be fair game for observation. But be careful. The right to privacy is not completely relinquished in public. The behavior of coming out of a hotel arm-in-arm with a member of the opposite sex may be public, but to record that behavior with a camera, say, so that the individuals could later be identified could conceivably have damaging consequences for them. So, it should not be done. In general, research in which specific individuals are identified as having been at a certain place at a certain time or in the company of certain others is considered to be an invasion of privacy. There are also widely shared social norms that operate in public to secure areas of privacy for individuals, and these norms should not be disregarded in observational research. For example, if you were in a restaurant and the people at the next table were talking loudly enough for you to hear, it would be perfectly acceptable to make notes on such overheard conversations. But to use a listening device covertly to enhance the audio level of conversations lost in the din of plates and silver would not be acceptable. By talking at a level so that their conversation is indeed lost in the surrounding din, people invoke a measure of privacy for themselves—even though they are in a public place.

Thus, even if you are observing naturally occurring public behavior, questions may still arise as to whether or not your observations constitute an invasion of privacy. If there is any doubt about the research you are planning, one thing you should not do is trust your own judgment. You are likely to pay too much attention to the possible usefulness, either practical or theoretical, of the research. Others, such as your Institutional Review Board or potential research participants, may be able to focus more clearly on the possible ethical risks involved. One of the suggestions of the APA Committee on Ethical Practices in Research that was mentioned earlier is this: Always obtain the advice of other people who are concerned about the potential risks to participants (American Psychological Association, 1992). But do not forget that even if those others see no problem and say "go ahead," you will be the responsible party if problems do arise. So, be careful: Always respect the privacy of those whose behavior you do observe.

One of the things that may help you to respect the privacy of those observed is to remember that any particular behavior is usually related to a variety of other behaviors, attitudes, beliefs, and values. Thus, whether or not the behavior you are focusing on is revealing something that the person would like kept secret may not be immediately obvious to you, but it might be to the person being observed. That is one of the reasons why it is a good idea to discuss your plans with others before beginning your research. They may help you see the implications of what you have in mind.

The idea that there are systematic relationships among behaviors is an important one. So far, the examples mentioned in this chapter have dealt with single aspects of behavior. The research described has taken one aspect of behavior—horn honking, seat chosen in a classroom, number of beers consumed at a party, manner of speech in an interview—and related it to some other aspect of the person or situation. This attention to individual aspects of behavior was intentional. It was supposed to get you thinking analytically about the varieties of behaviors that could be observed. It was also intended to introduce you to some general bugaboos that plague all observational research: the problems of validity, reactivity, and invasion of privacy. But it is clear that individual aspects of behavior do not occur in isolation. In fact, most observational systems focus on several different behaviors simultaneously. That vastly increases their power, of course, but it also multiplies the problems involved.

Observational Systems

The central component of all observational systems is what Hawkins (1982) has called a **behavior code.** A behavior code is a detailed description of the behaviors and events to be observed and recorded and includes a precise set of rules about how those observations are to be made. The purpose of developing a behavior code is to enable observations to be made that are not dependent on the particular characteristics and interests of the observer. That is, with a good behavior code, two or more people watching the same set of events should end up having seen and recorded the same things. The code tells them what to look for, and it does so in language that is as unambiguous as possible. (See Box 3 for a potential problem.) The price you pay for using a behavior code is tunnel vision. You focus on only a few specific behaviors that are of interest. In the process, of course, you miss a great deal of what occurs. But the benefit is that you, and others, can have faith in what you say about those specific behaviors—provided you follow a few simple rules in developing and using the behavior code. Before describing those rules, let us look at an example.

An Illustration: Interaction in Mutual Help Groups

A "mutual help group" is a group of people who get together to discuss their problems and provide each other with social and emotional support. Often, but not always, the members of such a group have a common problem or are going through similar stages of life. They may all be recently widowed, or divorced, for example. Or, they may all be survivors of a catastrophic disease,

Box 3

Halos at the Olympics?

During both the 1988 and 1992 Olympics, minor controversies erupted over the apparent subjectivity of the judges' ratings. In the figure skating events, for example, skaters are supposed to be judged separately on "technical merit" and "artistic impression." A skater loses points on technical merit for imperfections, or missed elements, in his or her routine. A botched landing, or a misstep, or a slip results in fractions of points being deducted from what the judge would have awarded for a perfect performance. A skater's artistic impression score, on the other hand, is based on choreography, musical interpretation, skating speed, facial expressions, and body posture. In the women's program at Calgary, many in the audience felt that one of the two top skaters had been given undeservedly high marks on artistic impression because of her sexy style and revealing costume (Associated Press, 1988).

The error that the judges were accused of making is referred to as the "halo effect." It means that their judgments of one attribute—the skater's sexy appearance—influenced their judgments of another, theoretically unrelated, attribute—her choreography. The halo effect can be a serious problem when observers are asked to categorize and/or make judgments about several different aspects of behavior. A positive, or negative, judgment about one aspect may all too easily spread to others. Our global evaluations of people, for example, may alter our perceptions of their specific attributes. If we like or approve of someone, for example, we may perceive that person as more attractive.

In many systems that involve making judgments about, or categorizing, different aspects of behavior, the halo effect is a potential threat to validity. Its detrimental effect can be reduced or prevented, however. For example, Bernardin and Pence (1980) asked subjects to make judgments about two instructors on 13 dimensions of performance. Prior to making the ratings, some of the subjects were warned about the halo effect and shown examples of ratings that did and did not exhibit the effect. Among those subjects, the halo effect was significantly reduced. However, Bernardin and Pence also argue that it is much more important to teach observers to observe accurately than it is to try to teach them about all the errors they might make. An observer who is consciously trying to avoid falling victim to the halo effect is likely to err in the opposite direction. But keep it in mind. If the ratings you obtain are all clustered at the positive, or negative, ends of the scales, you should be suspicious. You may need to devise ways for improving observer accuracy.

such as cancer. Mutual help groups often begin informally when people discover that several of their co-workers, or fellow church members, or neighbors, are having difficulties. They are typically led by one of the members themselves, not by a professional mental health worker.

Over the years, word has spread that mutual help groups have indeed proved to be beneficial for thousands of people. But, as Roberts et al. (1991) point out, very little is known about what actually goes on in such groups. The testimonials of ex-members are usually quite positive, and they suggest that some of the benefit stems from helping others as much as it does from being helped. That is an intriguing possibility, but the retrospective accounts of a few self-selected informants hardly qualify as hard data. As we have seen in the preceding chapter, memory cannot always be trusted, and it may be that group members who did not have such a good experience just keep it to themselves.

To get some evidence on the actual processes that occur in mutual help groups, Roberts et al. (1991) designed a set of behavior categories for coding interactions in these groups. They needed a set of categories that had the following characteristics. First, it had to capture some of the things that members said usually occurred in such groups, like "Helping Others" and "Receiving Support." In other words, some of the categories were shaped by an initial hypothesis, based on the reports of ex-members, about the sorts of interpersonal processes the observers would find in mutual help groups. Second, they wanted the categories to be exhaustive; that is, every comment made in the groups should be codable into one of the categories. Third, since the interactions were to be observed live, the categories had to be relatively few in number; otherwise the observers' job would be too difficult and much of the group process might be missed. They ended up with 12 categories, divided into 5 general areas. These are listed in Table 1, along with a brief definition of each.

Once the behavior categories had been decided upon, the next task was to train observers to use the categories reliably while observing group interactions. To do this, Roberts et al. made videotapes of mock group meetings and had would-be observers—actually, students—watch the tapes and practice coding the observed interactions into the 12 categories. The advantage of using videotapes for training observers, of course, is that the interactions depicted on the tapes could be coded very precisely in advance—by playing the tapes over and over until Roberts and her colleagues could agree on exactly what occurred, in what order, in the group. That is, for every verbalization on the tapes, they made a record of who said it, which category it was coded into, and what was said immediately before and after it. Thus the codings of the observer trainees could be compared with this record of what was "known" to be on the tapes. Trainees could watch and code the tapes again and again until their codings had reached an acceptable level of accuracy. According to Roberts et al. (1991, p. 722), it took the average coder about 40 hours of practice to master the task of watching group interactions and coding them, as they occurred, into the 12 categories seen in Table 1.

The actual data collection was spread over a 2-year period, with 10 different observers attending a total of 527 mutual help group meetings. Access to the meetings was gained through an organization called GROW International, which sponsored and organized the mutual help groups. As Roberts et al. note, "GROW is a mutual help organization for individuals with a history of emotional and psychological problems. (It) . . . offers a program for recovery and growth which includes weekly group meetings, reading and memorizing GROW literature, and friendly social contact among members" (p. 719). A typical meeting lasted 1½–2 hours and had an average attendance of eight people. After each meeting, the members of each group were asked to answer some questions and fill out some ratings of the meeting, the other group members, and the problems that had been discussed.

Table 1   The Twelve Categories Constituting the Behavioral Interaction Code (BIC) Used for Assessing the Processes that Occur in Mutual Help Groups

CATEGORY	DESCRIPTION
Helping Behavior	
Support	Comments that have the aim or effect of raising another group member's status; are nurturing, encouraging, or approving of another group member; or offer tangible assistance
Interpretation	Comments that interpret, analyze, evaluate, redefine, reconceptualize, challenge, summarize, or explain another group member's common behavior
Direct guidance	Comments that give concrete, direct, and specific suggestions, direction, or guidance about possible courses of action
Questioning	
Personal questions	Comments that request revealing information about an individual's feelings, motivations, opinions, or actions
Impersonal questions	Comments that ask for orientation, clarification, repetition, general factual information about the world, or impersonal ("safe," factual, or superficial) information about another individual
Task Orientation	
Group process	Comments that have the aim or effect of altering or reflecting on the immediate group process
Small talk	Comments that are not relevant to the group's current task or are non-sensical or inappropriate in the context of the group
Help-Seeking and Disclosure	
Self-disclosure	Comments that give specific personal information about the speaker or someone in the personal life of the speaker. "Personal" information includes any discussion of feelings, desires, expectations, or behaviors that are generally nonpublic and not ordinarily volunteered to others
Information giving	Comments that give clarification of previous comments or general, impersonal, trivial, vague, or abstract information about the world, the speaker, or other individuals
Request for help	Comments that directly request the group or a particular member of the group to provide the speaker with an evaluation, interpretation, suggestion, information, or guidance about the speaker's feelings, actions, personal life, or group behavior
Affective Response	
Agree	Comments that show agreement with an opinion or interpretation previously stated, show acceptance or acknowledgment of support or feedback, or verbally indicate that the speaker will comply with a suggestion or guidance
Negative	Comments that explicitly disagree with a previously stated opinion or interpretation; are resistant, closed, or defensive; or indicate disapproval of any part of the group method or philosophy, another group member, or the speaker him or herself

Source: Roberts et al. 1991, Table 2, pp. 20–21.

There were a number of interesting findings from the study, but we shall just summarize a few here before we focus on the methodology. Overall, the categories of behavior indicating a positive, supportive climate with the groups were scored seven times more often than those indicative of a negative atmosphere. Further, since the groups met repeatedly, it was possible to examine changes in the behavior of individuals over time. As anticipated, it was found that the longer people were in a group, the more they contributed. Specifically, over time, more and more of their comments consisted of support for others, interpretation, comments about group process, information giving, and impersonal questions. And the more they had engaged in supporting others, the more positive they felt about themselves at the end of the sessions. In contrast to the stereotype about what goes on in "touchy-feely" groups, it was found that impersonal and low-level disclosures (information giving) occurred much more frequently than self-disclosures, and that impersonal questions were much more common than personal questions. As Roberts et al. (1991, p. 733) put it: "Contrary to common belief, much of the discussion in mutual help meetings focuses on ordinary events and activities."

As mentioned earlier, the heart of any observational system is the set of categories into which your observations are coded. Roberts et al. used 12 content categories. Note that if they had observed precisely the same set of group interactions with a different set of categories, they would have had an entirely different study—and an entirely different set of conclusions. For example, they might have been interested in the relationships between health and spontaneous expressions of satisfaction and dissatisfaction among the group members. If so, the observers would have coded the group discussions into a set of positive and negative categories having to do with, say, jobs or families or presidential politics or last night's television programs. The point, again, is simply that the categories into which your observations are to be coded are the keys to the whole enterprise. Hence, they need to be constructed and used with care.

Category Construction

Category construction refers to the process of deciding which behaviors you want to observe and defining them clearly and unambiguously. The total set of different behaviors to be observed is referred to as a **category system,** and the process of actually observing ongoing behaviors and tabulating how frequently the behaviors in your category system occur is referred to as **coding**. The construction and use of a set of categories for recording observations of behavior is very similar to what happens in a method of research called content analysis. The major difference, as you will see in the following chapter, is that content analysis is used on printed text. It is also sometimes used on videotapes or films, but usually not on live, ongoing behavior. Conceptually, however, content analysis and the use of a category system for coding observed behavior are so much alike that about halfway through Chapter 4, you may start wondering why the two have been separated here.

They have been separated because there is an important difference in the nature of the categories that can be employed. With printed material, you can read a passage several times, examine your categories repeatedly, think about the big picture, and even ponder the meaning of life before coding any particular phrase or sentence into a category. Not so with live behavior, especially if you are observing the interactions of a group of four or five people. There is no time for contemplation. If you do not pigeonhole a particular behavior into one of your categories immediately, it is lost forever. Thus, the set of categories—the behavior code, in Hawkins's (1982) phrase—must consist of relatively simple, clearly observable behaviors when you are observing the action live. For example, Evans and Lepore (1993) were interested in the possibility that people who live in fairly crowded conditions might develop the habit of tuning others out as a way of coping with the stress of crowding. Hence, they recruited subjects from crowded and relatively uncrowded homes and observed them in a laboratory setting interacting with a confederate who, at a particular point, offered some socially supportive comments. The subjects' response was coded into one of three categories: (1) Not responsive, ignored confederate; (2) Minimal acknowledgment, brief comment, head nod; or (3) Very responsive, elaborated and embellished. In contrast to such relatively simple judgments, the categories employed in content analysis can require the coder to make much more complex discriminations. For example, in a content analysis of the writings of Robert E. Lee and his opponents, Suedfeld, Corteen, and McCormick (1986) employed a set of categories designed to assess complexity of thought (see Chapter 4). Excerpts of Lee's written works, as well as those of his opponents, were read and coded for *differentiation* (the ability to see different aspects of a problem) and/or *integration* (the perception of links or connections among those differentiated aspects). In addition, the coder had to decide whether there was a little or a lot of each of these two qualities present. Unless you were blessed with an unusually good memory, those would be difficult judgments to make on the spur of the moment while listening to someone talking and while continuing to make the same judgments about everything they had to say.

So, the first rule of constructing a category set to use in observing live behavior is this: Keep It Simple. Do not ask more of yourself—or others who may be observing for you—than is humanly possible. As Foster, Bell-Dolan, and Burge (1988) note, there is no firm rule about the number of categories that may be used. But you should begin with the simplest set conceivable, that is, the simplest set that will enable you to answer the question(s) of interest. There is, in fact, evidence that the simpler the code, the more accurate the observers (e.g., Dorsey, Nelson, and Hayes, 1986).

One thing you should look into before you begin is the possibility that someone else has already developed a set of categories that you could use. Using an existing category system saves you the time and effort that would have gone into making your own. There are numerous category systems already in existence—for observing classroom behavior, problem-solving groups, mutual help groups, family interactions, infants, disturbed children, rats—you name it. For example, Grotevant and Carlson (1989) summarize the information available on 13 different category systems that have been developed for observing interactions in families. If your interest is such that an existing category system can be used, there is another advantage: Your research is more likely to fit into a coherent body of literature. If, for example, you were able to use an existing system, chances are you would find that there were a number of relevant research reports pertaining to it. Those reports would probably be very helpful because they would give information on how to train observers to use the categories and the reliability that could be achieved in coding interactions into the categories. That information, of course, would benefit you personally. In a similar vein, there is a benefit to others if you use an existing system: Your results will be more easily comparable to other results in the literature because they will have been obtained using the same basic procedures.

But suppose you have examined the literature carefully, and there is nothing that seems to fit exactly what you had in mind. How do you begin to develop you own categories? The first step is to be explicit about the behaviors you want to observe. Once you have done that, you may find that even if there are no entire systems that fit your needs precisely, there may be parts of systems that you can use. For example, the behavior code that Roberts et al. used in the study described above was, in fact, developed by them, but some of the categories they employed were derived from other systems already in the literature.

Whether you generate them yourself or find them in existing systems, each of the categories you plan to use must be labeled and defined in great detail. Dictionary-like definitions are necessary, but they are definitely not sufficient. You are going to have to elaborate on those definitions, to point out how the behaviors that fit into each category differ from the behaviors that fit into other categories. Also, you will need to give some examples of behaviors in each category. The point, of course, is to remove as much ambiguity as possible and thereby increase the likelihood that different observers using the system will all categorize any given behavior in the same way. Consider this example. Years ago, a Harvard psychologist named Robert Bales (1950, 1970) developed a system for observing groups called Interaction Process Analysis. It has 12 categories, and the tenth one is this:

Disagrees, shows passive rejection, formality, withholds help.

Now, what really constitutes disagreement? Suppose somebody says, "Yes, I think you are absolutely right, *but*...". Or, suppose somebody simply raises an eyebrow at a suggestion, or rolls their eyes, or is slow to respond. You see the problem. Box 4 gives the directions that Bales developed to instruct observers how and when to score behavior in this category. Read them carefully and you will see that they are thorough instructions, but not excessively so. They give examples of things that would fit into the category, examples of things that would not, and even specify the context to be taken into account—that is, only the immediately preceding statement. The point, of course, is to try to anticipate all of the questions an observer might have

Box 4

How to Score Interaction Category 10

The following directions from Bales (1970) were developed to instruct observers how and when to score behavior in Category 10 (Disagrees, shows passive rejection, formality, withholds help).

Disagreement is an act with negative implications. But not all acts with negative implications are classed as disagreement in Category 10. Disagreement is defined more specifically in terms of where it comes in interaction sequences. Disagreement is the *initial* act of conveying the information to the other that the content of his proposition (his statement of information, opinion, or suggestion) is not acceptable, at least not immediately; for example, "No." "I don't think so." "I disagree." I don't agree." "I can't accept that." "Well, . . . " "But, . . . " Sometimes the information is repeated by a combination of two or three of these kinds of reactions. In this case a separate score is given for each act. Disagreement is a *rea*ction to the other's action. The negative feeling conveyed is attached to the content of what the other has said, not to him as a person. And the negative feeling must not be so very strong, or the act will seem unfriendly.

Mild degrees of disagreement are included, such as showing surprise, temporary disbelief, astonishment, amazement, or incredulity; for example, "What!" "You don't say!" "That can't be!" "Would you believe it!" One may also disagree by omission, failing to pay attention when the other is speaking, failing to give a requested repetition, or the like. Either verbal or nonverbal indications that the member is skeptical, dubious, cautious about accepting the proposal, hesitant, or critical, may be included as disagreement, provided the implications of ascendance or of hostility are absent. When these indications are present, the act should be scored as seeming unfriendly.

Unless there is repetition of disagreement as described above, only the *initial* act after the other speaks is marked as disagrees. The propositions that follow in making the argument, in the form of information about the situation, analysis of the facts, opinions, alternative suggestions, and the like are scored in their regular category, *unless* the tone of voice, the facial expression or bodily attitude conveys negative feeling. Whenever the observer sees or hears any actual signs of negative feeling or emotion directed at the other person, the act should be scored as seeming unfriendly.

But the simple fact that an argument stands in logical opposition to the content of the other's argument does not require that the argument be scored as Disagrees. For example, suppose that one person gives some information to another. Then the other reacts by saying, "I don't think so. It seems to me that there were more than that. In fact, I remember seeing at least five." The first reaction would be scored as disagrees, assuming there were no signs of negative feeling toward the other as a person. The second act would *not* be scored as disagrees, but as giving opinion, since it is neutral, and a conjecture. The third act would be scored as giving information, on the assumption that it is also neutral because it reports a concrete observation. The thing to note is that *after the initial act of disagreement, the scoring reverts to the neutral categories based upon the interaction form of the acts.* After an initial act of disagreement, "the slate is wiped clean," so far as relations of logical contradiction are concerned. If the slate were not wiped clean, one would have to continue to follow logical contradictions in an argument indefinitely. Finally, it might happen that everything said would be in logical contradiction to something said earlier. The category Disagrees would have become a "sink" into which all interaction would be drawn.

(continued)

The frame of reference within which disagreement is judged is thus short in time, consisting of one or more acts during which a logical position is taken, and the initial act only the rejoinder. The frame of reference for judging agreement is similar. If the reaction is an agreement, after the initial act of agreement, the scoring reverts to the neutral categories based upon the interaction form of the acts. Unless, that is, there is an emotional tone of seeming friendly.

Assume that another person's act of giving information is followed by these three acts: "I don't think so. It seems to me we should be more careful! You have no right to go around saying things like that!" The first act might be scored as disagrees, although in the context that follows one might also have felt some negative feeling in the phrase "I don't think so," in which case it might be scored as seeming unfriendly. The next two remarks, in any case, seem clearly to imply some negative feeling toward the other and so should be scored as seeming unfriendly.

about when, precisely, to code an act or behavior in that category. Such detailed definitional instructions must be developed for every category you plan to use. Often these instructions are bound together in what is referred to as an observer's manual, which brings us to the issue of observer training.

Observer Training

In training observers to use a category system, the first step is to have them memorize the manual—word for word! There are several reasons for this. The first is that they need to be completely familiar with the definition of each category. For example, if observers do not know precisely what "on task" behavior refers to in an observational system, they will not be able to tell whether the children they are observing are "on task" or "off task" at any given moment. That seems rather obvious, but it is an important point. The second reason for memorizing the category definitions is that it is important for observers to understand that the definition of any particular category is partially determined by its place in the system as a whole. "Support" in the system developed by Roberts et al. (1991) was defined, in part, with respect to what was categorized as "Direct Guidance." "Disagrees" in the Bales system mentioned above has to be distinguished from "Gives Opinion," another category in the system. In other words, the total category system has to be understood. That understanding facilitates judgments about the placement of specific behaviors within the system. There is more to be said about the relationships among categories in the following chapter on content analysis. For now, just remember that what has been said about individual category construction here will be just as relevant there, and what will be said about the system as a whole there is relevant here.

Once observers are thoroughly familiar with the category definitions, the next order of business is practice in using the system—lots of it. It is one thing to know the definitions and quite another to use them in categorizing live action under the pressure of time. Observers have to learn to use the system quickly and efficiently, to categorize an item of behavior and move on to the next. Observers also need to learn to stay calm, to not get upset when they realize they have missed something. They have to let it go and pay attention to what is happening at the moment.

But practice alone is not enough, in spite of the old adage that practice makes perfect. Practice alone only makes you tired. Practice with corrective feedback makes perfect. As Roberts et al. (1991) noted, the preparation of videotapes depicting the kinds and range of behavior to be observed with the system is quite useful in training observers. They can watch and code the action on the tape, and their coding can then be compared—behavior by behavior—with what is known to be on the tape. Misclassifications, omissions, and other errors can be discussed, and they can try again. And again. And again, until they get it right.

A study by Bass (1987) provides another example of how training can be done. He prepared a set of 6-minute videotapes showing five special education students and their teacher during an industrial arts class. The category system included such behaviors as handling materials, student talk, verbal and nonverbal praise by the teacher, and verbal and nonverbal efforts by the teacher to stop particular student behaviors. Using a computer-assisted system, the tapes were viewed repeatedly and scored for the presence of the behaviors. The purpose of the repeated viewing was to record—with 100% accuracy—exactly which of the behaviors were being exhibited, second by second, on the tape. Bass was then able to use the tapes to train observers in the use of the category system. As observer trainees viewed and attempted to score the tapes for the presence of the behaviors, the computer could compare what they claimed to have seen with what was "known" to be on a particular segment of the tape. Thus, observers could receive immediate, precise feedback about how they were doing, and they could go back and reexamine sections of the tape where they had made mistakes.

To maximize observer performance, then, you need simple categories, clear definitions, thorough familiarity with the system, practice using it, and feedback about mistakes. The point of these requirements is to give you faith that different observers using the system to observe the same behavioral sequences will all see and record identical things as having occurred. Another way of saying this is that the goal of developing such a system is to make observations independent of the particular observer. As Bakeman and Gottman (1987) put it, a well-developed and correctly used category system should take you beyond the impressionistic stage of observation. With such a set of categories, observation becomes systematic and replicable—that is, reliable. Let us look at this notion of reliability, and some of the problems in establishing it, a little more closely.

Observer Reliability

Reliability concerns the extent to which observations and other forms of measurement are repeatable. It would, of course, be nice if we could forget about the notion of reliability and just discuss observer accuracy. Usually we cannot, because in most studies there is no criterion against which to assess true accuracy. If you make videotapes of the events you are observing and recording using a system of categories, as Bass (1987) did in the study described above, then you can assess accuracy. Without such records of the actual events, you must fall back on trying to assess observer reliability instead.

The most common form of reliability assessment is a check on the extent to which different observers watching and coding the same events agree in what they record. This is usually referred to as **interobserver agreement**. For example, in the study mentioned earlier by Geller et al. (1989) in which two observers were stationed some distance from each other along the roadside to note seat belt use, it was found that they observed a total of 18,859 cars and drivers. Since they also recorded license plate numbers, they could tabulate how many cars they had both seen and then calculate the extent to which they agreed on whether or not the driver of a particular car was wearing a seat belt. There were 2885 cars that were seen by both observers. Using the following formula, it was found that the two observers agreed 88.3% of the time on whether or not the driver of a particular car was wearing a seat belt.

$$\text{Percentage of agreement} = (\text{Number agreed on}/2885) \times 100$$

It is important to note that if you cannot achieve interobserver agreement, something is clearly amiss. Without it, there is no guarantee that anything real is being recorded. The categories may be too broad, or too poorly defined, if observers are putting different behaviors into particular categories. Or it may be that the observers were not trained well, or that they did not have enough practice using the system. Whatever the problem, it must be found and corrected before the results of the observations can be used as evidence for, or against, anything.

The percentage of agreement among observers is useful information and is by far the most commonly reported measure of reliability in observational studies. But there are problems that preclude simple reliance on it. For one thing, it does not correct for chance. Two observers watching the same interaction and coding it into the same categories are going to agree sometimes even if they are just coding randomly. Fortunately, once you have tabulated the agreements and disagreements, there is a simple statistic you can calculate, called "Cohen's Kappa," that will tell you whether the percentage of agreement you have obtained is significantly greater than the percentage you would expect by chance alone (Cohen, 1960; Bakeman and Gottman, 1987). You should also be aware that what is an "acceptable" level of interobserver agreement may vary from situation to situation. If the observers are being asked to observe and code only two or three clearly defined and distinct behaviors, you might expect them to agree 100% of the time. With a more complex set of categories that require somewhat more judgment on the part of the observers, that might be too much to expect; 60% to 70% agreement might be all you could hope for.

There is another problem with interobserver agreement, however: a phenomenon called **observer drift**. If observers are able to see each other coding, or if they discuss the various behaviors being coded too much, they may well come to agree with each other in what and how they code, but drift away from what the manual says they should be doing. Thus, they would have high reliability—they would agree with each other—but they would not be coding behaviors correctly. So you should not place too much faith in interobserver agreement. If at all possible, obtain some measure of accuracy of coding as well. For example, Roberts et al. could have videotaped a few of the mutual help group interactions they observed. Then they could have coded the filmed interactions—very carefully—and used those codings as criteria of accuracy. Observer codings of those same live interactions could then have been compared with the codings of the filmed versions.

If you do not have fancy equipment, or if it is simply impossible to develop criteria with which coding can be compared, there are still several things you can do to prevent observer drift. Reid (1982) suggested that you not allow observers to watch each other as they code or to discuss disagreements about coding unless someone thoroughly familiar with the coding system is present. He also said that frequent review sessions and quizzes on the category definitions are a good idea—just to keep everyone on their toes.

There is an interesting irony involved in establishing and checking on the reliability of observers. As was pointed out earlier, one of the major problems with direct observation is the possibility that it will produce reactive effects. However, to check that the observers are doing their task properly, you must observe them. Hence, there is the possibility that your observations may change the behavior of the observers. When they know they are being checked, they will cut out the horseplay, pay more attention to the task, and do a bang-up job of observing and coding. When they know they are not being checked, they may relax and take the whole thing a little less seriously.

Topf (1988) has identified several strategies for dealing with the potential for decline in interobserver reliability. The first is something we have already discussed: that is, the fewer and the more clear-cut the categories the observers have to deal with, the more likely they are to continue to do the job of categorization well, even when they are not being checked. Another possibility is more thorough training in using the category system before turning the observers loose. That is, if the observers have had to learn to use the system with 100% accuracy, they may slip a little from time to time and still do well enough that the data they record can be trusted. Still another possibility is the continuous use of two or more observers, physically separated from each other, for every observation. That way, reliability could be assessed at any point at which there was any question about a particular observer's data. Periodic retraining in the use of the category system is also a possibility.

Of course, none of these strategies is guaranteed to work. But the point is to try to ensure that an observer continues to use the system as it was intended to be used. Learning the system well and practice using it are important, but if an observer does not use the system consistently, then you are likely to confuse changes in the observer with changes in the thing being observed.

Summary

Ethology, the study of the behavior of animals in their natural settings, forms a link between participant observation and the focus of this chapter: the use of observation by nonparticipants to test specific ideas. The approach advocated here is the rational approach, which involves the formulation of a specific question and decisions on which behaviors to observe in order to answer that question. The source of your question, not the methodology chosen to answer it, determines whether you will be doing basic or applied research. Basic research stems from questions intended to test or clarify theory. Applied research stems from questions arising from the need to make an intelligent decision in a specific situation.

Although most observational research has focused on verbal behavior, a variety of other kinds of behavior can be reliably observed, including nonverbal, extralinguistic, and spatial behaviors. The only reason, apparently, that verbal behavior has been so overutilized is that it is, generally, the easiest to observe. Whatever behavior you do choose to observe, it is absolutely crucial to document that the behavior is a valid indicator of whatever it is you are taking it to indicate.

One of the major problems with the use of direct, firsthand observation in research is that, in most settings, the presence of an observer is obtrusive. It may create changes in the behavior of those observed and thus bias the conclusions based on the observations. Such reactive effects may be due to evaluation apprehension, an attention-feedback-regulation cycle, or social facilitation. Whatever the explanation, it is your responsibility as an observer to demonstrate that your observations are not contaminated by reactivity. There are several ways of avoiding or minimizing reactive effects, including unobtrusive observation and concealment.

The ethical concern most often discussed in connection with observation is invasion of privacy. One way to avoid the possibility that you will be invading someone's privacy is to secure their permission, via informed consent, to observe them. If you choose that route, you need to be sure that there is no hint of coercion involved. For observation of public behaviors, informed consent is not necessary as long as specific individuals are not identified. Just to be safe, however, you should discuss your research with others who are concerned about the potential risks to participants before you begin.

Individual aspects of behavior rarely occur in isolation. Consequently, most observational systems focus on several different behaviors simultaneously. A study by Roberts et al. of the interactions among participants in mutual help groups was used to illustrate such an observational system. In this study it was found that group members were quite supportive of each other and that a member's satisfaction with the group was more a function of the amount of help he or she had given than the amount of help received. The central component of the Roberts et al. study was a set of 12 categories for coding group interactions. Such behavior codes, or category systems, must include detailed descriptions of the behaviors to be observed and recorded as well as a set of rules about how the observations are to be made.

If you cannot find an existing behavior code that suits your purposes, there are several things to remember about constructing and using such a set of categories. The first is to keep it as simple as possible. You cannot expect observers to make complex, subtle discriminations while observing and recording live behavior. You also need to define each category thoroughly (i.e., elaborately, with lots of examples) and have the observers memorize those definitions. You need to give the observers lots of practice using the system. You also have to identify the observers' mistakes, provide corrective feedback, and have them try coding again and again.

In the absence of any means of assessing the accuracy of observation, interobserver agreement is the most common substitute. In establishing a respectable level of interobserver agreement, you need to correct for chance agreement and try to prevent observer drift. Observer drift is the phenomenon of observers agreeing with one another, but drifting away from using the categories as they were intended to be used. Strategies for helping to ensure that observers continue to use the system as it was intended include initial overtraining, frequent retraining, and not allowing observers to watch each other coding.

Recommended Readings

Boehm, A. E., and Weinberg, R. A. (1987). *The classroom observer: Developing observation skills in early childhood settings* (2nd ed.). New York: Teachers College Press.

Boehm and Weinberg have written a straightforward, practical guide to developing and implementing an observational system for use in early childhood settings. Their focus is on the actual construction of a set of categories that will enable you to investigate the specific topic, or problem, of interest to you. Even if you are not interested in early childhood settings, the authors cover, in just over 120 pages of text, the essential topics you need to consider in developing a category system for any setting. They also provide a number of hands-on exercises, many with answers, that will enable you to test your understanding along the way. In addition, the book contains a bibliography on the development of observation skills and a partial listing of existing schedules and systems for use in observational studies.

Brinberg, D., and Kidder, L. (Eds.) (1982). *Forms of validity in research.* (New Directions for Methodology of Social and Behavioral Science, no. 12). San Francisco: Jossey-Bass.

If I were to pick out the two most important concepts in research, I would choose observation and validity. We have spent a considerable amount of time on observation in the preceding chapters, and we have introduced the notion of validity in several places. We shall return to it repeatedly in the chapters that follow and elaborate on its multiple forms. The volume by Brinberg and Kidder is a good introduction to those multiple forms of validity. It will help you to sort out their many names—internal validity, construct validity, external validity, concurrent validity, predictive validity, face validity, ecological validity, and more—and see how they are related. McGrath and Brinberg, for example, argue that there are really just three basic issues involved: correspondence, robustness, and value. The question of correspondence is that of fit between things, say, between your ideas and the ways you choose to investigate them. The question of robustness is that of generalization: Can you extrapolate your findings, say, to other groups of people or to related domains of inquiry? The question of value is one that used to be raised by Senator Proxmire: Are the events and phenomena that are the subject of research both real, or true, and important? If you do not make it through the entire volume, at least read the chapter by Kidder. It is an interesting discussion of the many faces of face validity.

Goodall, J. (1990). *Through a window: My thirty years with the chimpanzees of Gombe.* Boston: Houghton Mifflin.

Many of the early studies of animal behavior were severely criticized because they were carried out in what, for the animals, were peculiar, unnatural environments. The observations of chickens, for example, that led to the concept of a pecking order were carried out in barnyards. There, nearly all of the inhabitants are female, they are often cooped up in a relatively small, fenced enclosure, and they are fed at predetermined times. Under more natural conditions, they would spend their days roaming freely over a wide area in search of food, and their behavior might or might not be similar to that seen in a chicken coop. From the *observers'* point of view, the advantage of making observations in artificial environments is that it is usually so much easier than seeking out the animals' natural habitats. In spite of that, Jane Goodall and her associates have spent three decades observing chimpanzees under completely natural conditions at the Gombe Stream Research Center in Africa. Their tireless tramping through jungle grass, climbing trees, perching on mountaintops, peering through telescopes, and taking pictures have been rewarded with a number of significant findings. It was discovered, for example, that chimpanzees eat meat, whereas previously they had been thought to dine exclusively on nuts and berries. They were also seen using tools and even—surprise—making tools. This book provides a nice introduction to both the style and the substance of Goodall's approach to the study of chimpanzee behavior.

Rothfeder, J. (1992). *Privacy for sale: How computerization has made everyone's private life an open secret.* New York: Simon and Schuster.

Back in the 1940s, when George Orwell wrote his disturbing view of the future in *1984*, one of his primary fears was that a centralized government would weave its way into all aspects of daily life. Individual freedom and privacy would be lost forever. With telescreens and spies everywhere, Big Brother would be watching. According to Jeffrey Rothfeder, privacy in modern society is indeed in serious danger. But not from Big Brother. The danger stems from the proliferation of microcomputers coupled with the too easily accessible data sets containing all sorts of information about you, me, and everybody else. Just how easy is it to obtain supposedly private and confidential information about others? Rothfeder illustrates by obtaining former Vice President Dan Quayle's credit record, home address, Social Security number, credit card numbers, and unlisted phone number—all with a few keystrokes on his Macintosh home computer and a couple of telephone calls. Of course, information about credit records, medical histories, past criminal activities, and current employment can be useful for a variety of legitimate purposes. If you want to borrow money from someone, they have a right to be curious about your credit status. However, the compilation of this information and its availability to others for purposes for which it was never intended constitutes an invasion of privacy. This interesting book raises some serious questions about how people can control access to information about themselves. As you will see, there are surprisingly few legal protections available.

Weick, K. E. (1985). Systematic observational methods. In G. Lindzey and E. Aronson (Eds.), *Handbook of social psychology* (3rd ed.), vol. 2, pp. 357–451. New York: Random House.

Weick's chapter is one of the most literate and thoughtful discussions of observational techniques that you are likely to find. As he notes, there are a "staggering variety" of procedures and techniques that can be loosely assembled under the rubric of systematic observational methods. Rather than providing a mere catalog of this heterogeneous collection, Weick begins by offering a definition of systematic observation as "sustained, explicit, methodical observing and paraphrasing of social situations in relation to their naturally occurring contexts." Making use of numerous examples, he then uses most of the chapter to dissect and explain the implications of this definition. He points out that systematic observation has traditionally meant the use of a set of categories of behavior to be observed, and that the goal of using these categories was to focus the observer, to restrain the observer into looking only for behaviors that would fit into the categories. However, Weick argues that when the social situation is distorted by this process, the result to be hoped for is that systematic observation will destroy the observer's a priori categories and suggest more valid ways of understanding what is being seen. The chapter is tough going at times, but well worth the effort.

4

Archival Research and Content Analysis

Some of the richest sources of data bearing on social, psychological, and behavioral processes are the records and written materials produced in the course of everyday life. Vast stores of records and texts are continually being generated in every literate society: traffic statistics, newspapers, crime reports, speeches, marriage license applications, magazine articles, unemployment statistics, television scripts, factory production data, and much more. The most common uses, and often the intended purposes, of such materials are simply to describe events in society and to inform decision making. If the crime rates are increasing, perhaps more money should be allocated to the Police Department. If people are told about pollution of the nation's waterways, maybe they will do something about it. If the figures show that sales are down, perhaps the product needs redesigning, or a new advertising campaign. But with a little ingenuity, records and texts—even fiction—can often be used for purposes other than those for which they were originally intended.

Consider an example. Daily reports of maximum and minimum temperatures, of course, are meant to inform people about the weather. Similarly, police reports of violence are intended to keep the public and the government informed about criminal activity. But when records of temperature and violence are examined together, you will find that people are more aggressive when the weather heats up (Anderson and DeNeve, 1992). Of course, you may be able to think of one or two possible alternative explanations that need to be ruled out concerning this temperature–aggression link. Maybe people are just outside more in hot weather and, hence, there is greater opportunity for interpersonal aggression. But, assuming the relationship between temperature and aggression holds up under critical scrutiny, it is a basic, theoretically important fact about human behavior.

Existing data can also be useful for addressing practical, applied problems about behavior. For example, after years of complaints about accidents caused by "unintentional acceleration" of certain makes of cars, Tomerlin (1988) examined what was known about thousands of relevant cases. He found that the most reasonable explanation was not mechanical or electrical failure, but driver error—that is, mashing the gas pedal instead of the brake.

Some of the factors that led him to this conclusion were: (1) after incidents of unintentional acceleration, no mechanical or electrical malfunctions could be found; (2) incidences of unintentional acceleration were more likely to occur when the driver did not have much experience in the car in question; and (3) incidences of unintentional acceleration were more likely to occur among older, rather than younger, drivers. What Tomerlin's research suggested was that cases of unintentional acceleration could probably be reduced by such simple measures as greater physical separation of the brake and gas pedals or an automatic shift lock device—a gadget that requires your foot to be on the brake before you can shift out of Park or Reverse. Many manufacturers have now installed such devices.

Both of the above are examples of **archival research,** research that utilizes selected aspects of those mountains of records from the past to examine questions and hypotheses of current interest. Similarly, **content analysis,** which we shall discuss in the second half of this chapter, utilizes texts of all sorts—books, diaries, speeches, newspaper and magazine articles, and television and movie scripts—for the same purpose. As you will see, content analysis is not limited exclusively to preexisting materials. Investigators can and do ask people to generate materials—to write out self-descriptions or to keep diaries, for example—which are then subjected to content analysis. For the most part, however, content analysis and archival research still deal primarily with preexisting records and texts. To see what's involved, let's take them one at a time.

Archival Research

Most dictionaries define the term **archives** as "public records and documents." I would define it more broadly than that to include public and private records of any sort (see Box 1). But even if you stick with public records only, it is hard to conceive of the sheer mass of information that is out there. There are tremendous stores of official government documents maintained by the National Archives and Records Services, the Library of Congress, numerous presidential libraries, and other government agencies from the Internal Revenue Service to the Federal Communications Commission to the Bureau of the Census. These documents alone contain an incredible storehouse of information about all aspects of the nation's past: government, laws, people, wars, economics. In addition, there are literally hundreds of thousands of archives scattered across the country: City, county, and state governments, colleges and universities, businesses, churches, synagogues, social clubs, and professional societies all maintain records that might be helpful in our attempts to understand a little more about people.

Employing that information intelligently, however, can be a tricky business. The major problem in using archival data is that the most interesting questions about human behavior can rarely be answered with a simple descriptive statistic. If all you want to know is something on the order of how the per capita income of residents of New York State ($23,534 in 1992) com-

---

Box 1
Oral Histories

Prior to about 1940, archives consisted almost entirely of written material: diaries, records of transactions, birth and death certificates, letters, deeds, and numerous other public and private documents. The invention of wire, and then tape, recorders and their ever-increasing accessibility and affordability has made a different kind of record common: oral histories. An oral history is simply a tape-recorded interview with someone who has been selected because of his or her knowledge of a particular historical event, person, or way of life.

In contrast to the sometimes dry written record, oral histories can offer the fascination of listening to a good storyteller, an eyewitness who can tell you how it really was. Because of that immediacy, that feeling of listening to someone who was there, there is a danger of being less critical and cautious than one might be with other types of records. In evaluating the reliability and validity of material obtained from oral histories, you need to be just as skeptical as you are in evaluating other kinds of archival data—maybe even more so. Memory, after all, is notoriously fallible, and each witness to historic events has only one perspective—and that, of course, may be biased (e.g., Tonkin, 1992). In fact, it is usually a good idea to self-consciously ask yourself the following questions about recorded interviews:

- Why was the interview conducted?
- Who paid for it?
- How long after the events described did the interview occur?
- Is the account firsthand or secondhand?
- Who was the interviewer?
- Was the interviewer generally knowledgeable about the topic?
- Is the information in the interview internally consistent?
- Is the information in the interview consistent with other sources? If not, why not?

As Baum and Hardwick (1988) point out, "oral histories are recollections remembered—often many years later—and colored by succeeding events in the narrator's life."

---

pares with that of residents of West Virginia ($15,065 in 1992), you do not need a course in research methods to find out. You can consult one of the many almanacs that are published annually and that are filled with such esoteric facts and figures. But, as mentioned in Chapter 1, what we need are explanations. Why is the per capita income so much higher in New York than in West Virginia? Why do so many fewer women choose careers in science and engineering than men (Brush, 1991)? Why do suicides peak in the springtime and following holidays (Gabennesch, 1988)? It is rare that archival records speak for themselves on such questions. As Fischhoff (1980) has noted, records have to be delicately coaxed to shed any light on such issues. As for suicides and springtime, you might suggest the April 15 deadline for paying taxes as a possible explanation. That possibility can be ruled out, however, because suicides peaked in the springtime even before there was an income tax (Schachter et al., 1980). Gabennesch (1988) suggests that suicides peak in the spring, and following holidays, because the anticipated promise and happiness of those periods is not realized by the severely depressed. Disappointed again, their despair plunges to an even lower level and heightens the probability of suicide.

Do not misunderstand. We need descriptive information about the past to help us understand a variety of phenomena, and the major sources of such information, of course, are the multitudinous archives referred to above. But you should not assume that archives are useful only for such descriptive purposes. With some ingenuity and a little careful thought about what data are there, archives can also help tremendously in the search for explanations of behavior, for an understanding of why people do the things they do. As an illustration, let's examine one of the classic examples of archival research and a couple of more recent follow-ups of that study.

An Illustration: Threat and Authoritarianism

Following World War II, when the extent of the Nazi atrocities against the Jews became known, a number of personality and social psychologists began trying to understand how it could have happened. Was it a quirk of the German character? Could it happen here? Are there specific conditions under which humans become so inhumane? Utilizing questionnaire data and intensive clinical interviews, investigators pieced together a picture of what has come to be known as the authoritarian personality, characterized by a bizarre pattern of ideas and beliefs. The authoritarian syndrome, as sketched by Adorno et al. (1950), was indeed a complex web of contradictory impulses. In contrast to others, authoritarians seemed: (1) to greatly admire power and strength; (2) to have a cynical contempt for humankind; (3) to believe in mystical determinants of one's fate; (4) to maintain submissive attitudes toward anyone in power; (5) to reject those who violate in-group values; (6) to oppose efforts to examine the subjective and interpersonal aspects of experience; and (7) to be especially harsh toward those who violate sexual norms. Of particular interest, however, was the suggestion by Adorno et al. that environmental threats—such as an economic depression, a war, or a natural catastrophe—would bring about increases in authoritarianism. Someone who seemed relatively normal during good times might become rigidly authoritarian and punitive when the chips were down.

An interesting idea, but can it be tested? Some sort of pervasive threat with serious potential consequences for the individual would be needed to give the hypothesis that threat leads to increased authoritarianism a real test. It occurred to Sales (1973) that the economic disaster of the 1930s might have been just such a threat. The 1920s had been a time of unparalleled prosperity for the United States, but in the 1930s, the bottom fell out. Unemployment more than tripled from the 1920s to the 1930s, and the per capita income slid downward. Bread lines and soup kitchens were common during the 1930s, and the prospect of a global war was becoming increasingly real with Hitler's rise to power and his subsequent territorial claims for Germany. Thus, Sales chose a number of indices, or markers, that seemed to correspond to aspects of the authoritarian syndrome described above and compared the values of these indices for the 1920s and the 1930s.

For example, if authoritarians tend to demand submission to in-group values, then it should follow from the hypothesis that a time of increased threat (the 1930s) should lead to greater demands for conformity, for toeing the party line, than a time of low threat (the 1920s). Sales found that eight states passed statutes requiring loyalty oaths from schoolteachers in the 1920s. During the 1930s, however, 17 states passed such laws. This occurred in spite of the fact that at the beginning of the 1930s there was a smaller remaining pool of states without such laws than at the beginning of the 1920s. Thus, it appears that, as expected, increased demands for submission to in-group norms occurred during the 1930s.

A second index Sales chose was the amount of support for police forces during the 1920s and 1930s. If authoritarians condemn those who violate in-group values, it should follow that they will support the forces in society charged with apprehending and punishing the violators. During the times of increased threat, authoritarian tendencies should increase, which implies that support for such forces should increase. Looking at the proportion of the New York City and Pittsburgh budgets devoted to police, Sales found that during the 1920s police were allocated a significantly smaller percentage of the budget in those cities than during the 1930s. Although this fits with the hypothesis, it is ambiguous until some additional information is brought to bear. First, was crime on the increase? Consulting the Uniform Crime Reports for the United States, Sales found that, in fact, there was actually a decline in crime between the 1920s and 1930s. The second type of data needed is information on other aspects of the budgets. Maybe Pittsburgh and New York were generally increasing expenditures for services—police, garbage collection, fire departments—and cutting back in other areas. Selecting the fire department allotment for comparison, Sales found that the fire departments' shares of the budgets actually declined from the 1920s to the 1930s. Thus, it appears that, relative to other city services and in the face of a decline in crime (but in line with the hypothesis), in the 1930s New York City and Pittsburgh increased their support for police to a level higher than that given in the 1920s.

Another index that Sales selected was designed to see whether there was an increase in the harshness with which sexual offenders were treated during the period of increased threat (the 1930s). Going through the court records of Allegheny County, Pennsylvania, he found that during the 1920s, rapists received sentences averaging 3.41 years in prison. During the 1930s, the average sentence for rape was 4.65 years. For a major nonsexual crime selected for comparison purposes, no such increase in sentence length occurred between the 1920s and the 1930s. Again, the result is in line with the hypothesis.

Sales employed a series of additional indices taken from archival sources to test the hypothesis about the relationship between environmental threat and authoritarianism. Figure 1 depicts the results for two of the additional measures. Each of the indices used has limitations, of course; none of them is an infallible indicator. The result of each, however, was generally in line with the hypothesis: In threatening times, authoritarianism seems to increase. Sales's use of multiple indicators, each of which has its own unique problems and sources of error, increases our confidence that the relationship between threat and authoritarianism is real.

There is more to Sales's research. He did a similar analysis comparing the years 1959–1964, a period of low threat in the United States, with the years 1967–1970, a period of high threat. Again, the results derived from the analysis of a variety of indicators of authoritarianism (numbers of books on astrology, circulation of conservative periodicals, lengths of sentences for rape) were generally supportive of the hypothesis that authoritarianism increases during periods of high threat. Again, confidence in the reality of the relationship between threat and authoritarianism is increased a little by the comparison of these two additional time periods. If the relationship had held only for the 1920s to 1930s comparison, you might have suspected that it was spurious. You might have believed that there was something peculiar about the 1920s or the 1930s that made it appear that authoritarianism and threat were related when, in fact, they were not. Or, you might have suspected that authoritarianism was especially low in the 1920s and has been on the increase ever since. The additional data from the two periods in the 1960s help to establish the generality of the hypothesis that authoritarianism increases only during threatening times.

More recently, Doty, Peterson, and Winter (1991) have helped to clarify the relationship between threat and authoritarianism with a follow-up of Sales's research. Doty et al. point out that both of the earlier comparisons in-

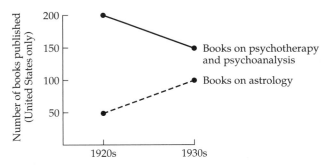

1 The number of books published on astrology increased during times of threat, while the number of books published on psychotherapy and psychoanalysis decreased. These data are consistent with the authoritarian syndrome discussed in the text. The hypothesis predicted that if threatening times (the 1930s Depression) increase authoritarianism, interest in astrology should increase and interest in psychotherapy should decrease. (Data from Sales, 1973.)

volved a low-threat period followed by a high-threat period. Suppose the high-threat period occurs first? Can it be demonstrated that authoritarianism then *decreases* in a subsequent low-threat period? And suppose the "threat" is not as extreme as those employed by Sales, that is, the Great Depression (1930s) and the turmoil of the Vietnam War era (1967–1970). Will less extreme threats also produce increases in authoritarianism?

Doty et al. examined a series of social and economic indicators to identify periods of high and low threat. They found that in 1978–1982, as compared with 1983–1987: (1) personal income was lower; (2) the Consumer Price Index was higher; (3) there were significantly more work stoppages; (4) the average rate of increase of the unemployment rate was significantly higher; (5) the prime interest rate was significantly higher; and (6) there were significantly more bombing incidents. Survey data collected by the Gallup Poll on a yearly basis also indicated that during 1983–1987, residents of the United States were significantly more optimistic about their financial future and significantly more satisfied with the way things were going than they had been during 1978–1982.

Thus, using 1978–1982 as the period of high threat and 1983–1987 as the period of low threat, Doty et al. then proceeded in a manner similar to what Sales had done 20 years earlier. They selected indicators that they believed would reflect authoritarianism and compared those indicators for the low- and high-threat periods. Increased authoritarianism, for example, should be accompanied by an increased affinity for symbols of power and toughness. Doty et al. found that a yearly average of 152,844 attack dogs were registered with the American Kennel Club during the high-threat period compared with an average of only 113,358 during the low-threat period. In contrast, registration of lapdogs increased during the low-threat period. Increased authoritarianism should also be reflected in increased support for conventional middle-class values. Examining the election results for the 30 most conservative and 30 most liberal members of Congress, Doty et al. found that relative to the 1978 (high-threat) elections, the liberals did significantly better than the conservatives in the 1986 (low-threat) elections.

In all, Doty et al. compared 20 indicators of authoritarianism for their low- and high-threat periods, including reported anti-Semitic incidents, Ku Klux Klan activity, and survey data on expressions of prejudice toward members of other races. Overall, their results again confirm the high threat–increased authoritarianism link. But not all of their indicators came out precisely as the threat–authoritarianism hypothesis predicts, and it is instructive to consider why. For example, one of the selected indicators was length of sentence for those convicted of rape. You will recall that this was one of the indicators used in the original study by Sales, and that he found, as predicted, that during periods of high threat, the average prison sentence given rapists was significantly longer than during periods of low threat. Doty et al. found just the opposite. Using data from the State of Michigan Department of Corrections, they found that minimum sentences for rape were significantly longer during the low-threat years (1983–1987) than during the high-threat years (1978–1982). Why should that be so? Doty et al. (p. 635) point out that views about the seriousness of rape have changed since the periods covered by Sales's research. Hence, increased sentences for rape in the mid-1980s may reflect changes in society and in judicial acceptance of those changes. The important point here is that simply because some indicator, or measure, has worked in the past, one cannot assume that it will continue to work. Its meaning may have changed. As Doty et al. put it, because of "changing historical context and effects of other variables, . . . isolated individual measures are likely to have limited historical generality. The researcher's task is to identify and construct measures that may be functionally equivalent across time and social change" (p. 637).

As noted in Chapter 1, when the same result is obtained using several different measuring instruments, several different research methods, or several different indices of some hypothetical phenomenon, the likelihood that the result is erroneous, artifactual, or unrepresentative of the real state of affairs is greatly diminished. The variety of indicators used by Sales and by Doty et al. to look at the consequences of perceived threat is an excellent example of what has been advocated here all along: triangulation of measurement. Operationalize your concepts in several different ways, and seek evidence on your hypotheses with several different methods. In archival research, operationalization translates into deciding on exactly what information you are going to extract from the records—what index or marker you are going to use.

Operationalizing Concepts

The measures, or indices, used in archival research are, in several respects, analogous to what geologists refer to as outcroppings. An outcropping is a projection of bedrock or some other stratum of stone through the soil. It is like the tip of an iceberg—it is not of great interest for itself, but for what it signifies. A small outcropping of coal, for example, may mean that miles of rich veins of coal lie hidden just beneath the surface. A geologist who recommended setting up an expensive mining operation on the basis of sighting one small outcropping, however, would probably not be taken too seriously. Other evidence in support of the inference that those veins were really there would have to be found before such a massive expense could be justified— other outcroppings, borings that yielded coal, soundings, information on other coal found in the vicinity.

Similarly, the indices used in archival research are seldom of intrinsic interest, and it is equally rare for their meaning to be so unequivocal that they can stand alone. Sales (1973), for example, was interested in the number of astrology books published in the 1930s only because of the hypothesized relationship between increased authoritarianism and increased interest in things mystical. The number of astrology books published in the 1930s, by itself, was and is essentially meaningless. Only within the context of the additional information Sales obtained could that number be used to support the inference that people become more authoritarian when things get tough. Note that "additional information" does not refer only to the other indices that Sales used—the percentage of municipal budgets devoted to police, the lengths of sentences given rapists. That additional information includes all the data Sales had to gather to rule out various alternative explanations for changes in the indices he used. For example, it was not sufficient to show merely that more astrology books were published in the 1930s than in the 1920s (see Figure 1). Maybe people had more time for reading all kinds of books in the 1930s. There were a lot of people out of work, with time on their hands. But Sales wanted to know if the demand for this particular type of book increased in the 1930s. Thus, he obtained the total numbers of books published on all subjects in the 1920s and 1930s and calculated the proportions of those two numbers that were astrology books. Sure enough, a significantly greater proportion of the books published in the 1930s were about astrology.

Note that in Sales's (1973) and Doty, Peterson, and Winter's (1991) research, a variety of indicators, or outcroppings, *other than* the ones actually chosen might have been used. Numbers of reported UFO sightings per year might have been used as an index of interest in things mystical instead of number of books on astrology. The only thing that limits the choice of indicators is your ability to make a plausible case that the chosen indicator reflects the phenomenon of interest.

As you can see, then, there are no general indices for use in archival research. The particular ones chosen are usually highly idiosyncratic to the research you are doing. There are, however, a couple of general principles to follow. First, you should have a specific research purpose, or question, or hypothesis, clearly in mind. There are some exceptions to this principle (see Box 2), but in general, random searches through records are unlikely to yield anything of value. Your hypothesis, of course, serves as a guide, suggesting which records are pertinent, where you should look. Consider two examples:

1. Evans (1988) was interested in the question of whether or not elderly automobile drivers are at increased risk for doing themselves, and others, harm. This possibility was suggested by data showing that certain sensory and motor abilities change with age. Reaction time, for example, has been shown to decline with advancing age (Olson and Sivak, 1986), and a quick reaction time might make the difference between a collision and a close shave. The National Highway Traffic Safety Administration of the U.S. Department of Transportation maintains a set of files, called the Fatal Accident Reporting System, that contain information such as driver age, sex, type of car, and time of day for every automobile accident in the United States that has involved a fatality since January 1, 1975. Evans extracted from these files information on all accidents between 1981 and 1985 in which the driver of an automobile was killed. He then obtained data from the U.S. Bureau of the Census (1987) report on the resident population of the United States by age and sex for 1981 through 1985 and plotted the number of fatalities per mil-

---

Box 2

Searching for That Needle

Epidemiology is the study of how diseases originate and spread through human populations. Its purposes are to identify environmental agents and other factors that may cause disease and to identify people who may be at high risk of developing a disease. Although it is not generally considered to be one of the more glamorous fields of medicine, in the last few years the fruits of epidemiological research have received a great deal of coverage in the popular press. Hardly a week goes by without an article appearing in the newspapers or a magazine in which you are given the opportunity to score yourself on risk factors for developing heart disease, cancer, or some other dreaded malady.

Much of the research substantiating the potential lethalness of those risk factors was archival research, carried out by combing through medical records (imagine trying to decipher the handwriting of all those physicians). It usually works like this. An epidemiologist will collect reports of a number of people who have, or had, a particular disease or disorder, the origin of which is unknown. The medical records of those people are then obtained and searched for anything that they all have in common. It can be a wild goose chase, of course, but it can also pay off handsomely. Gordis and Gold (1980) listed a few of the things that have been uncovered in this way: (1) an increased risk of cancer among those exposed to asbestos and vinyl chloride in their work; (2) an increased risk of cancer after exposure to radiation; (3) an increased risk of developing vaginal cancer among the daughters of women given a particular hormone during pregnancy; and (4) the knowledge that German measles contracted by a mother during pregnancy can produce congenital malformation in her child. The list goes on and is indeed an impressive yield.

Note, however, that this kind of archival research is not a purely random search through medical records for whatever will turn up. The investigator starts out with a well-defined group of people, people who have disease X. The investigator also starts out with the conviction that those people must have something else in common, that is, they must all have made contact with the cause of X. The task, of course, is to find that something else.

---

lion population against driver age. As you can see in Figure 2, there is indeed a relationship between driver age and the likelihood of being involved in a fatal accident, especially for male drivers: Beginning at about age 65, the probability begins to go up. Be sure to note, however, that Figure 2 also shows that for both males and females, the young (from the late teens through about age 30) are the most likely to be involved in fatal accidents.

2. Simonton (1988b) was interested in the conditions under which geniuses and great creative achievements are likely to emerge in a society. Specifically, he wanted to examine the possibility that geniuses are most likely to flourish in an atmosphere, or setting, in which there are many others of creative ability also working, although those others may be of somewhat lesser renown. Genius might be enhanced, then, by stimulation from one's peers, and the great creators of one generation might serve as models or teachers for those in the next. A contrasting possibility is that genius is an in-

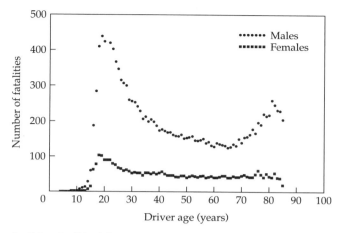

2 Driver fatalities (all motorized vehicles) per million population in the United States, 1981–1985. (From Evans, 1988.)

dividual phenomenon, determined by heredity. If this were the case, then geniuses would arise at random points in time, regardless of what else was going on in society at the moment, or who had been working in the preceding generation. To examine these possibilities, Simonton obtained the names of over 10,000 Chinese creators, leaders, and celebrities stretching back over 2820 years (from 840 B.C. to 1979 A.D.). The names were obtained from histories, anthologies, and biographical dictionaries covering the entire course of Chinese history. He then assumed that creative achievement peaks at about age 40 (for some evidence on this, see Simonton, 1988a) and that generations average 20 years. The results indicate that the most creative people—whether scientists, authors, poets, philosophers, mathematicians, painters, or musicians—tended to appear in eras when there were many other creative people at work. There also appeared to be evidence for a generational effect—that is, the more creative souls there had been in a particular generation, the more there were likely to be in the next.

What you seek to extract from archives, then, is guided by your hypothesis. The second general principle about selecting an index to suit your needs is, simply, trial and error. You propose an index and subject it to critical scrutiny. That scrutiny should be aimed at discovering what plausible interpretations are allowed by this index in addition to the one intended by the hypothesis. In other words, the problem of index construction is one of operationalizing your research questions in such a way that the measure you extract from the archives reflects the concept of interest and as little else as possible.

An example should help to clarify this point. Suppose you are interested in the effect on the crime rate of the introduction of a home-cruiser program, that is, allowing police officers to take their patrol cars home with them and use them when not on duty. The idea behind such a program is that it makes the police more visible in neighborhoods and at shopping centers, and that this increased visibility serves as a deterrent to crime. The data you will want to look at to check this hypothesis are contained in police archives—records of crimes reported, arrests made, convictions, and so forth. The point here is that whatever index you finally select, it cannot be a simple before–after measure of number of crimes reported. At the very least, your index must take population changes into account. Suppose the population is increasing rapidly. The home-cruiser program is instituted, and next year crime is up. Would you conclude that the home-cruiser program led to an increase in crime? Another thing you would need to worry about is seasonal variations in crime. If the home-cruiser program was instituted on June 1, and you compared the number of crimes reported in the previous three months with the numbers reported in the following three months, you might again be tempted to draw an invalid conclusion about the effects of the program. In general, crime increases in the summer.

The distinction between the index you use to reflect the phenomenon of interest (such as crime rate reflecting the effectiveness of the home-cruiser program) and the additional information you need to rule out alternative interpretations (such as an increase in crime due to an increase in population) is sometimes a little fuzzy. You could take care of the increased population possibility by using a simple ratio as your index, that is, number of crimes per 10,000 people rather than just the number of crimes (but see Box 3 first). Possible seasonal variations might be a little more difficult to incorporate into a single number. However, you could get the data from the preceding year and set up a comparison of the two years similar to that shown in Figure 3. What you would expect, of course, is that the number of crimes per 10,000 people would be roughly the same in the two March 1–May 31 periods, but that the number for the June 1–August 31 period would be smaller after the institu-

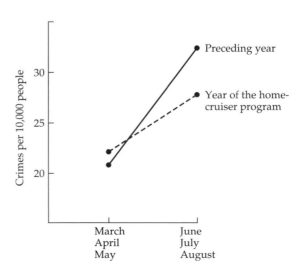

3 Hypothetical data on a home-cruiser program. If off-duty police officers are allowed to use their police cars, will this be effective in reducing crime? In both the year in which the program is instituted and the preceding year, crime increases in the summer months. However, following the introduction of the home-cruiser program on June 1, there is less of an increase than there had been in the preceding summer.

Box 3

Choosing the Right Denominator

When selecting an indicator, or measure, to operationalize the concept of interest to you, it is often useful to convert that indicator to a rate. For example, suppose you were interested in the relationship between religious preferences in a community and abortion. You might anticipate that the higher the proportion of Catholics in a community, the lower the rate of abortion. If that is your prediction, then it is more useful to know that there were 350 abortions per 1000 live births in community A than it is to know, simply, that there were 3897 abortions. The rate, 350 per 1000 live births, does two things for you. First, it facilitates comparison with other communities in a standardized manner; that is, you can meaningfully compare the rates for two different communities that are known to differ in their proportions of Catholics. Comparison of the rates allows you to rule out the possibility that the differences obtained are simply a function of different population sizes in different communities. Second, the rate tells you something about the relative prevalence of abortion in a community that a bare figure, such as "3897," does not. With the rate, you know that 350 of every 1350 pregnancies ended in abortion. With the bare figure, you have no idea whether 3897 is a lot or a little.

The choice of the denominator in constructing a rate is crucial. Unfortunately, this is an area in which mistakes are often made, with seriously misleading results. Your first thought in constructing a rate might be to use population figures: that is, how many __ per capita? For some indicators that might be appropriate, but for others it is not. For example, if you were interested in the amount spent on education, it would be more meaningful to use the amount spent *per child* than it would be to use the amount spent *per capita*. A city with a large elderly population might spend less per capita on education, but more per child, than a city with a different age distribution. Similarly, if you were interested in the incidence of sexual crimes against women, it makes little sense to refer to rapes *per capita*. It is more meaningful to refer to rapes *per female over age 10*. As Jacob (1984) points out, using *per capita* in this latter case makes rapes appear much less common than they, in fact, are.

Unfortunately, there is no general rule that will tell you the correct denominator in any given case. It depends on the concept that you are trying to measure. Simply being aware of the potential for problems here is the first step, and a careful, logical analysis of exactly what the rate you select will imply is the second.

---

tion of the program than in the preceding year, even though it might be larger than the numbers in either of the March-April-May periods.

One way to think of the process of operationalization is as a form of interpretation: The concepts of interest must be translated into measures, just as in switching from one language (the abstract concepts) to another (the concrete measures). And, you must be able to persuade others that you have not lost the original meaning of the concepts in the process. Of course, it is easiest to accomplish this when you have complete freedom to design the measures that you will use. Then, for example, if you are interested in the possibility that similarity leads to attraction, you can choose, or construct, the very best indicators of similarity and attraction.

With archival research, you often do not have such freedom, but must work with data that someone collected for a purpose totally different from the one you have in mind. The question, of course, is whether or not you can obtain from those data valid indicators of the concepts of interest to you. You will need to keep questioning yourself about the index you want to extract from the archives. Does it really reflect your hypothesis? What additional information is needed? In the example above, would you really expect all categories of crime to decrease following the introduction of a home-cruiser program? It is doubtful that such a program would influence white-collar crime, so maybe the index needs refining: Instead of all crimes per 10,000 people, maybe you should use only certain types of crimes. As was noted in Chapter 1, to assess whether your hypothesis accounts for something, you have to be able to rule out all the alternatives that might plausibly have produced that same result. In other words, you have to establish that your measures are valid indicators of the concepts of interest.

Factors Affecting Validity

In terms of validity, working with archival data has one distinct advantage over other research methods. If the data were collected for a purpose other than what you have in mind and if they have already been collected and filed away, then it is impossible for you to bias the data collection process. In that sense, the use of preexisting records and texts is relatively **nonreactive,** or unobtrusive. As we noted in Chapter 3, research, or measurement, is said to be reactive when it produces a change in the process or object of interest that would not have occurred otherwise. For example, suppose you were interested in voter apathy and decided to interview a number of people on the eve of the election about their voting intentions. Chances are that the questions on your interview schedule would remind some people who had forgotten that the election was tomorrow. Your research on voter apathy would, thus, be reactive: It would produce an effect on the voter turnout the following day. On the other hand, examining archival data to see whether suicide rates in countries around the world are related to the gross national product and/or the quality of life in those countries (Lester and Stack, 1989) would be completely nonreactive. There is no way that the examination of records from preceding years can influence the outcome. Archival research and content analysis are, generally, less reactive than other research methods.

There is something else that sets archival research apart from other methods, something that makes it very appealing to many people. It has a quality that research using interviews, questionnaires, experiments, and simulations lacks. There is a realism about the data that grabs you. As Tom Wolfe (1974) once said about good reporting, what makes it fascinating is that you know all this actually happened. Unfortunately, there is a problem. Even though all this may have actually happened, there may be a lot more that happened that never got recorded. The official name for this difficulty is **selective deposit,** and it can be a real annoyance. The information you are after may never have been filed away. Someone may have considered it too trivial to bother with, or too much trouble. There is also the possibility that the information of interest to you was incriminating to someone or, at least, would have made that person look bad, and as a consequence, was intentionally destroyed. The widely publicized Garbage Project (Rathje and Murphy, 1992), in which anthropologist William Rathje and his students collect and analyze samples of the garbage of Tucson, Arizona, is unlikely to turn up many letters from secret lovers. Such letters are more likely to be burned than thrown out with the trash—especially now that everyone in Tucson knows that Dr. Rathje will be going through their garbage. However, some years ago, a group of industrial spies was exposed, and it was found that their principal source of data had been the contents of a rival firm's trash bins. Since then, many companies have installed paper shredders. More mundane motives may also influence selective deposit, of course. Even such genuine public documents as the Congressional Record, a transcript of the words spoken on the floors of the U.S. Senate and House of Representatives, are subject to selective deposit. Senators and representatives are allowed to edit the record before it is published. That means, of course, that they can add or delete material and edit their more ungrammatical expressions.

Selective survival is a closely related problem. It is no accident that archaeologists tend to be pottery and burial experts. Pottery is durable and tends to survive the onslaught of the elements, and the ancients often took great care to preserve the bones of their departed. Paper, in contrast, is not so hardy, and ink fades. So, even when original records or correspondence or manuscripts have been preserved, they may not be there when you go to look for them. Hill (1993) points out that records may be missing for a variety of reasons. Even when the original record keepers had the best of intentions and intended to save everything for posterity, there is often a filtering process that determines what survives. Has the necessary space been continuously available to keep them? Have fires, floods, or other acts of nature intervened? Is there reason to believe the records might have been purposefully destroyed? Is it likely they would have reflected poorly on someone? Who was responsible for keeping those records, anyway?

That last question is quite an important one, and you need to ask it even—maybe especially—when you find the records you need. Cochran, Gordon, and Krause (1980) have described records as **proactive** to call attention to the fact that the record keeper's desires and beliefs about why the records are being kept precede, and thus shape, the record. If the records are going to be used to evaluate the record keeper's performance, there is always the possibility that the record keeper will simply fake them. But the effect is usually more subtle than that. Cochran et al. cite an example of some research by McCleary in which it was found that parole officers quite often failed to report parole violations by the people for whom they were responsible. The parole officers' freedom of action in handling cases turned out to be crucial in determining which violations were and were not entered into a parolee's record. Their ability to exercise a little discretion about what was entered into the record allowed the parole officers to use the record for a variety of purposes. Not entering particular violations, for example, helped a parole officer on occasion to avoid scrutiny by superiors. Conversely, entering a violation was sometimes used to threaten parolees—better straighten up, that's strike one! Not entering a violation and letting the parolee know that it had not been entered might help to establish or maintain a relationship with the parolee. From the parole officer's point of view, maintaining that relationship might be the means of doing the job well—that is, trying to keep the parolee from slipping back into a life of crime. Thus, rather than static descriptions of what happened, the records you seek may have been part of a dynamic system. They may have been tools used by record keepers for accomplishing their own goals.

That does not mean, of course, that records are useless for research. It does mean that you should learn as much as possible about the situation in which the records you want to use were generated. You need to become thoroughly familiar with the dynamic pressures affecting what record keepers write down. Take suicide rates, for example. It is commonly believed that the rates are biased, that suicides are underreported among the middle and upper classes. Why should that be so? Or, take worker productivity. Unless you have taken the trouble to find out the basis for worker compensation in the data being used, you may get several unexplainable peaks in productivity. Piece-rate workers may turn out more work just prior to Christmas and vacations in order to make some extra money. That would not be particularly surprising, but you need to be aware that the extra emphasis on productivity during such periods may lead to neglect of routine maintenance. That, in turn, might result in more equipment breakdowns and production declines in subsequent periods. Again, the point is simply that the more you know about the situation in which the records you want to use were produced, the more intelligently you can use those records.

In spite of the potential difficulties posed by selective deposit, selective survival, and all-too-human record keepers, I am enthusiastic about the largely untapped potential for research represented by the use of archival data. It is something of a paradox that, in a time when many are demanding answers, pertinent, unused data are lying around gathering dust. And one of the prime advantages of archival research is that it is generally quite inexpensive—in fact, it is downright cheap. Old newspaper files, public archives, and information almanacs are filled with data, waiting for you to put them to use. Many of the more important archives have put together guides to help you make use of their services (e.g., National Archives and Records Administration, 1991).

The Ethics of Access and Use

At first blush, access to government archives and those of public libraries and other such institutions would appear to present no problem. In our open, democratic society with freedom of speech and a free press, the concept of freedom of information has also taken hold. Both the American Society of Archivists and the American Library Association subscribe to the principle of equal access to archives (Danielson, 1989). But, as Hill (1993) notes, what sounds great in principle doesn't always seem to work in practice. The material contained in archives is often unique, noncirculating, and under the total control of the resident archivist, who, according to Hill, can thwart your access in a variety of ways. And, even if the archivist would really like to help, he or she may be bound by legal and contractual restrictions.

With individual records or the archives of businesses and other private institutions, there is, of course, no "right" of access. But what if the material, or information, you are seeking has been deposited in the archives of a public institution? It still may not be available. Several years ago, for example, a large body of Sigmund Freud's letters and papers was deposited in the Library of Congress (Malcolm, 1984). Should you want to examine them, however, there may be problems. The man who collected the materials and donated them to the library set two conditions for their use. First, access to them was to be strictly controlled; that is, only "selected" people were to be allowed to see them. The "selected" people, of course, are typically those known to be sympathetic to Freud and/or his view of the mind. Second, some of the papers will not be open to the public until the year 2150—that's still over 150 years from now. To many people, such restrictions, which are usually intended to protect the reputations and/or privacy of the famous, are inappropriate and unethical. But they exist in many places and could constitute a problem, depending on what information you are after. Of course, existing data that are not contained in public archives may simply be unavailable (see Box 4).

A second ethical problem in the use of archives concerns the use of data that may have been initially obtained in legal, but ethically questionable, ways. The Federal Bureau of Investigation, for example, can and does make surreptitious tape recordings of conversations when it has reason to believe that such recordings will reveal evidence of illegal activity. These tapes could be quite valuable to linguistic researchers. When people know their voices are being recorded, their speech patterns change. The subjects on the FBI tapes, of course, did not know they were being recorded. Therefore the tapes—and there are thousands of them—should contain evidence of natural conversational practices. But if you believe that you should obtain the informed consent of subjects prior to their participation in research, is it ethically acceptable to use these tapes, for which informed consent was not obtained? Shuy (1986) argues that it is, as long as certain other ethical safeguards are implemented, such as assuring the anonymity of individuals by changing names, dates, places, and other identifying characteristics revealed on the tapes. The same issue arises, of course, with many other types of archival data. For example, is it appropriate to use medical records in research when the individuals whose aches and pains and operations and medications are contained in the records never gave their consent? Most would argue that it is acceptable as long as the anonymity of those individuals is preserved.

On the other hand, there are some who feel that access to information about specific people has become too easy and too widespread. Boyd (1990) suggests that data about individuals, which may have been obtained for legitimate purposes, are increasingly being used in ways that constitute invasions of privacy. Many state and federal agencies, for example, collect detailed information about people. The Department of Motor Vehicles knows your height, weight, and visual acuity. The Internal Revenue Service knows

> **Box 4**
>
> **Data Sharing?**
>
> When someone mentions archival research, content analysis, or the use of existing data, what typically comes to mind is research making use of information and texts stored in government, business, or university libraries and/or data from large-scale surveys conducted in the past. However, in the past two decades, a number of people have argued that *all* data collected for scientific purposes should be available to anyone with a legitimate interest in examining them. Hedrick (1988) lists a number of reasons why such sharing of data might be advantageous:
>
> 1. It would reinforce an ideal that is at the very heart of all scientific inquiry—that is, that research is an open, honest process, all parts of which are to be available for inspection.
> 2. Sharing data would enhance the accuracy of public knowledge. If, for example, you had made a mistake in analyzing your data, someone else examining the data might find, and expose, the mistake.
> 3. Data collected for one purpose, or to test one hypothesis, might bear on issues and questions that would never occur to the person who originally collected the data. Another person, with a different perspective or a different interest, might be able to put the data to good use.
> 4. Sharing data might reduce duplication of effort. When different surveys ask respondents similar questions, for example, their time and energy—as well as the time and energy of the people doing the research—are wasted.
>
> There are other benefits to be gained by sharing data, but there are also some problems. Suppose, for example, that you had constructed an interview schedule, tracked down a number of Vietnam War veterans, managed to interview 50 of them about their readjustment to civilian society, painstakingly transcribed those interviews, carefully studied the transcripts, and—finally—written an article about the common themes and problems the veterans had encountered following their discharges from the Army. Someone reading your article and pondering the questions that you had asked might think of a different way of looking at what the veterans had to say. They might then write to you and ask you for copies of the interview transcripts. How would you feel about that? Should you comply with the request?
>
> It depends. If there is any identifying information about individual veterans in the interviews, then, of course, the interviews cannot be shared without the consent of the veterans themselves. There is also another, more selfish, but very real, consideration. Why should you do all that work—interviewing and transcribing—just to hand copies of the finished product over to a complete stranger to do with as he or she wishes? Some people would say that your having had the idea of doing the interviews and the work you invested in conducting them give you a proprietary right to the data and that there is no obligation to share. There is nothing to keep the other researcher from conducting similar interviews with other Vietnam veterans. In fact, that might be a good thing. The new interviews might replicate, or might refute, your findings. Either way, they would be informative. On the other hand, if you were not planning to make any further use of them, sharing your transcripts—with protection of confidentiality—might be the thing to do.

how much money you make and where you work. If you itemize deductions, it also knows how much interest you pay, how much you give to charity, and how much you spend on medical care. The problem arises when such information is used in ways in which it was never intended. Much government data can be obtained by nongovernment agencies and used without your knowledge and consent. Boyd (1990) cites some specific examples: sellers of health and diet products can buy lists of short, fat men assembled from data on driver's licenses; the names of individuals who have moved recently can be obtained from the U.S. Postal Service; and automobile dealers can target their advertisements by getting lists of everyone in their area who drives a car over 5 years old. The problem derives from the attachment of individual identifiers—name, Social Security number, driver's license number, tag number—to other information. Once that is done, any additional information to which the individual identifier is attached can be secured, collated, and used. The only ethical way to avoid contributing to the problem in doing archival research is to avoid identifying individuals.

In spite of the potential for abuse, archival research is usually less intrusive and less reactive than any other form of research. The interpersonal biases inherent in participant observation and survey research are absent, for example. And for some research problems, there is no alternative to archival research. But in order to make clear the advantages of archival research—and to alert you to a few more of its inherent difficulties—the discussion needs to be broadened to include content analysis. As you will see, content analysis and archival research are very closely related.

Content Analysis

In one respect, content analysis should be the most familiar of research methods. In an informal way, it is something we do all the time: every time we read a book, or watch a movie, or see a commercial on television. In trying to identify the message of a text, or decide what is being said or what images are being conveyed, we are, of course, analyzing its content. Similarly, literary and film criticism are forms of content analysis. The interpretation of a work of fiction, such as *The Adventures of Huckleberry Finn* or *Moby Dick*, involves trying to go beyond the surface level of the story line to understand its meaning. What does the river symbolize in Huckleberry Finn? Why was Ahab so obsessed with the white whale?

But, as you are probably aware, questions like these are more likely to provoke lively discussions than definitive answers (Greene, 1986). The reasons for this are not very mysterious. Everyone brings different sets of experiences and expectations to bear on a book like *Moby Dick* or a film like *Forrest Gump.* Therefore, interpretations may be idiosyncratic, filtered through each person's particular point of view. And, quite often, different people attend most closely to different parts of a text or a film.

Content analysis as a research technique goes beyond normal reading and viewing habits, as well as literary and film criticism, in requiring that you be explicit about the criteria you apply in deciding what a text contains and the rules by which you have applied those criteria. "Being explicit" means making it possible for another person to apply *precisely* the same criteria in *precisely* the same manner, and that when they do, they should arrive at *precisely* the same conclusions about the text in question. Content analysis, then, is a research technique by which certain characteristics of printed, spoken, or visual material are systematically identified (Stone et al., 1966). Before we elaborate on what we mean by "certain characteristics" and "systematically," consider a few examples.

Sexist Ads, Robert E. Lee, and Significant Life Events

On September 12, 1957, James M. Vicary, vice president of the Subliminal Projection Company, held a press conference. He wanted to announce the results of some field research conducted at a movie theater in Ft. Lee, New Jersey. While unsuspecting audiences were watching the main feature, every 5 seconds he had flashed the message "Hungry? Eat Popcorn" on the screen at speeds too fast to be consciously perceived. The result? Greatly increased sales of popcorn in the theater, according to Mr. Vicary. As it turned out, it was all a hoax. Mr. Vicary had fabricated his findings (Miller, 1990), and there was no evidence that subliminal advertising could increase sales of popcorn, or anything else. There still isn't (e.g., Pratkanis and Aronson, 1992). Subliminal messages are not an effective means of advertising.

But what about the converse of Mr. Vicary's claim? Can advertisements convey subliminal messages? One way to find out would be to do a content analysis of the "extra-message" components of ads. That is, other than a list of the good qualities of the product and saying "Buy It," what else do advertisements contain? That, of course, is too broad a question. Answering it would entail documenting everything contained in advertisements. A more specific version of the question, and one that has received a fair amount of attention (e.g., Bretl and Cantor, 1988; Hawkins and Aber, 1993) in the last few years is this: Do advertisements convey different images of males and females in our society?

In one of the numerous studies that have focused on this issue, Synnott (1988) selected six issues of the *New York Times Magazine* and searched for full-page ads containing pictures of one or more people. In those six issues, he found 72 such ads: 32 portraying women, 25 men, 12 couples, and 3 with mixed groups of children or adults. He then examined the ads and tabulated the ways in which the depicted men and women differed. For example, the women were, "without exception," young and beautiful. In contrast, the men were neither all young nor all handsome. Second, men were always portrayed as fully dressed. In contrast, women were often portrayed with "considerable body-display"—that is, in swimsuits, bra and panties, or see-through clothing. All of the beauty product advertisements featured women. Seventy-two percent of the women, compared with only 48% of the men, were advertising clothes. Ninety-one percent of the women, compared with 40% of the men, were depicted as being passive—that is, just staring off into space and looking pretty. The men were much more likely (60% vs. 9%) to be doing something. You get the picture. There is more, but the point here is simply that Synnott attempted to be explicit and objective about what he perceived to be the different ways in which men and women were depicted in the ads. He did not entirely succeed, and there are some things he did not do that he should have, but we shall come back to those. First, let's examine two somewhat different, and more complex, examples of content analysis.

Suedfeld, Corteen, and McCormick (1986) were interested in the question of military leadership, specifically, what is it that makes a great general? It cannot be simply superior might. There are too many examples of commanders who have won battles, and even wars, when all the odds were against them—poor equipment, too few soldiers, shortage of rations, and/or bad terrain to fight over. Conversely, there are many examples of defeated commanders for whom all the odds were initially favorable, yet, somehow, they managed to blow it. It occurred to Suedfeld et al. that the key variable might be how the commander thinks—that is, what he or she does with the information available at the time. As they put it:

> we would expect that innovativeness, tactical flexibility, the ability to guess the opponent's plans and state of mind, a willingness to search for information and to consider that information seriously—in other words, complex information processing—will be more helpful to a commander who faces superior forces. (p. 501)

Suedfeld et al. obtained some evidence on this by applying content analytic techniques to the writings of Robert E. Lee and some of the generals he faced in battles. They identified six major battles in which Lee had been opposed by Union forces that were considerably larger than his own army. He was victorious in three of these—against Generals McClellan, Burnside, and Hooker—and he was defeated in three—once by General Meade and twice by Ulysses S. Grant.

Samples of the writings of each of these men were obtained from official dispatches and orders in the published archives of the Civil War and from some of the published letters written by Lee. Because the manner in which we process information can change over time due to fatigue, stress, fear, depression, and a variety of other situational factors, it was important to obtain samples of the generals' writings at the time they faced each other in battle. Thus, for each of the six battles, the materials selected were written no earlier than one week before the battle and no later than the last day of the fighting. Five paragraphs from each general's writings at the time of the battles were randomly selected by someone who was not familiar with the hypothesis or the content analytic scheme to be applied to the writings. In addition to samples of Lee's writings at the times of each of these battles, five paragraphs each from his prewar and postwar writings were also analyzed for comparison purposes. Again, all of the paragraphs were selected by someone who was unaware of the purpose of the study.

The analysis made use of a set of categories devised by Schroder and his colleagues (e.g., Schroder, Driver, and Streufert, 1967, Appendix 2) to assess complexity of thought as revealed in language. The categories are based on

Table 1 Integrative Complexity Scale

LEVEL OF INTEGRATIVE COMPLEXITY	CATEGORY (SCORE)	DEFINITION	EXAMPLES
Low	1	Low differentiation, low integration	The country faces a great crisis that threatens us all and requires decisive action. Constantly rising inflation rates are eroding the economic security of our people, yet our government leaders seem impotent in the face of this threat. What shall we do? There is clearly only one solution to this critical problem: immediate drastic cuts in government expenditures.
	2		
Medium low	3	Moderate or high differentiation, low integration	The country faces serious economic problems: high inflation and high un-employment. To control inflation, we need major cuts in government spen-ding; to reduce unemployment, we need to encourage new investment.
	4		
Medium high	5	Moderate or high differentiation, moderate integration	The country faces two interrelated economic problems: high inflation and high unemployment. We con-front a painful trade-off here. To re-duce inflation, we need to reduce economic growth, thus risking greater unemployment. To reduce unemployment, we need to stimulate the economy, thus risking greater inflation.
	6		
High	7	High differentiation, high integration	The country faces both high unem-ployment and high inflation rates. To decrease government spending or in-crease taxes in an attack on inflation will exacerbate unemployment, un-less we combine a tough antiinfla-tionary policy with efforts to increase productivity and end regulatory excess. This combined policy will curb inflation and boost economic growth, thus increasing and creating new jobs.

Source: Tetlock, 1981.

Note. These integrative complexity categories were used by Tetlock in assessing changes in the speeches of presidents from before to after election. A scorer read a particular paragraph and decided to which category of thought it was most similar; this process is referred to as coding. Note that only categories 1, 3, 5, and 7 are defined. If a scorer had trouble deciding whether a paragraph represented category 1 or category 3, for example, it would be assigned to category 2.

two concepts: differentiation and integration. **Differentiation** refers to the ability to see different aspects of a problem and to take those various factors into account in making a decision. If you believe the only solution to crime is to lock up criminals and throw away the key, you have a relatively undifferentiated view of the causes of crime. A more differentiated view would recognize that crime has multiple causes, many of which would be totally unaffected by treating criminals more harshly. **Integration,** in Schroder's system, refers to the perception of links or connections among the differentiated aspects of a problem. As you can see, differentiation precedes integration. You have to be aware of the pieces before you can conceive of ways in which they might fit together. Utilizing these ideas about differentiation and integration, Schroder et al. defined the 7-step scale of integrative complexity of thought depicted in Table 1. Inspection of the scale and the examples reveals that higher scores reflect a greater understanding of the issue and a greater subtlety of thought. Using this scale, Suedfeld read each of the paragraphs from Lee's and the other generals' writings and assigned it a score. A reliability check was conducted by having a second scorer read a subsample of the paragraphs and assign scores.

The purpose of all this, of course, was to examine the complexity of Robert E. Lee's thought in comparison to that of the generals whom he faced in battle. The results are depicted in Figure 4, where it can be seen that at the outset of the war and during the first three battles, which he won, Lee's com-

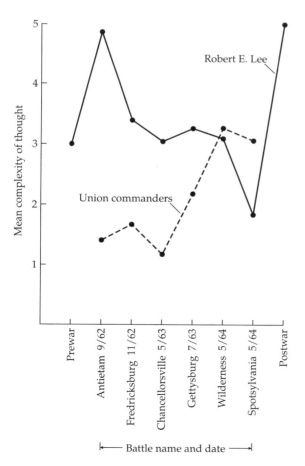

4 Mean complexity of thought for Robert E. Lee and six Union commanders whom he opposed in battle. The scale used in this study goes from a low of 1, indicating less complex thought, to a high of 7, indicating more complex thought (see Table 1). (From Suedfeld, Corteen, and McCormick, 1986.)

125

plexity of thought was much greater than that of his opponents. As the complexity of thought of the Union commanders increased and Lee's simultaneously decreased—at Gettysburg, Wilderness, and Spotsylvania—the Union commanders (Meade and Grant) prevailed. Several other things about the results are of interest. There appears to have been an overall decline in the complexity of Lee's thought throughout the war. That, of course, might have been due to a number of factors—fatigue, overconfidence as a result of early victories, mounting stress—as Suedfeld et al. (p. 505) point out. However, it is of interest that after the war, Lee's complexity of thought bounced back, suggesting that neither stress nor increasing age has a lasting negative effect on complexity of thought.

Some related research has been done by Suedfeld and Bluck (1993), who made use of the same content analytic scheme described above (see Table 1). Suedfeld and Bluck used the categories to analyze letters of 30 historically eminent men and women in the years prior to, during, and after significant events occurred in their lives. Their intention was to examine the effects of both positive and negative life events on complexity of thought. For each individual, biographical data were used to identify a major positive event, such as having a book published, and a major negative event, such as the death of a close friend. Paragraphs from the published letters of each of these people were then randomly selected from those written at six different points in time: during the positive event, during the negative event, 1–2 years prior to each of the two events, and 1–2 years after each of the two events. Identifying information about the author, the event, and the period of writing was blanked out by someone unfamiliar with the purpose of the study, and each paragraph was then read and scored according to the integrative complexity content analytic scheme depicted in Table 1.

The results indicated that positive life events had no effect on complexity of thought. And, for females, neither did negative life events. Somewhat surprisingly, however, male subjects showed a significant *increase* in complexity of thought during the period when they were experiencing negative life events. This result was unanticipated because prior research had suggested that just the opposite would be true—that negative life events would produce reduced, rather than enhanced, complexity of thought. Suedfeld and Bluck suggest that the key may be the nature of the negative events. Large-scale negative events over which an individual has little control, such as war or poverty, may indeed result in reduced complexity of thought. In contrast, complexity of thought may be enhanced when individuals are confronted with a negative event over which they have some degree of control and with which they must cope. As for why the effect was not found among females, there are several possibilities. It may be that females employ different, non-problem-solving, techniques for coping with negative life events. It may also be that more of the females in the study were confronted with negative life events, such as the death of a loved one, that are not amenable to problem solving.

With these examples of content analysis in mind, let us look at what is involved a little more closely.

Categories, Coding, and Reliability

As noted earlier, content analysis is a general procedure for objectively identifying the characteristics of textual material. But, as illustrated by the examples of content analysis that we have just seen, this can be done in several different ways. Synnott (1988), for example, did not specify in advance exactly what he was going to look for in his analysis of advertisements in the *New York Times Magazine*. Instead, he collected a sample of ads and then, from his inspection of the ads, devised a system for categorizing the ways in which males and females were presented. His approach, then, was empirical. He let the categories emerge from the ads themselves: Females were always attractive and young, usually passive, more likely to be modeling clothes or beauty products, and more likely to be displayed in various stages of undress. In effect, what Synnott did was to inspect the advertisements and construct a category system like that depicted below:

	FEMALES	MALES
Attractive	_____	_____
Model young	_____	_____
Fully dressed	_____	_____
Type of ad: Clothes	_____	_____
Beauty products	_____	_____
Other	_____	_____
Model active	_____	_____

Then he went back, examined each ad individually, and tabulated entries in the table as appropriate. Another way of saying this is that Synnott's category system was empirically derived. With another set of advertisements from a different newspaper or magazine, it might not work. Other categories might need to be added.

In contrast, the category system used by Suedfeld, Corteen, and McCormick (1986) was theoretically based and preceded their particular study. As noted earlier, it was derived from some considerations about the nature of human thought processes. Using that specific category system, Suedfeld and his colleagues set out to compare the levels of integrative complexity in the writings of Robert E. Lee and his opponents—before they had ever read any of those writings. The category system, along with detailed instructions for using it, was already available (see Table 1). All that had to be done was to thoroughly familiarize coders with the category definitions so that they could read the excerpts of the writings and assign each excerpt to the appropriate category: 1 if it reflected low differentiation and integration, 5 if it reflected high differentiation and moderate integration, and so on (see Figure 4).

Similarly, Suedfeld and Bluck (1993) were lucky in that the issue they were interested in could be investigated with a category system that already existed. Chances are you will not be so lucky. You will probably have to construct a category system to reflect those characteristics of text that you want to identify. Your set of categories will be determined by your hypothesis, of course—by what it is you are interested in. For example, suppose you were interested in comparing the relative occupational status of males and females depicted on prime-time television. You had come across a review by Hall and Briton (1993) suggesting that the expectations of others play a significant role in the display of gender-related behaviors. That started you thinking about the possibility that it is the expectations of others that give little boys and girls ideas about what they would like to do when they get older. But, where do they learn about those expectations with respect to occupations? If it is true that children watch as much television as surveys suggest, then the apparent occupations of males and females on television could be a major source of information about what is "appropriate" for them. So, you decide to draw up a list of occupations, lay in a supply of junk food, and get set for some heavy TV watching, ahem, research. You might begin with a list like the one depicted below:

	FEMALES	MALES
Professional	_____	_____
Technical	_____	_____
Farmers	_____	_____
Managers/administrators	_____	_____
Clerical workers	_____	_____
Laborers	_____	_____
Sales workers	_____	_____
Private household workers	_____	_____

You probably would not make it to the first commercial before you became aware of a number of problems with your categories. What, precisely, is the distinction between professional and technical? Are you going to put ranch owners with farm laborers? What are you going to do when you come across somebody who will not fit into any of your categories?

Holsti (1969) gives five general guidelines for constructing a set of content analysis categories that would help out in revising this initial set. The first is that the categories should reflect the purposes of the research. That seems obvious. But think about your list of occupations for a moment. Probably implicit in your reason for doing the research was the idea that the occupations of males, as depicted on TV, would be somewhat more glamorous or prestigious. If so, you need to incorporate that hypothesis into your category system by subdividing the occupations into groups: High Prestige, Medium Prestige, and Low Prestige. Or, you might do as Bretl and Cantor (1988) did in their analysis of the portrayal of males and females in television commercials: They categorized apparent occupations as "Relatively High Status," "All Other Occupations," and "No Depicted Occupation." Then, your refined hypothesis would be that a lower proportion of women on TV will be categorized as having a "Relatively High Status" occupation.

The second rule for constructing a set of categories is that they must be exhaustive. All that means is that there must be a category into which each relevant item can be placed. Many people finesse this exhaustiveness criterion by adding a "Miscellaneous" or "Other" category. But you need to be careful about this. Coding too many items into "Other" or "Miscellaneous" might indicate that your category system is missing something. For example, in his analysis of *New York Times Magazine* advertisements, Synnott (1988) used only three product categories: (1) Clothes; (2) Beauty Products; and (3) Other. This was fine for the female models, as the vast majority of them were in clothing or beauty product ads. But 52% of the male models ended up in the "Other" category, and we are left to wonder exactly what sorts of products they were selling.

The third guideline, that categories should be mutually exclusive, means that each item to be coded should be capable of being placed in only one category. With the occupations of television characters, that should not be too difficult. Problems could arise, however, if you came across a person who had two different occupations. You would have to draw up some special coding rules for such cases, such as "classify the person according to the way he or she was first depicted." You will recall from Chapter 3 that in constructing category systems for the observation of behavior, it is sometimes necessary to draw up very detailed instructions for coders, instructions in which you try to anticipate all questions and resolve all ambiguities. The same is true in defining categories for content analysis.

According to the fourth guideline, the assignment of one item to a given category should not affect the assignment of other items. This is referred to as independence of categories. It should give you no trouble with occupations of characters on television, because each character is a separate person.

Finally, categories should be derived from a single classification principle. That sounds a little heavy, but all it means is that you cannot mix different levels of analysis in the categories. You cannot have one category for oranges and another for fruit, because oranges and fruit are at different levels in the system of edible foods; the former is a subcategory of the latter. Likewise, physicians are a subcategory of professionals; hence, you could not have both in your occupational categories. That would not keep you from having physicians, lawyers, nurses, teachers, and other professionals as separate categories, however. Physicians are not a subcategory of Other Professionals.

To summarize briefly, there are five general guidelines to follow in constructing a set of content analysis categories: The categories should reflect the purpose of the research, be exhaustive, independent, mutually exclusive, and derived from a single classification principle.

It is important to be as precise as possible about the definitions of the categories and the rules for assigning items to the categories. The definitions and rules must be sufficiently clear that the categories can be used reliably. Whether you are interested in the values expressed in Girl Scout Handbooks (Auster, 1985), media coverage of religious cults (van Driel and Richardson, 1988), or differences between French and American advertisements (Biswas, Olsen, and Carlet, 1992), you must ensure that another person employing the same category system on the same textual or visual information would find exactly what you did. In their analysis of the integrative complexity expressed in the writings of Civil War generals, for example, Suedfeld, Corteen, and McCormick (1986) had a second coder read and categorize a subsample of the writings. The point of this was to establish that the ratings of integrative complexity made by the first reader were reproducible by anyone who knew how to use the scale and were not peculiar to the first reader. One of the shortcomings of Synnott's (1988) study of *New York Times Magazine* ads is that he did not establish the reliability of his findings. For example, he categorized all the females as "attractive," but for all we know, he may have a very unusual definition of what it takes to be attractive.

Once your categories are well defined, you simply read the text (or watch the movie) and record the frequency of category appearance. The usual technique for establishing reliability is to have two or more coders independently code the same portions of the text, as Suedfeld et al. did. It is best to keep the coders unaware of your hypothesis and of the sources of the material they are coding if at all possible. This strategy is known as **blind scoring** and will help to ensure that unintentional biases do not creep into their categorizations. If the degree of agreement about the relative frequency of occurrence of the various categories is high, you can have some faith that the coding scheme and categories are well defined. What you conclude from any given content analysis depends, of course, on the hypothesis you started with, the category system you constructed, how the text fits into the categories, and last, but certainly not least, the texts you decided to sample.

Sampling and Generalization

To sample something means to take a portion of the whole. The reason sampling is an issue in research is that many times it is impossible to do the research on the "whole"—usually referred to as the population—of interest. Note that *population* does not necessarily mean people, although it can. The population of interest may be everybody who lives in the United States, or all the ads that feature males and females, or all letters written by people suffering through negative life events. When you cannot reach everyone in the United States, or don't have time to look at every ad that features males and females, you have to settle for a sample—a small portion of what is available. That means you have to be concerned about whether the results you obtain with the sample will generalize—whether they will be similar to the results you would have obtained if you could have reached every unit in the population of interest. The notion of sampling will be discussed in detail in Chapter 6 (Survey Research) and in Chapter 8 (The Experiment). The purpose here is just to call your attention to the fact that decisions about sampling the texts or materials to be analyzed are often, but not always, a part of content analytic research. To see why, consider the following examples.

Suppose you were interested in the extent to which newspaper editorial support for a political candidate is reflected in biased news coverage. That would define the texts: You would look at editorials and news stories about candidates; you would not look at the candidates' campaign literature or television commercials or political billboards. Given that you would examine only newspaper editorials and news stories, however, there would still be a sampling problem. You could not possibly analyze all newspaper editorials and news items about all political candidates at all times and in all places. So, you would be forced to set up some rules for selecting a sample. You might decide to look only at coverage of the presidential candidates of the two major parties in the 1984, 1988, and 1992 elections. Further, you might (arbitrarily) decide to use editorials and news items from a random sample of 10 daily papers from the population of those with circulations of 100,000 or more. That is, for each candidate in each election, you would need to find 10 such papers that supported the candidate editorially. You would then have to choose a time period within which to sample. Would you examine news items in each paper for each day for three months preceding the election? Two months? Six months? Every third day for three months? Every fourth day for five months? The point is that even with a relatively clear-cut research question, as in this example, a series of important sampling decisions may have to be made in the process of selecting the texts to be compared.

Further, those sampling decisions define the universe to which you can generalize your results. If you sampled only presidential elections, you could say nothing about local elections. If you sampled only big-city newspapers, you could say nothing about what happens on small-town papers. As Krippendorff (1980) has put it, you should never lose sight of the ultimate aim of those sampling decisions. That aim is to yield samples that are representative of the phenomenon of interest. In the example of editorials and news coverage, the decisions outlined might not, in fact, do that. Using only presidential elections, elections in which a variety of newspapers and other media have numerous reporters observing the candidates' every move, there might be relatively little misrepresentation of what the candidates actually said or did. There would simply be too many alternative sources against which readers could check the facts and thus expose the bias. The phenomenon of interest, editorial support leading to biased coverage, might show up only in campaigns in which there is less public scrutiny of the candidates or in local elections in cities where one newspaper has a monopoly on the printed word. Another way of saying this is that you can generalize the results of your content analysis only to the population of texts from which you have sampled. And you should be able to demonstrate that you have an unbiased sample, because a biased sample may distort your results. Thus, when you want to establish the generality of a finding on the basis of content analysis of only a portion of the pertinent materials, appropriate sampling of those materials is crucial.

There are uses of content analysis, however, for which sampling is less of a problem. If you have the time and energy, or if the amount of material bearing on your hypothesis is relatively small, you can analyze everything that is relevant. For example, a few years ago, I was doing some research on the history of psychology and needed to examine the manner in which a well-known psychologist had been depicted in the *New York Times* (Jones, 1987). By checking the index of the *Times* for the period of interest—1906 through 1940—I found that he had been mentioned in the *Times* on 41 occasions during that 35-year period. With only 41 relevant articles, I could find, read, and analyze them all. Thus, there was no need to select a sample. Similarly, Hooper (1988) was interested in changes in child psychology as reflected in published "handbooks" of the field. Since only six or seven such handbooks have been published since the early 1930s, he did not have to sample them, but could read them all. (You might be interested in knowing that in successive editions of the handbooks, descriptive material on children's behavior has steadily decreased, while analytic and theoretical discourses have blossomed.)

In general, sampling is also less of a concern when you want to use content analysis to learn something about a specific event or a specific person, or simply to see whether something exists. For example, Messner, Duncan, and Jensen (1993) were interested in seeing whether male and female athletes were referred to differently during nationally televised sports events. So, they videotaped the men's and women's "Final Four" of the 1989 NCAA basketball tournaments and the last four days of the 1989 U.S. Open tennis tournament. Once they had the tapes, they simply examined how male and female athletes were referred to by the commentators. Note that these particular tournaments are in no way a "representative" sample of sporting events in which males and females participate. But, in this case, that is precisely why they are important. Because of their prominence, one would expect the very best, most professional coverage. And what did they find? As you probably guessed, male and female athletes were not, in fact, referred to in the same manner. As just one example, in the U.S. Open, women tennis players were referred to by their first names only over half the time. For the men players, this occurred only 7.8% of the time.

Take another example. Neisser (1981) compared the transcripts of tape recordings of two meetings between Richard Nixon and John Dean with Dean's testimony at the Senate Watergate hearings to see whether Dean's testimony about what was said at those meetings had been accurate. In terms of the details of the conversations, Dean was almost completely inaccurate, which is why Nixon claimed that the transcripts would vindicate him when they were released. However, at a deeper level—in terms of Nixon's knowledge of the Watergate cover-up and being in on the effort to secure hush money for some of the burglars—Dean was right. But, note that Neisser was not concerned with the issue of whether these two conversations were representative of all those between Nixon and Dean. About other conversations, Dean may well have been wrong. Rather, Neisser was interested in analyzing the two conversations and comparing them with Dean's testimony about them in order to explore some aspects of the nature of memory. Dean, for example, consistently recalled himself as having been more at the center of things than he actually was.

Sampling, then, may or may not be problematic for content analysis. It depends on your hypothesis and the focus of your research. The same thing could be said, of course, about archival research. In fact, it should be clear by now that content analysis and archival research are, in general, variations on a theme; one simply deals with text, the other with other kinds of records. Content analysis also has a lot in common with the systematic observational methods discussed in Chapter 3. For both, the development of a set of categories for coding material is the key. Content analysis, however, focuses on behavior once removed, that is, on recorded speech and writing. Thus, it has some problems and some advantages that the observational methods lack, and they need to be noted.

Uses and Abuses of Content Analysis

Focusing on text, recorded speech, and writing involves some of the same problems mentioned in connection with archival research: selective deposit and selective survival, for example. The really crucial documents needed for testing a certain idea may have been destroyed, or altered, or never written, or unavailable for a variety of reasons (Hill, 1993). Further, even when the documents of interest are available, content analysis can usually tell us nothing about the truth of assertions in the text or about such nebulous qualities as the aesthetic appeal of the text. Similarly, like archival research, content analysis is blind to some aspects of human behavior, such as nonverbal communication. As an example, read the minutes of the next meeting you go to and then compare their Spartan quality with your memory of what actually went on—who sat next to whom, the innuendo and sarcasm that occurred, the angry glances, the flirtations, the audible sighs when the more long-winded began to speak.

Unfortunately, content analysis also has something of a bad reputation. It has, in truth, been much abused. As Stone et al. (1966) put it, "a large proportion of studies bearing the label of content analysis have been mechanical, superficial tabulations of who says how much of what to whom." Or as Cartwright (1953) put it, "One of the most serious criticisms that can be made of much of the research employing content analysis is that the findings have no clear significance for either theory or practice. In reviewing the work in this field, one is struck by the number of studies which have apparently been guided by a sheer fascination with counting." This fascination with counting is likely to get worse instead of better as researchers learn to use computers to do their so-called content analysis for them.

On the other hand, it is clear that when appropriately employed, content analysis can be genuinely helpful. Often the only information you have about a particular issue or research question is in documentary form. With such data, content analysis forces you to make explicit the categories and coding rules on which your conclusions about such documents are based. In the absence of an explicit set of categories, detailed coding rules, and established reliability of coders, issues about documentary evidence are, unfortunately, likely to be decided by claims of expertise (or, by who can shout the loudest).

Another advantage that content analysis shares with archival research is a relative lack of obtrusiveness into the processes or phenomena of interest. Both are generally considered to be among the most unobtrusive, nonreactive methods available (Barzun and Graff, 1992). They are usually not confounded by the sorts of biases that are introduced when someone is aware of being a participant in research.

The pioneers of content analysis, in journalism and political science, used it almost exclusively with preexisting documentary materials, as in Suedfeld and Bluck's (1993) analysis of the letters of historically eminent people. In recent years, however, it has become increasingly common to use content analysis with textual material that subjects are asked to generate specifically for the research at hand. This is an especially appropriate use when something about the subjects' own language or thought is of interest. Much of the psychological research on self-descriptions, for example, has required subjects to check those adjectives on a list that seem to be descriptive of themselves or to sort previously prepared statements about their behavior in certain types of situations. One of the major problems with such procedures is that they restrict subjects to a fixed format and a preselected vocabulary. Thus, they may fail to provide subjects with categories that are relevant or meaningful with respect to their particular perceptions. Allowing people to describe themselves (and others) with terms of their own choosing and then employing content analysis on the resulting descriptions avoids this problem. If you think so-and-so is a jerk, you can say so and not have to resort to some less expressive substitute. And if the coders do not have a category for that one, the system will just have to be revised.

Summary

Archival research is an investigative technique that makes use of public or private documents pertaining to the past. In one example of such research, Sales used a variety of archival data to test the hypothesis that perceived threat leads to an increase in authoritarianism. The evidence seems to indicate that in the 1930s, as compared with the 1920s, cities devoted greater proportions of their budgets to the police; the proportion of books published on astrology increased; rapists were given more severe sentences; more states passed laws requiring loyalty oaths; and the proportion of books published on psychotherapy declined. An odd assortment of findings, indeed, but all were predicted by the hypothesis that threatening times bring out authoritarian tendencies. Follow-ups of Sales's research, using other indicators in other times and places, provide excellent examples of triangulation of measurement as well as additional models for archival research. These studies addressing threat and authoritarianism also illustrate that the indicators used in archival research are analogous to outcroppings in geology—although one small outcropping may hint at subterranean treasures, that inference must be shored up with additional data.

The construction (or selection) of indices for archival research is highly idiosyncratic to the problem at hand. Even so, it helps to have a specific hypothesis clearly in mind and to subject all possible indices to a process of careful scrutiny and revision if they turn out to allow too many alternative explanations. Several problems accompany the use of records in research; selective deposit and selective survival are among the most generally troublesome. It must also be kept in mind that record keepers use records for purposes of their own. Thus, you should become thoroughly familiar (if possible) with the situation of the record keeper whose records you want to employ.

Content analysis is an investigative technique similar to archival research that uses texts of all sorts. Research by Synnott using advertisements in the *New York Times Magazine* and by Suedfeld and his colleagues on the writings of Civil War generals and the letters of historically eminent men and women provide examples of content analysis. Synnott employed an empirical approach and let the categories emerge from his reading of the ads. Suedfeld et al. employed a preexisting set of categories that had been constructed to reflect theoretical ideas about the nature of human thought processes.

Whether it is empirically or theoretically derived, the category system that is employed by the researcher and into which the texts of interest must be coded is the key to content analysis. General guidelines for construction of the categories were illustrated in the context of a hypothetical example about the depiction of the occupations of males and females in television scripts. The categories must reflect the purposes of the research and must be independent, exhaustive, mutually exclusive, and derived from a single classification principle.

A series of sampling decisions is usually, but not always, involved in content analysis. The nature of those decisions, of course, determines the extent to which you can generalize your results.

Both archival research and content analysis are among the most unobtrusive research methods. Although they each have their limitations, they are both important tools, and they deserve to be utilized more than they have been in the past.

Recommended Readings

Barzun, J., and Graff, H. F. (1992). *The modern researcher* (5th ed.). Fort Worth, TX: Harcourt Brace Jovanovich.

I first came across this book many years ago, when it was in its second edition. It was then and is now an excellent guide to research. The authors are historians, but the value of the book is not limited to aspiring historical scholars. It will be of use to anyone who ever has to try to find out something about the past. That includes just about everyone, and it certainly includes everyone who does research in the social and behavioral sciences. This book contains information about reference books, how to take notes on what you read, separating fact from fancy, common fallacies and how to avoid them, the processes involved in verification, and much, much more. Many of the points are illustrated with detailed examples of actual research—both good and bad. In illustrating various points about the nature of research, Barzun and Graff often use examples that are tantalizing in themselves. Did you know that Joan of Arc was not really from Arc? And that Lord Acton, the man who supposedly said "Power corrupts and absolute power corrupts absolutely," did not quite say that? The book is divided into two parts, the first dealing with "The Principles and Methods of Research" and the second with "Writing, Speaking, and Publishing." It is well worth reading.

Davidson, J. W., and Lytle, M. H. (1992). *After the fact: The art of historical detection* (3rd ed.). New York: Knopf.

Like social and behavioral scientists, historians are usually forced to deal with probabilities, not certainties. Most events, of course, are shaped by a multitude of forces. But in their efforts to reconstruct and explain events, historians must often work with partial, missing, or fragmented data. Thus, the process of trying to understand the past can be an exciting, and sometimes frustrating, type of detective work. Evidence must not only be located, but must also be sorted and rearranged and questioned and sifted until a coherent pattern can be perceived and supported. In a series of 15 intriguing essays about some important events in our past, Davidson and Lytle show how this process works, how the raw materials of the past "come to be fashioned and shaped" into history. What kind of man was Andrew Jackson? What was really behind the Salem witch trials? Why did the Sacco and Vanzetti case arouse such passions? What was it like to live as a slave in America? Davidson and Lytle provide some intriguing analyses of these, and other, issues. More important, they demonstrate many of the facets of historical research—how history gets done—in the process.

Jacob, H. (1984). *Using published data: Errors and remedies*. Beverly Hills, CA: Sage.

The key to this small (63 pages) book is contained in its subtitle. It is a valuable introduction to some of the many pitfalls in using published statistics and archival data. As Jacob puts it, such data are "like the apple in the Garden of Eden: tempting, but full of danger." Take the Consumer Price Index, for example, an indicator that you see quoted in the news almost every week. It is used as a measure of the cost of living and for many years was partially based on the most recent mortgage rates. In the early 1980s, mortgage rates skyrocketed and, consequently, the Consumer Price Index went way up, apparently reflecting a large jump in the cost of living. But, as Jacob points out, the vast majority of homeowners were paying much lower mortgage rates than those on which the Index was based because they had purchased their homes years earlier when the mortgage rates were much lower. Hence, the Consumer Price Index was accurately reflecting the cost of living for only a very select group, those who had *recently* purchased a home. The point, of course, is that before you use a particular set of data or a particular indicator, it behooves you to know precisely how it was obtained and exactly what it means.

Rathje, W., and Murphy, C. (1992). *Rubbish! The archaeology of garbage*. New York: HarperCollins.

Since the early 1970s, William Rathje, an anthropologist at the University of Arizona, and dozens of student assistants have been systematically collecting and analyzing garbage. Their interest is not just cataloging what people throw away, but also what garbage tells us about the people who have thrown it out. They are, in other words, students of "material culture" who believe that physical artifacts "from the garbage in our waste baskets to the paintings on our walls" help define who we are. As part of their analysis of refuse, Rathje and his co-workers have developed a coding scheme with almost 200 categories—including everything from "Potato Peel" (no. 44) to "Local Newspapers" (no. 181). Their category system, just like those discussed in the last two chapters, includes detailed instructions for sorting items, such as this for category no. 44: "Do *not* count individual peels; weigh them as a group." In addition to picking up garbage right off the curb in front of homes—the courts have ruled that once it is on the curb, it is no longer private property—Rathje and his colleagues have dug and bored into landfills all around the country. They have also been able to compare survey data on what people report about their consumption habits with what their garbage pails reveal. This unusually messy, smelly work has been rewarded with a number of interesting findings. One they label the Lean Cuisine Syndrome: that is, "People consistently underreport the amount of regular soda, pastries, chocolate, and fats they consume; they consistently overreport the amount of fruits and diet soda" (p. 70). The project has also discovered some interesting things about landfills. For example, they are not being overwhelmed with plastic, as many people feared. But even for biodegradable materials, the supposed decomposition that takes place way down there is *very* slow and often just stops.

United States Bureau of the Census (1878–). *Statistical abstract of the United States.* Washington, DC: U.S. Government Printing Office.

Available in hardback or paperback and with a new edition each year, the *Statistical Abstract of the United States* is a veritable gold mine of facts and figures. If you want information on the percentage of 35–44-year-old females who are working outside the home, or changes in the number of television stations owned by newspapers, or the life expectancy of a 28-year-old white male living in Rhode Island, or the number of motor vehicles registered in California, it's all there, and much more besides—the 1993 edition, for example, has nearly a thousand pages of tables and charts and data. It is, indeed, a valuable resource. Just remember that before you use any of the data that you find there, you should make sure you know how the data were obtained. If that can't be done, you should proceed with caution.

5

The Interview

One of the easiest ways of gathering information is simply to ask someone who knows whatever it is you want to know. If you want to know what your friends think of the president's chances for reelection, ask them. If you want to know what was said in the class you missed last week, ask someone who went. If you want to know whether your true love "really" cares, just ask. Whether you are seeking knowledge of others' opinions and beliefs, a report of the facts, or an expression of someone's heartfelt attitude, the most direct route is often a simple, straightforward question. Asking questions is, in fact, a remarkably efficient way to obtain information from and about people. But, as we shall see, whether or not you put much faith in the answers you receive depends on many things, including who you ask, what you want to know, and how you phrase the question.

Questions and answers, of course, are the defining characteristics of that most sociable of all research tools, the interview. In its broadest sense, an interview is simply a social interaction between two people, one of whom wants to get information from the other and attempts to do so by asking questions. Note that the phrase "wants to get information from the other" indicates that the interview has an objective and that that objective has been defined ahead of time. The interaction between interviewer and interviewee, whether face-to-face or voice-to-voice, as over the telephone, is what differentiates the interview from a questionnaire, even when the questions and possible answers are identical. Whether you are a consultant trying to understand the operation of a small business, a reporter trying to get the facts for a story, or an experimenter discussing a procedure with subjects in the laboratory, skill in the formulation and asking of questions is a necessary element of success.

The interview is not generally considered a complete research method by itself. Although the interview is an integral part of survey research, for example, there is more to survey research than simply asking questions. But there, as in other research settings, questions are the essential research tools, the picks and shovels with which information is accumulated. A very large proportion of the data on human behavior is generated, or obtained, by interview (or the interview's half-sibling, the paper-and-pencil questionnaire).

The difference between the sorts of general discussions and conversations that we are all familiar with and the research-oriented interview is that the latter never loses track of its objectives. The **research interview**, then, is a social interaction between two people in which one, the interviewer, initiates and varyingly controls the exchange with the other, the respondent, for the purpose of obtaining information bearing on predetermined objectives. Within this broad definition, there are several different subtypes of research interviews. We are going to focus on two in the pages that follow: qualitative interviews and standardized interviews. As you will see, these two types actually define the ends of a structural continuum. At one end is the very open **qualitative interview**, which might appear almost conversational to an eavesdropper. The interviewer has the freedom to adapt the questions and question ordering to what a particular respondent has already said—as long as the general purpose of the interview is adhered to—and the respondent is encouraged to discourse at length on the topics raised by the interviewer. At the other end is the highly structured **standardized interview**, in which the interviewer must ask each question precisely as it is worded and cannot vary the order of the questions. The respondent, in turn, must typically respond by selecting one of a limited number of predetermined answers to each question.

There are gradations between these two types, with varying degrees of openness and structure. But once you are thoroughly familiar with both, you should be able to design what you need, depending, of course, on the purposes of your research. As you will see, there is a parallel between these two types of interviews and the two uses of observation that we discussed in chapters 2 and 3. The analogy goes like this: Qualitative interviewing is to participant observation as standardized interviewing is to the use of observation to test ideas. But let's take them one at a time.

Qualitative Interviewing

To push the analogy a little further, note that the ultimate goal of qualitative interviewing is quite similar to the typical goal of participant observation. You will recall that in participant observation, the aim is to become intimately familiar with a particular setting in order to develop an understanding of the social and psychological processes occurring in that setting. Similarly, with qualitative interviewing, the goal is to develop an understanding of the social and psychological processes that have occurred in a particular setting, or among people who have had particular sets of experiences—but not by immersing yourself in the setting and observing. Rather, the goal is achieved by interviewing people who have been in the setting of interest, or who have had the experiences you want to focus on.

As Weiss (1994) points out, qualitative interviewing has many aliases. It has been referred to as "intensive interviewing," "depth interviewing," "unstructured interviewing," and "unscheduled interviewing." The conversational style often employed by the qualitative interviewer bears a resemblance to that of a "non-directive" therapist, that is, "attentive, non-judg-mental, and receptive" (p. 208). But there is a difference. Stewart and Cash (1991, p. 9) point out that in a nondirective interview, the interviewee may be allowed to control the purpose, pacing, and subject matter of the interview. Not so in the qualitative research interview. There the interviewer controls the purpose and the subject matter, although there may be occasional mean-derings with a particularly interesting and articulate interviewee.

Just as with participant observation, there are a variety of reasons why one might undertake a qualitative interview study. Weiss (1994) lists a num-ber of general research aims for which such a study is appropriate.

1. *Developing detailed descriptions.* You might, for example, want to know what life is like for laid-off executives who cannot find another job com-parable to the one they had (Lohr, 1994). What do they do each day? How do they structure their time? How has their family life been af-fected? How do they feel about the company that laid them off after all those years?

2. *Integrating multiple perspectives.* To understand the day-to-day operation of a company, you may need to gather information from everyone from the janitorial staff to the board of directors. It is a safe bet that you will get different kinds of information from such diverse groups. But, for a complete understanding of the company, all those different views must be taken into account.

3. *Describing process.* As Kunda (1992) did in the study described earlier, you may want to describe the processes and techniques used by organi-zations to exact loyalty from employees. What sorts of events and oper-ations elicit feelings of obligation from employees? How does loyalty develop? What sanctions are applied to employees who do not join in?

4. *Learning how events are interpreted.* You might be interested in how peo-ple react to and perceive major events in their lives. How do victims of catastrophic illnesses make sense of their lives? What do they think about what has happened to them? Who do they blame?

Within these general categories—developing descriptions, integrating per-spectives, describing process, understanding interpretations—your specific focus would depend on what it is you are interested in, that is, on your spe-cific research objectives.

Developing the Interview Guide

What keeps the qualitative interviewer on track are, indeed, those research objectives, as expressed in a more or less well-developed **interview guide**. This guide specifies the classes of information needed. It may be as simple as a reminder of the topics and subtopics that the respondent should cover dur-ing the interview, either spontaneously or with some probing and prodding. Or it may be as specific as a list of questions. The interviewer using an inter-view guide is free to make decisions about how and when to ask questions based on what is already known, or can be judged, about the respondent (such as age or educational background) and the feedback obtained during the interview as to the respondent's knowledge of and ease in discussing various subjects. But the interview guide is there to remind the interviewer that all the listed topics are to be covered at some point in the interview.

Once you have decided what it is you are interested in, the next task is to find out what is already known about the topic. What are the relevant issues? How do they relate to one another? What sorts of things should I ask about? (For some examples of the importance of background information to the success of qualitative interviews, see Box 1.) Thinking through the issues pertinent to the topic of interest is the way you begin to construct the inter-

---

Box 1

Necessary Background Knowledge

In the example of the interviews with laid-off executives used in the text, the amount of background information necessary to construct an interview guide was minimal. Common sense suggests that people who have recently lost a job will experience changed economic and social circumstances, and that assumption, in turn, dictates the areas to explore in the interview. In many instances, such minimal preparation will not be sufficient for the construction of a meaningful interview guide. In other words, it is sometimes necessary to prepare for qualitative interviews by learning all you can about the topics and people of interest. An interviewee who has nothing to say is less than useful, but an interviewer who has no idea what questions to ask is even worse. Below are some examples that illustrate how much background information and preparation the interviewer must have for a successful interview. The first is from an interview by Bill Moyers (1990) with Nobel Prize-winning author Toni Morrison. The second is from an interview by Jonathan Cott (1987) with actor and playwright Sam Shepard. The third is from an interview by Richard Evans (1989) with noted psychologist Albert Bandura.

- Moyers: Well, you also created a twentieth-century woman in *Sula*. She's out there, independent, uncontained, and uncontainable, you said. You called her the New World black woman. Why?
- Cott: In many of your plays, your characters talk a lot about and often perform music on stage; and the "feel" of your plays is often that of a jazz improvisation or an extended country, blues, or rock-and-roll song. When did your preoccupation with music begin?
- Evans: Among your various contributions, your theory of modeling appears to be quite significant. I wonder if you might talk about how Miller and Dollard's book, *Social Learning and Imitation*, contributed to your theory of modeling.

Moyers had clearly read Morrison's novels and knew enough about their differences to ask about comparisons of the characters depicted. Cott, obviously, had seen and thought about most, if not all, of Shepard's plays. Similarly, Evans was well aware of Bandura's work on the modeling of behavior and its theoretical background. Other examples of this sort of informed, probing interview abound on television news programs. The next time you see an example, be sure to note how different the result is from what happens when a talk show host says to a guest: "Well, how's it going?"

view guide—that is, the list of areas to be covered in the interviews them-selves along with subtopics and, possibly, specific questions to be asked. The interview guide is essentially an outline to help you remember what to ask and to help you recognize relevant information from the interviewee even if that information does not come when you expect it (Stewart and Cash, 1991). Consider this example.

Suppose you were interested in the life situations of laid-off executives and wanted to learn about their ways of attempting to cope with their new status and circumstances. Think about what is likely to happen to such peo-ple. Typically, there are a number of immediate adverse effects: Economic cir-cumstances deteriorate, daily routines are disrupted, and relationships with friends and co-workers may be ended, or at least made more difficult. There-fore, you might begin with a list of topics to ask about, such as the following:

1. The company they used to work for
2. Efforts to find new work
3. Effects on family
4. Effects on other relationships
5. Current economic circumstances

That is a pretty sparse list of topics, but it is merely a starting point. Now each topic can be developed into a line of inquiry that can be taken up with the former executives. Fleshing out the topics with a few actual questions and di-rections in each area, we construct an interview guide that looks like this:

1. *Former companies.* Ask about the respondent's employment history. What companies? The nature of his/her most recent position? Could you tell me what a typical day was like in your last job? How did you find out that you were going to be laid off? What were your thoughts at the time? What were your concerns and feelings at that time? How do you feel about the company now?

2. *Efforts to find new work.* I wonder if you could tell me about what you have done to find new employment. Exactly what sort of work were/are you looking for? If unable to find the type of job you want, what types might you be willing to accept? What types of jobs do you feel qualified for? What other alternatives are you considering?

3. *Effects on family.* How has unemployment affected other members of the family? What sorts of changes/adjustments has your husband/wife had to make as a result of your unemployment? What was your spouse's reaction when he/she found out that you were going to be laid off?

4. *Effects on other relationships.* Ask about friends at the former company. Do they still keep in touch? How has his/her social life changed? Has he/she made any new friends or met any new people since being laid off?

5. *Current economic circumstances.* Ask about current income and/or savings. What kind of severance package was there from the company when he/she was laid off? If married, ask about spouse's employment. Ask about prospects and willingness to take part-time, nonprofessional jobs to make ends meet.

Note that the interview guide does not specify each and every question that the interviewer might ask. The interviewer's task is to get the respondent talking about the topics in the outline and to keep him or her from wandering too far afield. Some questions are suggested, but even they may not be necessary. In response to a question such as, "I wonder if you could tell me about how your friends at IBM responded to your being laid off," the respondent may begin talking and cover everything the interviewer intended to ask on that topic.

It should be obvious that the research objectives—as expressed in the interview guide—determine who should be interviewed. If you are interested in the experiences of recently laid-off executives, you are going to have to find some recently laid-off executives. If you are interested in single parents, you will have to find some single parents willing to be interviewed. With such groups, it is usually impossible to know how many potential respondents are out there or how you might get in touch with them all. But you have to start somewhere. You might advertise for volunteers, or contact companies known to have cut back their workforce recently, or ask workers at a day care center for names of clients (in the hope that some will be single parents). Once you have identified one or more members of the group you are looking for, you might ask them for names of others like themselves—a procedure known as **snowball sampling**.

Weiss (1994) suggests that for many qualitative interview studies, it may be best to intentionally seek out respondents who are as different as possible. That is, if you are interested in single parents, you would want to interview both male and female single parents, black and white single parents, rich and poor single parents. Such a diverse sample is referred to as one chosen to maximize range. The hope is that because of their diversity in everything except being a single parent, the respondents will have experienced "single parenthood" in every possible way it can be experienced, and be able to tell you all about it.

Chances are, however, that some of the respondents may not be particularly forthcoming and articulate. The tasks of the qualitative interviewer are to get them talking and to make sure the topics in the interview guide are covered—without putting words in their mouths, or constraining their responses. How can that be done?

Questions, Language, and Meaning

Part of the answer has to do with the nature of the questions employed in qualitative interviewing. Typically, the questions in a qualitative interview are what are referred to as **open-ended questions**. As you can tell from the examples above, open-ended questions are those to which it is expected that the respondent can and will respond as he or she wishes. As Stewart and Cash (1991, p. 55) put it, such questions are "broad, often specifying only a topic, and they allow the respondent considerable freedom in determining the amount and kind of information to give." Some examples of open-ended questions are these:

- What have you learned from this research methods course?
- How do you feel about being laid off after 20 years at IBM?
- What is a typical day like for you?
- What things do you like best about your job?

Technically speaking, some open-ended questions are not even questions. They may be imperatives, or simply statements, informing the respondent about the topic you would like to hear about next.

- Tell me how you got interested in vintage automobiles.
- I would really like to hear a little more about your experiences with alligators.

Open-ended questions have as their most obvious advantage the freedom of the respondent to volunteer whatever information he or she deems most appropriate in response. As Stewart and Cash (1991) point out, they also convey interest in the respondent's views and trust in his or her judgment. On the other hand, open-ended questions also have certain disadvantages. They may, for example, elicit more information than you really need and provide you with material that is difficult, if not impossible, to make sense of. It has also been suggested that open-ended questions are likely to generate superficial responses—that is, that respondents may answer them with those salient bits of relevant information and/or opinions that come most easily to mind—and that such "top-of-the-head" answers may not reflect respondents' "true" knowledge and/or attitudes. However, some research by Geer (1988, 1991) and the transcripts of qualitative interviews suggest that this concern is not too serious.

What is sometimes a serious problem with open-ended questions is getting the respondents to give a full, detailed response. Thus, it is often necessary for the interviewer to probe for an answer. A **probe** is any verbal or nonverbal behavior on the part of the interviewer that is intended to encourage the respondent to continue, amplify, or clarify an answer. As Fowler and Mangione (1990, p. 41) note, probing open-ended questions is one of the hardest tasks for interviewers to do correctly. First of all, the use of probing at any given moment will depend on the interviewer's running assessment of whether or not a response is adequate. Second, it is difficult for interviewers to avoid suggesting the nature of the additional information they are seeking.

If the respondent is giving relevant answers in the detail and depth required, there is, of course, no need to elaborate on the original questions or to do more than look interested and make sure the recorder is still working. But if the respondent seems to lose interest, grows uncomfortable, or begins to give inadequate answers, then the interviewer can turn to one of a variety of probes, which include:

- *Direct questions.* Perhaps the single most useful probe is the word "Why?" Other direct questions might be, "How do you mean that?" "Can you tell me more about that?" "Is there anything else?"
- *Requests for specific additional information.* "When did you do that?" "Exactly what did he say?"
- *Repetition of the original question.* For example: Interviewer: "What kind of work do you do?" Respondent: "I work up at the University." Interviewer: "I see. What kind of work do you do there?"
- *Echo or repetition of the respondent's last words.* Respondent: "Well, I tried studying for finals, but it didn't work." Interviewer: "It didn't work?"
- *Silence.* When the interviewer looks expectant, waits, and says nothing, that in itself can be taken as a signal that the respondent is doing fine and the interviewer wants to hear more. However, the value of silence as a probe diminishes very quickly.

There are three basic guidelines for the construction, or the spontaneous creation, of probes. First, you must be sensitive to the effect of any probe on the individual respondent. Some people will need more encouragement and probing than others. And, occasionally, respondents who are made uncomfortable by silences may jump into irrelevant answers simply to fill time. Others may misinterpret "uh-hum" type encouragements, feeling that the interviewer is trying to hurry them along. Second, probes should always be neutral. Although probes act to selectively lengthen responses, they should not also bias the direction of answers. Finally, probes should be recorded along with everything else. The transcript of an interview should include not only your questions and what the respondent had to say, but also the context in which each answer was given—and that clearly includes the probes necessary to evoke it.

The fact that respondents are sensitive to silences and to both verbal and nonverbal expressions of approval from interviewers calls attention to the obvious fact that the token of exchange in interviews is speech (Mishler, 1986). Every culture has rules that govern the use of language and the construction of meaning via communication. What that means is that if the end product of an interview is to be intelligible, then both the interviewer and the respondent must adhere to certain culturally shared rules about how they talk to each other. As Clark and Schober (1992) point out, one key principle is that when speaking to another person, we take into account the current common ground—that is, the knowledge, beliefs, and assumptions that we believe we share with them at that moment. For example, if you were asked what you liked best about your new blazer, you would be extremely unlikely to answer how pleased you were by the fact that it has only two sleeves, although you certainly would not have bought one with three sleeves, no matter what other glowing attributes it possessed. But there is a tacit assumption between you and your questioner that coats have only two sleeves and that therefore the fact is inconsequential, in spite of its predominant importance to you as a coat buyer. That unspoken assumption, of course, is part of the common ground of the transaction.

Extended transactions, such as qualitative interviews, build on what has gone before—that is, the common ground accumulates. In other words, the interviewer must take into account what the respondent has already said. If, in answer to a question about how being laid off has affected family life, the respondent covers the family's current economic problems in detail, then the interviewer would not later ask about current economic circumstances. If that were done, the respondent might well be offended and assume that the interviewer had not been listening. This freedom not to ask questions that have already been covered by the respondent, or to pursue a topic intended to be covered later when it is mentioned spontaneously by the respondent, helps to establish and maintain rapport in the interview. This flexibility is important. As Weiss (1994, p. 80) puts it: "The best questions fit in so well with what respondents are saying that they seem almost to be continuations of the respondents' own associations. They encourage respondents to say more about what is already in their minds."

In any interaction, the participants have another responsibility that is basic to the way we use language: They are responsible for making sure that what has been said does indeed become a part of their common ground (Clark and Schober, 1992). Each must make sure that what the other means has been properly understood. The flexibility of the qualitative interview should make this easy. If the interviewer does not understand what the respondent is saying, then the question can be rephrased, or the interviewer can ask for clarification: "How do you mean that?" "Let me make sure I understand what you're saying." "Could you elaborate on that a little?" But even in qualitative interviews, this strategy does not always work. Riessman (1987) gives an example from a study of the experience of separation and divorce. In her interviews, she attempted to elicit chronological narratives from respondents. But one respondent seemed unable to develop a coherent sequence of events and insisted on talking about several apparently unrelated episodes concerning the use of leisure time and families and work situations. Repeated attempts at probing and requests for clarification did not help. Only later, in reading over the transcripts, did Riessman see what the respondent had intended. She was telling a story about cultural conflict and how her husband's family and their "old-world" orientation had created problems in the marriage, problems that eventually led to the divorce.

Making Sense of It All

Riessman was eventually able to discover what her respondent intended to convey because she had available a transcript of the interviews with the respondent. In other words, her interviews were tape-recorded and, subsequently, transformed into a typed verbatim text. Thus, Riessman was able to read, reread, and study what the respondent had said—every word, every "er," every pause. Without that transcript, the respondent's meaning would have been lost forever in a few cryptic and hastily scribbled notes. There is a strong consensus among those who do qualitative interviews that tape recording and transcribing are *essential* (e.g., Mishler, 1986; McCracken, 1988; Seidman, 1991; Weiss, 1994). McCracken (1988, p. 41) is most emphatic on this point: "Interviews must be recorded on tape. … Interviewers who attempt to make their own record of the interview by taking notes create an unnecessary and dangerous distraction."

Of course, transcribing an interview takes time, but it is time well spent. It creates a full and permanent record of the respondent's words for analysis and reanalysis as needed. Even with an adept note taker, the condensations, summaries, and key words that make up notes of an ongoing conversation leave out as much as, if not more than, they include. For example, Weiss (1994, p. 54) points out that even though he is "fairly good" at shorthand, he regularly has to leave out a great deal when taking notes—things that are considered unimportant at the moment, parenthetical expressions, details, and a great deal of what is said when people speak rapidly. Of course, what is considered unimportant at the moment and all those details and parenthetical expressions may turn out to be of great importance later on. In addition to producing an accurate record of the interview, tape recording and transcribing have another key advantage: By releasing the interviewer from the need to take notes, they make it easier to attend to what the respondent is saying. That, in turn, makes it more likely that the interviewer will be alert to those points on which clarification is needed and can make sure that the topics in the interview guide are covered in appropriate depth and detail.

Once you have transcripts of the interviews in hand—or, preferably, in the computer—analysis proceeds in a manner analogous to that described in Chapter 2 for analysis of a participant observer's field notes. Actually, the analysis may have already begun. That is, way back when you were contemplating your research objectives, reading the relevant literature, and constructing the interview guide, you may have come up with a few hunches about what you were likely to hear. These initial ideas, of course, constitute the beginnings of an analytic system for making sense of the interview data. As the interviews themselves are conducted, you will find that other ideas occur to you about the processes and the nature of the problem you are examining. Hypotheses and hunches will be suggested, and repeated themes may emerge. Jot them down and keep a list. These ideas, questions, hunches, and themes will form the basis from which you will construct your analytic files.

You will recall from Chapter 2 that analytic files are simply a set of abstract categories. Their purpose is to help you make sense of what the respondents have said. For example, suppose you had conducted a set of interviews with recently laid-off executives using the interview guide that was described earlier. In reading through the transcripts of those interviews, you find several different ways in which the respondents are attempting to cope with their new circumstances. Some appear to be beginning a pattern of withdrawal from their former business and professional interests and plotting a course of, at least partial, permanent retirement. Others appear to be taking their situation as an opportunity for reinvention of themselves. They are looking into opportunities for retooling, examining new careers, and, perhaps, going back to school. Still others seem to have developed a fixation on their old careers and are devoting all their time and energies to finding a new job that is just like their old one. It is important to note that each of these three general patterns of behavior may have been expressed in very different ways by individual respondents. So, the first task is to read through the transcripts carefully, marking everything that you think is an example of *withdrawal,* everything that seems to indicate *reinvention,* and everything that looks like *fixation*—in each case, keeping track of which respondent said it, of course. These marked excerpts are then collected in three files. It used to be that the "files" were actual physical folders, or designated piles on a tabletop, and the excerpts were actually cut out of the transcripts, labeled, and placed in the file (or on the pile). Nowadays, of course, it is more likely that they are locations on a computer disk, and that the excerpts are simply marked blocks of text that are copied from a master file containing the complete transcript to the appropriate analytic file.

Your reading of the transcripts may, of course, have produced other ideas, calling for files in addition to the three mentioned above. But, considering just those three, once you had scoured the transcripts for every quotation that even hinted at withdrawal, reinvention, and fixation, your next step might be to study the excerpts in the individual files in relation to which respondents they came from. It could well be the case, for example, that the three modes of coping with the trauma of being laid off are characteristic of distinctly different subgroups among the ex-executives you interviewed. That is, those who take their bad luck as an opportunity for reinventing themselves might be predominantly younger—say, early to mid-40s—and have a working, professional spouse who is willing to support them for a while. In contrast, withdrawing into semi-retirement may turn out to be characteristic of the 55–60-year-olds among those you interviewed.

Even with such a simple example, of course, there are many other possible analytic schemes. What they might be depends on (1) the ideas and theoretical hunches you had when you constructed the interview guide—because those preconceptions determined the topics that would be covered in the interviews; (2) the way you happened to phrase specific questions and probes in working your way through the interview guide; (3) what the respondents actually said in response to your questions and probes; and (4) the ideas and expectations you have as you read the transcripts. Another way of saying this is that the analytic concepts and conclusions that result from a qualitative interview study are to some extent imposed—by you, your own knowledge, questions, and expectations—and to some extent emergent—suggested by the way in which the respondents describe their experiences. That's all well and good. The purpose of qualitative interviewing is to collect information, perhaps in order to understand some phenomenon not fully understood, or perhaps in order to generate some hypotheses about the phenomenon. But it is important to note the major consequence of this dual imposed/emergent character of the results of qualitative interview studies: that is, someone else starting out with the same interview guide and conducting the same study might come up with an entirely different set of analytic categories and reach an entirely different set of conclusions.

Does that mean that qualitative interviewing is like trying to determine the size of a football field with a rubber yardstick? No. But it does mean that qualitative interviews are not the appropriate research tool when we want to directly compare the responses of two or more people or groups. When that is what we want to do, everything that might influence those responses—except the respondents themselves—must be held as constant as possible. Although that goal turns out to be more difficult to attain than people used to think (e.g., Mishler, 1986), there is a format for attempting to reach it.

Standardized Interviewing

Consider two brief examples. In June of 1989, the Massachusetts Mutual Life Insurance Company sponsored a nationwide survey in which 1200 randomly selected adults were interviewed over the telephone. The intent of the survey was to gain an overview of American beliefs and attitudes about various family arrangements, values, and concerns. Asked about the quality of family life, for example, only 44% reported it to be "good" or "excellent." Quittner, Glueckauf, and Jackson (1990) interviewed mothers of deaf children to examine some hypotheses about the stress of parenting a disabled child and its relation to the mother's social support network. As you might anticipate, mothers who perceived little emotional support from others tended to be the most chronically stressed.

Think about those two examples for a moment. In order to conclude anything meaningful about "American" beliefs concerning the family, or about the relationship between emotional support and stress, it is important that the same information be obtained from the different respondents in each study. If you want to know what percentage of people believe X, as opposed to Y, you have to ask them all about X and Y. Similarly, if you want to know whether there is a relationship between their answers to X and their answers to Y, you have to ask everybody X and Y. Another way of saying this is that when the data from interviews are to be used to make comparative statements about the attributes of various groups, you cannot ask some people X and other people Y. The information obtained from all respondents must be comparable. And the best way to make things comparable is to quantify them (Fowler, 1993).

The basic assumption underlying **quantification** is that if something exists, it can be measured. The simplest form of measurement, of course, is just yes/no: Is something present, or is it absent? The process of quantifying, or determining how much of something is present, seems quite natural when the units of measure are a familiar part of our culture. For example, not only are we taught height as a concept, but also we are taught to think in terms of inches and feet. The question "How tall is he?" includes the concept of height and the way in which to measure it. But the assumption underlying quantification is more daring than that: It involves faith that entities for which the units of measurement have not been so clearly spelled out can be measured. Most of us would agree that romantic love exists. Many of us would admit to having experienced it. (Cynics or the recently betrayed can substitute some other emotion in which they do believe, such as cynicism.) One way to quantify love would be to set up some units of measurement, perhaps a simple scale of (1) love a lot, (2) love somewhat, (3) love a little, or (4) that was last week. Having set up these units on a rather intuitive basis, we could then ask people where they fit concerning their feeling toward their most significant other. But what do they know? Love is not just blind, isn't it different for everyone? Maybe, maybe not. But if we want to find out, we have to be very clear about what we are asking. Thus, the tricky part of measuring something for which the units of measurement are not spelled out is the operationalization of the concepts of interest—the process by which you define specifically and exactly what it is you are talking about. And, in standardized interviewing, the major part of the process of operationalization boils down to deciding how to word questions and answers.

Questions, Answers, and How People Think

Although they often include a few open-ended questions, the predominant question format for standardized interviews is the **closed-ended**, or **closed**, question, also referred to as a **fixed-response** question. There are dozens of variations of the closed-ended question, but the defining characteristic of them all is that specific acceptable answer options are provided, and the respondent is expected to choose one of the provided options. Here are some examples from actual surveys:

- "Do you do any sports or hobbies involving physical activities, or any exercise, including walking, on a regular basis?" __YES __NO (Fowler, 1992)

- "Are we spending too much, too little, or about the right amount on improving the nation's education system?" __TOO MUCH __TOO LITTLE __ABOUT RIGHT (Rasinski, 1989)

- "Do you think the government is trying to do too many things that should be left to individuals and private businesses, do you think the government should do even more to solve our country's problems, or haven't you thought much about this issue?" __TOO MANY __EVEN MORE __HAVEN'T THOUGHT (Bishop, Tuchfarber, and Oldendick, 1986)

- "Which best describes your present occupation?" __CLERICAL __MANAGERIAL __TRADE __PROFESSIONAL __STUDENT __MILITARY __SALES __UNEMPLOYED __OTHER (*Folio Weekly*, 1989)

Other types of closed-ended questions may ask the respondent to make a rating: "On a scale from 1 to 10, in which 10 is 'absolutely fantastic,' how would you rate the food in the dining hall?" Or, the respondent may be asked whether he or she "strongly agrees, agrees, has no opinion, disagrees, or strongly disagrees" with each of a series of statements. Again, the variations are endless, but there are certain common problems that must be considered.

The purpose of a question, of course, is to obtain information. The sought-after information may be subjective—such as a report of the respondent's attitude toward abortion—or objective—such as a report of how many drinks the respondent had last week. In either case, the goal of writing a good closed-ended question is twofold: (1) to have the question and response alternatives mean the same things to each respondent; and (2) to have the question and response alternatives mean the same thing to all the respondents as they do to you, the question writer. That can be tricky for a variety of reasons. For starters, you have to make sure that the words you use in the question capture what you really mean. That sounds obvious, but it is crucial. It has been shown repeatedly that even slight changes in the wording of questions can make big differences in how respondents answer. Take a couple of examples. If you are interested in studying attitudes toward those unfortunate members of society who are unable to make ends meet, it makes a tremendous difference whether you refer to them as "the poor" or "those on welfare" (Smith, 1987). "The poor" and "those on welfare" are different concepts, with quite different connotations, and people respond to them differently. Similarly, compared with those asked about "assistance to big cities," those asked about "solving the problems of big cities" are much more likely to agree that too little money is being spent (Rasinski, 1989).

Therefore, the first rule of question writing is to be precise about the concepts you are interested in asking about. If you think there may be some ambiguity about what you are asking, you can word the question to define, at least partially, what you mean. For example, Fowler (1992) points out that the following question is ambiguous: "What is the average number of days each week you have butter?" The problem is that many people would not know whether "butter" included margarine or not. And, indeed, when the question was changed to begin with the phrase "Not including margarine," many fewer people reported using butter more than once a week. Ambiguity may also stem from words that have more than one meaning, especially if the context is unclear. Such words are the source of much humor ("Do you believe in infant baptism?" "Believe in it, hell, I've seen it!"), but if you are interested in obtaining valid answers, they are no laughing matter. Similarly, the question "Do you work alone?" needs to specify whether "working alone" refers to who helps or to who is in the room. As noted in Box 2, ambiguous words must be avoided in the response options provided as well as in the questions asked.

Being precise and defining ambiguous terms, or avoiding them altogether, are the first steps to making sure that the respondent will understand

---

Box 2

One Person's Constantly Is Another's Hardly Ever

In the movie *Annie Hall* there is a couple who are having problems with their relationship, and each is independently seeing a psychiatrist. When asked about the frequency with which they have sexual intercourse, the woman replies, "Constantly, about three times a week." When asked the same question, the man tells his psychiatrist, "Hardly ever, about three times a week." In the movie, it's hilarious. For the survey researcher, it's not so funny. Indeed, all too many people seem to have adopted the attitude that "when I use a word, it means just what I choose it to mean, neither more nor less."

Relative frequency expressions such as *always, frequently, very often, sometimes, seldom,* and *never* are pervasive response categories in questionnaire and interview items. But only for a few such expressions is there agreement on exactly what they mean. How often, after all, is *often*? As you might expect, the expressions on which there is agreement are the ones that define the ends of the scales: *never* and *always*. To some extent, the definitions attributed to frequency expressions depend on the context. If you are discussing rain in Seattle, *very often* will have a meaning different from the one it has when you are discussing earthquakes in California. It also may depend on whom you ask. If you go to the movies every week, then you may believe that the behavior of someone who goes only once a month could be appropriately described as *seldom* going to the movies. But to a person who never goes to the movies, going once a month may be perceived as going *very often*.

The problem is actually more complicated, however. Schaeffer (1991) points out that different groups may use relative frequency expressions to mean different things. She reports an analysis of a survey conducted by the National Opinion Research Center in which blacks and whites were asked how often they felt excited and how often they felt bored. Those who selected a relative frequency term other than *Never* in response to these questions were then asked, "About how many times a week or a month did you mean?" Answers to the latter question, of course, are absolute frequency estimates. The results suggest that in a number of cases, relative frequency terms were indeed used differently. For example, the reported relative frequency of boredom was significantly greater for blacks than for whites. But when the absolute frequency estimates were examined, there appeared to be no differences in frequency of boredom. Hence, your conclusion about the black–white difference in boredom would be different depending on whether you used the relative or absolute frequency reports.

What to do? As Schaeffer points out, there is no simple answer to this question. If you are asking about highly memorable events, events the person is likely to recall every single instance of clearly, then it may be best to ask for an absolute frequency report. If you are asking about regularly recurring events, which a person is likely to be able to enumerate mentally, you might use alternatives like these:

a. More than once a day   d. 2 or 3 times a week

b. Once each day   e. Once a week

c. 4 to 6 times a week   f. Less than once a week

As Schaeffer notes, whether absolute or relative frequency response alternatives are more appropriate will depend on how respondents make the specific judgment that is being requested. And, unfortunately, in many instances that may not be known.

the question as it was intended. But there is much more that can be done. Other things being equal, it is better to avoid long questions because they are more difficult to understand and remember, especially if the respondent also has to remember a list of response alternatives. In fact, Fowler (1992) has demonstrated that breaking up long questions into one or more shorter questions tends to produce more accurate responses. And Presser and Zhao (1992) have found that short questions are more likely to be read exactly as worded. With short questions, it is also easier to make sure that each question is really only one question. If you ask, "Do you favor smaller classes in larger rooms?" and the answer is "Yes," you cannot be certain what that means. Maybe the respondent is simply answering whichever part of the question registered with them. Or, maybe the respondent's opinion on one part of the question—smaller classes—was influenced by their opinion on the other—larger rooms. Such questions are often referred to as **double-barreled questions**; the answers to these two-part questions are completely uninterpretable.

Many questions used in standardized interviews ask respondents about events in their personal history: "How many times in the last 6 months did you visit a dentist?" "How many times in the last 3 months did you eat in a restaurant?" Such questions are referred to as autobiographical questions. The evidence seems to suggest that recall of such information, especially if the events asked about occurred long ago, is not very good (Bradburn, Rips, and Shevell, 1987). There is some evidence, however, that when respondents are asked about relatively distinct events—such as grades, or specific courses taken in college—allowing them time to formulate an answer improves their accuracy (Burton and Blair, 1991). When asked about how they arrived at their answers to such questions, the vast majority of respondents report trying to remember and enumerate each episode.

If you ask about something the respondent has experienced many times, however, memory for autobiographical episodes is particularly bad. It's as if the repeated, similar episodes blend together in memory and become impossible to recall individually and enumerate. What can be done? Allowing respondents to consult records may help, but often this is not practical or even possible in an interview. It does seem to be the case that if the question asks about events, or behaviors, that occur regularly, many respondents do not even try to remember each occurrence. Rather, they decompose the question, calculate a rate for a short term, and then multiply. For example, if respondents are asked how many times they ate out in the last 3 months, they may recall the number of times they ate out in the last week—say five times—then multiply by 12 or 13 weeks to arrive at the answer: "Well, I guess I've eaten out between 60 and 65 times in the last 3 months." Bradburn, Rips, and Shevell (1987) suggest that such decomposition does, indeed, appear to improve accuracy of recall for regularly occurring events and might even be worth suggesting to respondents when they do not adopt it spontaneously.

Bradburn, Rips, and Shevell (1987) also suggest that prompts, such as cues about locations where events took place or what other people were present, may improve accuracy. People organize memory into meaningful sequences of events. Therefore, questions should specify exactly the time and place of the information you want. A question about "when you were young" can mean almost anything. (A newspaper column recently proclaimed the good news from a study of college women: They thought "older men" were the most attractive. And now for the bad news, added the columnist: The women defined "older men" as being about 30. If you fail to see the humor in this, do not worry—you will when you are older.) Because of this possibility of different perspectives (Suchman and Jordan, 1992), the question must provide the one you intend. Ask instead, "When you were still in high school…" or, "When you were about 10 years old…"—or whatever is relevant to the question.

Being precise about the time and place the question refers to is, of course, an attempt to provide the respondent with the appropriate context for answering the question. For many autobiographical questions, context is crucial because the behavior of interest may be somewhat poorly defined (Figure 1). When that is the case, as Schwarz (1990) points out, respondents may use the provided response alternatives to define the context. He gives the example of asking someone how often they get "really irritated" (p. 108). If the response alternatives range from "several times a day" to "several times a week," then the degree of irritation implied by the question is apparently less than if the response alternatives range from "several times a month" to "several times a year." The available response alternatives help the respondent to understand the question. By defining the target behavior more clearly in the question, the impact of differing sets of response alternatives should be reduced—theoretically, at least (Schwarz, 1990). There is a danger here, however. You do not want to suggest the nature of the response that you are seeking. Questions that imply that a particular answer is preferred are called **leading questions**, and they are to be avoided at all times. You do see the logic behind that advice, don't you?

Another tactic for improving the accuracy of responses to autobiographical questions and simultaneously reducing the impact of available response alternatives is to ask questions, if possible, in terms of the respondent's specific experiences rather than generalities. For example, suppose you ask, "How much television do you watch on an average day?" and provide a set of response alternatives ranging from "Up to half an hour" to "More than 2½ hours." Respondents are likely to use those response alternatives to define the range of "normal" television watching and pick an answer somewhere in the middle. If you ask the same question and provide a set of possible answers ranging from "Less than 2½ hours" to "More than 4½ hours," you are likely to get a much higher estimate (Schwarz, 1990; Schwarz and Bienias, 1990). A better approach is to make the question specific and not suggest a range of possible answers. Ask, for example, "What television shows did you watch yesterday?" and then read the respondent a list of the shows that aired yesterday and let them indicate which they watched.

1 A question without a context. Questions for which a context has not been specified are unlikely to turn up useful information. (Cartoon © Sydney Harris.)

Of course, that might be difficult, especially if the respondent has cable television. When you do provide response alternatives, it is important that they be exhaustive, providing categories into which all possible responses can be fitted. Clark and Schober (1992) point out that respondents typically assume that they "should" be able to answer any question asked by an interviewer and that they may be embarrassed if they cannot. What that means is that unless respondents are provided with an explicit "Don't Know," "Haven't Thought Much About It," or some other "Other" option, they may express opinions on issues about which they know little or nothing, or claim to have done things that they really have not (Bishop, Tuchfarber, and Oldendick, 1986). It is also important that response alternatives be mutually exclusive, such that either only one answer is right, or the instructions specifically state that the respondent is to choose the one best answer or the answer closest to his or her own experience or opinion.

In the standardized interview, there is often a trade-off between validity and reliability, with precision the currency of exchange. Questions that separate respondents into those who love, feel neutral about, or despise their mates may be both valid—in that they actually measure what they purport to measure, in this case, the degree of affection—and reliable—in that the questions consistently evoke the same responses when asked at different times or by different interviewers. Other questions with more response options—say, ones that differentiate people's feelings toward their mates along a continuum of ten levels—will be far more sensitive to differences (thus, they are more valid), but this same precision may decrease their reliability. Collapsing that 10-unit scale is likely to increase reliability again, but at the expense of validity. What this means is that response alternatives should be adequately divided to capture the respondents' views, but no more so than necessary. There is some evidence that 7-point scales are good for many purposes in terms of reliability and respondents' ability to discriminate between scale values (e.g., Cox, 1980), but the best number of alternatives will depend on what is being rated.

It is important to remember that if you are interested in your respondents' opinions and experiences, you do not want to suggest which alternative should be chosen. In other words, biased or loaded questions are to be avoided at all costs. It is surprisingly easy to bias a question. "Do you agree with the President's proposal that . . . ?" is a very different question from "Do you agree with the recent proposal that . . . ?" and even more different from "Do you agree with the Minority Caucus proposal that . . . ?" even when what follows is identical. Words matter. Even the numeric values used to define the ends of rating scales matter. Schwarz et al. (1991) report a study in which respondents were asked to rate how successful they had been in life on an 11-point scale. For half of the respondents, the scale ran from "0 (Not at all successful)" to "10 (Extremely successful)." For others, the scale ran from "–5 (Not at all successful)" to "+5 (Extremely successful)." Of the respondents using the 0–10 scale, 48% selected a number between 0 and 6, but only 22% of those using the –5 to +5 scale selected the formally equivalent numbers between –5 and +1. Schwarz et al. note that what appears to happen is that with the 0 to 10 scale, respondents interpret the low numbers simply to mean the *absence* of success. But, with the –5 to +5 scale, the low numbers are interpreted to mean the *presence* of failure. They recommend that the numeric values used to label scales reflect whether the attribute being rated is unipolar or bipolar. For unipolar attributes, a zero-to-positive values format should be used "to emphasize that the question pertains to the absence or presence of this specific attribute, rather than the presence of its opposite" (p. 578). For bipolar attributes, negative-to-positive value labels are best.

Even when questions are clear and well constructed, with appropriate and unbiased response alternatives, and respondents are able to understand them and can accurately retrieve the information that is being requested, there may still be a problem: The respondent may simply be unwilling to tell you what you want to know. Answering the question truthfully may put the respondent in a socially undesirable light. People, generally, are reluctant to reveal negative things about themselves, a phenomenon known as the **social desirability bias**. As Fowler (1993) notes, there may simply be a limit to what can be asked in a standardized interview. There are some strategies that may help, however, when questions focus on potentially sensitive topics. Fowler suggests that the interviewer can emphasize the confidentiality and anonymity of the data, or attempt to convey a nonjudgmental attitude. Sometimes it is possible to rephrase questions so that the awkwardness of having to admit specific shortcomings is reduced. For example, the question "Did you finish high school?" may require an admission of failing to do so. "What was the last grade you completed?" permits a positive answer. You can also incorporate face-saving phrases into the beginning of the question: "Do you happen to know who the congressman is from this district?" "As you know, more than half the registered voters in this county were not able to get to the polls last May. Were you able to vote?" In a similar manner you can make it easier for people to reveal what might be considered unacceptable opinions or behaviors: "Some people feel it's important to report all income for taxes; other people feel this isn't necessary in all circumstances. What would your feeling be?" A final possibility is that questions on sensitive topics can be asked near the end of the interview, after some degree of rapport has developed. Where questions appear in the interview can make a difference.

Sequence and Context

There are a number of ways in which the ordering of questions in a standardized interview can influence the answers received. As we have noted several times, respondents often assume that the rules that govern ordinary conversation have not been completely suspended in an interview. One of the consequences of this is that they are likely to interpret successive questions as related, unless you tell them otherwise (Clark and Schober, 1992). Therefore, the sequence of questions should make sense to the respondent. To the extent possible, the questions should fit with one's experience and order of things, chronologically perhaps, or moving among naturally associated topics. As Sudman and Bradburn (1982, p. 222) put it, once you have the respondent thinking about a particular topic, "it is logical to ask *all* the questions about that topic before switching to another topic." New topics should be marked by clear transition statements, such as, "Now I'd like to ask some questions about your own experiences with armadillos," so that the respondent does not spend time and energy trying to answer a new question in the context of the old ones.

The sequence of questions should also work to establish and maintain rapport and good feeling between the interviewer and the respondent. Experienced interviewers recommend that interviews begin with questions that are both easy to answer and enjoyable. They recommend *not* beginning with age, marital status, occupation, and income because some respondents will perceive these topics as personal and threatening (Sudman and Bradburn, 1982, p. 219). When the respondent has become more confident, the interview can shift to more personal, or difficult, questions. The assumption is that over the course of the interview, some degree of rapport will develop, so that potentially sensitive, or threatening, topics can be raised toward the end. Another practical advantage of putting such questions at the end is that if the respondent decides he or she does not want to respond to them and terminates the interview, you will already have most of the information you were seeking. It is important to remember that the principles of informed consent give respondents the right to terminate an interview at any point.

There are several other types of context effects that can be important. While there are no definite guidelines about how long, or short, a standardized interview must be, there are several indications in the literature that respondents—being human, after all—can get tired, and with long interviews may give less accurate answers to questions near the end (e.g., Tourangeau and Rasinski, 1988, p. 311). How long is too long may depend on the topics, of course, and how interesting they are to the respondents. Pretesting the interview, as we shall see, can help to determine appropriate length. And speaking of length, Tourangeau (1984) points out that even within individual questions, a lengthy list of response options can create problems. Respondents listening to a lengthy list of options being read to them may simply adopt—that is, give as their answer—the first one that comes close to what they really mean, or believe. For this reason, long lists of response options are often rotated for different respondents. With options "A" through "M," for example, some respondents will be read the list in that order; for others, the list will be read "B" through "M," then "A," and so on until the list starts with "M" for the 13th respondent and goes back to "A" for the 14th. (See questions 2a and 2b in Figure 4 for examples.) Of course, reading the response options in a different order for each respondent means that the interviewer has to keep track of which option to begin with for each respondent.

The most intriguing context effects, however, and for many years the most puzzling, are the ones that occur among related sets of questions in an interview. In some cases, later questions may simply clarify what was meant by an earlier question that was not well understood, so changing the order of the questions will change the answers (Colasanto, Singer, and Rogers, 1992). When you have a series of questions on a given topic, there are, of course, many different ways in which you can order them. In one of the most common arrangements (e.g., Stewart and Cash, 1991), called the **funnel sequence**, general questions are asked first, and each successive question is related to the previous question, but more specific. For example, if you were interested in life satisfaction, you might begin by asking:

> "Now I would like you to tell me how satisfied you are with LIFE IN GENERAL by picking a number on a 7-point scale. If you are dissatisfied you would pick the number 1. If you are satisfied…" (McClendon and O'Brien, 1988)

Then you would ask a series of more specific questions about various subtopics within this general area:

"Now I would like you to tell me how satisfied you are with your MARITAL STATUS by picking a number…"

"Now I would like you to tell me how satisfied you are with your STANDARD OF LIVING by picking a number…"

In contrast to this ordering, there is the **inverted funnel sequence**, which moves from the specific questions to the more general.

The problem is that such variations in the ordering of questions influence the answers you get (e.g., Benton and Daly, 1991). Why is that? Schwarz, Strack, and Mai (1991) suggest that part of the reason has to do with an everyday conversational norm that respondents import into the interview setting: In normal conversation, we are not supposed to be redundant. If you ask me about how satisfied I am with my marriage and then ask me how satisfied I am with life in general, I am going to assume that you want to know about parts of my life *other than* my marriage. So, I will leave that out when answering the more general question—in other words, that specific part will be contrasted with the whole. On the other hand, if you have just asked me a series of questions about how satisfied I am with my marriage, my work, my neighbors, my colleagues, and my house, and then ask me a question about satisfaction with life in general, you'll get a different answer. In that case, I assume that you are asking a summary question, and I will include all those topics when answering—in other words, the specific parts will be assimilated to the whole. The evidence seems to indicate that such processes do occur in the interview setting. As Schwarz, Strack, and Mai (1991, p. 18) put it:

If only one specific question is asked, the most plausible request for new information bears on other aspects of one's life. Accordingly, respondents interpret the general question as if it were worded "Aside from what you already told us…" If *several* specific questions are asked, however, a final integrative judgment would conform to the conversational practice of "summing up" at the end of related thoughts.

As Tourangeau and Rasinski (1988) point out, context can also affect what is remembered and considered as respondents attempt to answer particular questions. They point out that attitudes are made up of interrelated sets of beliefs, not all of which are necessarily consistent with one another. Prior questions in an interview may cause some of these beliefs to be retrieved, but not others. Subsequent questions are then more likely to be answered in the light of these previously activated, and hence more easily accessible, beliefs. Note that such context effects should occur only among respondents with mixed views—that is, those who have some beliefs on both sides of an issue. As illustrated in Figure 2, such a respondent's answer to a question about abortion may vary depending on whether prior questions called to mind beliefs about

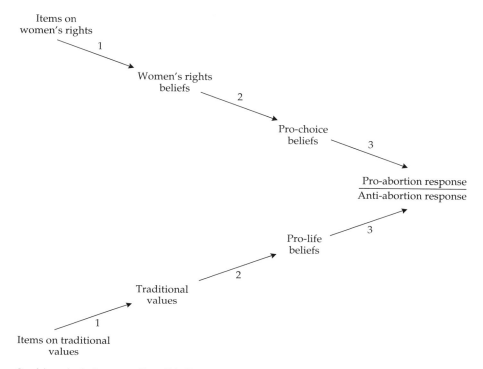

Items on
women's rights

1

Women's rights
beliefs

2

Pro-choice
beliefs

3

Pro-abortion response
Anti-abortion response

3

Pro-life
beliefs

2

Traditional
values

1

Items on traditional
values

2 A hypothetical context effect. This illustrates how the responses of respondents who hold mixed views on the issue of abortion can be influenced by prior questions in an interview. The first process (1 in the figure) is retrieval of beliefs related to the context items, which pertain either to women's rights or traditional values. Activation then spreads to related beliefs about the target issue (2), rendering a response on one side of the issue more likely (3). Tourangeau and Rasinski (1988) report (p. 304) that the data support this hypothetical sequence: "Respondents who answered four items on women's rights showed greater support for legalized abortion than did respondents who answered four questions concerned with traditional values. A group that received neutral context items exhibited intermediate levels of support." (From Tourangeau and Rasinski, 1988.)

traditional values or beliefs about women's rights. Such context effects might be eliminated by getting respondents to think carefully about the issue before answering. That could be done by calling attention to both sides of the issue, either in prior questions or in the stem of the question of interest.

The multiple ways in which the sequence and context of questions can influence answers in the standardized interview are, unfortunately, not fully understood. However, in addition to the suggestions mentioned earlier, Tourangeau and Rasinski (1988) call attention to these three caveats: (1) with an unfamiliar issue, make sure the question defines the issue; (2) avoid questions requiring complex judgments; and (3) encourage respondents to admit when their feelings are mixed, or when they do not have an opinion.

Constructing the Interview Schedule

Making up questions and asking them are acts that occur almost simultaneously in conversation. And, as we saw in our discussion of the qualitative interview, such spontaneity can occur there as well. But it is characteristic of standardized interviews that making up questions and asking them are conspicuously separated in time and space. Standardized interviews may be conducted in a variety of places—in the laboratory, or the respondent's living room, or over the telephone, or at the mall. But the questions, response alternatives, opening and closing statements, and all instructions for the interviewer must have been constructed ahead of time. Thus, by the time the interviewer meets with the respondent, the course of the interview itself has been firmly plotted out, and there is no latitude to make changes.

The issue of unvarying presentation of interview questions is such a key one in standardized interviews that the entire script is written ahead of time, with an eye to keeping everything as constant as possible from one respondent to the next, regardless of who is doing the interviewing (e.g., Fowler, 1993). This detailed written plan for the interview is known as an **interview schedule**. It always includes the items in the following list, but may include other types of instructions and directions to the interviewer as well.

1. An opening statement to the respondent, explaining who you are and what you want.
2. A list of questions to be asked verbatim and in an indicated order.
3. Instructions to the interviewer about specific questions and what to say at various points in the interview.
4. Space and directions for recording responses.
5. A list of probes to be used for any open-ended questions.

The opening comments to the respondent are very important, especially if the interview is to be conducted over the telephone (Lavrakas, 1993). In the space of a few seconds, you have to identify yourself and your affiliation, explain what it is you want, mention the topic of the interview and how long it will take, and ask the respondent if he or she is willing to participate. The opening statement might look something like this:

> Hello, my name is _____ and I am calling from the University of North Florida Survey Research Center. We are conducting a study, sponsored by the Duval County Sheriff's Office, on perceptions of crime in the greater Jacksonville area and would like to ask you a few questions. It will only take about 10 minutes of your time and your cooperation would be greatly appreciated. Your responses, of course, will be completely confidential.

The point of the opening statement is to elicit cooperation. The ideal is to have as few people as possible decline to participate, because—as we shall see in the next chapter—high refusal rates can create problems. As Fowler (1993) points out, however, it is clear that some interviewers are better at delivering this opening gambit than others. He suggests that starting out with the assumption that there is no question but that the respondent will be happy to take part—a "confident assertiveness," as he calls it—may help.

It is important that the opening remarks be as clear as possible and anticipate any reasonable questions the respondent might have about who you are and what you want (Figure 3). If not, some respondents may ask for more information, and if you give more information to some respondents and not others, then the context in which the subsequent questions are asked and answered will not be the same for all of the respondents. Many respondents will assume—especially if they are interested in the topic, your opening is pleasant, and you sound like a reasonable person—that this is going to be just another conversation (e.g., Clark and Schober, 1992). In order to keep things under control, you are going to have to disabuse them of that notion without, of course, being rude. Fowler and Mangione (1990, p. 51) recom-

3 Why are you here and what do you want? The introductory comments to a respondent are very important. To avoid misunderstandings, introductory comments should convey, clearly and concisely, exactly why you are there and what will be expected from the respondent. (Cartoon © Clarence Brown.)

mend that right after the opening remarks, a paragraph like the following be read:

> Since many people have never been in an interview exactly like this, let me read you a paragraph that tells a little bit about how it works. I am going to read you a set of questions exactly as they are worded so that every respondent in the survey is answering the same questions. You'll be asked to answer two kinds of questions. In some cases, you'll be asked to answer in your own words. For those questions, I will have to write down your answers word for word. In other cases, you will be given a list of answers and asked to choose the one that fits best. If at any time during the interview you are not clear about what is wanted, be sure to ask me.

Now, if the respondent has trouble with a question, or asks what a word means, the interviewer can politely say something to the effect that "I understand why people might have difficulty with that question, but you'll recall that I am only allowed to read the questions exactly as they are worded. Let me just read the question again for you, and just give me the best answer you can." Similarly, a number of other problems—such as the respondent talking too fast or not wanting to choose one of the provided alternatives—can be handled by gently reminding the respondent of the rules of this particular type of interview.

The main part of the standardized interview schedule—the body, according to Stewart and Cash (1991)—consists of the questions, instructions to the interviewer, and the response alternatives, or spaces for answers. It is important to note that in addition to the questions, the schedule has *every word* the interviewer is to say to the respondent *written out*. This includes, of course, the opening and general instructions noted above, but also includes all transitional statements for introducing new topics: "Now I'd like to ask you a few questions about your views on the school system." Special instructions having to do with specific questions are also included. To help the interviewer avoid confusing the questions with these instructions, the latter are often printed in a different format, like this:

16. Do you have any children under 18 years of age?
__Yes (SKIP TO QUESTION 20)
__No

The words in capitals are, of course, instructions to the interviewer. If the respondent answers "Yes," then the interviewer should ask question number 20 next. The questions in Figure 4 contain some other examples of instructions to interviewers. With question number 51, for example, the "IF QUALIFIED" means that the interviewer has to decide—based on how the respondent has answered prior questions— whether he or she should be asked this question. With question 12, the interviewer is instructed to "WRITE OUT PERCENTAGE." And with question 7, if the respondent answers "Stronger," the interviewer is to skip to question 9, but if the respondent answers "Weaker," then the interviewer is instructed to go on to question 8.

Although most questions in standardized interviews are, as we have noted, fixed-response questions, many such interviews include a few open-ended questions. And, as was discussed in connection with the qualitative interview, open-ended questions often require that the interviewer use probes to elicit complete and detailed answers. Fowler and Mangione (1990) recommend that with such questions in standardized interviews, interviewers be limited to four, and only four, probes. That is, if the interviewer believes that the question has not been answered, or that the answer is not clear, or not detailed enough, the options are limited to these:

1. Repeat the question.
2. How do you mean that?
3. Tell me more about that.
4. Anything else?

On the interview schedule, these probes can be printed in the margin below each open-ended question, and the interviewer can circle each one that it was necessary to use.

The purpose of all these detailed instructions and the emphasis on asking questions exactly as they are worded is to try to make the question mean the same thing to all respondents. That means using not only the same wording, but the same presentation by the interviewer, and the same probes, if any are needed. The context too must be identical, including the reasons given or implied for asking the questions and the encouragement or reinforcement given for answering them. And, as we have seen, because preceding questions help to shape the context of subsequent questions for the respondent, the sequence of topics and questions must be identical. When all of this is true, when the interview schedule is as clear, precise, and detailed as possible, we should be able to assume that any variations in responses to the questions are attributable to actual differences among the respondents and not to variations in the questions themselves, or the order in which they are presented. Unfortunately, there are still a few other things that must be done before we can feel confident about that assumption.

Pretesting and Interviewer Training

After all the questions have been carefully worded and placed in a sequence within the interview schedule, some trial runs are in order. The whole package needs **pretesting**—that is, it needs to be tried out on some respondents to see if what seems perfectly clear to you is clear to others. Fowler (1992) points out that, unfortunately, pretesting has usually been unsystematic and subjective. A few interviewers administer the interview schedule to a few respondents to "see if any problems arise," without knowing precisely what they are looking for. Of course, a few of the more blatant ambiguities in question wording or arrangement might be picked up in this way, but pretesting needs to be more systematic, and it can be. One possibility is to tape-record an initial set of in-

2a. Which of the following things gives you the most pleasure? (ROTATE)

2b. Which gives you the second greatest amount of pleasure?

1st	2nd	
_____	_____	your work
_____	_____	your family
_____	_____	your friends
_____	_____	your involvement in the community
_____	_____	your religious involvement
_____	_____	your philosophy of life
_____	_____	recreational activities
_____	_____	your car, house, or other personal belongings
_____	_____	don't know/no answer/other (volunteered)

3. In general, how would you rate the quality of American family life today? Would you say family life in the U.S. is excellent, good, only fair, or poor?

___ excellent   ___ good   ___ only fair   ___ poor   ___ don't know

7. Generally speaking, do you think family values have gotten stronger in the U.S. recently, stayed about the same, or have family values gotten weaker—or aren't you sure about this?

___ stronger (GO TO Q. 9)   ___ same (GO TO Q. 9)

___ weaker (GO TO Q. 8)   ___ aren't sure (GO TO Q. 9)

8. Which of the following do you think is the most important cause of family values having gotten weaker?

_____ schools not teaching about values

_____ parents having less time to spend with their families

_____ there have been no tragedies like war or depression to bring families together

_____ the value we place on material things has become more important

_____ people moving away from their original homes and their extended families

_____ economic conditions becoming more difficult

_____ government policies that are not helping families

_____ parents are not disciplining their children enough

_____ don't know/no answer/other

12. Over the course of an average week, please tell me about what percentage of your waking time you spend being with your family?

___ less than 10%   ___ 11–20%   ___ 21–30%   ___ 31–40%

___ 41–50%   ___ 51–75%   ___ 76–100%   ___ don't know

(WRITE OUT PERCENTAGE) _____

13. Would you say you spend too much time, about the right amount, or not enough time with your family?

___ too much   ___ right amount   ___ not enough   ___ don't know

14. Which of the following statements comes closest to your definition of family?

_____ a group of people that is related by blood, marriage, or adoption

_____ a group of people living in one household

_____ a group of people who love and care for each other

_____ not sure about this

26. Now I'm going to list some institutions to which some families turn for help with family problems. After each, please tell me whether or not you have ever turned to that kind of individual or group for help with a family problem. (ROTATE)

Yes	No	
_____	_____	your church or synagogue
_____	_____	community centers
_____	_____	parents support group
_____	_____	schools
_____	_____	your company
_____	_____	the local, state, or federal government
_____	_____	social worker, doctor, or other professional

51. (IF QUALIFIED) About how many miles away from you does your oldest child live?

___ 1–10   ___ 11–25   ___ 26–100   ___ 101–500   ___ 501–1000

___ 1001–2000   ___ More than 2000   ___ don't know/no answer

4 Excerpts from an interview schedule. Note that the schedule includes not only questions for the respondent, but instructions for the interviewer as well. In several instances, the interviewer uses a prior answer to determine which question to ask. When this is done smoothly, the interview can sound much more conversational than it appears on paper. (From MassMutual American Family Values Study, 1990.)

terviews and then tabulate for each question how many respondents ask for clarification or give an inappropriate answer. If more than a certain, very small, percentage of respondents do either of these for a particular question, then the question and/or response alternatives can be reworded.

In a similar way, as Sanchez (1992) notes, the physical layout of the interview schedule itself can be examined. In many instances, even with fixed-response questions, the interviewer's task is a complex one. If the respondent selects one alternative, for example, the interviewer may be required to skip a few questions, or ask the respondent to "specify" what is meant. If the respondent selects a different alternative, the interviewer may be required to move to a different section of the questionnaire and ask 13 questions about the experience of having yellow fever. Again, by tape-recording an initial set of interviews, those questions that interviewers miss, ask incorrectly, or fail to follow up can be identified. Thus, not only can the wording be fine-tuned, but the accompanying directions and the physical arrangement of the schedule can be improved.

Pretesting, of course, adds to the cost of standardized interviews—in money, in time, in respondents—because, obviously, the responses of those in the pretest group(s) cannot be included in the final analysis. After all, the questions asked them were hardly contextually identical, and, in fact—thanks to their reactions—may well be changed for the final interviews. Pretesting, however, more than pays its way by increasing both the validity and reliability of the final results. As Fowler (1993, p. 102) puts it, there is clear evidence for the value of using tape recording and behavior coding in pretesting interview schedules.

Similarly, there is clear evidence of the value of—read, necessity for—training interviewers. The standardized interview is, as we have seen, different from normal conversation. Consequently, interviewers have to learn a few new rules: to read questions exactly as worded and with no improvisations, for example. They also have to learn to suppress a few old habits, such as rephrasing what the other person says when they are not sure they understand. And, of course, they have to learn the specifics of the interviews that they will be conducting. Thus, the most important phases of interviewer training might be labeled "general" and "study-specific" (e.g., Frey, 1989; Lavrakas, 1993). The first phase consists of a general orientation to the requirements and routines of standardized interviewing. This can be done by means of lectures, demonstrations, and videos, and might include, for example, information about reading questions as worded, the meaning of different instructions on interview schedules, and demonstrations of nondirective probing. Fowler (1993, p. 113) notes that it is a good idea to provide interviewers with a general manual in which all this information is written out. The second phase of training is specific to the study being planned. It involves thoroughly familiarizing interviewers with the purposes of the study, the specific questions to be asked, the layout of the interview schedule, and the nature of the respondents to be interviewed. And, most important, interviewers should actually conduct some supervised practice interviews during this phase of training.

Fowler and Mangione (1990) report a detailed study of interviewer training in which four different levels of training were compared. They recruited 57 interviewers, none of whom had had any prior professional interviewing experience, and gave each of them a manual describing the skills and techniques that they would be taught. Some of them were then given less than half a day of training, which consisted primarily of a lecture and a demonstration interview. A second group was given the same treatment, but in addition saw a movie on general interviewing techniques, were allowed to discuss the training and ask questions about procedures, and took part in some supervised practice interviewing. Their training lasted 2 days. A third group took part in a 5-day training session with all of the same components, but more extended versions of them. For the fourth group, training lasted 10 days—with even more of the same, but also with practice evaluating interviews, exposure to some research findings on interviewing, and a short, supervised practice interview in a respondent's home. Following their training, all the interviewers were given addresses of 40 people whom they were to contact and with each of whom they were to conduct a standardized half-hour health-related interview. One-third of the interviewers in each group were required to tape-record their interviews so that the manner in which they actually conducted the interviews could be examined.

There were a variety of interesting results. The clearest, perhaps, was that a half-day of training was simply inadequate. On almost every measure—from the percentage of questions read correctly to the probing of open questions properly to avoidance of biasing interpersonal behavior—those who had had only half a day of training did significantly worse than the other groups of interviewers. A second finding was that 10 days of training appeared to be too much. By the end of training, those who had been at it for 10 days appeared to have gotten bored. They scored lower in the practice interviews than those who had had either 2 or 5 days of training, and also seemed to conduct themselves in a less standardized manner in their actual interviews. The interviews of those who had had either 2 or 5 days of training were more likely to be rated as excellent or satisfactory in a variety of categories, including reading questions as worded, probing open-ended questions, and recording answers to both open-ended and closed-ended questions. Fowler and Mangione (1990) point out that supervised practice is what really "pays dividends in interviewer skills and data quality" (p. 119). They also note that the length of training needed will, in many cases, be a function of the specific details of the study being planned, but that for teaching basic interviewing skills, 2–4 days may be the optimal length of training for most standardized interview studies (e.g., Billiet and Loosveldt, 1988). As we have seen, the interviewer's skill in conducting the interview does make a difference. But what about other characteristics of the interviewer? Do they make a difference as well?

The Interview as a Social Occasion

The short answer to that question is "Sometimes, but not as often as you might expect." It is true, of course, that the interviewer and respondent arrive at the interview with different histories, personalities, attitudes, and values. It is also true that they may differ in gender, age, race, social class, and a variety of other characteristics. And sometimes those differences count—but when?

There is, in fact, a long—and continuing—history of relevant research on this issue. Consider a few examples. Benney, Riesman, and Star (1956) found that when interview questions turned to sexual habits, the least inhibited communication occurred when both interviewer and respondent were young people of the same sex. The most inhibited? People of the same age but opposite sex. At about the same time, Hyman (1954) demonstrated that black interviewers obtained significantly more reports of resentment and dissatisfaction with various American institutions from blacks than did white interviewers. Even earlier, Robinson and Rohde (1946) reported that the more apparently Jewish an interviewer, the less likely respondents were to express anti-Semitic attitudes. More recently, Lavrakas (1993) reported a study in which male respondents were less likely to admit having sexually harassed someone if the interviewer was female than if the interviewer was male. Finkel, Guterbock, and Borg (1991) reported finding a race-of-interviewer effect in preelection polling: Specifically, when the interviewer was black, independent and Democratic voters reported greater support for a black Democratic candidate than when the interviewer was white.

Is the pattern becoming clear? Most of the evidence seems to suggest that interviewer effects appear only when the characteristics on which the interviewer and respondent differ are relevant to topics covered in the interview, especially if the topics are sensitive ones. That is likely to be the case in a very small percentage of interviews. Thus, except in those few cases, Fowler (1993, p. 110) recommends using the best interviewer(s) available, regardless of their demographic characteristics. And "best," of course, is defined by good training and careful supervision.

Summary

Asking questions of others is a remarkably efficient way to obtain information, and a tremendous proportion of the knowledge we have about people has been obtained in just that way. The research interview is a social interaction between two people in which one, the interviewer, initiates and varyingly controls the exchange with the other, the respondent, for the purpose of obtaining information bearing on predetermined objectives. Within this broad definition, there are several different subtypes of research interviews. This chapter focuses on two types, defining the ends of a structural continuum of openness from qualitative interviews to standardized interviews.

In the qualitative interview, the interviewer has the freedom to adapt the questions and question ordering to what a particular respondent has already said, as long as the general purpose of the interview is adhered to. The objectives of the interview are outlined in an interview guide, which is constructed prior to the interview, and the respondent is encouraged to discourse at length on the topics raised by the interviewer. Questions in the qualitative interview are typically open-ended. When necessary, they are followed by nondirective probes to urge the respondent to continue and/or provide more detail. Several guidelines were suggested for the construction of probes. It was also pointed out that respondents import into an interview setting certain assumptions about the common ground they share with the interviewer. Understanding what the respondent has to say will often depend on taking these assumptions into account.

For analytic purposes, qualitative interviews must be recorded and transcribed. In a manner analogous to what is done with a participant observer's field notes, analysis proceeds with careful readings of the transcripts and the development of a set of theoretical concepts to account for what the transcripts contain.

The purpose of the standardized interview is to obtain precisely comparable information from each and every respondent. The typical question format here is the closed-ended, or fixed-response, question, although a few open-ended questions may appear in some standardized interviews. Because measurement and comparison are the objectives of the standardized interview, everything about it is intended to be the same for each respondent. Thus, a great deal of effort and thought goes into constructing the questions, response alternatives, probes, sequence of questions, and opening remarks, as well as training interviewers.

The goal of writing questions for a standardized interview is to have them mean the same thing to all respondents. To achieve that goal, the following guidelines were suggested: (1) be precise about the concepts of interest; (2) define, or avoid, ambiguous terms; (3) avoid long and double-barreled questions; (4) take into account the foibles of human memory; (5) be specific about the context of the question; (6) do not let the response alternatives suggest what is normal; (7) avoid loaded, or biased, questions; (8) provide respondents with a Don't Know option, or its equivalent; and (9) be especially careful in the way sensitive topics are broached. It was also pointed out that sometimes it matters where a particular question appears in the interview. Questions on sensitive topics might best be placed near the end of an interview, but questions requiring detailed responses might not work best at the end, especially if the interview is a long one. A series of related questions should all be placed together, but the interrelations among them should be made clear; that is, respondents should be told whether or not their answers to prior questions are to be considered in answering subsequent questions on related topics. Similarly, prior questions may make certain beliefs and/or information accessible to respondents and thus bias answers to subsequent questions. Once the questions and their order have been decided, the entire interview schedule is laid out with everything the interviewer is to say and do written out in complete detail. Once that is done, the schedule must be tried out, corrected and improved, and used to train interviewers to stick to the script.

Various characteristics of the interviewers themselves may, on occasion, make a difference in the nature of the responses they receive. Several strategies for dealing with this problem were discussed. The evidence seems to indicate, however, that the problems produced by poorly trained interviewers are much greater than those produced by the demographic characteristics of the interviewers.

Recommended Readings

Fowler, F. J., Jr., and Mangione, T. W. (1990). *Standardized survey interviewing: Minimizing interviewer-related error*. Newbury Park, CA: Sage.

In fewer than 150 pages of text, Fowler and Mangione provide a detailed look at the nature of the errors produced by interviewers, brief reviews of relevant research, reports of their own research on interviewer error and training, and advice on how to avoid such errors. They take a hard line on measurement in the social sciences—and in survey research in particular. As they put it, "measurement in the social sciences can be just as rigorous and valid as in any other of the sciences. We cringe when someone says interviewing or question design is an art, not a science" (p. 9). Not everyone would agree, but Fowler and Mangione make a strong case that interviewer error can be identified and, in many cases, minimized. What is the hardest skill for an interviewer to learn? According to Fowler and Mangione, it is the delicate "art"—of course, they would not like that term—of probing inadequate answers. Is it possible that *more* interviewer training would overcome the problem? Only up to a point. The key to training is *supervised practice*, and more is not always better. My advice: Read this book.

Morgan, D. L. (1988). *Focus groups as qualitative research*. Newbury Park, CA: Sage.

A "focus group" is basically a group interview, but it is not an interview in the traditional sense in which there is an alternation between interviewer's questions and respondents' answers. Rather, it is a group discussion and interaction centered on topics, or issues, supplied by the researcher. The end product is simply a transcript of the discussion. According to Morgan, such groups are useful for, among other things, (1) learning about a new field; (2) generating hypotheses; (3) discovering how participants perceive and interpret events, products, and/or issues; and (4) suggesting areas to be covered in interview schedules and questionnaires. Although widely used in marketing research, focus groups are not as well known among social scientists. However, they appear to have potential in this field, particularly in the exploratory stages of research and when coupled with participant observation and individual interviews. Morgan's slim (70 pages of text) introduction to focus groups is part of a series entitled Qualitative Research Methods, which is edited by John Van Maanen. There are several other titles in the series that you might also find useful.

Payne, S. L. (1951). *The art of asking questions*. Princeton, NJ: Princeton University Press.

This is an unusual book. First published in 1951, it has since been reprinted many times—a sure sign that people are still buying it and, presumably, finding it useful. It focuses, almost exclusively, on how to word individual questions in a survey. There are chapters on problem words, loaded questions, the dangers of taking too much (or too little) for granted—all profusely laced with examples. Consider this example: "How do you feel about your income tax—that is, the amount you have to pay the government on the money you take in during the year?" As Payne points out, this question would insult nine out of ten people by telling them that you assume they do not understand what income tax is. But simply reversing its internal order makes the question much more acceptable. Then it reads, "How do you feel about the amount you have to pay the government on the money you take in during the year—your income tax?" Now the explanation does not sound like an explanation. Payne's advice on question wording is thorough, detailed, and well documented. But, best of all, it is conveyed in a pleasant, entertaining style that makes the book very easy and enjoyable to read.

Tanur, J. M. (1992). *Questions about questions: Inquiries into the cognitive bases of surveys.* New York: Russell Sage Foundation.

This book was sponsored by the Committee on Cognition and Survey Research of the Social Science Research Council. The Committee brought together a number of sociologists, cognitive and social psychologists, anthropologists, linguists, and other social scientists to explore the ways in which language, thought, and memory processes influence how people respond to survey questions. In a series of 13 chapters, Tanur presents some of their more exciting and promising lines of inquiry. For example, in a chapter on the assumptions underlying language use, Clark and Schober discuss the importance of understanding a speaker's *intentions*. If a listener fails to take into account the assumed personal and cultural common ground shared with the speaker, the actual meanings of words may be ambiguous. The chapter by Pearson, Ross, and Dawes presents some intriguing data on how people construct answers to questions about what they were like in the past. In many instances, they appear to first note their present standing on the attribute in question and then invoke an implicit theory of stability, or change, to calculate what they must have been like in the past. In other words, when they cannot really recall what they were like—which is often—they construct an answer that may bear little relation to the truth, even though they may sincerely believe it.

Terkel, S. (1988). *The great divide: Second thoughts on the American dream.* New York: Avon Books.

In social science research, interview questions are usually formulated to gather information relevant to specific theoretical or practical issues. However, the interview can also be used in a more open, exploratory manner. Qualitative interviews can be used to find common themes that spontaneously emerge in discussions with different people. Studs Terkel, a Chicago writer and radio personality, has spent many years interviewing people from all walks of life. His method of operation is quite simple—he just turns on a tape recorder and gets people talking. Terkel talks with truck drivers, novelists, housewives, teachers, the famous and the infamous—everybody. He asks about how things are going, their hopes, their fears, their concerns. *The Great Divide* illustrates the depth and breadth of material that can be gathered in open-ended interviews. It also illustrates one of the most powerful ways of presenting such material, that is, direct quotation—just letting people speak for themselves.

6

Survey Research

For the average person, survey research is probably the most visible and pervasive form of research in the social and behavioral sciences. Even if you escape the dubious honor of being personally interviewed by academic opinion gatherers, it is hard to get through a day without having information about your opinions and behaviors solicited on items that range from trivial to tragic. Restaurant managers want to know how they are doing, and they stick a little card between the salt and pepper shakers for you to fill out. How was the service? How would you rate the food? Comments? Telephone pollsters want to know whether you think the president is doing a good job and if the election were held tomorrow, for whom would you vote? Census takers want to know how many people live in your house and how many bathrooms you have. Magazines print questionnaires they want you to answer, tear out, and mail in. Market researchers want to know whether you prefer brand X or brand Y, and why.

Of course, you can refuse to participate, and as we shall see, there is evidence that in recent years more and more people are doing just that (e.g., Groves, 1989). But even if you do "just say no," you will find it more difficult to avoid being exposed to and affected by the results of survey research. The results of the latest poll appear in the news with ever-increasing frequency, especially during election years. Political careers are aborted because of the results of polls. New products are marketed. Policies are changed. Thus, to the general public, survey research is not only the most frequently encountered social science method, but may also be the most influential (e.g., Bradburn and Sudman, 1988).

Why Do a Survey?

The purpose of **survey research** is to gather information about selected opinions, beliefs, behaviors, or other attributes of a group of people, or of objects, by asking questions of the people themselves, or people familiar with the objects of interest. The focus might be anything from opinions about the current political scene to how much they earn to how many drinks they had last week. Gathering this information often involves interviewing—either face-to-face or over the telephone. But a preprinted questionnaire that each person, or respondent, fills out on his or her own may also be used, and it can be mailed instead of being delivered in person. Typically, the people who are asked the questions in a survey are a subset—a sample—of all those of interest, the larger group being referred to as the population of interest.

The most common objective of survey research, then, is **description**, pure and simple (e.g., Lavrakas, 1993). What percentage of the voters in lower Slobovia favor candidate Zerky? What are the most popular programs on public radio? How often do males aged 40-49 visit a dentist? Description, of course, is what the U.S. Census Bureau is charged with: that is, to provide a profile of the distribution of ages, living arrangements, incomes, and other attributes of the population of the United States every 10 years. But the Census Bureau conducts numerous other, more limited surveys, as do many other government agencies (U.S. Bureau of the Census, 1993). And most surveys do not collect data from the entire United States population. That would be too time-consuming and expensive. Rather, some smaller, more specific sample is defined. For example, when President Clinton's health care reform plan was being debated, *Time* hired Yankelovich Partners, Inc., to conduct a survey for a story that was being written about the plan. The survey was conducted by telephone, in one day (February 10, 1994). A sample of 500 adult Americans were asked, among other things, "How well would you say you understand current proposals to change the health care system?" In response, 21% of the respondents claimed to understand it "Very Well," 57% replied "Somewhat," and 21% confessed "Not Very Well" (Greenwald, 1994). These answers, along with the answers to the other questions that were asked, provided a descriptive snapshot of what people were thinking about the health care plan at that particular point in time.

Another, slightly more complex, type of descriptive information can be obtained with a survey by asking the same questions of two or more different groups of people. The answers are then used to document, and compare, the differences among various groups and subgroups. For example, based on questions asked in the National Health Interview Survey, the National Center for Health Statistics (1990) reported that 57.8% of white Americans eat breakfast almost every day, compared with 46.9% of black Americans. And, 51.3% of Americans who have never been married exercise regularly, compared with only 39.4% of currently married Americans. Such comparisons, of course, are typically more informative than a simple statistic about a single group. Imagine trying to decide how you did on a difficult test. Knowing that you scored 237 points is important, but it is better to know both your score and the class average. Without that average, you can't know whether you did well or poorly. The descriptive information obtained from surveys is useful for a variety of practical purposes, from predicting election outcomes to marketing attractive products to suggesting policies that need to be implemented.

Survey research may also be used in our attempts at **explanation** of why people behave and feel the way they do. To explain a phenomenon means to give a reason for it, to make it comprehensible. It is something people do, or try to do, all the time. When survey research is used for this purpose, some of the questions asked must be selected to reflect theoretically relevant variables, that is, those variables that we think may account for the thing we are interested in. For example, suppose you were interested in the determinants of levels of aspiration. Why is it that some adolescents seem clearly bound for college and professional careers while others, who may be equally intelligent or making equally good grades, do not? Maybe it has something to do with the level of their parents' education, or their financial resources, or, possibly, even their religious orientation. A survey in which teenagers are asked about their career plans, as well as these other factors, could provide the information needed to explain why some have higher aspirations than others. Maybe more of those whose parents have a college education have learned that it is reasonable to aspire to that for themselves. If so, then parental education would help us to understand differences in levels of aspiration. Even if that were true, there might still, of course, be other factors that contribute to such differences.

Whether you want to describe the attributes of a population, compare the relative standing of different groups in terms of those attributes, or explain relationships among some of those attributes, there are a number of decisions that must be made in designing a good survey. Our purpose in the pages that follow is to help you understand the nature of those decisions and how they are interrelated. We begin by introducing the notion of Total Survey Design.

Sources of Error and Survey Design

The goal of a survey, of course, is to secure answers from respondents that are as error-free as possible. Each and every aspect of the entire process of constructing and administering a survey must be shaped with that goal in mind. This process is referred to as **Total Survey Design** (Dillman, 1978; Fowler, 1993). It is the process of examining all potential sources of error and their interrelations, and then shaping each component to achieve the highest quality data possible. Note that this does not necessarily mean that you will be able to achieve perfection. As Groves (1987) points out, the final form of any survey is a compromise among competing sources of error.

The Overall Plan

In order to achieve the best design possible—within the means available to you—it is essential to be aware of all the possible errors that can throw you off (see Box 1). Survey errors fall into two general categories, roughly corresponding to errors of omission and errors of commission. Groves (1989, p. 11) refers to them as errors of nonobservation—failure to question some members of the population of interest—and errors of observation—obtaining inaccurate answers from those who are questioned. In order to give us a frame-

---

Box 1

The Tip of the Iceberg

When reporting stories that include data from a survey or poll, many newspapers and magazines now include brief descriptions of how their data were collected. Usually this information appears in a footnote or a small box inserted into the text of the article. This practice is intended to convey information about when the survey was done, how it was conducted, and who the respondents were so that the reader will have some basis for judging the validity of the results. The problem is that these information blurbs may actually mislead readers about the accuracy of polls by calling attention to only one type of error—sampling error. Consider this box that appeared in the summer of 1990 in a *New York Times* article (Oreskes, 1990):

How the Poll Was Taken

The latest *New York Times* Poll is based on telephone interviews conducted Aug. 9 and 10 with 670 adults around the United States, excluding Alaska and Hawaii.

The sample of telephone exchanges was selected by a computer from a complete list of exchanges in the country. The exchanges were chosen to assure that each region of the country was represented in proportion to its population. For each exchange, the telephone numbers were formed by random digits, thus permitting access to both listed and unlisted numbers. The numbers were then screened so only residences would be called.

The results have been weighted to take account of household size and number of residential telephone lines

and to adjust for variations in the sample relating to region, race, sex, age, and education.

In theory, in 19 cases out of 20, the results based on such samples will differ by no more than 4 percentage points in either direction from what would have been obtained by seeking out all American adults. The potential sampling error for subgroups of the full sample is larger. For example, for those who said they were following news about Iraq's invasion of Kuwait "very closely" it is plus or minus 6 percentage points.

In addition to sampling error, the practical difficulties of conducting any survey of public opinion may introduce other sources of error into the poll.

Indeed they may! But the impression conveyed by this box is that most of the results are within 4 or 5 percentage points of the truth. Potential errors introduced by ambiguous questions, order effects, poorly trained interviewers, lack of telephones in some homes, and refusals to be interviewed by some people who did answer their phone are all lumped under "practical difficulties." The reader is likely to conclude—mistakenly, of course—that since these sources of error were not dignified with a percentage estimate, they must not be too serious.

work for examining where these errors are likely to show up, I have sketched out a rough sequence of the major decisions involved in designing a survey in Table 1. It begins with deciding what it is you want to know—the general purpose of the survey—and who you want to know it about—the population of interest. Next is the process of conceptual clarification and honing your general interest(s) into specific research questions. That is followed by a decision about how the survey will be conducted and an initial attempt to write and arrange the actual questions that will be asked. The final stages involve selecting and training interviewers, if they are to be used, and revisions to erase any remaining ambiguities in the questions themselves or the manner in which they are presented. In the pages that follow, we will examine each of these components of the process and make a special note of the kinds of errors that can enter at each stage. Note that several important parts of the process—drafting questions and training interviewers, for example—have already been covered in Chapter 5. And, as you will see, there are several steps that can be omitted if you decide to use a questionnaire to conduct your survey. But let's take it from the top.

You begin, of course, by deciding—in general terms—what it is you want to know. What do you want to describe, or compare, or explain? Are you interested in the relationship between television viewing habits and community violence? Do you want to predict who is going to win the "at-large" seats on the city council? Whatever it is you want to know, you are going to have to convert your ideas and general research interests into specific items on an interview schedule or questionnaire. In other words, you are going to have to operationalize them, a process that should be thoroughly familiar by now from the preceding chapters. But, just to refresh your memory, a concept is operationalized by specifying instances of it, by saying what you would have

Table 1 Sequence of major decisions involved in designing a survey

What do you want to know?

Who do you want to know it about?

Are the concepts clear?

What are the research questions?

Given available resources, how will the survey be conducted?

Are you interested in changes over time?

How are the questions to be worded and arranged?

Are the questions understood as intended?

What revisions are needed?

Who will administer the instrument?

Are ambiguities still present?

What final revisions are needed?

How will nonresponse and follow-ups be handled?

DATA COLLECTION

to see or hear or touch or smell in order to be convinced that the thing referred to by the concept was present. And, as we saw in connection with constructing a standardized interview schedule, this process of saying what you are going to take as indicators of your concepts boils down to deciding which questions to ask and how to word them. Before you can start writing specific questions, however, there are several decisions that have to be made. The first, and most important, because it is actually a part of what you want to know, is this: Who do you plan to get the information from?

Sampling

It is always nice to find a way of doing things that will save you time and energy, provided that you do not sacrifice quality in the process. In survey research, sampling is just such a time and energy saver. Furthermore, when done properly, it not only does not sacrifice quality, but may actually improve the quality of the data obtained. To show you why this is so, the first order of business is to define a few terms.

In any survey, the focal group about which we want to learn something is referred to as the **population of interest.** The population may be composed of individual people, in which case each person is considered to be an **element** of the population. An element of the population is also referred to as the **unit of analysis,** the unit about which information is to be obtained and conclusions drawn. For example, the National Park Service conducts periodic surveys to help it plan changes in the facilities that it provides for the public (National Park Service, 1993). The population of interest in this case consists of all potential users of the National Park System. The elements, or units of analysis, of course, are individual people. But it is not always the case that individuals are the units of analysis. You might be interested in the relationship between family composition and socioeconomic status, in which case families would be the units of analysis—even though you might obtain all your information about each family from only one family member.

Now, if the population of interest to you is fairly small, you are in luck. You simply administer your questionnaire, or interview schedule, to all of them. If you want to know how the people on your block feel about that proposal to route an interstate highway through the neighborhood, you can make up your questions and poll everybody on the block. Usually, however, the populations of interest in survey research are somewhat larger and more geographically dispersed. Thus, it is very difficult to contact each and every member of the population. What is typically done is that a relatively small portion, a **sample,** of the population is contacted. When the National Park Service attempts to survey potential users, for example, it makes no attempt to contact *all* potential users. That would mean tens of millions of people, maybe more. It probably would have to close down all the parks to get the necessary workers to do that many interviews, and even then it would take years. What it does instead is interview a sample of potential users. In one of its surveys, for example, the National Park Service interviewed a national sample of 5757 people over the course of a 9-month period. Thus, **sampling** can save you time and energy by decreasing the number of people you have to contact. That means fewer interviewers to be trained and monitored, or fewer questionnaires to be administered. It also means that money is saved and the study can be completed in a more reasonable period of time.

The danger, of course, is that the preferences of those 5757 people—26% of whom said they liked to jog—may differ from the preferences of the population of all potential park users. The Park Service would not want to spend a lot of time and money putting in jogging trails if only 2 or 3% of the park-goers used them. More generally, the question is, how representative is the sample of the population as a whole? Are the distributions of attributes, opinions, and beliefs in the sample the same as their distributions in the population? Are the relationships among variables in the sample the same as in the population? If the Park Service had asked a *different* set of 5757 people the same questions, it might have found that 23%, or 31%, or 19%, liked to jog. Different samples from the same population may indeed produce different results—a phenomenon known as **sampling error**. In other words, when you cannot contact everyone in the population of interest, the results of a survey are partially a function of the particular sample that you did contact. Representativeness is, thus, the major issue in sampling, and the reason for its importance is simple: You want to be able to make inferences about the population as a whole based on what you find to be true of the sample. If the sampling error is large—if different samples yield vastly different results—then your conclusions about the population are likely to be incorrect. (For an all-too-common example of sampling error, see Box 2.)

So, how are you to obtain a **representative sample**—that is, a sample in which the distribution of attitudes, opinions, and all other attributes is similar to their distribution in the population of interest? The first thing to do, of course, is to decide on the population of interest. Then, one way to proceed is to construct what is referred to as a **sampling frame**, a list of each element in the population. If the population of interest to you consists of students enrolled at your college, then the sampling frame is a list of the names of all students currently enrolled. That sampling frame would be fairly easy to construct because, presumably, somewhere in the bowels of the registrar's computer, all the ingredients exist. With a little updating—additions for late enrollments, deletions for drops—you could fairly quickly come up with a list in which you had confidence. Other populations are not so easily listed. As a result, another error—referred to as **coverage error**—is introduced into the survey process. Members of the population of interest who do not appear in the sampling frame, of course, can never be a part of a sample. And, if those who are not listed in the sampling frame differ in terms of the attributes of interest from those who are listed, then your results will be partially a function of coverage error.

Box 2

Self-Selection and Biased Samples

A **self-selected sample** is one in which the respondents themselves decide who will and who will not be in the sample. Such samples might arise either by respondents seeking out the opportunity to be included or by their refusing to be included. Many magazines, for example, include questionnaires on various subjects from time to time and ask their readers to take a few minutes to fill out the questionnaire and mail it in. For several reasons, the results of such surveys should be regarded with suspicion. First, most magazines appeal only to particular types of readers. *Cosmopolitan* and *Fortune* are not oriented to the same audiences; neither are *Time* and *Rolling Stone*. Thus, the people who even see a questionnaire in a magazine are already unrepresentative of the general population. They are only representative of people who seek out exposure to that particular magazine. Second, it is very doubtful that the results of such surveys are even representative of the opinions and attitudes of the readers of the magazine in question. Most people who buy the magazine will not bother to fill out the questionnaire. Further, chances are that at least some of those who take the trouble to fill out the questionnaire will never get around to mailing it. Thus, when the results of the survey appear in a later issue of the magazine, they are likely to consist of the opinions and attitudes of those readers of the magazine who (1) are most interested in the topic, (2) have the least to do, and (3) happened to have a stamp handy.

The problem, of course, is that it is usually impossible to know how much the people who self-select themselves into a survey differ from those who do not. There have, however, been a few studies that were able to compare randomly sampled respondents with self-selected respondents. Walsh et al. (1992), for example, selected a random sample of 300 oceanographers from the subscribers to a computer network called SCIENCEnet. These people were asked to respond to a 93-item survey, and they could respond electronically over the network, print the questionnaire and mail it in, or request that a copy be mailed to them. While the survey was being conducted, a message was posted on the network bulletin board inviting others to take part. An additional 104 subscribers to the network asked to participate and completed the survey. Thus, Walsh et al. were able to compare the results for the sample of 300, whom they had selected, with the sample of 104, who had selected themselves. The results from the two samples differed in a variety of ways. The self-selected respondents gave higher-quality responses—their answers to open-ended questions were longer and their fixed-alternative responses had fewer missing values. They knew more than other oceanographers, subscribed to more group distribution lists, had more positive attitudes toward computer networks, and wrote more about the benefits of electronic communication. In general, the self-selected group was more motivated and produced a different pattern of results than the randomly selected group—a pattern of results that would have led to biased conclusions about the population of interest—that is, all oceanographers who subscribed to SCIENCEnet.

Of course, no one keeps a list of shade tree mechanics, or part-time poets, or joggers. If such esoteric populations are of interest to you, you may be tempted to settle for what is referred to as a **convenience sample**: those shade tree mechanics you can find easily, the part-time poets in the English department, joggers you happen to know. You can often learn a great deal from a convenience sample (e.g., Brecher and Brecher, 1986). Just be sure you keep in mind that the sample may be completely unrepresentative. That means you should always preface any comments about it with something like, "The four joggers I was able to talk to one Saturday over in Middleton Park said …"

But suppose you are able to construct a sampling frame fairly directly. You have a list of all the registered voters in your county, or all Mercedes owners in the state, or all soccer players in your school district who drive green mopeds, or whatever other population has piqued your interest. Now what? You select your sample from that list, of course, but you have to select it in such a way that every name on the list has an equal chance of being included in the sample. Your sample will then be a **random sample** of the population. If there are 2000 names on your list, for example, and you want a sample of 200, you might select every tenth name. In this case, you would refer to the sample as a **systematic random sample** with a **sampling interval** of 10, because you selected every tenth name. Or, you might write each of the numbers from 1 through 2000 on little slips of paper, put them all in a box, and draw out 200. You then take the names from your list that correspond to those numbers as your sample. In this case, you would have a **simple random sample.** You could also use a table of random numbers, which will be described in Chapter 8, to select your sample.

For scientific purposes, convenience samples are not acceptable because they are usually **unrepresentative samples**—that is, their characteristics typically do not correspond to those of the population of interest. But it is often an almost impossible task to construct a sampling frame that lists every element in the population of interest (e.g., Groves, 1989). Fortunately, it is possible to devise a sampling frame without listing every single element in the population. This method is referred to as **multistage cluster sampling**. Essentially what you do is divide the population into segments, or clusters, of elements. Then you take a sample of those clusters. That means you have to list only the elements in the clusters that are in your sample, not every element in the entire population. You then take a sample of the elements from each cluster included in your sample of clusters. For example, if you were interested in the population of a particular city, you might first divide the city into blocks or groups of blocks that have approximately the same number of residences in each. Next you would take a sample of blocks. Then you would select 10 residences, say, from each of the blocks included in your initial sample and interview someone from each of those residences.

You might even get a little more sophisticated and create what is referred to as a **stratified sample**. For example, suppose that in that population of 2000 that was mentioned earlier, there are 800 females and 1200 males, and you have reason to believe that sex is an important variable with respect to whatever it is you are interested in. It often is. Therefore, you want to make sure that males and females are included in your sample in appropriate numbers, that is, in proportions that correspond to their presence in the population. You could treat males and females as separate populations and take a 10% sample from each. Or, you could just rearrange your sampling frame so that the females are all listed first, and then take every tenth name. Either way, you would end up with 80 females and 120 males in your sample. When taking a systematic sample like this from your sampling frame, there is one thing to beware of: You need to make sure that your list does not have some sort of periodic ordering that corresponds to your sampling interval, or to some multiple of your sampling interval. For example, Mosteller (Kruskal and Mosteller, 1981) revealed that he once found himself sampling every thirty-second soldier from roster lists of bunkhouses, each of which contained 32 men. The problem was that the roster lists had been arranged in order by rank. So, taking every thirty-second soldier gave a sample in which everyone had the same rank. The bunkhouse population, however, had a variety of ranks and, hence, the sample was unrepresentative.

There will be more to say about sampling in the chapter on experimentation, in which you will be introduced to the notion of quota sampling. But it is important at this point to have a feel for why the variations on random sampling usually produce a representative sample. The basic assumption is really quite simple: When all the elements in a population have an equal chance of being included in the sample, the characteristics of the elements included in the sample should turn out to be about the same on average as the characteristics of all the elements in the population. With a sample of only one or two, of course, that is not a safe assumption, but with larger numbers, it usually is. For now, let us give the preceding discussions of operationalization and sampling a little more focus with an example.

Outlining the Research Questions

As we saw in Chapter 5, there is a great deal of evidence that the way in which questions and response alternatives are worded can influence respondents' answers. Similarly, in many instances, the position of a question in an interview schedule, or on a questionnaire, can also influence respondents' answers. Thus, the interview schedule or questionnaire you construct—that is, the measuring instrument itself—can be a major source of what we referred to above as errors of observation (Groves, 1989). For that reason, the initial writing down of specific questions is a task that many people approach with some trepidation. Knowledge of all the different ways in which it can go wrong, and produce erroneous results, can be paralyzing.

The goal, of course, is for the questions, and answers, to be interpreted in the same way by everyone. There are several strategies that will help you get started on the path to that goal. For example, Fowler (1993) suggests that early in the process of designing a survey, it can be very helpful to make use of **focus groups**. Focus groups are small groups of, usually, 6 to 10 people similar to those you plan to survey who are willing to discuss the concepts of interest. Their value is that they may be able to point out ambiguities, hidden assumptions, or conceptual complexities that you might have missed. If you are interested in health care, for example, what will it really mean if you ask someone how often they visit a doctor? Does a telephone consultation count? Suppose the person went to the doctor's office, but only saw the nurse. Will that count? The more such ambiguities you catch at this stage, the less trouble you'll have later.

At some point, of course, you will have to commit yourself to a few draft questions, but it is important that you first be clear about why you want to conduct the survey. Sudman and Bradburn (1982, pp. 13-14) suggest the following:

1. Restrain the impulse to write specific questions until you have thought through your research questions.

2. Write down your research questions and keep them handy while you are working on your questionnaire.

3. Every time you write a question, ask yourself, "Why do I want to know this?" Answer it in terms of the way it will help you to answer your research questions. "It would be interesting to know" is not an acceptable answer.

If everyone adhered to these simple rules, the world would be a better place, for respondents at least. Questionnaires and interview schedules would not be so long and cluttered.

One thing that may help you in thinking through your research questions is to take each area of interest or concern and make a list of exactly what you think is involved in it. Start with the general topic and then get more and more specific. At each level, write down all the issues that come to mind and any implications or implicit meanings you can think of. Let's try an example. We shall develop this one in a little more detail than usual in order to use it to illustrate a number of points in the sections that follow.

Suppose you are interested in attitudes toward the use of the insanity defense in criminal cases. Based on newspaper editorials and public reactions to several well-known cases in recent years, one might have developed the impression that people, generally, are quite negative about the use of that defense. There is something that seems to rub many people the wrong way about the practice of finding defendants "not guilty by reason of insanity," especially when the defendants clearly committed the dastardly deed in question. What you want to know is why that upsets people so, why are people so negative toward that particular legal maneuver? The first thing to remember is that an impression that people are negative does not count as evidence. Your first step, then, would be to get some data on the validity of that impression. That means the survey would need one or more questions assessing people's attitudes, pro or con, about the insanity defense. As was mentioned earlier, you do not need to explain why something is so until you have established that it is.

The next thing to ask is why. What are some possible reasons why people would support the use of the insanity defense? What are some reasons why people might oppose its use? It could be that people are simply uninformed—that is, that they do not know the legal definition of insanity. Perhaps some are negative because they believe that those who are found not guilty by reason of insanity will be set free, put back out on the street to do others harm. Or perhaps this view has more to do with a general philosophy that people should always be held responsible for their actions. On the other hand, maybe it is really due to a fear of the unpredictable, a belief that the truly insane are capricious people who lash out randomly at those around them. Maybe people want to deny that there is such a thing as insanity because they find the very idea threatening to their sense of safety and invulnerability. Maybe those who favor the use of the insanity defense believe that human nature is basically uncontrollable and that the threat of punishment is not really a deterrent to crime. Maybe… and so on.

As you see, it can get complicated very quickly. Indeed, you could probably come up with a number of additional reasons why someone might be positive or negative toward the use of the insanity defense. What happens as you go through this process, however, is that you realize that you could not possibly test all of these ideas in a single survey, and the questions of greatest interest become clearer. In no time at all you end up with a list that includes the phenomenon of interest, two or three possible explanations you want to test, and notes about additional information that might be pertinent and, hence, worth asking about.

Note that since you are interested in *explaining* something, you will need to think carefully about which variable is the cause (the **independent variable**) and which the effect (the **dependent variable**). Here the dependent variable is attitude toward the insanity defense: Is the respondent's attitude positive or negative? And above, we sketched out several possible independent variables—things that might explain why it is positive or negative. In this example, the determination of which is the independent and which the dependent variable was based purely on logic, and quite often, that is all you will have to go on. You will have to make a case that A could plausibly cause B, and, unless your logic is sound, people will argue with you about it. There are some instances in which the nature of the relationship between the two variables will help you to decide which is the independent and which the dependent variable—that is, if the values of one variable occur prior to or are determined before the values of the second variable, then the one whose values are determined first can only be the independent variable. For example, for many years there was some controversy about the clarity of the evidence that smoking causes cancer (e.g., Eysenck, 1980), but nobody argued that cancer causes smoking, because smoking comes first, cancer later. Similarly, good high school grades may lead to acceptance at the college of your choice. But acceptance at the college of your choice usually comes too late to produce good high school grades. Even when there is a clear time order to the variables of interest, however, you still have to be able to make a reasonable argument for how the first causes the second.

Now, having ruminated over the possible causes of both positive and negative attitudes toward the insanity defense, our outline of research questions might look something like this:

Research Questions
I. Attitudes toward the insanity defense
    A. Negative?
        1. Believe it lets the guilty go free
        2. Know the legal definition of insanity?
        3. Believe in individual accountability
        4. Believe that punishment deters crime
    B. Positive?
        1. A general trust-others attitude
        2. Member of the helping professions
II. Relevant additional demographic information
    A. Education: more highly educated, less negative?
    B. Sex: females less negative?
    C. Religious orientation: Hindus less negative?

There are several things to note about this outline. First, one of the nice features of survey research is that you can obtain evidence on a number of possible explanations for the phenomenon of interest simultaneously, that is, in the same questionnaire or interview schedule. All you have to do is include appropriate questions about each. Second, in constructing those questions, one of the best sources of inspiration is previous research on the topic. For example, in a telephone interview, Hans and Slater (1983) asked respondents the following question, which you might be able to use:

> How strongly do you agree or disagree with the following statement: "The insanity defense is a loophole that allows too many people to go free." Do you strongly agree, agree, disagree, strongly disagree, or neither agree nor disagree with that statement?

On second thought, you probably cannot use it. The question is loaded. The word loophole has a clear negative connotation. This sounds better: "How do you feel about allowing defendants accused of crimes to plead 'not guilty by reason of insanity'? Would you say you are strongly in favor, in favor, undecided, opposed, or strongly opposed?" Using other people's questions for inspiration, you see, does not mean you have to copy exactly, although that is perfectly acceptable (Fowler, 1993, p. 97). If you can find a question that has been used previously and that suits your purpose, use it. It will enable you to compare your results with those obtained in other research.

The third thing to note about the preceding outline is that there is (or should be) a reason behind each entry. If you cannot think of a reason why a person's age might be related to his or her attitude toward the insanity defense, then do not ask people how old they are. It will only take up time, and the answers you obtain will never be used. Finally, note that the outline indicates that you are going to have to ask respondents several different types of questions: questions about their *attitudes* toward the insanity defense, questions about their *knowledge* (what is the definition of insanity?), questions about specific *beliefs* (does punishment deter crime?), questions about *demographic characteristics* (what was the highest grade in school you completed?), and questions about their *general orientation* to life. That mixture of question types is actually a good thing. It will make the interview, or questionnaire, a little more interesting for the respondents and, thus, help keep the respondents' interest and attention.

Mode of Presentation

With the research questions outlined, there is still a major decision to be made before you actually start writing questions: How is the survey to be conducted? Do you plan to use face-to-face interviews, telephone interviews, a mailed questionnaire, or some combination of these? This decision must be made before you write questions because it affects nearly all facets of the questions themselves and the way in which they are arranged on an interview schedule or questionnaire. Each style of data collection has its strong points, of course. And combinations of the three can also be useful under certain circumstances. As Frey (1989) points out, the choice depends on what it is you are studying, the population of interest, and the resources available to you. To help you make that choice, let's consider some of the major advantages and disadvantages of each.

QUESTIONS   The decision about whether to use questionnaires, face-to-face interviews, or telephone interviews depends in part on the kinds of questions you plan to ask. Generally speaking, the face-to-face interview is the most flexible in terms of the types of questions that can be asked. Open-ended questions are no problem at all, especially if the interview is being recorded. With a well-trained, relaxed interviewer, they often sound like spontaneous conversation. With closed-ended questions having several response alternatives, the interviewer can hand the respondent a card with the answer options printed on it, as in Figure 1A. It is also best to ask knowledge questions in face-to-face or telephone interviews. Filling out a questionnaire in the privacy of his or her home, a respondent might be tempted to look up the answer before proceeding. A variety of props can be used to test knowledge or preferences, or both, in the face-to-face interview. To test geographic knowledge, for example, the respondents can be shown a map and asked to label the parts (Figure 1B). To test musical knowledge, they can be played a tape and asked to name the composer. Pictures and products can be displayed and preferences, aesthetic and otherwise, solicited.

In contrast to this high level of flexibility, the telephone interview and the mailed or self-administered questionnaire are somewhat more constrained. The telephone interview is entirely dependent on what can be communicated verbally. Hence, the options of visuals and props available to the face-to-face interviewer are eliminated. In addition, the respondent in a telephone interview must

STRONGLY IN FAVOR
MODERATELY IN FAVOR
DON'T CARE
MODERATELY OPPOSED
STRONGLY OPPOSED
DON'T KNOW

(A)

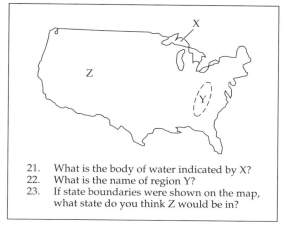

21. What is the body of water indicated by X?
22. What is the name of region Y?
23. If state boundaries were shown on the map, what state do you think Z would be in?

(B)

1 Props can be used in a face-to-face interview. (A) For closed-ended questions, a card with the response options can be handed to respondents to help them keep all the options in mind when making a choice. (B) An outline map can be shown to respondents, who are then asked a series of questions about it to test their knowledge of geography.

remember each word or phrase of the question and all the response alternatives (Dillman, 1978). Thus, long, complex questions are more likely to be misunderstood, and the telephone interviewer does not have access to nonverbal cues—quizzical looks, for example—that would flag the respondent's lack of understanding. Similarly, with the mailed questionnaire, open-ended questions must be kept to a minimum because people do not like to write out long answers. Also, questions intended to apply to only some of the respondents are more likely to create problems. **Contingency questions**, which are to be answered only if a prior question was answered in a certain way, are more likely to be skipped or misunderstood. One additional disadvantage of the questionnaire is that you are unable to control the sequence in which respondents answer the questions. And there is nothing to prevent respondents from going back and changing answers to questions if a later question suggests something that they had not thought of earlier. As Dillman (1978, p. 59) put it, if the sequence of questions is important in your survey, you cannot trust the mailed questionnaire.

PERSONNEL   While the mailed questionnaire does not rate too well in terms of question flexibility, it must be considered if personnel are in short supply. In fact, if all you've got is yourself—and maybe a friend or two—the questionnaire is likely to be your best bet. For example, not too long ago, two students and I (Jones et al., 1992) sent a brief, two-page questionnaire to a sample of 180 elderly people. We were interested in their concerns and information needs, and being able to talk to each of them individually would have been ideal. Unfortunately, we lacked the money to hire interviewers, and each of us had other obligations that prevented us from doing the interviews ourselves, so we opted for the mailed questionnaire.

One of the major reasons that the telephone interview has become more typical of survey research than the face-to-face household interview has to do with personnel. The face-to-face approach simply requires many, many more people. Frey (1989, p. 41) estimates that face-to-face surveys of a national sample can require up to 100 trained interviewers and several supervisors. In contrast, a telephone survey of a national sample may need only a dozen or so interviewers and one or two supervisors. The reason for the tremendous difference, of course, is that the telephone interviews can be conducted from a single location equipped with several phone lines. Also, a supervisor in a telephone survey can listen in to portions of actual interviews as they are being conducted and monitor several different interviewers simultaneously.

So, in terms of personnel requirements, face-to-face interviews are usually the most demanding. Differences between the personnel needed for face-to-face and telephone interviews can be expected to decrease, of course, the more geographically concentrated the sample you plan to interview. If the potential respondents are all living in the same school district, for example, you may not need any more interviewers for a face-to-face household survey than for a telephone survey. But there are a couple of complicating factors. First, depending on the school district, there may be safety concerns for interviewers going around knocking on doors—and if you have to furnish a bodyguard for each interviewer, you double the personnel requirements. Second, if no one is home on the first try, it is much less time-consuming—and, hence, requires fewer personnel—to simply dial the number again later (or tomorrow) than to make another trip to that front porch later (or tomorrow).

SPEED OF ADMINISTRATION   If timeliness is crucial, the telephone survey is the usually the most efficient. Even allowing 2 or 3 days for training new interviewers (see Chapter 5), telephone surveys can be conducted in a fraction of the time required for mailed questionnaires to be returned, or for household interviewers to fan out across the landscape. Respondents often put mailed questionnaires aside and answer them later, when they are not busy. Household interviewers have to travel to the respondent's place of residence, and must return the next day if nobody is home. Telephone surveys of national samples are now commonly done in a couple of days or less. That New York Times telephone survey mentioned in Box 1, for example, was conducted in 2 days. Bradburn and Sudman (1988) point out that it is the speed with which results can be obtained that has made the telephone survey the most popular form among politicians and political pollsters. The reactions of constituents to world and national events can be obtained almost overnight.

FACILITIES AVAILABLE   Of course, conducting a telephone survey depends, to some extent, on having access to the necessary equipment. At a minimum, that would include telephones and tables and chairs for the interviewers. Chamblin (1993) reports a telephone survey concerning attitudes toward sex education in the public schools in which the interviewers were college students with minimal training and the "facilities" were the telephones and desks in vacant faculty offices in the late afternoons and early evenings. Lists of telephone numbers were furnished to the interviewers, and respondent answers were recorded on printed interview schedules.

At a more advanced level, many colleges and universities now have survey research centers equipped with computer-assisted telephone interviewing (CATI) systems of varying degrees of sophistication (Spaeth, 1987). These consist of individual workstations for interviewers with computers that have been programmed to handle many aspects of the data collection process. Typically, the questions to be asked are displayed on the screen, the interviewer speaks to respondents via a headset, and their answers are typed directly into the computer. As Carpenter (1988) points out, CATI systems do wonders for the telephone interview process. For example, when an interviewer has to read questions from a printed form and write down the answers, the amount of contingent branching to different sets of questions is limited by the ability of the interviewer to keep track of prior answers and branching instructions. But with a CATI system, the computer keeps track of all prior answers and displays the appropriate next question on the screen. All the interviewer has to do is read it. Table 2 lists some of the types of computerized contingent questioning capabilities currently available in CATI software packages. In addition to creating greater questioning flexibility, CATI systems usually handle

Table 2 Some Contingent Questioning Capabilities Available in Computer-Assisted Telephone Interviewing Software

CAPABILITY	DESCRIPTION
Single-question branching	The question asked depends on the answer to the previous question
Multiple-condition branching	The question asked depends on the answers to several previous questions
Online math calculations	Numbers from the responses to various questions are manipulated and used for checks before another question is presented
Math logic for branching	Similar to conditional branching, but the question asked is determined by mathematical logic relating to one or more previous answers
Personalized questions	Individuals' names or other personal information is inserted into questions or statements throughout the questionnaire
Insertion of previous answers	Answers to previous questions constitute part of a question
Re-presentation of data	Similar to insertion of previous answers, but a set of data is presented as a matrix
Prompted recall	The respondent receives information from a database that aids his or her recall of past events

Source: Carpenter, 1988, p. 355.

a variety of other tasks for the interviewer, including generating random digits for telephone numbers, automatically dialing numbers, controlling the
number of callbacks, and even displaying an interviewer's screen for a supervisor, who can thus see what the interviewer sees while simultaneously
monitoring what the interviewer says. Of course, the more elaborate the features, the more the software package costs. And, as House and Nicholls
(1988) point out, with these systems, questionnaire construction becomes a
complex computer programming task.

In contrast, the facilities needed to conduct a survey by mail are usually
much more modest: Access to a typewriter or computer for printing the questionnaire, some form of duplicating machine for making multiple copies, and
a worktable for folding the questionnaires and stuffing envelopes are about
all that is needed.

COST   The cost of any survey is a function of a variety of factors (Groves,
1989). Some of the more obvious are the geographic dispersion of the sample, the sample size, and the number of attempts that are made to reach respondents not available on the first try. It can be difficult to compare the costs
of different modes of presentation because most reports of surveys in the literature do not mention costs. But, in almost every instance in which cost comparisons have been made (Dillman 1978, pp. 68–72), the mailed questionnaire
has been found superior to—that is, cheaper than—a series of face-to-face interviews. It is also usually less expensive than telephone interviews, unless
you plan on doing all the telephone interviews yourself and calling only people in your local dialing area. For that two-page mailed questionnaire mentioned above (Jones et al., 1992), our total costs were a box of envelopes, a
ream of paper, two mimeo stencils, $72 in postage, a little time licking stamps,
and a couple of paper cuts. To have gone out into the community and tracked
down each of those 180 people would have been much more time-consuming
and expensive. There are exceptions, of course, but when they are feasible,
self-administered questionnaires are generally the cheapest source of survey
data, even if you have to pay postage both ways.

AVOIDING NONRESPONSE   When we were discussing the construction of an interview schedule in Chapter 5, it was pointed out that the opening comments
to respondents—whether face-to-face or over the telephone—are very important. As Groves, Cialdini, and Couper (1992) point out, in those initial few
seconds of contact, the respondent makes the crucial decision whether to participate in the survey or not. If the respondent decides not to participate, the
component of total survey error referred to as nonresponse error is increased,
and to the extent that nonrespondents differ from respondents who agree to
participate, the results of the survey will be biased. As Groves and Lyberg
(1988) point out:

> Nonresponse is perhaps the most inscrutable of survey errors. Many other sur-
> vey errors can, at least theoretically, be dealt with if the researcher has adequate
> financial and administrative resources. Nonresponse in voluntary surveys,

however, is the result of behavior of persons who are outside the researcher's control. (p. 191)

Unfortunately, it appears that all types of surveys—face-to-face interviews, telephone interviews, and mailed questionnaires—have been increasingly plagued by nonresponse in recent years (Groves et al., 1988; Groves, 1989).

The face-to-face interviewer has an advantage when it comes to soliciting cooperation. As Oksenberg, Coleman, and Cannell (1986) point out, in the face-to-face setting there are a number of things that may help the interviewer overcome a respondent's hesitation—a friendly smile, a neat appearance, and a pleasant demeanor. Over the telephone, all the interviewer can convey has to be conveyed via his or her voice. And there is some evidence that vocal characteristics do make a difference.

In monitoring telephone interviewers at the University of Michigan's Survey Research Center, Oksenberg et al. noted that there were some who had *consistently* high nonresponse rates—more than 20 or 30% of the people they called refused to be interviewed—and others who had consistently low rates—fewer than 10% of those they called refused. Since all interviewers read the same opening remarks, and since most refusals occurred before they could get to the first substantive question, it had to be something about the voices. Right? To check on what that something was, Oksenberg et al. recorded the opening remarks of several interviewers who had high refusal rates and several who had low refusal rates. They then asked two groups of naive subjects to rate the recordings on a variety of dimensions. They found that those interviewers whose voices were higher in pitch and who exhibited greater variations in pitch, as well as speaking louder, faster, and clearer, were perceived to be more attractive and competent—and these were the ones who had the lowest refusal rates.

Another potential contributor to nonresponse error in telephone surveys is the increasingly widespread use of answering machines to screen, or avoid, unwanted calls. Piazza (1993) reports that in a recent telephone survey in California, answering machines were encountered at 31% of the households contacted. Xu, Bates, and Schweitzer (1993) found that a somewhat lower percentage of first calls encountered an answering machine. But the good news is that the eventual contact rate and the likelihood of completing an interview were both significantly higher for households with an answering machine than for those where the first call went unanswered. Xu et al. also found that leaving a message on the answering machine significantly decreased the eventual refusal rate. They speculate that the message may work this magic by introducing the study without making any immediate demands on the time and energy of the potential respondent. Or, it may simply help the respondent decide that the request is a legitimate one and not a disguised sales pitch.

With the mailed questionnaire, overcoming nonresponse is even more of a problem. There is no friendly interviewer. There are no applicable social norms, such as returning calls and not hanging up in people's faces. Typically, all you have to motivate the respondent with are these ingredients: (1) the appearance of the envelope in which the questionnaire arrives; (2) a cover letter describing the study and requesting participation; (3) the questionnaire itself; and (4) the envelope for returning the questionnaire. As Dillman (1978) has pointed out, each of these has motivational significance; that is, they *will* affect the respondent's decision to participate or not. Therefore, they all have to appear to minimize the costs and maximize the rewards to the respondent of filling out the questionnaire and returning it. The proportion of potential respondents who do return the questionnaire is referred to as the **return rate**, and it is crucial to try to maximize it.

The cover letter should briefly describe the study and its importance. If the respondent is going to take the time to fill out the questionnaire, it is essential that you convey quickly how and why the results will be useful. Respondents do not want to waste their time. For example, even though you are legally required to respond to the decennial census, the U.S. Bureau of the Census includes several brief messages about the importance of the census on an attractively printed page that accompanies the mailed forms. Here are the first two paragraphs from the page that was sent out in 1990:

HERE IS YOUR OFFICIAL 1990 CENSUS FORM.

It is very important that you fill out the form and mail it back by April 1. Your answers are needed to help you and your entire community.

YOUR ANSWERS HELP FUND SERVICES EVERYONE NEEDS.

By putting yourself in the picture—answering the census and being counted— you help make sure your community gets its fair share of federal and state funding for essential programs and services: for schools, health centers, parks, highways, services for the elderly, child care, employment and training and much more.

With all those good things, who could refuse? Well, no one, actually, because a few paragraphs further on is this sentence: "Federal Law, Title 13 of the U.S. Code, requires that you complete the enclosed form to the best of your knowledge." But you see the point. In answering the questions, your time will be well spent; important and useful things will result. That is what a cover letter should convey.

Also, with a mailed survey, the actual physical appearance and layout of the questionnaire are extremely important—more important than the layout of an interview schedule, even though the two may contain the same questions. The interview schedule is read by an intelligent, trained interviewer who has practice using it. With the questionnaire, you have only the questionnaire itself to elicit the answers—and the respondent has never seen it before. There are a few physical design features that are similar for interview schedules and questionnaires. You will recall from Chapter 5 that in constructing an interview schedule, we recommended starting out with questions clearly related to the topic of the study, grouping related questions, and putting potentially sensitive, or objectionable, questions toward the end. Those suggestions also apply to questionnaires.

But that's about where the similarity ends. As Dillman (1978) has pointed out, with the questionnaire, it is much more important that the first questions be easy, neutral, and clearly apply to everyone. To repeat, the physical appearance of the questionnaire is crucial: An attractive, brief, well laid out questionnaire with lots of white space that looks as if it would be a snap to answer is, in fact, much more likely to be answered (Dillman, 1978). To see what this means for individual items, let's go back to those research questions we outlined earlier regarding attitudes toward the insanity defense and actually translate a couple of them into questions as they might appear on an interview schedule and a questionnaire. Here is how they might appear on an interview schedule:

1. How do you feel about allowing defendants accused of crimes to plead "not guilty by reason of insanity"? Would you say that you are strongly in favor, in favor, undecided, opposed, or strongly opposed? __SIF __IF __UN __OP __SO

2. Currently, when a person is found "not guilty by reason of insanity," which of the following do you think is most likely to happen to that person? Would the person be set free, put on probation, confined in a mental institution, or sent to jail? __Set free (A) __Put on prob (B) __Confined in inst (C) __Sent to jail (D)

   IF C OR D, ASK: How long do you think they would be kept there? __(WRITE IN ANSWER)

3. What is your sex? __Male__Female

Those same questions on a questionnaire would look like this:

1. How do you feel about allowing defendants accused of crimes to plead "not guilty by reason of insanity"? (Circle number of your answer)
   1. STRONGLY IN FAVOR
   2. IN FAVOR
   3. UNDECIDED
   4. OPPOSED
   5. STRONGLY OPPOSED

2. Currently, when a person is found "not guilty by reason of insanity," which of the following do you think is most likely to happen to that person? (Circle number of your answer)
   1. SET FREE
   2. PUT ON PROBATION
   3. CONFINED IN A MENTAL INSTITUTION
   4. SENT TO JAIL

   (If you answered 3 or 4) How long do you think they would be kept there? (Fill in answer)

   _____

3. What is your sex? (Circle number of your answer)
   1. MALE
   2. FEMALE

In the latter format, there is much more open space, making for a more attractive and uncluttered appearance. The vertical spacing of the answer options is also important, for two reasons. First, with the answers placed vertically, there is less opportunity for confusion—for example, if you want to answer "Male," do you put your check before or after the word? Second, with the vertical spacing, respondents will move down the page and through the questionnaire much more quickly, making it more likely that they will actually complete the questionnaire. The openness and vertical spacing also make the questionnaire look as if it will be easier to answer.

Dillman (1978) points out that the Total Survey Design approach, when applied to mailed questionnaires, means that there must be attention to even the most minute details: clear and well-worded questions, spacing of questions on the page, precise instructions for answering, good-quality paper and printing, an appealing logo or letterhead on the cover letter—anything and everything that might affect respondents' perceptions of the questionnaire and the survey of which it is a part. And there is evidence that if all those details are properly attended to, nonresponse error can be minimized.

Cross-Sectional versus Longitudinal Surveys

In planning a survey, there is another design decision that is intimately related to the research questions providing the motivation for the survey: that is, do you want to trace changes over time in the variables of interest? If not, you will be conducting what is referred to as a cross-sectional survey, in which data are collected at one point in time to describe and/or explain something at that time. For example, in November 1983, the *New York Times* conducted a telephone survey of 1309 adult men and women (Dowd, 1983). Respondents were asked questions about whether or not they worked outside the home, how much they liked their jobs, if they had ever been discriminated against in the workplace, and other issues such as how working affected their parental roles and responsibilities. In connection with the latter issue, the poll found that 59% of the females thought that women employed outside the home were just as good, or better, mothers than women not employed outside the home. Only 44% of the males interviewed held that view. Another example of a cross-sectional survey is the study mentioned earlier by Hans and Slater (1983). Between June 28 and July 1, 1982, they conducted telephone interviews with 434 men and women from New Castle County, Delaware. Only a week prior to that, John Hinckley, Jr., had been found not guilty by reason of insanity of the attempted assassination of President Reagan. Hans and Slater were interested in reactions to that particular trial and verdict. They found that 65.7% of the respondents did not think Hinckley was insane, and that 87.1% thought the insanity defense was a loophole, but only one respondent (out of 434) knew the legal definition of insanity. The cross-sectional survey is by far the most frequently encountered variety, and, as Babbie (1990) has noted, if your goal is one-time description, it is for you. It provides a snapshot in time, a capsule of information about what the respondents have to say right now, today.

However, there are many research questions for which a **longitudinal study** is required, a study that gives you information about changes over time. For example, suppose you were interested in how getting married affects social relationships with same-sex peers. The popular stereotype is that when people get married, they gradually, or abruptly, quit going out with the boys or the girls. You could try examining the issue with a cross-sectional survey by selecting some respondents who are married and some who are not and asking them all about how frequently they see their friends. If you did, and if you found that those who were married had fewer friends, or saw their friends less often, or both, you still would not be able to say that their getting married was the reason for that. Someone would quickly point out that the married people may have had fewer friends before they got married. In fact, it is entirely possible that they got married because they were lonely.

You need to do a **panel study** (Markus, 1979) to answer questions involving changes over time. You select a group of respondents, all of whom are single, and interview them about their friends: "How many friends do you have?" "How often do you see them?" "Do you enjoy being around them?" Then, at some later time, you interview exactly the same people again. Presumably, in the interval, some of them will have gotten married. If the newlyweds now see their friends less often, you will be in a much better position to argue that getting married produced the decrease. Of course, if it turns out that in the second round of interviews even the confirmed singles are seeing less of their friends, you are going to have to look for another cause for the decrease in sociability. Maybe everyone is working overtime to keep their standard of living up. Panel studies tend to be quite time-consuming, as you probably can guess from this example. You might have to wait a long time for any sizable number of the initial group to get married. There is also the danger that you might not be able to reinterview all of the initial group: some may move and leave no forwarding address; some may die; some may simply refuse to be interviewed a second time. The loss of part of the original group of respondents at the second or third round of interviewing is referred to as panel **attrition**. If there is some systematic reason for panel attrition, you end up with an unrepresentative sample. Another potential problem with panel studies, especially when the waves of interviewing are fairly close together, is that the answers the second time may be affected by the fact that the respondents just answered all the same questions not too long ago.

Given the expense and effort involved in keeping track of all the members of a panel, it is sometimes possible to employ a substitute design that will still let you examine issues of change over time. In a panel study, the same sample of respondents from a population is contacted repeatedly. In a **cohort study** (Glenn, 1977), different samples from a given population are contacted. For example, suppose you wanted to examine how attitudes toward the insanity defense change with increasing education. You could interview a sample of tenth-graders, wait 2 years, and interview those same people again. If you did that, you would have conducted a panel study. However, it would be easier and quicker to interview, simultaneously, a sample of tenth-graders and a sample of twelfth-graders from the same schools. If you did the latter, you would have conducted a cohort study. But be sure to note the hidden assumption: you would have to assume that in the 2 years since the current twelfth-graders were tenth-graders, there have been no changes in the general population of tenth-graders. In other words, you would have to assume that the tenth graders of today are just like the tenth-graders of 2 years ago. It is because subtle changes may occur in the total population over time that cohort studies can be tricky. The tenth-graders of today may not be like the tenth-graders of 2, or 20, years ago. If the population has changed, any comparison between cohorts will be confounded by those changes.

There are other ways to approximate the kinds of longitudinal information that you can obtain with a panel study without going to all the time and effort required to conduct a long-term study. You might, for example, be able to find an earlier study that asked questions similar to the ones you are interested in. You could then compare your results with those earlier results. In her discussion of the *New York Times* survey mentioned earlier, Dowd (1983) did just that. She compared the results obtained in November 1983 with the results from a 1970 survey sponsored by Virginia Slims. In 1970, 53% of the women surveyed cited motherhood as "one of the best parts of being a woman." In 1983, only 26% of the women surveyed said that. When you do try to use previously collected data to compare with your own, ask yourself the following questions: Are the samples of respondents really similar for the two surveys? Are the questions they were asked sufficiently similar to allow comparison? If the answer to either of these questions is no, the comparison will not be very informative.

Mixing Modes

It should be clear by now why you cannot wait until all your questions have been written and a sample selected before you decide how the survey is going to be conducted. Question format and arrangement are intimately related to the mode of the survey. Some things that would work beautifully in a face-to-face interview would be a total disaster on a mailed questionnaire. On the other hand, it might be possible to reach a national sample via a mailed questionnaire, even with very limited resources. Conducting face-to-face interviews with that national sample could strain the budgets of entire academic departments. But there is another possibility that we have not considered: There are some survey purposes for which it makes sense to use more than one mode.

A mixed-mode survey is simply one that makes use of two or more modes of data collection: face-to-face *and* telephone interviews; questionnaires *and* face-to-face interviews; telephone interviews *and* mailed question-naires. Dillman and Tarnai (1988) identify six types of mixed-mode surveys, which are presented in Table 3 along with an example of each type. Each of the mixed modes outlined in the table has certain advantages, of course. A telephone follow-up for respondents who have not returned a questionnaire may decrease the nonresponse rate and reduce the time needed to complete the survey. Face-to-face interviews for an initial survey followed by subsequent telephone contact may produce higher overall rapport and cooperation. It will also reduce costs, compared with conducting both initial and follow-up face-to-face interviews.

There are other combinations that may prove useful under certain circumstances. For example, during face-to-face interviews, respondents might be given a brief questionnaire to fill out on their own—without the interviewer seeing their answers—as one way of handling sensitive topics that might be embarrassing for them to verbalize. An initial contact via mail may enhance cooperation in a subsequent telephone or face-to-face interview. Here is an example, a postcard that I received in the mail not long ago. Note how carefully worded it is: "You count," "invite you," "nothing to sell," "no one will visit your home."

YOU COUNT IN THE RADIO RATINGS!

Chris_____ of Arbitron Ratings will call your home in the next few days to invite you to tell us what you listen to on radio. Chris_____ has nothing to sell. We've been conducting ratings surveys like this for more than 40 years. Whether you listen a little, a lot, or not at all, radio stations are counting on people like you to be in the survey.

Won't you please talk to Chris? We think you'll enjoy being in the radio survey.

Cordially,

Jane_____
Arbitron Ratings Survey Director

P.S. No one will visit your home and your name will *not* be revealed to anyone. If you have any questions, our toll-free number is 1-800-555-7091.

Sure, I'd be glad to help Chris. Just tell him to give me a call.

As you can see, mixed-mode surveys offer many options that may help in your effort to get the most accurate data possible within the means available to you. As Dillman and Tarnai (1988) put it, creatively mixing modes allows you to tailor the entire data collection process to take advantage of the best way of solving whatever survey problems you face.

Table 3 Six Types of Mixed-Mode Surveys

PURPOSE OF SURVEY	EXAMPLE
To collect same data from different respondents in a sample	Mail for early respondents; telephone and/or face-to-face interviews for respondents who could not be contacted
To collect follow-up panel data from same respondents at a later time	Face-to-face interview for initial survey; telephone for panel study follow-up interview
To collect same data from different sample frames in same population for combined analysis	Dual frame survey using area probability sample for face-to-face interviews and random digit dialing sample for telephone
To collect different data from same respondents during a single data collection period	Mail questionnaire to respondents immediately after completing a telephone interview
To collect data from different populations for comparison purposes	Telephone used to collect data from a national household sample for comparison with mail questionnaires from a list frame sample
To increase response rate for another mode	Telephone contact used to encourage response to mail survey

Source: Dillman and Tarnai, 1988.

Revise, Revise, Revise

If you look back at Table 1, you will notice that several of the major steps in the process of designing a survey involve obtaining information that will help you revise what you have done up to that point. You will recall that Fowler (1993) suggested using focus groups early in the process to help clarify the concepts of interest and alert you to ambiguities before you start writing questions. Of course, a few critical, intelligent friends may be able to serve the purpose for you if resources are limited.

Once you have an initial draft of the questionnaire or interview schedule, another reality check is called for. What is needed now are a few people willing to go through the questionnaire in detail, or to have the interview schedule administered to them, and identify any ambiguities or difficulties with the opening statement (or cover letter), the questions, the response alternatives, the instructions for answering, the directions for branching questions—anything and everything. The people you need here are ones who will be willing to discuss the individual questions at length—maybe thinking aloud as the question is read and as they attempt to formulate a response. This is not really a pretest in the sense that we discussed in Chapter 5. Rather, it is a series of in-depth interviews with a small number of people to see whether the questions are comprehended and can be answered as intended (Forsyth and Lessler, 1992). The information obtained from these people is then used to revise anything that appears problematic: questions, opening remarks, layout of the questionnaire—anything.

Once those revisions have been made—and interviewers trained, if they are to be used—then a pilot test of the questionnaire or interview schedule is in order. It is at this stage that the pretesting we described toward the end of Chapter 5 is called for. In the case of face-to-face interviews, the interview schedule is administered to 20 to 50 respondents similar to those who will be used in the survey proper. Recordings of the interviews are then analyzed to identify problems (Oksenberg, Cannell, and Kalton, 1991). Are there questions that the interviewers have trouble reading correctly? Are there transitions that are too awkward? Are there questions that provoke too many requests for clarification? With mailed questionnaires, as Fowler (1993) points out, this process is a little more difficult. The best alternative in this case may be to have the pilot respondents fill out the questionnaire and then conduct a group discussion to get at their perceptions of problems with the questionnaire.

Whether you are working with an interview schedule or a self-administered questionnaire, the end result of the pilot test is the same. You *revise again* and attempt to eliminate any and all problems that were identified. The pilot test is a crucial part of survey design. In fact, it is so important that Sudman and Bradburn (1982, p. 283) say: "*If you do not have the resources to pilot test your questionnaire, don't do the study.*"

Summary

Survey research is probably the most visible and influential variety of research in the social and behavioral sciences. The information obtained from surveys is useful for a variety of purposes, from the marketing of attractive consumer goods to getting the attention of recalcitrant politicians. Three of the most important functions of surveys are description, comparison, and explanation. The descriptive use of surveys is the most familiar: that is, the use of surveys to obtain information on the attributes of the population of interest. By obtaining data from two or more groups, that descriptive information may be used to compare the groups in terms of the attributes in question. Of greatest interest in social science circles, however, is the use of surveys to gather information that will help to explain relationships among variables.

Constructing and conducting a survey involves a number of design decisions. The concept of Total Survey Design was introduced to highlight the process of examining all potential sources of error and shaping each component of the survey to achieve the highest quality data possible. It was also noted that a survey is typically a compromise between competing sources of error: (1) errors of nonobservation, stemming from the failure to question some members of the population of interest; and (2) errors of observation, stemming from inaccurate answers from those who were questioned. The first step in survey design is to get clearly in mind exactly what you want to know and who you want to know it about. The people you want to know about are referred to as the population of interest. There are several ways of obtaining a representative sample of that population. The concepts of sampling error and coverage error were introduced to alert you to some of the difficulties involved in obtaining a representative sample. Sampling error refers to the possibility that two samples drawn from the same population may differ—not only from the population, but also from each other. Coverage error refers to the possibility that all members of the population are not available to be sampled.

Once you have determined what you want to know and how you will obtain a sample of the population of interest, the next steps are to clarify the concepts of interest and make a list of the issues you want to be able to address with the results of the survey. You then use that list to write out the specific questions you want to ask each respondent. Before actually deciding on the wording of questions, however, you have to decide how the survey will be conducted. Data can be collected in one or more of three basic ways: face-to-face interviews, self-administered questionnaires, or telephone interviews. Each format has certain advantages and disadvantages. The questionnaire approach is usually cheapest, but is fairly constraining in the types of questions you can ask. The face-to-face interview is the most flexible in terms of the types of questions that can be asked, but conducting a number of face-to-face interviews can be quite time-consuming and expensive. Face-to-face and telephone interviews require training and supervision of interviewers and may require facilities that are not available to you. On the other hand, they tend to result in lower nonresponse rates than mailed questionnaires. Nonresponse is another (potentially serious) source of error. One possible way to lower nonresponse rates is a mixed-mode design; for example, one in which questionnaires are mailed out and respondents telephoned either before the mailing (to request their cooperation), or after (to remind them to send the questionnaire back), or both.

Another basic design decision involves the choice of a one-time, or cross-sectional, survey versus the use of survey data collected at several points in time in order to trace longitudinal changes in the attributes of interest. For longitudinal surveys, you might select a panel study, in which the same people are repeatedly contacted, or a cohort study, in which different samples from the same population are contacted. A potentially serious source of error with a panel study is attrition. With a cohort study, dissimilarity of cohorts can be a problem.

Once you have a draft of the questions you would like to ask, it is a good idea to pretest it on a few people. There are several ways in which this can be done. One is to ask respondents to think aloud as they respond to the questions, alerting you to ambiguities and misunderstandings. Another, as we saw in Chapter 5, is to administer the survey as intended to a small sample of respondents. In this way questions that trigger too many requests for clarification and/or inappropriate answers can be identified. If respondents do not understand what you are asking or if their answers seem weird, revise your questions. Then try it again. And again.

Recommended Readings

Frey, J. H. (1989). *Survey research by telephone* (2nd ed.). Beverly Hills, CA: Sage.

As noted in the text, because of its relative speed, convenience, and lower cost, the telephone survey has gradually replaced the face-to-face survey in many areas of research. Frey provides an interesting, readable, and brief introduction to all the major components of telephone surveying—including sampling, random digit dialing, and questionnaire design. However, he begins with an interesting history of the telephone itself and its impact on social relations and other aspects of human behavior. As he notes, the telephone quickly became an instrument of personal freedom and geographic dispersion. It made industrial decentralization possible by allowing manufacturing firms, for example, to locate different parts of their operations in different parts of the country, and even abroad. As the telephone became common, norms of telephone usage developed, norms that in fact can help you if you want to conduct a telephone survey. One, for example, is that the person who makes a call also terminates that call. There is much more, but perhaps the most valuable part of the text is a point-by-point comparison of the advantages and disadvantages of face-to-face, telephone, and mail surveys.

Groves, R. M. (1989). *Survey errors and survey costs*. New York: Wiley.

This is a comprehensive text in which Groves brings together the statistical and social science perspectives on survey design. It is richly detailed and illustrated, focusing on the interrelationships among the different types of errors in surveys. The major error sources discussed are those we have mentioned in the text: those due to nonobservation (coverage, nonresponse, and sampling) and those due to observation (interviewer, questions, respondent, and mode of data collection). Designing a survey is seen as a series of trade-offs or compromises among the varying error sources that are constrained by cost considerations. With a fixed budget for conducting a survey, any given source of error—such as insufficient training of interviewers—can be reduced only by cutting back resources for some other area—such as the size of the sample that can be interviewed—and that, of course, increases the likelihood of sampling error. With unlimited resources for conducting a survey, cost considerations would not be important. But, as Groves points out, resources are always limited. The important question is how to maximize survey quality given the resources available. This book will help guide the way.

Moore, D. W. (1992). *The super pollsters: How they measure and manipulate public opinion in America*. New York: Four Walls Eight Windows.

David Moore is a professor of political science at the University of New Hampshire. His book provides a very readable overview of the history of political polls in America. But it is more than just a historical overview of the use of polls by politicians. Moore traces the gradual evolution and improvement of the polling process itself. Along the way, he discusses the infamously incorrect *Literary Digest* poll of 1936, in which biased sampling appears to have been the culprit, and the equally wrong "Dewey Defeats Truman" headlines of 1948, in which poor timing of the last preelection polls may have caused the error. His final chapter provides a cautionary methodological tale about question wording, a tale that begins with George Gallup's invention of the "split-ballot" technique in 1939. The story of the rise and increasingly widespread use of polls is, indeed, an interesting one. Although there is reason to believe that he is somewhat biased about it, Moore claims that it may be "the most important social science development in the 20th century" (p. *ix*).

Tufte, E. R. (1983). *The visual display of quantitative information*. Cheshire, CT: Graphics Press.

Data graphics are visual displays of measured quantities, including bar graphs, pie charts, distribution maps, and a host of different types of pictures and drawings. Newspapers and magazines often use graphics to display at least the main results of surveys and other types of research. But, as Tufte eloquently demonstrates with examples selected from a variety of sources, graphics often lie. Unless carefully drawn, they distort the data—usually by exaggerating apparent change, or apparent differences. Tufte proposes a series of principles that, if adhered to, would greatly enhance graphical integrity. The first seems so basic that it is difficult to argue with, yet it appears to be routinely violated: The representation of numbers, as physically measured on the surface of the graphic itself, should be directly proportional to the numerical quantities represented. The book is profusely illustrated and a delight to read. Its true value is that it will teach you how to view visual displays of data with a critical eye.

Turner, C. F., and Martin, E. (Eds.) (1984). *Surveying subjective phenomena* (Vols. 1 and 2). New York: Russell Sage.

In the late 1970s a number of events occurred that raised questions about the reliability and validity of survey data, especially data concerning attitudes, beliefs, and opinions. For example, it had become apparent to those conducting and using survey data that there was a decline in the willingness of people to take part in surveys. There were also several instances of apparently similar surveys conducted at approximately the same time producing very discrepant results. These and related concerns prompted a group of prominent survey researchers to convene a panel for the express purposes of (1) improving the practice of survey research and (2) understanding the processes that produce errors in survey data. The panel's work, which extended over several years in the early 1980s, resulted in these two rather weighty tomes. The volumes cover everything you ever wanted to know about survey research—from the role of the respondent to why surveys disagree to how public understanding of surveys can be improved. They are valuable, well-documented source books, containing clear presentations of all the major issues.

7

Quasi-Experiments and Field Experiments

To many people, the notion of experimentation implies activity and excitement. To experiment is to be alive, to try new things, to change something, to grab the world—or, at least, your corner of it—and shake it in order to see what will happen. The world is constantly changing. New laws are passed, new products are marketed, new programs are introduced, new drugs and medical procedures are made available. Modern civilization seems at times to overwhelm us with change, but it is unclear how much of that change is real progress. Progress, of course, is a wonderful thing. But change and progress are not always identical, and it behooves us to be able to distinguish the two.

Consider an example. In 1986 the city of Detroit was experiencing a dramatic upswing in the number of homicides committed. As a result, late in the year the Detroit City Council passed a law imposing a mandatory jail sentence for anyone convicted of carrying a concealed firearm without a permit (O'Carroll et al., 1991). The new law received extensive media coverage in the weeks following its enactment, and it went into effect on January 10, 1987. The intent of the law was to preserve "the public peace, health, safety, and welfare of the people." But, as you can see in Figure 1A, homicides by firearms in Detroit generally continued on the upswing.

Think about that for a moment. Would you be willing to conclude that passing the law was a futile gesture, a waste of time? That would be a little hasty at this point. You need more information before you can decide. What about other homicides—that is, those not committed with a gun? Maybe they were rising at an even faster rate in 1987. And would you really expect the threat of a mandatory sentence for carrying a concealed weapon to affect all homicides by firearms equally? As O'Carroll et al. point out, the law did not say anything about possession of firearms in the home. Therefore, it probably should have had its effect—if any—on murders committed in public places and little or no effect on those committed indoors. As Figure 1B shows, that indeed appears to be the case. In the months following the beginning of enforcement of the law, the number of murders committed indoors continued to soar, while the number of murders committed outdoors did not. You can probably think of some more information we would need before we could decide whether the Detroit City Council's quasi-experiment was really a success or not. That, by the way, is what

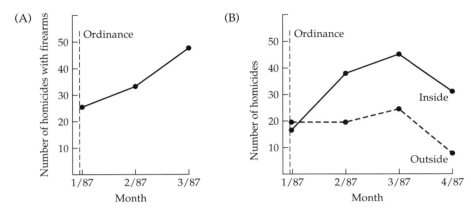

1 Homicides in Detroit following the passage of an ordinance imposing a mandatory jail sentence for anyone convicted of unlawfully carrying a concealed firearm. (From O'Carroll et al., 1991.)

the passing of the ordinance was—a quasi-experiment—although the City Council probably did not know it. The Council had all the elements necessary for a quasi-experiment: a change in the existing state of affairs (the ordinance against carrying concealed weapons), an outcome measure by which to evaluate the effectiveness of the change (the number of homicides by firearms in 1987), and a number of comparisons that they could have made to help them decide whether the new law really had any effect on the murder rate.

Actually, a **quasi-experiment** can take several different forms. It can involve any of a number of situations in which some people are exposed to an event or intervention and others are not, and in which you can assess what happens after the intervention, but in which you are not able to assign people randomly to the intervention and nonintervention groups. A **field experiment** may also take a variety of forms. Again, there must be at least two groups, one exposed to the intervention or manipulation and one not, and you must be able to assess what happens after the intervention. But in a field experiment, as opposed to a quasi-experiment, you are able to control—usually by random assignment—who is exposed to the intervention and who is not. A field experiment differs from a laboratory experiment, which we shall discuss in the next chapter, only in its setting. It is carried out in the "field," that is, away from the laboratory. What quasi-experiments and field experiments have in common is that their "real-world" settings give rise to many of the same problems.

The major purpose of this chapter is to alert you to the kinds of comparisons you need to make and the kinds of questions you need to ask yourself whenever you are trying to determine the results of a given change in the existing state of affairs. Whether it is you, the City Council, or the brute force of nature that introduces the change, the questions are the same.

Interventions and Naturally Occurring Changes

At first blush, the task sounds simple. If you have reason to believe that a change in the existing state of affairs will be followed by certain consequences, then after the change has occurred, you look to see whether those consequences are present or absent. The problem is that in many situations there are likely to be a number of **plausible alternative explanations** for the consequences that you are interested in. The apparent consequences of planned interventions and naturally occurring changes often can be attributed to a variety of more or less plausible causes other than the intervention or change in question. That means your task is not just to look and see whether the anticipated consequences are present, but to think of ways—preferably, ahead of time—of eliminating all of those additional plausible explanations for those consequences. This thinking of ways to eliminate plausible alternative hypotheses is what is meant by **research design.**

The task can be quite tricky because most interventions and naturally occurring changes are relatively complex phenomena. For example, on March 24, 1989, the supertanker *Exxon Valdez* ripped a hole in its hull on some underwater rocks in Prince William Sound, Alaska. The millions of gallons of oil that flowed out into the sound created an environmental disaster, one that directly affected residents of a number of nearby communities. A group of alert investigators from southern California thought that the spill might be an excellent opportunity to study naturally occurring reactions to such disasters. Thus, some months following the spill, Palinkas et al. (1992) conducted interviews with hundreds of residents in the region directly exposed to the oil spill. They asked questions about how lives had been affected by the spill and cleanup operations, how family relationships had been affected, what sorts of psychological difficulties had occurred, and, generally, tried to assess how people were coping with the aftermath of the mess. Surprisingly, they found that different groups of people were reacting in quite different ways. Compared with residents of Euro-American background, Native Alaskans appeared to have been much more directly affected by the spill. They were more likely to have taken part in the cleanup and to have had areas where they hunted and fished damaged by the spill. They were also more likely to report symptoms of depression and disruptions in their social relations following the spill. The point here is that interventions and naturally occurring changes are often complex and may interact with components of the preexisting situation in peculiar ways. You need to develop a thorough knowledge of both the change itself and the situation into which the change is introduced (see Box 1). You will recall from Chapter 2 that developing intimate familiarity with the situation is a crucial component of participant observation. It is also critical for well-conducted quasi-experiments.

Nonequivalent Groups

There is another circumstance that makes the task of understanding the effects produced by interventions and naturally occurring changes difficult: They usually happen only once, and to one group. Quite often, because of the cost or logistics involved, even planned interventions cannot be duplicated—much less oil spills. For example, Marvell (1989) points out that between 1965 and 1985, 38 states passed no-fault divorce laws. For the purposes

---

Box 1

Things Are Different in the Field

It is important to remember that the results of research are determined, at least partially, by the setting in which the research is conducted. For example, an examination of the results of laboratory studies of attitude change leaves the clear impression that attitudes are easily changeable. Subjects exposed to brief persuasive communications often show massive shifts in attitudes, sometimes changing completely from one side of an issue to the other (e.g., Eagly and Chaiken, 1993). On the other hand, field experiments on the effectiveness of mass media leave one with the impression that attitude change is genuinely rare. The millions of dollars spent in prolonged election campaigns, for example, often appear to change the attitudes of only a very small percentage of the voters.

Why the difference? In a classic analysis, Hovland (1959) suggested a number of variables that may account for it. First, there is a difference in *discrepancy*. In laboratory studies of attitude change, subjects are usually exposed to communications arguing for positions quite different from their own. In field settings, however, a great deal of self-selection takes place. That is, those people who show up to hear candidate X are likely to agree already with most of what he or she has to say. Hence, not much change is possible. A second difference concerns the *nature of the issues*. Laboratory studies of attitude change quite frequently use noninvolving issues, issues of no great import. In contrast, field research is typically concerned with socially and politically significant issues—issues deeply rooted in the respondents' worldviews, lifestyles, and reference groups. A third difference is the *timing of measurement*. In laboratory research, measurements of attitude are often made within minutes after exposure to the persuasive communication. In field research, attitude assessment may not take place for days, or even weeks, following exposure to the communications or events intended to change attitudes.

There are other differences between the two settings, but the point here is simply that the circumstances into which you introduce an intervention or treatment can make a tremendous difference in its apparent effectiveness. Another way of saying this is that psychologically important variables may vary across situations. That is why it pays to develop a thorough understanding of the situation into which you plan to introduce the manipulation of interest.

---

of evaluating the effects of those laws on divorce rates, it would have been convenient if they could have been made to apply only to randomly selected samples of married couples living in each state. Then one could compare the subsequent divorce rate among those couples with the rate among couples in another randomly selected sample to whom the law did not apply. Such legal arrangements, of course, are impossible. The laws had to apply to everybody, or they would have been laughed out of court. As you will see in Chapter 8, when you can randomly assign subjects to treatment and no-treatment groups, it solves a lot of problems.

If all you can do is make some observations or measurements after an intervention or change has occurred, you will have what is referred to as a **one-shot case study.** For the purpose of inferring whether or not an intervention made a difference, the one-shot case study is useless. To help you see why that is so, a couple of symbols will be useful. Following Donald Campbell and his colleagues (Campbell and Stanley, 1966; Cook and Campbell, 1979), let X stand for an intervention (or change, or treatment, or manipulation) of some sort and O stand for the observation (or assessment) of effects. Then, the one-shot case study looks like this:

$$\underrightarrow{X \qquad O}$$
(Time)

The reason it is useless for the purpose of inferring whether or not the intervention has an effect is that you have nothing to compare the O to.

The no-fault divorce law in the state of Utah became effective in April 1987. Suppose someone had done a one-shot case study of the effects of the Utah no-fault divorce law. What that researcher would have been able to say would have been something like: "In April 1987 the Utah no-fault divorce law became effective, and in July 1987 there were 349 divorces in Utah." You see the problem. For all you know, there might have been 349 divorces in Utah every month for the last century. The one-shot case study gives you no explicit data with which you can compare your observations. When people conduct one-shot case studies, there is often a comparison implicit in their expectations about what their observations would have been if X had not occurred, but that is not acceptable. Their expectations may be cockeyed. You need data! Do those 349 divorces per month represent an increase or a decrease? (We'll return to the no-fault divorce laws later; Marvell actually did have a better plan for determining their effects.)

Let's consider some of the things you would have to add to the one-shot case study to make it into a more respectable design for the purpose of inferring cause-and-effect relationships. What do we have to start with? A change has occurred, and we have some observations made after the change. The simplest step toward building a better design would be to secure observations both before and after the change. That seems to presume that the change is planned, but it does not have to be. It depends on what you select as your indicator(s) of the effects of the change. There are archives full of records that might contain information about conditions prior to the change. In any event, if you can obtain some information about the state of affairs prior to the change, the one-shot case study becomes the **one-group pretest-posttest design** and looks like this:

$$\underrightarrow{O \qquad X \qquad O}$$
(Time)

That is an improvement, but not much of one. To understand why, think about that Utah no-fault divorce law again. It became effective in April 1987 (the X above). Assume that in March 1987 there were 325 divorces in Utah (the first O). Then in July 1987 there were 349 (the second O). Would you be willing to conclude that the divorce law had had an effect? You should not be, because the number of divorces in Utah might have been increasing at a steady rate of six per month for a long time. That would mean that between March 1987 and July 1987 there would have been an increase of 24 divorces regardless of any new law: 331 in April, 337 in May, 343 in June, and 349 in July. For this and other reasons, it would be foolish to attribute the changes in the number of divorces to the no-fault divorce law.

Try another improvement. The one-shot case study lacks a basis for comparison; if you could find another group that was not exposed to the intervention (or treatment, or oil spill), that would provide one. Then the design could be diagrammed like this:

$$
\begin{array}{lcc}
\text{Group 1} & \text{X} & \text{O} \\
\text{Group 2} & & \text{O} \\
\hline
& \text{(Time)}
\end{array}
$$

That is certainly an improvement. The problem, of course, is that Groups 1 and 2 may be **nonequivalent groups.** If they turn out to differ at the time of observation, there will still be the nagging suspicion that they may have differed before Group 1 was exposed to the intervention. If they did, then it is very difficult to argue that exposure to X is what produced the difference at the time your observations, the O's, were made. Of course, the more evidence you can summon to support the argument that Groups 1 and 2 were indeed equivalent before the occurrence of X, the stronger this design will be for discovering whether or not X has made a difference for Group 1. This design has two names. Campbell and Stanley (1966) referred to it as the **static group comparison.** Cook and Campbell (1979) preferred the more descriptive **posttest-only design with nonequivalent groups.**

Many naturally occurring changes are, of course, unanticipated. The earthquake that shook San Francisco on October 17, 1989, was certainly not planned. With such events, the posttest-only design with nonequivalent groups may be able to give you useful information about the consequences of the change. For example, in the weeks immediately following that San Francisco earthquake, Wood et al. (1992) examined the frequency and content of nightmares among college students in the Bay Area. They used as a comparison group students attending college in Tucson, Arizona—that is, students who were in college at the same time as the Bay Area students, but who had not experienced the earthquake. Remember, the key to the usefulness of the static group comparison design is your ability to convince yourself (and others) that the two groups were similar prior to the intervention. Are students attending college in Tucson really similar to those in San Francisco? To try to answer that question, it was necessary for Wood et al. to collect a good deal of demographic information about the students in the two groups.

With planned interventions, there is a better way. If you know when and to whom an intervention is going to occur, you can document the standing of the two groups on the measures of interest before its occurrence. Then, after one of the groups has been exposed to the intervention, you observe both groups a second time. If you do all this, the design you will be using is referred to as the **untreated control group design with pretest and posttest.** It is diagrammed below:

$$
\begin{array}{llll}
\text{Group 1} & O & X & O \\
\text{Group 2} & O & & O
\end{array}
$$

According to Cook and Campbell (1979), this may be the most frequently used research design in the social sciences. As an example of a situation in which it might be employed, suppose you were interested in the effect of handing out samples of food—say, pizza—on sales of that food in supermarkets. You might record pizza sales in two different supermarkets for a week, hand out free samples in one of them for a second week, and then record sales in both supermarkets again for the third week. If sales were up during the third week in the supermarket in which you had handed out pizza, but not in the other one, you might be able to conclude that free samples do enhance sales.

But then again, you might not. Now that you have been introduced to a few quasi-experimental designs, let us focus a little more closely on some of their shortcomings. Earlier, it was mentioned that the major purpose of this chapter is to acquaint you with the sorts of questions you should ask yourself when trying to determine the results of a given change or manipulation. That is the topic we must discuss before describing any additional designs. As you will see, there are a few things you would need to worry about before you could conclude that handing out pizza slices enhances sales. The mere fact that sales went up in the store in which you did hand out pizza, but not in the other one, is not enough (see Box 2).

Problems in Making Causal Inferences

Mark Twain once said that we should be careful to get out of an experience only the wisdom that is in it. He had probably never heard the phrase **internal validity,** but he seemed to have a feel for what it means. Simply stated, the question of internal validity is the question of whether an intervention or change does, indeed, make a difference (Figure 2). Did handing out those hot slices of pizza really cause pizza sales to increase in store A—or was it the fact that a nearby pizzeria went out of business that third week? Did that concealed weapons ordinance in Detroit really make a difference in the homicide rate—or was it simply followed by normal seasonal fluctuations in the number of murders?

The concept of internal validity was formulated by Donald Campbell almost 40 years ago, in 1957, and has been extensively developed by Campbell and his colleagues (Campbell and Stanley, 1966; Cook and Campbell, 1979; Campbell, 1986). They have made explicit a number of general **threats to internal validity,** possible contaminating factors you must be able to rule out before concluding that the intervention or change of interest to you really made a difference. There are a baker's dozen of these threats to internal validity, and they are defined and briefly illustrated below. Following the defi-

---

Box 2

Getting the Results You Expect Is Not Enough

When a field experiment turns out as you anticipate it will, you should be especially careful in your attempts to evaluate alternative explanations. There is a real danger that because the intervention seemed to work, you will be less than thorough in your efforts to think up plausible alternative hypotheses that could predict the same result.

Eysenck (1965) has reported an interesting historical example that illustrates the potential for being misled about a causal explanation when two hypotheses predict the same result. It concerns the famous Broad Street pump in London, England. The pump was one of the main water sources for an area of London that was beset by an epidemic of cholera. An epidemiological study by Snow found that, for the most part, members of households whose water supply was not obtained at the Broad Street pump did not get cholera. Thus, Snow arrived at the hypothesis that cholera was being transmitted via polluted water from the Broad Street pump. He removed the handle from the pump so that it could not be used, and ended the cholera epidemic. However, a man named Farr also had conducted a series of studies that led him to a different conclusion. He had become convinced that the most important factor in the transmission of cholera was elevation above sea level. Thus, his recommendation was that people be moved from the low-lying areas of the city, which included the region served by the Broad Street pump, to higher inland regions. The point is that if Farr's suggestion had been followed and the population of London had been evacuated to the higher inland districts, the cholera epidemic would have ended—just as it ended when the handle was removed from the Broad Street pump. If the people were out of reach of the Broad Street pump, they would no longer have been obtaining their water there. Thus, the success of an intervention is not necessarily evidence for the hypothesis on which the intervention was based. You have to be able to rule out any and all plausible alternatives first.

---

nitions, we shall see how some of the quasi-experimental designs introduced in the last section measure up. There is a related concept, called *external validity*, which will be discussed in the following chapter.

The first threat to internal validity is **history**—all the events going on in the world at the time of your study, other than your intervention, that might reasonably account for the outcome of interest. If any of those events could plausibly have produced the same change that you were hoping your intervention would, you are in trouble. If there really was a nearby pizza place that closed down during the same week you were trying to assess the effect of giving free samples of pizza at the supermarket, that would provide a plausible explanation for the rise in pizza sales at the supermarket.

The second threat to internal validity is **maturation**. People are constantly changing. They get older, wiser, heavier, all on their own—that is, without regard to your research. If the effect you are looking for could plausibly be attributed to normal maturation processes, no one is going to believe that it was produced by your intervention. Maturation can be a genuine problem if your research is in an educational setting, or involves children, or both. For example, if you were interested in whether taking a year of Latin—yes, some of us actu-

"Lately I've been very happy, but I don't know if it's me or vitamins."

2 Internal validity is basically an attributional issue: Has the intervention (treatment) made a difference, or did something else cause the change? (Cartoon © *The New Yorker*.)

ally did that—improves vocabulary, you could not simply give a vocabulary test to students before and after their year of Latin classes. Chances are their vocabularies would increase in size over the year even without the Latin classes.

The third and fourth threats to internal validity are referred to as **testing** and **instrumentation**. Testing is the problem posed by the possibility that if you give the same test to people on more than one occasion, their responses the second and third time may be influenced by the mere fact of having taken the test before. (This is one reason why so many eleventh-graders take the Practice Scholastic Aptitude Test.) People who have taken a test before may remember their previous answers, for example, or they may consciously try to change their answers. Thus, testing refers to the possibility of a change due to repeated test-taking or measurement. In contrast, instrumentation refers to the possibility of a change in the tests or observations themselves. For example, suppose that as part of your research you were having observers code classroom interactions between teachers and students. After a couple of weeks, the observers might become bored and begin missing things because of inattention. Thus, the results would look as if the teachers were interacting less with the students as the semester progressed, but, in fact, it would have been the observers who had changed. They were simply missing more interactions as the semester dragged on.

Statistical regression is the fifth threat to internal validity. It stems from the fact that people tend to vary somewhat in their performance from time to time. Thus, if you score really well on a test, you may not do so well the next time. Or, if you really blow it, chances are you will do a little better next time. What this means for research is that you have to be very careful when you select people for participation in the research because they had either a very high or a very low score on some measure. For example, suppose you select people for a compensatory reading program because they did extremely poorly on a test of reading comprehension. You then administer the program and retest them. If they do better the second time, at least part of the improvement may be due to statistical regression, and you will have to be able to rule that out before skeptics will believe your program is effective.

The sixth and seventh threats to internal validity are **selection** and **mortality**. As noted earlier, many interventions and changes can be administered to—or happen to—only one group. That means the group you use as a comparison group may not be equivalent. Selection simply refers to this notion that people in different groups are, indeed, often different. In many instances people select themselves into certain groups. Those who take Latin in high school, for example, are different from those who take shop. They have different interests and career plans, and hence could not be considered equivalent groups for most research purposes. Mortality refers to another kind of self-selection: the fact that some people may drop out of a group during the course of your research. (Attrition is actually a better word for this, because the respondents do not usually die off.) If that happens, it will be more difficult to decide at the end whether the intervention made a difference. It could be that any difference between the pretest and posttest observations is just due to the fact that some people dropped out and left a biased sample of the original group.

The eighth threat to internal validity is actually a cluster of threats—all the things that can produce an **interaction with selection**: history, testing, maturation, and instrumentation. For example, suppose you administered an educational program to a group of 11-year-old girls and used as a comparison group 11-year-old boys. At the pretest, the two groups were equivalent in terms of their scores on standardized tests and achievement, but at the posttest, a year later, the girls did significantly better than the boys. Would you be willing to conclude that the educational program had made the difference? That would be questionable, because at the 11–12-year-old stage, girls and boys are maturing at different rates, and girls are, generally, doing better in school at that age than are boys. Not only is there the possibility of a selection-maturation interaction in this case, but there is also the possibility of a selection-history interaction. Different things are happening to 11-year-old girls and 11-year-old boys outside of the classroom; hence, you could not necessarily attribute the girls' greater achievement at age 12 solely to your educational program. As for the possibility of a selection-testing interaction, you might anticipate that because the girls in your study are really doing better in school and maturing at a faster rate than boys, they would also benefit more from taking the same test twice—that they would be more likely to have developed good test-taking habits and, possibly, would be more likely to remember their answers from the previous test. Again, this experience will make them look better than the boys on the posttest, but it will not be due to your educational program. Selection-instrumentation interactions can also be a problem if differential assessments of your groups are due to the nature of the measuring instruments you use. Suppose you were using classroom observers to assess the quality of answers given in class by the girls and by the boys. The observers might quickly come to expect that the girls generally give better answers. Once that expectation develops, the observers are no longer unbiased. From then on, they may very well see what they expect to see (Jones, 1977).

The ninth threat to internal validity is **ambiguity about the direction of causality**. As you no doubt recall from Chapter 1, at a minimum, a cause always has to precede an effect. In quasi-experiments there is usually a clear temporal relationship between the intervention, or change, of interest and the assessment of its consequences. So, ambiguity about the direction of causality is usually not a problem in quasi-experimentation because the intervention obviously precedes the observation of its effects. If your intervention initiates a cycle involving feedback (for example, warm instructor, pleased students, even warmer instructor, even happier students) and you do not make your observations until sometime later, it could be a problem. However, as Cordray (1986) has pointed out, even if such feedback is not a problem, you will still need a credible rationale linking your intervention and its consequences. And, as you also recall from Chapter 1, you have to be able to rule out all other plausible explanations for the outcome. Ambiguity about the direction of causality is most likely to be a problem in cross-sectional survey research in which all the variables of interest are assessed at the same time by self-report.

The tenth and eleventh threats to internal validity are closely related: **diffusion or imitation of treatments** and **compensatory equalization of treatments**. Communication among subjects in the various groups can cause problems for your research in several ways. If you have set up a quasi-experimental design in which one of the groups gets to do something fun, there is a danger that members of the groups not exposed to that intervention will hear about it and do it on their own. For example, if you were trying to assess different weight-loss plans and started one group of overweight volunteers on a regimen of daily aerobic dancing and another group on a bland diet, some members of the latter group may imitate the former group by taking up aerobics, which is much more fun than dieting. Similarly, compensatory equalization of treatments may occur if one or more of the treatments appear to be better than the others. If people with the power to do something about it become aware of this, they may feel obligated to do something for those not receiving the better treatment.

The final two threats to internal validity are also closely related: **compensatory rivalry** and **resentful demoralization** on the part of those who find out they are receiving less desirable treatments. In the former, those who find out they are receiving less desirable treatments may try harder just to show they can do it on their own, that is, without the advantage of your treatment, whatever *it* may be. This, of course, will spuriously reduce the differences between the groups at posttest time. In the case of resentful demoralization, those receiving the less desirable treatment may simply quit trying altogether, out of spite. This too may spuriously increase the differences between the groups at posttest time. In either case, you will not be able to get an accurate assessment of just how much difference your treatments have made.

These threats to internal validity are summarized in Table 1. It is a good idea to commit them to memory and mentally check them off each time you think you have a foolproof design. They are all potential alternative explanations that can be troublesome whenever you are trying to determine whether the intervention or treatment of interest to you really made a difference. If the apparent effect of the intervention can plausibly be attributed to one or more of the threats to internal validity, you will not be able to tell whether or not the intervention really did anything. That can be very frustrating, especially if you have invested a lot of time, effort, and, possibly, money—not to mention ego—in the research. Therefore, what you want to do is avoid getting yourself into that state of attributional ambiguity—of not knowing whether it was the treatment, or selection, or maturation, or something else, that made the difference—in the first place. To accomplish that goal, you must try to anticipate which threats to internal validity are likely to be operating in the circumstances under which you will be doing the research. You must then design the research, as best you can, to obtain the evidence necessary to rule out the influence of those threats to internal validity.

Ruling Out Alternative Explanations by Design

Remember the one-shot case study? It should be clearer by now why it is scientifically useless. Not only does it provide you with no explicit basis for comparison, it also provides no means of controlling for any of the relevant threats to internal validity. Cook and Campbell (1979) have noted that there are several different ways in which the word *control* is used, so let me be clear about exactly what is meant here. *Control* is sometimes used to refer to the practice of holding constant all extraneous factors in the situation in which the research is conducted. That is often feasible in laboratory research, as you will see in Chapter 8. Unfortunately, it is usually not feasible in quasi-experiments and field experiments. But the fact that it is impossible to hold extraneous factors constant does not mean you can ignore them, or just wish them away. They may crop up in one or more of the threats to internal validity—for example, as a part of history.

Because you cannot hold extraneous factors constant, you have to find a way to demonstrate that they did not have a determining influence on the observations of interest to you. That usually means adding another condition or two to your design—for example, another group of people who experi-

Table 1   Thirteen Threats to Internal Validity

THREAT	DESCRIPTION
History	Events other than the intervention that occur during the course of the research
Maturation	Changes in respondents that may occur during the research, such as growing older and (one hopes) wiser
Testing	The effect of repeated testing on subjects' performance levels
Instrumentation	Changes in the measuring instruments over time
Statistical regression	The likelihood that if respondents are selected on the basis of extreme scores on a pretest, their scores will be less extreme on a posttest, regardless of the intervention
Selection	The possibility that the respondents in different conditions differ at the outset of the study
Mortality	The possibility that if subjects drop out of some conditions, you may end up with different kinds of people in different conditions, depending on why the dropouts occurred
Interactions with selection	The interactions of maturation, history, testing, and instrumentation with selection
Ambiguity about causality	The possibility that it will be unclear whether your intervention produced the effect of interest or vice versa.
Diffusion or imitation of treatments	The possibility that subjects in one research condition will find out that those in another condition are getting a more desirable treatment and will find a way to get that desirable treatment for themselves outside of the research setting
Compensatory equalization of treatments	The possibility that someone with the power to intervene will find out that subjects in one research condition are being denied a beneficial treatment that other subjects are receiving and will find a way to get the beneficial treatment for those subjects
Compensatory rivalry	The possibility that subjects in one research condition will find out that those in another condition are getting a more desirable treatment and will attempt to demonstrate that they can do better even without that treatment
Resentful demoralization	The possibility that subjects in one research condition will find out that those in another condition are getting a more desirable treatment and will, on the other hand, just get annoyed and quit working at their normal level

Source: Cook and Campbell, 1979.

ence the same extraneous events, but not the intervention. These other groups, or conditions, are referred to, of course, as control groups. Thus, if you add a control group to the one-shot case study, it becomes

Group 1   X   O
Group 2   O

which is the posttest-only design with nonequivalent groups. With this design, if you obtain a difference between the two groups at the time of your observations, you *may* be able to rule out history, testing, and instrumentation as having produced that difference. You may—if both groups experienced the same historical events and were tested with the same instruments at the same time. But do not forget that you have nonequivalent groups, so selection might still be a threat to internal validity. The point here is that in quasi-experiments and field experiments, the notion of control has to do with particular threats to internal validity and the need to eliminate those threats by the way you design your study and carry it out. The results of this approach to control are often referred to as **tailored** or **patched-up designs** (e.g., Trochim, 1986). In such designs, features are added to control specific factors that you think might be operating in the situation in which the research is to be carried out.

But how, exactly, do you go about it? It is very difficult to give specific advice in answer to that question. So much depends on the intervention, or change, of interest to you, on what you anticipate will be the effect of the intervention, on the situation into which the intervention is introduced, on the people who will be affected by the intervention, and so on. As Trochim (1986) put it, you cannot rely on "prefabricated designs." Rather, you must piece together your own design by focusing on the logic of what each added condition or additional item of information will tell you. However, there are a couple of general guidelines that may help you. Ellsworth (1977) has suggested that one way to proceed is to imagine the intervention producing exactly the effect you hypothesize that it will. Then ask yourself this question: What are the most likely alternative explanations that people could offer for that effect if I told them about it? Make a list of those explanations, and then figure out what information you will need to counter each item on the list. You may need an extra condition or two to get some of the information. In other cases, the solution may be as simple as asking the participants in the study a few additional questions. Marvell (1989), for example, in his study of no-fault divorce laws, decided that he needed long-term data on the number of divorces in each state. He used that data to rule out the alternative hypothesis that the increase in divorces from the months immediately before to the months immediately after the enactment of each law was no larger than the typical month-to-month increase. Similarly, in their study of that Detroit ordinance requiring a mandatory jail sentence for carrying a concealed firearm, O'Carroll et al. (1991) had to separate homicides committed indoors—which they did not anticipate would be affected by the law—from homicides committed outdoors.

Ellsworth (1977) has also pointed out that if you are able to choose the setting for your study—the situation into which the intervention is introduced—the availability of appropriate control groups should be one of the major considerations in your choice. As she put it:

> It is my hunch that many investigators devote a great deal of effort and creativity to finding a setting or population that provides a good embodiment of the treatment variable and that they then cast about hurriedly at the last minute for some sort of control group. The control group is exactly as important as the treatment group in research, and in fact it is impossible to separate the value of one from the value of the other.

She cautioned that quasi-experimental designs require particular attention to the question of appropriate control groups because there will usually be a number of ways in which the control and treatment groups are not equivalent, and each of those differences may pose a threat to internal validity.

Let's work through an example illustrating this notion of patching together the information and control groups needed in a particular setting. Imagine that you are employed in a college of medicine and are a member of the curriculum committee. One of the problems facing the committee is how to handle a stream of student complaints that too much material is being covered in lectures in the physiology course. (Sound familiar?) Because of the tremendous amount of material to be learned in physiology, the faculty (naturally) say they cannot cut down on what is presented. Thus, if any change is to be made, it must somehow be in the area of increasing what the students absorb from the lectures. It occurs to you that one possibility is to have the audiovisual department record the physiology lectures, make multiple copies of the cassettes, and allow students to check out those cassettes so that they can listen to the lectures again—and again and again and again, if necessary—until every last detail has found a home in their heads.

The committee is quite willing to try out your suggestion, but the dean says that if she is going to be asked to find the money to pay for all those cassettes, she wants some evidence that the scheme is either useful or not useful. (Deans tend to be a little conservative about anything concerning money.) So, having taken a course in research design some years ago, you decide that a pretest-posttest design with a control group is needed. In case it has slipped your mind, this is the design:

Group 1	O	X	O
Group 2	O		O

Your idea is that this year's first-year medical students will serve as Group 1—the complaints were from last year's class, and the committee is meeting in late August, before the semester begins. Someone then suggests that next year's class could serve as Group 2, but that is rejected by the committee because if the taping appeared to be beneficial for students, they would want to continue it.

219

After all, you want all those future doctors to know as much as is humanly possible. That means you will have to go back and use last year's class as Group 2.

The next problem is how to establish that this year's class and last year's class are really equivalent. Everybody is always talking about raising standards, and if the admissions committee was a little tougher in admitting students to this year's class, that could present a problem. It might be that what last year's students thought was a real crusher of a course, this year's students will take in stride. Fortunately for you, there is a standardized test that all applicants to medical school have to take. It is called the MCAT (or Medical College Admissions Test). There are national norms available for the MCAT, and it is a good measure of the general scientific knowledge of college seniors. Therefore, you decide to use the average MCAT scores of the two classes as the pretest. If the average MCAT scores turn out to be about the same for the two classes, you will be willing to assume that on entering their first year of medical school, the students in the two classes were about the same in terms of academic preparation and such relevant skills as study habits. That is probably a safe assumption. The data for the pretest are already available: They are in the files with the applications that every student in this year's and last year's classes submitted. All that is going to be required is to go through the files and extract the numbers—a version of archival research that you should remember well from Chapter 4.

What next? Probably the next decision is what to use for the posttest. You might use grades in the physiology course. Grades, however, often reflect things other than knowledge, and besides, the physiology faculty may just throw their tests together the day before the exam—that is, the tests may not be particularly well constructed. However, at the end of their second year, all medical students are required to take an exam referred to as National Boards, Part One, which tests their knowledge of the basic sciences relevant to medicine: biochemistry, anatomy, behavioral science, pharmacology, pathology, and, yes, physiology. So you decide to use the performance of the two classes on the first part of the National Boards as the posttest. This means, of course, that you are going to have to wait 2 years before the data for this year's entering class will be in. One other thing: So that the pretest and posttest will be directly comparable, you are going to have to convert the average scores of the classes on each to a percentage of the maximum possible score.

Pretend that everything goes according to plan.* There are no missing MCAT scores in the files, the dean agrees to foot the bill for the tapes and the taping, no students drop out of either class, the college librarians are willing to dispense and collect the tapes, and everybody takes the National Boards on schedule. Two years later, you eagerly tabulate the results, and they look like those shown in Figure 3A. Elated, you take this graph to the dean and proudly announce that your idea was a success. She takes one look at the graph and

---

*You realize, of course, that this is ridiculous. Several of Murphy's laws apply here, including: "Everything takes longer than expected" and "Nothing goes according to plan."

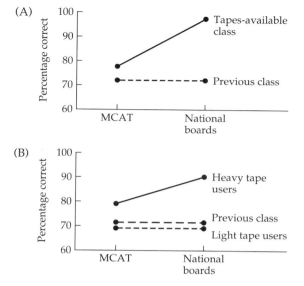

3 Two hypothetical outcomes for the quasi-experiment in which one class of medical students is provided with tape recordings of lectures. (A) Members of the class with access to the tapes appear to do better on their National Boards than members of the preceding class, which did not have the tapes available. (B) A further analysis, however, shows that only those students who actually use the tapes do better.

says, "Don't be silly! So, the average performance of the two classes on the MCAT was about the same. How do you know that it was really the tapes that made a difference? Maybe the students for whom the tapes were available simply thought that the faculty members were more interested in them and concerned about their doing well, hence, they were inspired to put forth a little more effort. Haven't you ever heard of the Hawthorne effect? I suggest you try reading about it in the original, which, I believe, is Roethlisberger and Dickson (1939)." The dean, it appears, is no slouch (see Box 3).

Thoroughly chagrined, you go back to your office and ponder this for awhile. Then it occurs to you that the librarians, bless their souls, have records of who checked out the tapes and how often. If you could get those data, you could take the class for which the tapes were available and break it down into two groups: heavy and light tape users. After another day or two of digging around in the librarian's files, your design has become a little more complex. Now it looks like this:

	MCAT SCORE	TAPES	NATIONAL BOARDS
Heavy tape users	O	X	O
Light tape users	O	X	O
Previous class	O		O

When you graph the results, you find that tape use seems to make a difference, even though those who used the tapes the most had the highest scores on both the pretest and posttest (see Figure 3B).

Box 3

The Hawthorne Effect

Beginning in the 1920s, a series of studies that were destined to become quite famous were conducted at the Hawthorne Western Electric plant in Chicago. In what is perhaps the best known of the studies, a group of women whose job it was to assemble electrical relays for telephones was separated from other workers and placed in a special room. There the people conducting the research (Roethlisberger and Dickson, 1939) made a number of changes in their working conditions. For example, the workers in the Relay Assembly Test Room, as it was called, were given free lunches, rest pauses, and shortened work hours, and were allowed to participate in a small group incentive payment plan. In addition, there was a change in the nature of the supervision to which they were subjected. The new style of managerial discipline was unusually friendly and easygoing and was designed to get the workers to relax and be more open about the things that bothered them. The purpose behind this new managerial style was to allow the evaluation of changes in the work environment, such as changes in lighting, hours of work, and length of rest pauses, without contamination. It was thought that if supervisors were open and willing to listen, workers would be more honest and straightforward in reporting what they liked and did not like, and a better assessment could be made of the optimal working conditions.

It turned out, however, that the only thing that really seemed to have an effect was this new attitude on the part of the supervisors. Now they appeared to be interested in the workers, and in return, the workers seemed to work harder in response to the many physical changes that were introduced into the work setting. The **Hawthorne effect**, as it came to be known, refers to this serendipitous finding that workers, and, presumably, subjects in research, are very responsive to the mere fact that someone has taken an interest in them. In recent years some questions have been raised about the quality of the original research at the Hawthorne plant and whether or not a Hawthorne effect was really demonstrated there (Jones, 1992). But, as Adair, Sharpe, and Huynh (1989) have noted, it is possible to interpret the Hawthorne effect as a motivation to please—or to perform as expected—produced by subjects' knowledge of someone's having taking an interest in them. It can be a real problem in trying to evaluate the effects of an intervention or treatment, especially if subjects do figure out what is expected of them. Thus, you will need to be able to rule out the Hawthorne Effect before you can conclude that it was the specific nature of the intervention of interest that made a difference.

In pondering the graph, it occurs to you that the dean is still not going to be convinced that it was the tapes that made the difference. What she is going to say this time is something to the effect that you have identified an interaction between selection and maturation. (The dean once took a course in research design also.) "The good students were the ones who made use of the tapes. They were better prepared to start with—note their higher MCAT average—and they were maturing, academically, at a faster rate. So naturally they ended up with even higher scores on the National Board Exam. The tapes were a waste of money."

How can you counter that argument? Well, you will need to show that even though the heavy tape users may, in general, have been better students all along than the light tape users, the tapes produced an additional increment in performance for them. In order to demonstrate that, you will need some indicator of the relative academic standing of the groups *prior to* the time they took the MCAT. Your design will become what is referred to as a time series design.

Interrupted Time Series

Remember Marvell's study of the no-fault divorce laws? The design he actually employed was a version of what is referred to as an **interrupted time series**. It is an elegantly simple design and is very similar to the one-group pretest-posttest design described earlier. The difference is that in the interrupted time series, instead of one set of observations before the intervention and one set of observations after, you use multiple observations before the intervention and multiple observations afterward. It looks like this:

O O O O O O X O O O O O O

It is a vast improvement over the one-group pretest-posttest design, in which all you know is the size of the change, if any, from pretest to posttest, and you have nothing with which you can compare that change. In the interrupted time series design, you can tell whether the magnitude of the change from just before to just after the intervention is different from the magnitude of the changes between the other adjacent pairs of observations. You can also tell whether there is an overall trend in the data, that is, an increase or decrease over time. If the intervention really does have an effect, you can expect some sort of sharp change in that overall trend in the observations immediately following the intervention. For example, Mesch and Dalton (1992) examined data on thousands of workplace disputes at a large public utility company over a 6-year period. Halfway through this period, a change in the grievance procedure was introduced: A "fact-finding team" composed of one union and one management representative was instituted to investigate newly filed grievances. Following the change, Mesch and Dalton found that the grievance rate went up, but so did the percentage of compromise outcomes. In addition, the introduction of the fact-finding procedure resulted in grievances being resolved at a lower level, saving everybody time and money.

With the addition of an untreated control group, the interrupted time series design becomes considerably more informative. With such an addition, the design becomes:

Group 1 O O O O X O O O O
Group 2 O O O O   O O O O

Now you can see whether the trend in the data for Group 1 differs from the trend for Group 2. If the intervention has made a difference, there should be an abrupt discontinuity in the trend for Group 1 immediately following the intervention, but no such abrupt change for Group 2 at that particular time.

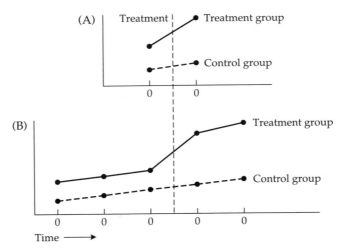

4 A pretest-posttest design does not rule out the possibility of an interaction between group selection and maturation. (A) It is possible that the treatment group in this hypothetical study had been improving at a faster rate than the control group even before the treatment was administered. (B) The interrupted time series design allows you to assess the improvement rates of the two groups prior to treatment. In this case, it appears that the two groups had been improving at similar rates before the treatment, but that the treatment increased the rate of improvement of the group exposed to it.

Note that this design may enable you to rule out the effects of history and instrumentation as threats to internal validity, whereas the simple one-group time series will not, because the two groups observed are presumably experiencing the same extraneous external events, and the observations being made are the same for both groups. This design also enables you to assess whether there is an interaction of selection and maturation, which the simple pretest-posttest with nonequivalent groups cannot do. To see what makes the difference, look at Figure 4. The point here is not for you to memorize which designs take care of which threats to internal validity. Rather, it is to show that if you understand the basic nature of the threats to internal validity, a little carefully applied logic and common sense will help you to piece together the best design possible under your particular circumstances.

For example, that study by Mesch and Dalton (1992) mentioned above actually involved an additional group in which the "fact-finding team" was not introduced. That group consisted of another utility company, in the same geographic region, whose employees were represented by the same labor union and whose grievances were handled by the same local union officers. In this comparison company, there was essentially no change over the entire 6-year period in the rate of grievances, the level at which they were resolved, or the proportion of compromise solutions. An additional feature of the situation investigated by Mesch and Dalton was that at the end of the fifth year, the fact-finding teams were discontinued in the company in which they had been introduced 2 years earlier. In other words, the real design consisted of 6 years of observations of an untreated control group and 6 years of observations on an experimental group in which the treatment was introduced at the end of the third year and withdrawn at the end of the fifth year. Now, if it was really the introduction of the fact-finding teams that produced the changes found by Mesch and Dalton during the fourth and fifth years, then with the removal of the fact-finding teams, those changes should disappear. And indeed they did. During the sixth year, the grievance rate and proportion of compromise solutions in the experimental company dropped, and the level at which grievances were settled rose. When a treatment appears to have an effect that goes away when the treatment is removed, confidence that it really is the treatment that is making the difference is enhanced somewhat. But note that this will not work for some types of interventions—that is, some interventions or treatments initiate self-sustaining changes, and when the treatment is removed, things will not go back to the way they were before.

Note that there is no particular reason why the number of observations before and after the treatment must be the same. They were not in the Mesch and Dalton (1992) study, for example. It simply looks better that way in a diagram. If your initial observations are simply meant to establish the comparability of the two groups, you might have a design that looks like this:

Group 1   O   X   O   O
Group 2   O   O   O

This is very similar to the design used by Baum, Fleming, and Singer (1982) to examine reactions to the decontamination procedures used following the nuclear reactor accident at Three Mile Island. Group 1 in this case consisted of residents of Three Mile Island. Group 2 consisted of residents of Frederick, Maryland, a town some distance away from the reactor. The treatment was the venting of radioactive gases from the contaminated building into the atmosphere, and the observations were a variety of performance, self-report, and biochemical measures taken before and after the venting took place.

There are other variations on the interrupted time series design that can enhance its value for establishing a cause-and-effect relationship between the treatment and what follows. One that is particularly useful is referred to (Cook and Campbell, 1979) as the **interrupted time series with switching replications**. The idea is that the intervention is introduced to more than one group, but at different points in time. It looks like this:

Group 1   O   O   O   X   O   O   O   O   O   O
Group 2   O   O   O   O   O   O   X   O   O   O
          ⋮   ⋮   ⋮   ⋮   ⋮   ⋮   ⋮   ⋮   ⋮   ⋮
Group 38 O   O   O   O   O   X   O   O   O   O

This is the basic design used by Marvell (1989) in his investigation of the effects of no-fault divorce laws mentioned earlier. He examined the divorce rates in 38 states that passed no-fault divorce laws between 1965 and 1985. Different states, of course, passed the laws at different times during that period (the Xs above). So, for each state, Marvell could compare the increase in the divorce rate in the year following the passage of its law with the annual increases for that state over a 20-year period. The nice thing about this design is that it gives you the opportunity to see whether the treatment works in each of the different groups at different points in time. If it does, that should increase your confidence that it really is the treatment that is making the difference. If it works for some groups, but not for others, you will have a puzzle on your hands. It could be that the time of introduction is crucial, or that there is some characteristic peculiar to the groups in which the treatment worked that is crucial to its success.

There are a number of other variations on the basic interrupted time series design. But with each, the key is to decide what data you need to make a case that it was, indeed, the intervention of interest that changed the nature of the series and to rule out each of the threats to internal validity. As Cook and Campbell (1979) point out, your best tools in this endeavor are logic, common sense, and a clear understanding of the nature of the intervention and its anticipated effects. A word of caution is in order on this last point: For the greatest interpretability when using any of the time series designs, the intervention (or treatment) should produce its effects quickly. For interventions that are implemented over a long period of time or for interventions that have delayed effects, the data from the time series design are likely to be ambiguous because the effects may not show up in the observations immediately following the onset of the intervention. That means it is going to be more difficult for you to establish that it was the intervention that produced the effects. People will look at the data from the observations immediately following the intervention and say, "See, nothing has changed." There are several strategies that will help in such situations. One is to have a strong, plausible, theoretical explanation for why the effects of interest should be delayed (e.g., Cordray, 1986). Another, which Cook and Campbell (1979) recommend, is to try the time series with switching replications. When you can demonstrate similar delayed effects in more than one group, it becomes more believable that they were produced by the intervention.

An Illustration: The North Carolina Seat Belt Law

Confronted with ever-increasing numbers of accidents and deaths on the nation's highways, many states have enacted seat belt laws in the hope of saving lives and reducing injuries. One such law was enacted in the spring of 1985 by the legislature of the state of North Carolina. The North Carolina law required motor vehicle drivers and other front seat occupants to have their safety belts properly fastened while their vehicle is in motion. It was to become effective on October 1, 1985, but for the first 15 months thereafter, only warning tickets would be issued to violators. Then, beginning on January 1, 1987, those not wearing their seat belts would be subject to a $25 fine. The law applied only to front seat occupants of passenger cars, light trucks, vans, and utility vehicles. It did not apply to rear seat occupants of those vehicles, nor to front seat occupants of vehicles not covered by the law. And, needless to say, the law did not cover several other groups who are often victims of vehicular accidents: pedestrians, cyclists, and farm equipment operators.

As part of the statute, the North Carolina legislature included a proviso requiring that an evaluation of the law's effectiveness be conducted and that a report of the evaluation be provided to the legislature 3 years after the law went into effect. After all, if the law had no effect, or had a detrimental effect, the people responsible for it ought to be told so that it could be changed, or dropped altogether. Two questions needed to be asked to evaluate this law. First, it was important to find out whether the law really did what it was intended to do: get people to buckle up. The second question was: Does buckling up really make a difference? Do vehicular injuries and fatalities decrease?

Given the lead time of 6 months between the enactment of the law and the beginning of the warning phase (October 1, 1985), Reinfurt et al. (1990) were able to set up a system of observation to estimate seat belt usage in North Carolina starting one month prior to the commencement of the warning phase. They selected 72 geographically dispersed intersections around the state, from the mountains to the sea and from cities to rural areas. Then, beginning in September 1985 and at 2-month intervals through August 1988, pairs of observers noted seat belt use by drivers for 1½ hours at each of these locations. The observers used a sampling plan that allowed some observations at rush hours, some at off-peak hours, and some on weekends. The data they collected are presented in Figure 5. There you can see in panel A that at the beginning of the warning phase, seat belt usage by drivers increased from 25% to 45%. It continued at about that level—varying from 41% to 49%—throughout 1986. Then, with the beginning of the citation phase—when getting a ticket for not wearing your seat belt would cost you money—seat belt usage jumped to almost 80%. Throughout 1987 and 1988, however, it gradually tapered back down to about 64%. Still, that's a vast improvement over the 25% in September 1985.

Now, did this increased seat belt usage make a difference in the number of deaths and injuries? To determine that, Reinfurt et al. (1990) obtained reports of motor vehicle accidents in North Carolina from January 1981 through June 1988. Injuries in all accidents were categorized into three levels of severity: fatality, serious injury, and moderate injury. The proportion of accident victims covered by the seat belt law who were seriously injured or killed is depicted in Figure 5B. There it may be seen that at both the beginning of the warning phase and the beginning of the citation phase, there were sharp drops in the proportion of covered victims who were killed or seriously injured. In fact, during the citation phase, serious or fatal injuries for those cov-

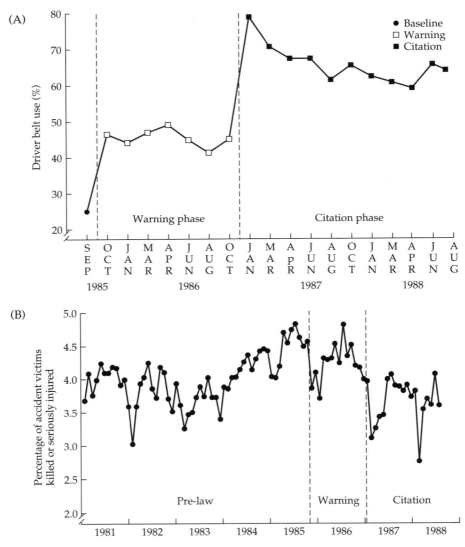

5 Seat belt use and serious injuries and fatalities before and after the enactment of the North Carolina seat belt law. (A) Seat belt use by drivers, September 1985–August 1988. (B) Serious injuries and fatalities among people covered by the seat belt law, 1981–1988. (From Reinfurt et al., 1990.)

ered by the new law were almost 15% less than expected based on previous trends. That translates into an *annual* reduction for the covered group of over 2300 serious or fatal injuries.

But was it really the law that made the difference? To help make that argument, Reinfurt et al. (1990) did similar analyses for two other groups, groups not covered by the law. The first group included rear seat occupants of vehicles covered by the law and front seat occupants of vehicles not covered by the law. Again, these people were not required to buckle up after October 1, 1985. For these noncovered occupants, there was no significant reduction in serious and fatal injuries during the citation phase. And for other noncovered accident victims—pedestrians, cyclists, and operators of farm vehicles—there was actually a slight increase in serious and fatal injuries after January 1, 1987. In other words, the law had essentially no effect on these two control series—that is, the fatalities and serious injuries occurring among two groups of vehicular accident victims who were not covered by the law.

It appears that the North Carolina seat belt law did indeed have the intended effect of reducing traffic fatalities and serious casualties. But before we can feel completely confident about that conclusion, we need to consider a few more threats to its validity. First, inspection of Figure 5 seems to indicate that maturation is not a factor. Neither seat belt use nor serious injuries and fatalities following October 1985 and January 1987 appear to be continuations of trends that had started prior to those two dates. Also, there is no reason to believe that testing or instrumentation are relevant threats here. It is possible that the observers got a little better over time in noting seat belt use, but the dramatic increases in recorded use in October 1985 and January 1987 are not likely to be due to changes in the observers. Also, the procedures for recording traffic accidents and casualties were well established, and there is no evidence that they changed with the beginning of enforcement of the new law. Neither is regression a plausible alternative to the finding that the new law produced dramatic increases in seat belt use at the expected times. And, as Figure 5 shows, the months preceding October 1985 and January 1987 were not particularly unusual in terms of the number of deaths and serious injuries on North Carolina highways.

Reinfurt et al. (1990) point out that there are several reasons why the seat belt law was not even more effective in reducing deaths and serious injuries. First, as noted earlier, the law did not apply to everyone, not even everyone in passenger cars. In fact, approximately 30% of the people involved in vehicular accidents in North Carolina were not covered by the seat belt law. And, even among those who were covered by the law, not everyone complied. Figure 5A shows that by August 1988, seat belt usage among drivers of covered vehicles had fallen off to 65%. Also, during the years from 1981 to 1988, the population of North Carolina had increased, as had the number of vehicles on the highways and the number of miles driven, making more severe accidents increasingly likely. Further, the maximum speed limit on North Carolina highways was increased from 55 miles an hour to 65 miles an hour in mid-August 1987—again, increasing the likelihood of more severe accidents. It is true that roads and highways were being upgraded continuously during the 1980s, but the improvement of roadways and traffic control were ongoing projects that did not make quantum leaps forward on October 1, 1985 and January 1, 1987.

One of the nice things about this study was that some of the data necessary to evaluate the effects of the new law were already being routinely collected, and had been for years. Information on vehicular accidents was sitting in the archives waiting for Reinfurt et al. to make use of it. No one was inconvenienced, no one's routine was interrupted, and no one was made to feel like a guinea pig. Unfortunately, research in natural settings is not always like that. The interventions and treatments utilized in some quasi-experiments and field experiments do interfere with people's lives, and that poses some ethical problems.

Some Ethical Considerations

Imagine yourself at a provincial park in upper Canada. You have spent a long day canoeing and hiking, and after dinner at the lodge, you plan to take in the free movie in the recreation room. You show up at 7:55 P.M., find a seat, and promptly at 8:00, the movie begins. Surprise! It is not the movie that was advertised on the bulletin board. Instead, it is a film about alcohol abuse and safety in the national parks. It does contain some interesting facts. You learn, for example, that approximately one-third of drownings in provincial parks are related to alcohol use. Even so, you feel puzzled. But the film is short. It is over in 15 minutes. Then the lights go on again, and the park ranger asks everyone to fill out a brief questionnaire. Your puzzlement increases, as do the grumblings in the back of the room, but rather than make a scene, you quickly fill out the questionnaire. Finally, at 8:25 P.M., the lights go off again and the movie you came to see begins. The next day you ask the ranger what was going on and find out you have been in a field study conducted by the Addiction Research Foundation in Toronto. They are interested in changing attitudes toward drinking and are showing the film you saw to some people and simply asking others to fill out the questionnaire without seeing the film.

How would you feel about that? No one asked whether or not you would be willing to participate. No one paid you for the 25 minutes of your time that the film and the questionnaire took. The columnist from the *Toronto Star* to whom this actually happened was more than a little annoyed (Jones, 1984), although he was quite sympathetic to the need for action on alcohol-related accidents. As he put it, he was a "bit short" with park personnel the next day. The issue, of course, is lack of informed consent and, possibly, invasion of privacy—although he could have refused to answer the questions on the questionnaire. There was also some deception involved. If the columnist had not complained and inquired about what was going on, he would never have known who was sponsoring the research or why the research was being done.

The columnist's reaction to his involuntary research participation is, apparently, not an unusual one. Wilson and Donnerstein (1976) described eight field experiments to a variety of people aged 17 to 85 and asked them how they would feel if they found out they had been subjects in such research. Two of the eight field experiments were as follows:

1. A woman and a confederate experimenter visit shoe stores at times when there are more customers than salesmen. The woman is wearing a shoe with a broken heel. She rejects whatever the salesman shows her. The confederate, posing as a friend of the customer, surreptitiously takes notes on the salesman's behavior (Schaps, 1972).

2. People sitting alone on park benches are asked to be interviewed by an experimenter who gives the name of a fictitious survey research organization that he claims to represent. At the beginning of the interview, the experimenter asks a person sitting nearby, who is actually a confederate, if he would mind answering the questions at the same time. The confederate responds with opinions that are clearly opposite those of the subject and makes demeaning remarks about the subject's answers: "That's ridiculous"; "That's just the sort of thing you'd expect to hear in this park" (Abelson and Miller, 1967).

These field experiments had actually been done, and they represent a strategy of accosting individual subjects to secure their participation in the research. Wilson and Donnerstein found that a large percentage of the people to whom such research was described did not believe it was justified. Many also reported that they, personally, would have felt harassed if they had been singled out for participation.

One of the major reasons that investigators attempt such unobtrusive research, of course, is that it avoids many biases that are present when subjects know they are taking part in an investigation. For example, if they do not know they are taking part in research, they are less likely to respond in a socially desirable manner or to be concerned about what the investigator will think of them. But, as Cook and Campbell (1979) pointed out, "from ethical and perhaps legal perspectives, much technically feasible unobtrusive experimentation is not desirable since it violates the ethical requirement of 'informed consent.'" However, as Aronson, Brewer, and Carlsmith (1985) have noted, if the research involves simple observation in public places with no possibility of identifying information being recorded, it probably is not a problem. If what the subjects are asked to do in such research is innocuous, takes very little time or effort, and is within the range of the subject's normal experience, then the research probably can be ethically justified. For example, placing apparently lost letters in different locations to see whether the people who find them will mail them (Milgram, 1969) does not seem objectionable.

A problem with such innocuous treatments, however, is that they are not likely to deal with anything of real significance in the respondents' lives. When the treatment is something that will make a difference in the subject's life, a new set of ethical concerns arises. As you know by now, untreated control groups are usually essential for establishing that a treatment does have a certain effect. But if the treatment is a beneficial one—or even a potentially beneficial one—it may be difficult to justify withholding it from some people while giving it to others (Levine, 1986). In fact, some people would argue that withholding a known beneficial treatment cannot be justified. But there are exceptions, and there is at least one way around the problem. One exception consists of those circumstances in which the available resources are simply not sufficient to treat everyone in need. For example, if you were interested in the issue of whether admission to a home for the aged was beneficial or harmful, you would have to work within the capacity of the homes that were willing to cooperate in your study. One possibility is that people on the waiting lists could serve as the untreated control group; that is, you could compare the health and well-being of those admitted to the home with that of similar people on the waiting list. Lieberman (1961) used such a design in his examination of mortality rates among people admitted to the Orthodox Jewish Home for the Aged in Chicago. During the period between 1947 and 1959, 860 applicants were placed on the home's waiting list after an initial physical and mental screening. Of these 860, 700 were later admitted to the home, 78 withdrew their applications, and 82 died while still on the waiting list. The waiting period for the 700 actually admitted averaged 6.4 months following completion of the screening tests and interviews. Lieberman computed the mortality rate for those admitted to the home for the first year following admission and found a 24.7% first-year mortality rate. The comparable rate for those who died while still on the waiting list was only 10.4%. Those are surprising figures, and they may say something about the expectations that many people have about homes for the aged, that is, that they are places where one goes to die. But the point here is simply that Lieberman could not have done the study if the home in question could have accommodated everyone who applied as soon as they applied. There would have been no people who died while still on the waiting list with whom to compare the people admitted to the home.

The Lieberman study suggests a way around the ethical problem posed by the necessity of withholding a beneficial treatment from some in order to evaluate the effects of the treatment—although in Lieberman's study, it appears that withholding what people sought was beneficial. In any event, there are circumstances in which treatment can be temporarily withheld from one group of subjects. Patients applying for psychotherapy, for example, often are put on a waiting list until the therapist has a free slot in his or her schedule. The patients on the waiting list could conceivably be used as controls for those currently in therapy, and the relative improvement in the two groups over the ensuing weeks could be compared. It may have occurred to you that what is being advocated here is a version of a time series design we discussed earlier, the interrupted time series with switching replications.

Note that the ethical problem posed by an untreated control group is a problem only when you have reason to believe that the treatment will indeed be beneficial. When the treatment is of unknown efficacy, there is no problem with having an untreated control group. In fact, you may have done the members of that group a favor if the treatment turns out to be harmful.

Summary

To establish whether or not a given intervention has certain effects, it is usually necessary to have some basis for comparison: that is, you need some information about what the situation would have been like without the intervention. The problem is that many interventions and naturally occurring changes occur only one time and to only one group of people. Thus, to establish a basis for comparison, it is often necessary to use another, nonequivalent group in which the change did not occur. That can result in ambiguity because every way in which the two groups differ is a possible threat to the validity of any inference concerning the effects of the intervention. A research design such as the untreated control group design with pretest and posttest can be helpful in this regard because the data from the pretest enable you to establish the preintervention similarity of the two groups.

There are at least 13 threats to internal validity; that is, 13 possible contaminating factors that you must be able to rule out before concluding that the intervention or change of interest to you really made a difference. These threats are history, maturation, testing, instrumentation, statistical regression, selection, mortality, interactions with selection, ambiguity about the direction of causality, diffusion or imitation of treatments, compensatory equalization of treatments, compensatory rivalry, and resentful demoralization. In addition to this standard list of things to watch out for, there may be specific factors in the setting in which you plan to do research or specific aspects of your procedure that can cause problems. Imagine the intervention producing exactly the change you expect, then ask yourself, "What are the most likely alternative explanations that people could offer for that effect if I told them about it?" Then decide what additional data you will need to rule out those alternative explanations.

Interrupted time series designs, especially those with an untreated control group and those with switching replications, can be excellent ways of ruling out most of the threats to internal validity. In addition to enabling you to establish the effects of an intervention more clearly than do the designs discussed earlier, the interrupted time series designs also enable you to see trends over time and changes in those trends. They enable you to rule out such threats to internal validity as interactions between selection and maturation, which you cannot do with the simpler untreated control group design with pretest and posttest. As an added benefit, the interrupted time series design with switching replications avoids the ethical problems of withholding a possibly beneficial treatment from a control group because all groups are exposed to the treatment, just at different times.

The usefulness of quasi-experiments and field experiments has been illustrated by studies of nightmares following San Francisco's earthquake, Detroit's ordinance against concealed weapons, no-fault divorce laws, a hypothetical example concerning taped lectures, and, finally, the effects of the North Carolina seat belt law. In each of these examples, the emphasis was on obtaining the data needed to rule out plausible threats to internal validity, that is, threats to the inference that it was the intervention in question that made a difference.

Ethical problems can arise in quasi-experiments and field experiments. These include lack of informed consent, invasion of privacy, and withholding of beneficial treatments from people who could profit from them. More will be said about these issues in Chapter 8.

Recommended Readings

Bowen, R. W. (1992). *Graph it! How to make, read, and interpret graphs.* Englewood Cliffs, NJ: Prentice Hall.

If a picture is worth a thousand words, then a well-drawn graph is probably worth at least 763. As you have seen in the preceding chapter, a graph can convey at a glance a relatively complex set of data. As Bowen puts it: "Graphs are intended to make it easy to read, understand, and remember a relationship found in a set of data" (p. 4). A clear, uncluttered, and easy-to-read graph facilitates communication and enhances memory for what the graph depicts. And, in ten easy steps, Bowen shows how to make your graphs clear, uncluttered, and easy to read. He also introduces a number of terms—from "direct accelerated" to "monotonically decreasing"—that will help you describe and understand relationships among variables. The book itself is easy to read and profusely illustrated with all sorts of graphs. A 106-page cure for graphophobia.

Gardner, M. (1992). *On the wild side.* Buffalo, NY: Prometheus Books.

Martin Gardner is a journalist who writes about science and pseudoscience. The essays, reviews, and columns reprinted in this collection offer fascinating glimpses into some strange and unbelievable belief systems. From faith healers and parapsychologists to astrologers and rainmakers, Gardner presents an array of cranks and mystics who seem unable to understand the nature of and necessity for scientific evidence, at least as far as their particular obsession is concerned. Some are relatively harmless. They are amusing to read about, and you wonder how anyone could really believe such bunk—speaking in tongues, indeed. But others are not so harmless. As Gardner points out, there is reason to believe that during the Reagan years at the White House, astrologers were consulted on a regular basis—and that their advice was heeded. In Russia, a scientific fraud named Trofim Lysenko—who happened to have the right political connections—created havoc in the agricultural production system and did serious harm to Soviet science. Whether the claim is that vitamin C will cure the common cold, or that the earth is a living organism, or that the position of the stars can predict the future, what is really surprising is how resistant these ideas are to disconfirmation. In many cases it seems that the results of one well-designed field experiment would clear away the fog. But don't bet on it.

Jaffe, A. J., and Spirer, H. F. (1987). *Misused statistics: Straight talk for twisted numbers.* New York: Marcel Dekker.

This is an excellent text on how to spot misuses of statistics whenever and wherever you run across them. And you do not need a background in math or statistics to understand it. Using real examples culled from newspapers, magazines, political speeches, and, yes, even scholarly journals, Jaffe and Spirer illustrate misuses ranging from misleading graphical presentations to the consequences of changing definitions of crime and disease. What does it really mean when an advertisement reports: "In a blind taste test, 50% of Michelob drinkers preferred Schlitz to their own brand"? It may not mean what the Joseph Schlitz brewing company thinks it does. Or, how do you interpret the statement: "The average American family lives in a house with 7 rooms"? Do you really know what counts as a room? And, how can it be that—according to the U.S. Bureau of the Census—the Native American population *increased* sixfold between 1860 and 1890? Jaffe and Spirer will alert you to some of the basic questions you should ask yourself when you confront such "facts." Their advice ranges from "Never take headlines seriously" to "Take nothing for granted." Reading this book should make you both a better methodologist and a more intelligent consumer of research findings. It will also increase your CQ (that's Cynicism Quotient) by a few points.

Kohn, A. (1986). *False prophets*. New York: Basil Blackwell.

Kohn provides a detailed discussion, with numerous examples, of various kinds of ethical misconduct in scientific research. He begins with an overview of the norms of science—which include disinterestedness, honesty, and objectivity—and points out that not all misconduct is intentional. There are many instances, even in the so-called "exact" sciences, in which investigators see what they expect to see—even when it isn't really there. In the 1920s and 1930s, for example, hundreds of papers were published reporting Mitogenetic Rays, supposed ultraviolet rays emitted by plant and animal cells when they were dividing. Mitogenetic Rays turned out not to exist. As Kohn points out, however, all those hundreds of investigators were not dishonest. They were led astray by wishful thinking and by trying to observe something that—had it existed—was right at the threshold of what was possible to see with the human eye. But intentional deception does exist, and Kohn discusses its many varieties—from the Piltdown Man to plagiarism to withholding data that do not fit one's hypothesis. He uses the examples to raise a number of important ethical questions and is forthright in making his position clear on each.

Roberts, R. M. (1989). *Serendipity: Accidental discoveries in science*. New York: Wiley.

Many people have called attention to the role of accidental discoveries, or serendipity, in research. Unfortunately, they all seem to cite the same two or three well-known examples, such as Fleming's discovery of penicillin in 1928. They then quote Pasteur—"Chance favors the prepared mind"—admonish you to prepare your mind, and go on to another topic. After seeing the same two or three examples over and over, you begin to wonder whether the role of serendipity is overstated—if there are only two or three examples, it is hardly worth learning to spell the word. Thus, Roberts has done us all a service by bringing together a variety of documented examples of serendipity—and what he refers to as pseudoserendipity. In the "pseudo" variety, an accident leads to a discovery that was actively being sought. "Real" serendipity is discovering something you were not seeking. Whether "real" or "pseudo," the tales of discovery that Roberts relates range from the invention of Velcro to the discovery of the Dead Sea Scrolls. Pasteur is there, of course, and so is Fleming, but there are many more, and they are indeed fascinating reading.

8

The Experiment

The laboratory experiment is probably the most powerful technique available for demonstrating causal relationships between variables—that is, for demonstrating that a change in one variable produces a change in another. That is quite a strong statement, even with the hedge "probably" included. But it is true! The only reason for hedging at all is that an experiment, like other research methods, may not be feasible for investigating particular problems, or in particular settings. If you are interested in understanding what led to the demise of the Babylonian civilization and the ascendance of the Assyrian one, experimentation is not going to help you very much. For such a question, experimentation is definitely not the most powerful technique available. But if your problem is one that can be attacked experimentally, you are in luck.

Compared with participant observation, archival research, and interviewing—all of which were familiar to Aristotle—experimentation on psychological, behavioral, and social processes is relatively new. There are, however, occasional reports of attempted experiments scattered throughout history. One story, for example, has it that an ancient king wanted to know whether children raised without exposure to language would develop a language on their own. So, a couple of unlucky babies were selected, isolated, and tended to only by slaves who were even unluckier—they had had their tongues cut out so that they could not talk. In spite of such legends, which reveal at least a rudimentary understanding of some of its elements, experimentation remained a seldom-used tool for investigating human behavior.

Things began to change in the 1800s, however. Toward the end of the century, with the mounting successes of the experimental approach in fields such as physiology, physics, and medicine, it was almost inevitable that some enterprising spirits would try it out on behavior. One of the first to take the plunge was a psychologist named Triplett at the University of Indiana. In going over the official records of the Racing Board of the League of American Wheelmen, Triplett (1897–1898) noticed that bicycle racers seemed to do better when they were paced by a swift multicycle, or when they were in competition with others, than when they were out on the track by themselves. In other words, when they were simply racing against the clock, they did not do as well. Apparently others had noticed this phenomenon too, because several ideas had been put forward to explain it. One such idea was termed suction theory. The notion was that the pacing machine created a slight vacuum behind it, which drew the huffing and puffing bicycler forward at a little better speed than he could manage on his own. One of the strongest arguments in favor of this theory was the fact that a man named Anderson had been able to exceed 60 miles an hour on a bicycle at Roodhouse, Illinois, when paced by a railroad locomotive. Another suggestion was that sustained attention to the revolving wheels of the pacing machine in front of him produced a sort of hypnosis in the pursuing rider that allowed him to ignore fatigue and pain to push himself beyond his normal limits.

The archival records that Triplett consulted established, very clearly, the fact of better performance under competition and paced conditions than during solitary time trials. However, there was no way to distinguish among the various explanations offered for that fact. Too many things were happening at once. There was even some evidence of self-selection—that is, that riders who were particularly good in competition would not participate in the solitary time trials, and vice versa. Triplett decided to study the issue of competition versus solitary performance in a way that would allow him to rule out some of the possible explanations for the effect. He designed a simple laboratory experiment in which people were asked to wind fishing reels. Again, he found that people did better (reeled faster) when competing with others than they did when alone. Now the list of possible explanations for this phenomenon was greatly reduced. Suction theory, for example, was simply no longer appropriate. Self-selection was ruled out because Triplett had the same people wind reels under both conditions.

Note what Triplett did. First, he observed an aspect of behavior—bicycle riders performing better against others than when alone—for which there were many plausible explanations. Second, he conceptualized this behavior as an instance of a general cause-and-effect process: Competition leads to improved performance. What he wanted to know, of course, was why, or how, competition leads to improved performance. So, third, he designed a setting in which this general process could manifest itself, but a setting in which the plausible explanations for its occurrence would be greatly reduced in comparison to the number of explanations that could be invoked in the natural setting. In short, he designed an experiment to establish why the presence of one variable (competition) changed something about a second variable (performance).

It sounds simple, and it can be. It can also be fun. But before going into the details, you might be interested in knowing the fate of this once-seldom-used tool for investigating human behavior. By the mid-1960s and early 1970s, the experiment had become tremendously popular as a research method, particularly among psychologists, and it remains so. In 1988, for example, over 60% of the articles published in the *Journal of Personality and Social Psychology* involved experimentation (West, Newsom, and Fenaughty, 1992).

In fact, the experiment has become so popular that it has generated something of a backlash. Many people have felt called upon to point out that there are, after all, other research methods available, and that there are some issues of importance that cannot be investigated experimentally. You, of course, already know that, so you are ahead of the game. But let us look at what is involved to see if it can be made clear why the experiment has enjoyed such a surge in popularity since Triplett's time.

The Essence of the Experiment

Basically, an **experiment** is a form of research in which you actively manipulate or change something (the independent variable) in order to see what effect that change has on something else (the dependent variable). There is more involved, but before describing the rest, it is important to point out that there are several ways in which the experiment is simply an extension of the methods discussed in the preceding chapters. For example, all research methods may be thought of as techniques for insulating your observations and inferences against error (Kaplan, 1964). There is a constant temptation to infer more than you should from your observations and to read into your own experiences lessons that may not really be there (see Box 1). Thus, research methods help keep you honest by forcing you to be explicit about (i.e., to acknowledge) the conditions under which your observations have taken place. Similarly, many research methods have as their goal the provision of evidence about causal relationships between variables. Whether the variables of interest are as complex as patterns of child rearing and adult personality or as simple as caffeine ingestion and hand tremor, the point of the research is usually to demonstrate that one leads to the other. Doing this, of course, requires a commitment to the notion of comparison. In fact, it is probably not going too far to say that the concept of comparison is the single most important concept in research. And, again, research methods help you to be explicit about what precisely you are comparing: the patterns of child rearing in Samoa and those in the United States; drinking three cups of coffee and drinking one; and so on. The factor that differentiates the experiment from other research methods is its ability to provide you with the most unambiguous information possible about a causal relationship between variables. The question is this: What are the features of an experiment that enable it to do that?

Manipulation

The first such characteristic of experimentation is **manipulation**, which, as you are no doubt aware, simply means changing something. If you are interested in improving the look of your living room wall, for example, you might try a nice picture instead of that old Stop sign. If you want people to stand closer when you talk, you might try cutting down on the garlic for breakfast. As these examples imply, manipulation is usually done with a purpose in mind, to see "what will happen if…" Similarly, in an experiment, the goal is to see what happens when some aspect of the setting is changed. Does that change make a difference in how people respond to the setting?

<u>Box 1</u>

Did It Really Make That Much Difference?

There is a poem by Robert Frost called "The Road Not Taken," which goes:

> Two roads diverged in a yellow wood,
> And sorry I could not travel both
> And be one traveler, long I stood
> And looked down one as far as I could
> To where it bent in the undergrowth;
>
> Then took the other, as just as fair,
> And having perhaps the better claim,
> Because it was grassy and wanted wear;
> Though as for that the passing there
> Had worn them really about the same,
>
> And both that morning equally lay
> In leaves no step had trodden black.
> Oh, I kept the first for another day!
> Yet knowing how way leads on to way,
> I doubted if I should ever come back.
>
> I shall be telling this with a sigh
> Somewhere ages and ages hence:
> Two roads diverged in a wood, and I—
> I took the one less traveled by,
> And that has made all the difference.

(Frost, 1949, p. 131)

Mr. Frost was an excellent poet, but it is clear that he could have profited from a quick course in research methods. There is simply no way of knowing whether taking the less traveled road made any difference at all.

In looking back on their lives, many people identify choice points that, in retrospect, seem to have been quite important. They decided to go to Harvard instead of Yale. They chose the Army instead of the Navy. They spent a year in Europe instead of joining the Peace Corps. And while they were at Harvard or in the Army or in Paris, they met this guy who . . . And the tale unfolds. They ignore the fact that they have no data on what would have happened had they chosen the other alternative. Their life might have been even more exciting if they had gone to Yale or joined the Navy or spent a couple of years in the jungle. They have assumed that the forgone alternative would have led to a dull, uneventful, or impecunious life, a fallacy we might term the "unfounded implicit baseline comparison." So the next time one of your friends starts reminiscing about what smart decisions they have made, you might point out that they are missing some data. Of course, you might want to make sure you have a few spare friends before you do that.

Note that with the exception of a few of the quasi-experimental designs discussed in Chapter 7, this concept of manipulation is not a part of the other research methods we have described. Quite the contrary! In survey research, participant observation, and archival research, the researcher's usual goal is to leave the research setting, or participants, or both, exactly as he or she found them. Thus, in a very real sense, the experiment provides a more active role for the person doing the research. That may, in fact, be part of its appeal. The experimenter gets a chance to get into the lab and tinker—try it, and if that does not work, try something else.

The concept of **control** is closely tied to the notion of manipulation. If you change something, you usually will want to know whether the change has any effect. Suppose you switch to Super Unleaded gas and get your car tuned up in an effort to stop the ping in your engine, and that you do both of these things on the same day. If the ping stops, you will not know whether or not the new gasoline had an effect. Similarly, if you stop eating garlic for breakfast, get a new wardrobe, start using mouthwash, and make it a point to be nicer to people, chances are that people will indeed seem friendlier. But you will not know whether mouthwash had anything to do with it. In other words, when you are interested in knowing whether a given manipulation of some aspect of the environment has any effect, you need to control, or hold constant, other aspects of the environment.

Of course, you cannot hold all other aspects of the environment constant. It is impossible to run the clock back and replay situations at will, once with and once without your manipulation. You can never know exactly what would have happened had you done A instead of B in a particular circumstance. You can only try doing A in the future in similar circumstances. Given that you cannot hold everything except your manipulation constant, what things should you attempt to control? You need to hold constant, or control, those other aspects of the environment that might plausibly be expected to interfere with or obscure observations of the change produced by your manipulation.

For example, suppose you develop a hunch that attitude change is a gradual process, that people take in information relevant to an attitude and mull it over for a while before it affects their attitude on the issue. Further, suppose you design an experiment in which you plan to test this idea by exposing people to a persuasive communication advocating abolition of the death penalty and measuring their attitudes toward the death penalty immediately afterward and again a week later. If you have such a plan, you had better pray for an outbreak of peace and good will during the week between measurements. A sensational murder case breaking into the news that week would very likely confound your results. You might control for this possibility by conducting the experiment at a summer camp, where you could confiscate all the radios or otherwise censor the news coming into the camp.

The aspect of the environment that is manipulated in an experiment is usually referred to as the independent variable. One of the basic decisions facing the would-be experimenter is how to present the independent variable. Aronson, Brewer, and Carlsmith (1985) have pointed out that it usually boils down to the question of manipulation by instruction (i.e., by what you say to the subjects) versus manipulation by event (i.e., by something that happens to the subjects). As an example of the instruction type of manipulation, Macrae (1992) simply had subjects read a brief description of a woman who gets food poisoning after eating in a restaurant. The independent variable in this case was whether the restaurant was described as (1) one she often ate in or (2) one she had never been to before: Half of the subjects read a paragraph in which she was described as having eaten in a familiar restaurant and half read a paragraph in which she was described as having eaten in a new restaurant. An example of the event type of manipulation can be found in an experiment by Greenberg (1988), in which workers at a large insurance company were temporarily assigned to new offices during a period of renovation and refurbishing. One aspect of this situation that was manipulated was the apparent status of the temporary office assignments. Some workers were assigned a new office that was larger, more private, had its own door, and contained a larger desk than their usual one. Others were assigned a new office that was smaller, more public, had no door, and contained a smaller desk.

As you can see from the two examples above, when you manipulate an independent variable by something that happens to the subjects, you are likely to have more impact on them. They will sit up and take notice. Think about how you might feel if you were told on a Thursday afternoon that beginning next Monday you are going to have to give up your nice corner office with the fantastic view and move into a cramped little cubicle down in the basement—and, by the way, you'll be sharing it with Smith and Jones from accounting. Only temporary, you understand. Beside such a vivid, involving manipulation, the use of instructions or printed information to manipulate an independent variable seems to pale by comparison. But there is a trade-off built into this event versus instruction decision about how to manipulate your independent variable. Events are likely to be relatively complex and are likely to introduce some ambiguity about what, precisely, is being manipulated. In the Greenberg (1988) study, the intention was to manipulate only the perceived status of the temporarily assigned offices, but other aspects of the work situation may have been changed as well—the availability of valued friends and co-workers, access to the coffee machine, the ability to hide from the boss. Instructions of the type used by Macrae (1992) to manipulate the perceived availability of alternative courses of action (familiar versus new restaurant) usually allow you to be more precise about what is being manipulated. But you may pay for that precision by failing to really capture the subject's attention and/or interest. (We'll come back to this event versus instruction issue later.)

When you have an independent variable such as high-status or low-status offices, it is usually said that the independent variable has two levels. But you can have more than two if you like. Greenberg, for example, actually had four levels of status in his temporary office assignments: (1) lower than one's own; (2) same as one's own; (3) slightly higher than one's own; and (4) much higher than one's own. When you have a variable you want to manipulate, the different levels, or degrees, of the variable are referred to as **treatments**. A common procedure is to expose some subjects to one treatment, some to another treatment, and some to no treatment at all. The latter are usually referred to as **no-treatment control subjects**. For example, suppose you were interested in the effect of varying degrees of food deprivation on the tendency of subjects to see food-related items in ambiguous shapes such as those formed by inkblots. You might deprive some subjects of food for 24 hours prior to asking them what they see in the inkblots, some for 48 hours, and some not at all. You would need the data from the undeprived subjects as a control or comparison in order to interpret the data from the two experimental conditions (24 and 48 hours of deprivation). If, for example, the undeprived subjects saw just as many food-related items as the others, then length of deprivation would not suffice as an explanation for seeing such items.

The aspect of the environment that you examine or measure to determine whether your change in the independent variable has had any effect is usually referred to as the dependent variable. If your hypothesis is correct, changes in the dependent variable will depend upon changes in the independent variable. In the food deprivation example, the dependent variable might be the total number of food-related images seen in five different inkblots. The independent variable, of course, would be the length of deprivation. In Macrae's study of accidents following routine or exceptional circumstances, the dependent variables were judgments about the negligence of the restaurant and compensation for the victim. Subjects judged the restaurant to be more negligent and awarded greater compensation to the victim of food poisoning when the poisoning was described as occurring in a new restaurant than when it occurred in one she routinely patronized. In the study by Greenberg (1988), the major dependent variable was worker productivity during the time of the temporary office assignments. Workers who were temporarily assigned to higher-status offices became more productive, and those assigned to lower-status offices became less productive.

The purpose of any experiment, of course, is to determine whether changes in the independent variable produce changes in the dependent variable. As mentioned earlier, in order to do that, you must hold constant those aspects of the experimental setting (other than the independent variable) that might plausibly be expected to influence the dependent variable. In a typical experiment there are many things that have the potential to produce changes in the dependent variable, but the most recurrently troublesome are preexisting differences among the subjects exposed to different levels of the independent variable. Consider a couple of techniques that have been devised for handling this problem.

Assigning Subjects to Conditions

Typically, an experiment involves comparisons of the responses of subjects exposed to the independent variable with the responses of subjects not exposed to the independent variable, or it involves comparisons of the responses of subjects exposed to different levels of the independent variable. If the subjects in these various conditions are systematically different to begin with, their responses may very well differ even in the absence of the independent variable. Take an extreme example. Nobody who was interested in the effects of caffeine on weight-lifting ability would compare the weights lifted by male college students who had had a cup of coffee with the weights lifted by female college students who had not had a cup of coffee. The comparison would be worthless, except as an example of how not to do research. The two groups of subjects (coffee drinkers and nondrinkers) differed systematically prior to their exposure to the independent variable.

There are basically two techniques for ruling out, or controlling, the influence of such preexisting group differences. The first, called **matching**, involves trying to equate the subjects in different conditions on the basis of certain known characteristics. For example, suppose you were interested in various ways of reducing stress, and you designed an experiment to compare the relative effectiveness of transcendental meditation, jogging, and biofeedback. If you believe that age and sex might be important variables determining how people respond to stress—and would respond to your three stress reduction programs—you would want to match on these variables. For every 50-year-old male assigned to the jogging condition, you would have to assign a 50-year-old male to the TM condition and another to the biofeedback condition. (For a better design, you should also have a no-treatment control condition, which would mean a fourth 50-year-old male.) On the other hand, you would probably be safe in assuming that hair color is unlikely to be related to stress reduction. Hence, you would not find it necessary to match subjects in the various conditions on hair color—although stereotypes about redheads suggest that maybe you should (Jones, 1982).

Table 1 illustrates the use of a **quota matrix**, a device that can help you match subjects. First, you decide what variables you intend to use in matching. In the stress reduction experiment, suppose you decide that, in addition to age and sex, you want to match subjects on body weight—that is, whether they are overweight or normal. Then you draw up a matrix like that in Table 1A, in which you categorize the people potentially available to participate in your experiment. Finally, you assign equal numbers of persons from each category to each condition, as shown in Table 1B. If you have 16 overweight males who are between 30 and 40 years old, for example, then 4 of these would be assigned to each of your four conditions.

According to Box, Hunter, and Hunter (1978), we may define a *block* as a subgroup of the available subjects (e.g., overweight males between 50 and 59 years of age) who can reasonably be expected to be more similar to one another than to the remaining subjects. Thus, the technical term for what you are doing when you use a quota matrix like that in Table 1 is **blocking**. There are several statistical advantages to blocking, which we need not go into here, but you can see how it would help to make comparisons of the various treatments more precise. In the example, age, sex, and weight of the subjects should not contribute to any differences among the conditions.

The problem with blocking and, more generally, with matching is that you can never be sure that you have matched subjects in the various conditions on the really important variables. The earlier reference to redheads was not entirely facetious because it seems to be the case that personality type is a more important determinant of reaction to stress than either age or sex (e.g., Taylor, 1991). Matching can promote a false sense of security by leading you to believe that your experimental and control groups were really

Table 1 Matching Subjects to Experimental Conditions by Using a Quota Matrix

A. Subjects Available for Experiment

AGE GROUP (YEARS)	OVERWEIGHT SUBJECTS		NORMAL SUBJECTS	
	MALE	FEMALE	MALE	FEMALE
20–29	8	7	16	18
30–39	(16)	19	25	29
40–49	21	23	18	△17
50–59	11	10	8	9
60+	7	4	◇5	3

B. Distribution of Subjects to Four Experimental Conditions

1 NO-TREATMENT CONTROL	2 JOGGING	3 TRANSCENDENTAL MEDITATION	4 BIOFEEDBACK
④	④	④	④
1	1	1	1
△4	△4	△4	△4
◇1	◇1	◇1	◇1

Note: All subjects potentially available for research are first categorized by their age, sex, and weight. Subjects are then assigned to each condition:

◯ Male subjects: overweight, 30–39

☐ Male subjects: overweight, 60+

◇ Male subjects: normal, 60+

△ Female subjects: normal, 40–49

Not all of the subjects will actually be assigned. For example, because there are only three females of normal weight who are over 60 years old, there are not enough subjects in that category to enable assignment of one subject to each condition.

equated at the outset, when in fact they were not equated at all on a host of variables.

The second solution to the problem of controlling for or ruling out preexisting differences among experimental groups is a better one. It is the process of randomly assigning subjects to conditions, or **randomization**. In principle, randomization is simple. If your design called for an experimental condition and a control group, for example, you would simply need to ensure that for all potential subjects, the probability of being assigned to the control group was equal to the probability of being assigned to the experimental group. With only two conditions, you could flip a coin—an unbiased one, of course—for each subject. Heads means that subject is assigned to the experimental group, and tails means that subject is assigned to the control group.

When your design has more than two conditions—and most designs do—you can use a **table of random numbers** to help you randomize subjects to conditions. I have provided such a table for you in the appendix to this book. If you look at the table, you will see that it consists of rows and columns of the digits 0 through 9. The table was generated by a computer that was instructed to print out the numbers in such a manner that for each successive entry in the table, any of the digits 0 through 9 was equally likely to be selected. That is, the table is a random arrangement of the digits.

The table is used in the following manner: Suppose you had five conditions and 100 subjects, and you wanted to randomly assign the subjects to the five conditions. First, number the subjects 00 through 99. Then pick an arbitrary point in the table—say, the beginning of the sixteenth row on the first page. Reading across that row, look at each successive two-digit number: 01, 92, 93, 21, … . Assign the first 20 subjects whose numbers you see to Condition 1, the next 20 to Condition 2, and so on. This is a very simple way of randomly assigning subjects to conditions. Just in case you have trouble following the example, however, there are a couple of additional examples on how to use the table at the beginning of the appendix.

In practice, achieving true random assignment can be very difficult, and all sorts of subtle biases may operate in determining which subjects get assigned to which group. Using volunteer subjects in one condition or treatment and paid or coerced subjects in another would be a potentially serious error because the motivations of the two groups could differ sharply, and that, in turn, could influence how attentive they were to experimental procedures and requirements. Similarly, using an 8 A.M. section of students in the experimental condition of a study and a 10 A.M. section of students enrolled in the same course in the control condition would also be an example of non-random assignment to conditions. Students who schedule their classes for 8 o'clock may be quite different from those who schedule their classes for 10 o'clock.

In general, randomization is better than matching for ruling out the possibility that preexisting group differences, rather than the different levels of the independent variable, account for any differences you obtain on responses to the dependent variable. Randomization assumes, of course, that when all subjects have the same likelihood of being assigned to any of the conditions, the personal characteristics of subjects in the various conditions should average out about the same. For large numbers of subjects, that is usually a safe assumption. For small numbers of subjects, it may not be so safe. If you have only four or five subjects in each condition, then one really weird guy in the control group, say, could throw off your whole experiment. So you need to be a bit skeptical about the effectiveness of randomization when using small numbers of subjects. As Campbell and Stanley (1966) have pointed out, randomization may assure unbiased assignment of subjects to groups, but it does not always guarantee the equivalence of such groups.

One way in which you can check on the initial equivalence of groups is to give some sort of premeasure or pretest after the groups have been constituted. For example, if you are planning an attitude change experiment, you might want to administer a questionnaire to assess attitudes on the pertinent issues prior to introducing your experimental manipulation—just to make sure that the subjects in the various conditions have similar attitudes to begin with. The major problem, of course, is that such a pretest might sensitize subjects to what you are interested in, and, as a result, they might not respond naturally to the manipulation. Lana (1969) recommended several ways of overcoming this problem. You might, for example, embed the crucial pretest item in a long questionnaire with a variety of items, or separate the pretest in time from the actual experiment, or collect the pretest data in a different setting from that in which the experiment is conducted.

Before going on, take a moment to look at the following list. These are the major concepts that have been discussed since the beginning of the chapter. If you understand them, you already have a basic grasp of the experiment. Give yourself a test. See how many of them you can define without peeking at the Glossary.

- Manipulation
- Independent variable
- Levels
- Treatments
- Manipulation by instruction
- Manipulation by event
- No-treatment control subjects
- Dependent variable
- Matching
- Blocking
- Quota matrix
- Randomization
- Table of random numbers
- Pretest
- Plausible alternative explanation

They are not all new, of course. You probably thought I beat the notion of plausible alternative explanations to death in the last chapter, and randomization should at least be familiar from the chapter on survey research. To illustrate these concepts, and some others to be mentioned later, I would like to describe an experiment on one of the things that stereotypes do for us.

An Illustration: Stereotypes as Energy Savers

The term **stereotype** was originally employed in the printing and newspaper industries. It referred to a one-piece metal sheet that had been cast from a mold taken of a raised printing surface, such as a page of set type. The stereotype was used to print—over and over and over—whatever figures or words had been cast into its surface. Many years ago the term was adopted by Walter Lippmann (1922) to refer to the pictures in our heads of various racial, national, religious, and other groups. The connotation that Lippmann apparently intended was that of an unvarying form or pattern, of fixed and conventional expression, and of having no individuality, as though cast from a mold. To stereotype members of a particular group, then, means to think about and refer to members of that group as though they were all the same (Jones, Hendrick, and Epstein, 1979; Jones, 1982).

For many years stereotypes were simply considered biases to be overcome, preconceived notions about groups of people that would fade away if we simply had more accurate and detailed knowledge of those groups. But research found that stereotypes seemed to be ubiquitous, and that they often proved remarkably resistant to change. Thus, people began to wonder whether the use of stereotypes was not somehow an integral part of the way we process information and navigate our way through the social world. Think about it for a moment. What function might be served by the use of stereotypes in perceiving other people? Or, to put it another way, what does a stereotype do for you? One thing it does is allow you to categorize a person on the basis of one, or at most a few, clues. And once you have categorized the person—as, say, a professor, or a potential date, or a salesperson—ambiguity about how to respond to that person is reduced, and you can get on with the business at hand. In other words, the use of stereotypes may be a means of simplifying the complexities of our social worlds. And, given the extremely limited amount of information that we can attend to and process in any given instant, it follows that the use of stereotypes is more likely the more overwhelmed we are with information. As Macrae, Milne, and Bodenhausen (1994) put it, the available evidence seems to suggest that stereotypes simplify processing by providing a mental framework for taking in and organizing information. Without this preexisting framework, making sense of information about others is much more time-consuming and effortful. We have to pay close attention to each new item of information and try to figure out how it fits with the others.

While this certainly seems plausible, Macrae, Milne, and Bodenhausen (1994) found that there is surprisingly little direct evidence that the use of stereotypes does indeed free up cognitive resources for other tasks. So they designed a simple laboratory experiment to see if they could obtain some. The first thing they had to do was decide which stereotypes they wanted to work with and find out what characteristics were considered to be components of those stereotypes. To do this, they generated a list of social categories—doctor, lawyer, Indian chief—and then asked subjects to rate the extent to which a long list of personality traits were or were not characteristic of the members of those categories. They then chose four categories—doctor, artist, skinhead, and real estate agent. For each of these categories, they chose five traits that had been rated as characteristic of members of that category. They also selected five traits that were neutral with respect to members of each category. "Neutral" here means that the traits were neither especially characteristic nor uncharacteristic of members of the category. The four categories and the 10 traits for each are presented in Table 2.

Macrae et al. used the traits and categories in Table 2 to present subjects with an impression formation task. Each subject was seated in front of a computer screen, and one of the names at the top of Table 2 (Nigel, Julian, John, Graham) would appear on the screen. Below the name, in random order, each of the 10 traits assigned to that person would then appear—one at a time for 3 seconds each. Then a second name would appear on the screen, and the 10 traits attributed to that person would appear. And so on, until each subject had seen all four names and all 40 traits. For half the subjects, stereotypes were invoked by providing the label for the person's category just below the

Table 2   Stereotype Labels and Personality Traits for the Impression Formation Task

NIGEL (DOCTOR)	JULIAN (ARTIST)	JOHN (SKINHEAD)	GRAHAM (REAL ESTATE AGENT)
Characteristic Traits			
Caring	Creative	Rebellious	Pushy
Honest	Temperamental	Aggressive	Talkative
Reliable	Unconventional	Dishonest	Arrogant
Upstanding	Sensitive	Untrustworthy	Confident
Responsible	Individualistic	Dangerous	Unscrupulous
Neutral Traits			
Unlucky	Fearless	Lucky	Musical
Forgetful	Active	Observant	Pessimistic
Passive	Cordial	Modest	Humorless
Clumsy	Progressive	Optimistic	Alert
Enthusiastic	Generous	Curious	Spirited

Source: Macrae, Milne, and Bodenhausen, 1994.

name—that is, as the 10 traits describing "Julian" were being presented on the screen, the word "Artist" appeared just below the name "Julian." For the remaining subjects, these category labels did not appear with the names. So, in the space of 2 minutes, subjects saw 40 different traits flashed on the screen, each attributed to one of four different people. For half the subjects, the four people were labeled by name only; for the other half, the four were labeled by name and social category. The subjects were told ahead of time that they were going to be tested for accuracy of recall—that is, that they were going to have to remember which traits were attributed to which people.

Difficult! But there is more. Remember, Macrae et al. were anticipating that the benefits of invoking a stereotype are likely to show up only when subjects are overwhelmed with information, when they have more information to process than they can handle. So, in order to make sure that the subjects were overwhelmed, they were asked to perform a second task *simultaneously* with the impression formation task. This second task involved listening to a 2-minute prose passage with basic facts and figures about the geography and economy of Indonesia—at the same time they were attending to the traits and names on the computer screen. The subjects were told that they would be tested on the material about Indonesia immediately afterward. And, sure enough, as soon as they were done with the two tasks, they were given a sheet of paper with the four names from Table 2 at the top and asked to recall as many of the traits as possible and attribute them to the right person. They then were given a 20-item multiple-choice test on the material in the passage about Indonesia: "Djakarta is found on which coast of Java?"

That is the whole experiment. The first thing to notice is that Macrae et al. used not one, but two independent variables. That is, they manipulated two things: (1) whether a stereotype label was present or absent as subjects viewed the traits they were to remember; and (2) whether the traits they were asked to remember were consistent with that stereotype or neutral with respect to that stereotype. In tabular form, you might depict the experimental design like this:

	TRAITS	
STEREOTYPE LABEL	**CONSISTENT**	**NEUTRAL**
Present	1	2
Absent	3	4

As you can see, there were four conditions (1–4), and subjects were randomly assigned to the present or absent conditions. Such a design, in which each of the levels of one independent variable appears in conjunction once and only once with each of the levels of the second independent variable, is called a

factorial design. Because there are two levels of the first independent variable (stereotype label: present vs. absent) and two levels of the second (traits: consistent vs. neutral), the technical name for this particular design is a 2×2 factorial with repeated measures on the second factor. The latter means that the same subjects were exposed to both the consistent and the neutral traits.

Note that if Macrae et al. had been interested only in measuring memory for stereotype-consistent and stereotype-neutral information immediately after invoking a stereotype, the design would have looked like this:

TRAIT	STEREOTYPE LABEL PRESENT
Consistent	1
Neutral	2

In this case they would have needed only one group of subjects, and the design would have been called a **single-factor design** with repeated measures. Or, they might have been interested only in whether memory for stereotype-consistent information is enhanced by the presence of the stereotype label. In that case, they could have employed a single-factor design like this one:

STEREOTYPE LABEL	TRAIT CONSISTENT
Present	1
Absent	3

The major advantage of combining two such single-factor designs into one factorial experiment is that you can look at the **interaction** of your independent variables. Two variables are said to interact if the effect one has depends upon, or changes with, changes in the other. Perhaps that can be made clearer by first showing you Macrae et al.'s actual results and then showing you a couple of other ways in which their results could have turned out. The actual results are depicted in Figure 1. The major result can be summarized fairly succinctly by saying that the presence of the stereotype label significantly enhanced recall for stereotype-consistent traits but not for stereotype-neutral traits. In other words, there was an interaction between the presence or absence of the stereotype label and the nature of the traits recalled. But remember, the point of the entire experiment was to see whether the invocation of the stereotype freed up cognitive resources for other uses. Did the use of the stereotype to help them remember some of the traits make it easier for the

1 Mean number of traits correctly recalled as a function of the presence or absence of a stereotype label. (Data from Macrae, Milne, and Bodenhausen, 1994.)

subjects to pay more attention to the information about Indonesia? Apparently so. On the 20-item multiple-choice test about Indonesia, subjects for whom the stereotype labels had been present did significantly better than those for whom the labels had been absent.

Figure 1 also reveals that subjects generally did better at recalling the stereotype-consistent traits than the neutral ones. Or, to use the proper phrase, there was a main effect for consistent information. To say that there is a **main effect** for some variable, such as consistent traits, simply means that overall, the nature of the traits (consistent vs. neutral) made a difference. In this case it is not exactly clear what that means. Perhaps as a group, the consistent traits in Table 2 are slightly more memorable than the neutral traits. But, again, the key result is the interaction: Stereotype activation enhances recall only of traits consistent with the stereotype.

The two graphs in Figure 2 show other outcomes that might have occurred in the Macrae et al. experiment. Figure 2A shows a simple main effect for stereotype-consistent information; that is, stereotype-consistent traits are recalled better whether or not the stereotype label is present. Such a result might suggest one of two things. First, it might be that subjects are invoking the stereotype label on their own when the traits start appearing on the screen: "'Dangerous,' 'rebellious'—Hey, this guy sounds like a skinhead." Or, such a result might suggest that those traits chosen for the impression formation task because they were consistent with the stereotypes to be used were simply easier to remember than those selected because they were neutral. Figure 2B shows another possible interaction between trait type and the presence or absence of the stereotype label. In this case, the interaction suggests that invoking a stereotype label actively interferes with memory for traits that are not consistent with that label.

Before leaving the Macrae et al. experiment, there is one last point to mention, which has to do with the preparation of the sets of traits consistent with and neutral with respect to the four different stereotypes. Suppose that Macrae et al. had used only one set of traits and invoked only one stereotype by telling subjects that the person being described on the screen was, say, an artist. Had they done that, their results would have been much less convincing because we might have suspected that there was something peculiar about that particular set of consistent and neutral traits. By using four stereotypes and four different sets of traits—and getting the same results with all four—they decreased the plausibility of any argument that their stimulus materials were biased. Macrae et al., in effect, conducted an internal replication of their experiment.

To replicate something simply means to duplicate or reproduce or repeat it. As can be seen in Box 2, there are several varieties of replications; unfortunately, none of them is very popular. In fact, replication is one of the most neglected aspects of research in the social and behavioral sciences. It is not too difficult to see why. A full-scale replication of any experiment would be as time-consuming and costly (probably more costly with inflation) as the original experiment, without its advantages. And you get very little credit for creativity in the scientific community if you appear to be doing what someone else has already done. But there are many ways of carrying out partial replications, as Macrae et al. did by using four stereotypes, without the added time and expense of a complete second study. For example, you might have

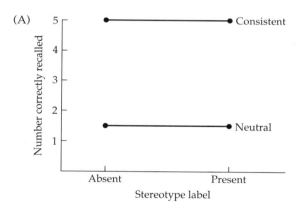

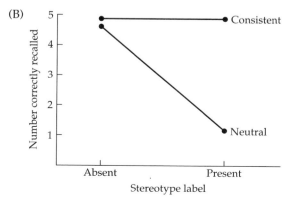

2 Two hypothetical outcomes for the experiment described in the text. (A) There is simply a main effect for trait type: Stereotype-consistent traits are remembered better. (B) There is an interaction suggesting that invoking the stereotype label interferes with memory for traits that are not part of the stereotype.

Box 2

Replicate, Replicate, Replicate!

One of the things that should be very clear to you by now, after having plowed through the preceding chapters, is that there are multiple ambiguities surrounding research in the social and behavioral sciences. Because of that, one demonstration of a given cause-and-effect sequence is never sufficient. Any experiment needs to be repeated with different manipulations and measurements (to probe its internal validity) and in different settings and with different subjects (to establish its external validity). Replication, in short, is not only the road to progress, it is absolutely essential even if all you want to know is where you are at the moment—that is, what you really know at the moment.

Replications come in several varieties. An exact replication of research is one in which all aspects of the original research are duplicated precisely. For most of the hard sciences, exact replications are routine. In chemistry, for example, at 10° Centigrade under atmospheric pressure with constant humidity, hydrogen and oxygen would be expected to combine in the same manner in Israel as in England. In an experiment on human behavior, however, Israelis and English would not necessarily be expected to react in the same manner to a given stimulus. You might argue that if we chose a stimulus that had the same meaning to both, we would get the same reaction. If we did that, and assuming there were other differences in setting, such as time of day and experimenters, we would have changed the hypothetical Israeli-English study from an exact to a conceptual replication. According to Hendrick (1990), a conceptual replication is one in which we "attempt to convey the same crucial structure of information in the independent variables to subjects, but by a radical transformation of the procedural variables" (p. 45).

In research on human behavior, exact replications are usually not possible: Experimenters, subjects, and settings are almost sure to differ, even when you manipulate and measure your variables in the same way as in the original research. Conceptual replications are thus more natural for the social and behavioral sciences, but they can pose problems. If your conceptual replication fails to reproduce the original result, you may not be able to say why. It could be because the new way you chose to manipulate the independent variable was flawed, or it could be because you used male subjects instead of female subjects, or it could be because.... .

Suppose that in reading a research report you notice a flaw in the procedure. It occurs to you that because of the way in which the author operationalized the independent variable, he or she has really manipulated something other than what is claimed. In short, you are able to suggest a plausible alternative explanation for the findings, and you want to do the research to demonstrate that your explanation is more valid than the author's. The type of experiment you need to conduct under these circumstances is called a balanced replication. In a balanced replication, you include all of the conditions necessary to duplicate the original conditions as precisely as possible as well as a new condition(s) in which you change or eliminate the flaw that you think is responsible for the original results. Inclusion of the original conditions is necessary to show that with your different setting and subjects you can duplicate the author's findings. Then, when you also demonstrate, by means of your additional condition, that the procedural change suggested by your alternative explanation for those findings produced a different set of results, you will have won your case.

two different experimenters each run half of the subjects in every condition. That is not ideal, but if the results are the same regardless of experimenter, you can place more confidence in those results than in the results of a single experimenter. The plausibility of the argument that two experimenters biased the results in exactly the same way is considerably less than the plausibility of the argument that any given experimenter may have biased the results.

Designing What You Need

The key thing to remember about the process of designing an experiment is that it is an exercise in simple, everyday logic. You do not need a knowledge of esoteric statistical techniques. You do need to be very clear about the hypothesis you want to test. Quite often one of the first things that happens when you begin to think about ways of testing a hypothesis is that you realize you are a little fuzzy about exactly what the hypothesis is. Variables that seem clear-cut when you are just toying with them may turn out to be extremely complex when you give them a little serious thought. Group size is a good example: On the surface, it seems very straightforward, but it is really quite complex. If your initial hypothesis is something like "Members are less satisfied in large work groups than in small work groups," a little analysis might suggest that it is not really size but ease of communication that is the important thing. It just happens that in large groups it is usually more difficult to communicate with other group members than it is in small groups. So, your revised hypothesis would be, "The greater the ease of communication in groups, the greater the member satisfaction." Whatever the subject you are interested in, the point is simply that the first step in designing any experiment is to specify your hypothesis as precisely as possible. Only when you have done that can you begin to set up the appropriate conditions to test it.

Some Standard and Not-So-Standard Designs

"Testing the hypothesis" simply means demonstrating that changes in the independent variable produce changes in the dependent variable. An experimental design that allows you to do that is said to be internally valid, or to have internal validity. As Cook and Shadish (1994) point out, identifying specific threats to internal validity and finding ways to overcome them remain the keys to good experimental design. An internally valid design is one that enables you to say that your experimental treatment, your manipulation, did make a difference. Although you may not be banished to outer darkness for constructing a design that lacks internal validity, you will be cursed with uninterpretable results.

It is, of course, impossible to foresee everything that might interfere with your ability to make causal inferences linking the independent and dependent variables in a specific setting. But, as you will recall from Chapter 7, there are a number of threats to internal validity that can be foreseen and dealt with, with varying degrees of success, by design. Cook and Campbell (1979) listed 13 such threats, which are summarized in Table 1 in Chapter 7, just in case they have slipped your mind. In fact, it would be an excellent idea to memorize them so that you can check them off mentally when you are designing an experiment. (I tried to think of a good mnemonic for you by using the first letters of each, but what can you spell with HMTISSMIADCCR? If you want to try it, you can get another vowel by substituting *Attrition* for *Mortality*.)

The basic design that qualifies as a true experiment—the bare minimum, so to speak—is one in which you randomly assign subjects to two conditions, expose subjects in one condition to your manipulation, and then have subjects in both conditions respond to your dependent variable. The official title of this design is the posttest-only control group design. Let R stand for random assignment of subjects to conditions and let X and O stand for the manipulation and measurement, respectively (which, of course, you remember from Chapter 7). The design may be diagrammed like this:

$$
\begin{array}{ccc}
R & X & O \\
R & & O
\end{array}
\longrightarrow \text{Compare}
$$

This design is simple, but elegant. It rests on the assumption that because subjects are randomly assigned to conditions and because measurement occurs at the same point in time for both conditions, any differences at the time of measurement must be due to the manipulation, X, in the experimental condition. There is only one comparison to make.

An example of a study using this design is one in which Dandoy and Goldstein (1990) attempted to replicate some earlier research on psychological stress and the coping process. The subjects were male and female college students who watched a brief film depicting several "gruesome" accidents in a woodworking plant. While they watched the film, their galvanic skin response was monitored. (Galvanic skin response is a measure of the electrical conductivity of the skin and is a fairly standard indicator of physiological arousal.) Following the film, the subjects were asked a number of questions about it as well as some questions about their own emotional reactions to the film. The manipulation was simply what subjects were told prior to watching the film. Half the subjects were randomly assigned to a control condition in which they were just told about the general content of the film they would be watching. The remaining subjects were given that information also, but in addition, they were asked to examine the film in a more "intellectual" manner as they were watching it. That is, they were instructed to "reflect upon the psychodynamics revealed by the interchanges between the people, and be analytical about the devices used by the foreman to influence the men in the shop, that is, the psychological processes that are involved" (p. 281). Subjects who watched the film in this frame of mind were significantly less distressed by its content.

Before commenting on how the posttest-only control group design fares with respect to the threats listed in Table 1 in Chapter 7, let me introduce you to two more true experimental designs. You will no doubt discern a certain family resemblance among all three. The pretest-posttest control group design is arrived at simply by adding a pretest to each of the conditions in the posttest-only control group design. Diagrammatically, it looks like this:

Now, however, there are three comparisons of interest. Comparison 1 will tell you whether or not your random assignment really worked. Comparison 2 will tell you how much of an effect history, maturation, testing, and statistical regression have had on your posttest. Comparison 3 will tell you whether your manipulation had any effect, and if so, how much. The latter statement assumes that Comparison 1 indicated that randomization did work—that is, that there was no difference between groups on the pretest.

If you take the two preceding diagrams and place one on top of the other, you will have a third experimental design. This one is called the **Solomon four-group design** (Solomon, 1949), and it looks like this:

Group 1	R	O	X	O
Group 2	R	O		O
Group 3	R		X	O
Group 4	R			O

As you can see, there are a number of comparisons that could be made here. The basic advantages of this design are that it enables you to estimate (1) the magnitude of the effects due to pretesting and (2) the interaction of pretesting with your independent variable (X). Rearranging the design as a 2 × 2 factorial design emphasizes the comparisons available:

	NO X	X
No pretest	4	3
Pretest	2	1

To determine the main effect of pretesting, you would compare the average response on your dependent measure from Groups 3 and 4 combined with the average response from Groups 1 and 2 combined. To determine the main effect of your manipulation, you would compare the average response from Groups 3 and 1 combined with the average response from Groups 4 and 2 combined. In addition, of course, you would be able to look at the interaction (or lack of interaction) between pretesting and your manipulation. It might turn out that your manipulation is effective only after subjects have been pretested; that is, the average response from Group 1 is greater than that from Group 2, but Group 3 does not differ from Group 4. If that result did occur, it would mean that you could generalize your results only to pretested groups.

The key to understanding experimental design, however, is not to try to memorize every design that might be possible. The point is to realize that the design you will need depends on your hypothesis and the setting in which you choose to test it. Both the hypothesis and the setting may dictate that certain conditions be added to achieve the comparison(s) of interest to you or to rule out various alternative explanations. For example, several years ago I was interested in the stability of physiological reactions to nicotine (Jones, 1986). That meant I had to monitor subjects' reactions before, during, and after smoking a cigarette. Then I had to get those same subjects back into the laboratory 6 months later to see whether the nature of their reactions had changed. Or, to take another example, Glass and Singer (1972) were interested in the possibility that noises, such as the noises of traffic and people and machines that one might be exposed to in a large city, are stressful at least in part because they are uncontrollable. Uncontrollable noises, of course, are noises that you cannot turn off and you cannot make go away. To test this idea, Glass and Singer needed at least three conditions: (1) controllable noise; (2) uncontrollable noise; and (3) no noise. Again, the point is simply that the number and nature of the conditions necessary when you design an experiment depend on the nature of your hypothesis.

Which brings us back to the threats to internal validity. The three standard designs mentioned earlier—the posttest-only control group, the pretest-posttest control group, and the Solomon four-group—are, indeed, *intended* to control for, or rule out, several of the threats to internal validity. For example, when your dependent measure shows a difference between the experimental and control groups, you may be able to rule out history as an explanation for that difference *if* the same historical events have occurred to both groups, with the exception of your manipulation. Similarly, selection, maturation, and statistical regression may be ruled out as threats by randomization, which is supposed to ensure that subjects in all conditions are equivalent to start with.

But before you can really make the judgment that these and the other threats to internal validity have been ruled out, you have to see all the details of the experimental procedure. It is like a football coach drawing X's and O's on a chalkboard. Everyone can see how things are supposed to work and why certain things are supposed to be done, but out on the field it is a different story. The concern switches from why certain things are supposed to be done to how to do them. It is one thing to understand why that guard is supposed to be moved backward and to the left (so the ball carrier can race through the opening thus created), but it is quite another thing to actually move that 265-pound mass of muscle.

Designing an experiment often presents the same sort of problem. It is easy to see why Glass and Singer (1972) needed one condition in which subjects would be exposed to controllable noise and one in which the noise would be uncontrollable. That was what they were interested in. But how, precisely, were they to set up those two conditions while keeping the amounts of noise constant in the two? If the noise really was controllable in one condition, then what would keep subjects in that condition from turning it off when it became unbearable and, thus, experiencing less noise? If they did experience less noise, then you would not be able to tell whether the differences between the controllable-noise and uncontrollable-noise conditions were due to controllability, or noise, or both.

Setting the Stage

The point, of course, is that once you have decided what conditions you need to test your hypothesis, you have to decide on a procedure. The decisions about what conditions you need are on a relatively abstract level. If you had reason to believe that the expertise of a communicator was an important variable in his or her effectiveness, then you might decide to have one condition in which a highly expert communicator presents a message, one condition in which someone low in expertise presents the same message, and a no-message control condition. On the other hand, the decisions about your procedure must be very precise and concrete. You have to decide how you are going to manipulate and measure the variables of interest. How, exactly, is expertise to be manipulated? To assess attitudes, will you use a 5-point scale, a 7-point scale, or a 31-point scale? How will the questions be worded? What do you plan to say to subjects when they arrive at the appointed time and place? What appointed times and places do you plan to use? How will the experimental room be furnished? In short, everything from the first to the last second of your contact with the subjects has to be planned. If it is not, the results of your experiment may be uninterpretable because of variations in what you said or did to different subjects, variations that may have influenced how they responded to your dependent measures.

This is the point at which experimental design becomes more of an art than a science. You must write, produce, and direct, as well as serve as prop manager and stagehand for, a one-act play. Remember the care and detail that went into Macrae, Milne, and Bodenhausen's (1994) study of stereotypes? First they had to determine which traits were considered consistent or neutral with respect to a variety of stereotypes. Then they had to program a computer to present the names, stereotype labels (for half the subjects), and traits (in random order) for 3 seconds each. In addition, they had to compose and record a 2-minute prose passage with facts and figures about Indonesia and generate a 20-item multiple-choice test about those facts and figures. The payoff, of course, was a tightly controlled presentation of the variables of interest.

Another example of what is involved in setting the stage for an experiment is provided by a classic experiment on conformity. Asch (1952) arranged a situation in which naive subjects were confronted with a clear discrepancy between what they saw in front of them and what a group of apparently similar others said was there. The stimulus materials Asch used were simple lines. Subjects were shown a number of different sets of cards and asked to judge which of three comparison lines on one card was the same length as a standard line on a second card. For every set of cards, each member of a group of seven to nine subjects was to make this judgment aloud and in turn. There was only one catch: In each group there was only one real subject. All of the others were accomplices of the experimenter who had been instructed to make incorrect judgments on certain trials. Thus, the naive subject, who was always maneuvered into a seat so that he or she would make a judgment after most of the other group members, was repeatedly confronted with a discrepancy between what he or she thought was correct and what the group said was correct. The results were dramatic. Compared with control subjects who made the line matching judgments alone, subjects confronted with the conflict between what they saw and what the group appeared to see made five times as many errors in matching the standard and comparison lines.

You may have noticed that both Macrae, Milne, and Bodenhausen's (1994) and Asch's (1952) experiments involved deception. Macrae et al.'s deception was relatively minor. At the outset of the experiment they simply told subjects that they were interested in the ability to perform tasks simultaneously. That, of course, was not what they were interested in. Asch's deception was somewhat more elaborate. He recruited a number of accomplices, had them pose as naive subjects, instructed them to give a number of incorrect responses, had them take certain seats in the room so that the real subjects would be in the position of giving a judgment after the accomplices had given theirs, and, finally, administered the whole session with a straight face. The one real subject in each group was led to believe that the experiment was about visual perception, when in reality it was about conformity. But if Asch had told his subjects that he was studying conformity, chances are he would not have observed a single error on the line judgment task.

The use of deception in experimental research has prompted a number of heated exchanges over the last few years. Some have gone so far as to say that deception should be avoided at all costs (Baumrind, 1985), and dire predictions have been made about the long-term consequences of its continued use in research. However, the available evidence seems to indicate that the use of deception in research has not resulted in the predicted loss of trust among potential subjects (Sharpe, Adair, and Roese, 1992). Nor has it been perceived as harmful by actual subjects (Christensen, 1988). If you can manipulate and measure the variables of interest without using deception, you should, of course, do so. But if your design can be realized only by a minor, temporary deception that is not in any way harmful to subjects, then I see no problem. Just be sure you note the key words in that last sentence. "Minor" and "not harmful" should be self-explanatory. "Temporary" means that one of the obligations you incur should you decide to use deception is that of thoroughly explaining the entire experiment and the reasons for the deception to all subjects as soon as the experiment is over. The technical name for this procedure is **debriefing**, and it is an important part of the experiment. Debriefing usually takes the form of a casual, relaxed, postexperimental discussion. Not only will it give you a chance to find out whether subjects saw through your deception, but it will also enable you to solicit suggestions from them about how the experiment might be improved.

There is some evidence, however, that if debriefing is done too casually, it may not "take." That is, beliefs or self-assessments that are induced as part of the experimental procedure may persist, even if subjects are later told that what they were led to believe was part of a cover story and not really true. For example, Misra (1992) reports a study in which subjects were asked to work on a set of difficult problems with ambiguous solutions. Some subjects were led to believe that they had succeeded in solving most of the problems, while others were led to believe that they had failed miserably. All subjects were then asked to rate some magazine advertisements. Subsequently, half of the subjects were debriefed in the "conventional" manner—that is, they were simply told that the feedback on the problem-solving task had been false and that it was necessary to deceive them to see whether their "state of mind" influenced their perceptions of the advertisements. The remaining subjects were given a more "explicit" debriefing, which included an explanation of the necessity for the deception, but which also pointed out how false beliefs—such as those about their problem-solving ability—often persist even when the evidence on which those beliefs are based has been discredited. Finally, all subjects were asked to rate their own ability at problem solving. Sure enough, the self-ratings of the subjects who had been debriefed in the more casual, conventional manner still reflected the false feedback they had been given earlier; that is, those who had been given the (false) failure feedback rated themselves as less able than those who received the (false) success feedback. The self-ratings of subjects who had been given the more explicit debriefing did not reflect those differences. As Misra (1992) notes, these findings suggest that the responsibility to conduct a thorough debriefing should be taken seriously.

You need to be aware, however, that debriefing can create other problems. As indicated by the last few threats to internal validity described in Chapter 7, subjects can and often do inform others about what goes on in an experiment. When those informed subjects participate in the study, their data may be worthless. They are not likely to tell you that they knew ahead of time that you were going to deceive them, not after they have just deceived you by going through the whole procedure as if they were naive about it. Indeed, Adair, Dushenko, and Lindsay (1985) note that several studies have been found in which debriefed subjects told their classmates about the research they had participated in, classmates who subsequently participated in the research themselves. Campbell (1988) points out other disadvantages of debriefing: "It provides modeling and publicity for deceit. … It reduces the credibility of the laboratory and undermines the utility of deceit in future experiments." Related to this is the fact that debriefing often informs the subject of his or her own gullibility, and for some people this could be very damaging to their self-esteem. Thus, one could argue that it might be better not to debrief subjects when the deceptions are minor. The deception in the stereotype experiment, for example, seems to fall into this category.

If it is at all possible to investigate what you are interested in without the use of deception, however, you are better off doing so for practical as well as ethical reasons. Parents often tell their children that it is simply easier to be honest because then they do not have to remember the lies they have told. Similarly, in an experiment involving deception, you usually cannot get away with one little misrepresentation of what is going on. From the subject's point of view, everything about your procedure has to make sense. That means you have to have an overall, coherent **cover story**, a pseudo-rationale for everything the subject is asked to do (or put up with). Asch's cover story was that he was studying visual perception; hence, it made sense that subjects would be asked to make judgments of line lengths. Further, an ideal cover story is constructed so that the manipulation of your independent variable and the measurement of your dependent variable seem natural within the context of the story. If Asch had been studying visual perception, it would have been natural to ask other subjects to state what they were seeing (the independent variable), just as it was to be expected that the real subject would have to state what he or she was perceiving (the dependent variable). You might note that in terms of our earlier discussion of manipulations, Asch's manipulation was clearly of the event variety, and it certainly had an effect on the subjects.

The major problem with an elaborate cover story is that in adding all the little details of procedure that will make it believable, you are likely to introduce a number of extraneous variables. If one of these supposedly extraneous variables can plausibly be related to the changes in your dependent variable, you are in trouble: The internal validity of your experiment will be lost. The more elaborate the cover story, the greater the number of extraneous variables, and the more likely it is that at least one of them will have some effect on your dependent variable.

Several terms are used to refer to the effects of these extraneous variables that mar the interpretation of results and destroy the internal validity of an experiment. The most common one is the word "confounded." The dictionary defines *confounds* as "causes to become confused" and "fails to distinguish." If you divided your class into short people and tall people, you would be confounding sex and height, because males are typically taller than females. Similarly, a manipulation would be confounded if it actually changed several different things at once. You would not know which of those changes produced changes in the dependent variable—in fact, they all might. For example, instead of presenting their stimulus materials as traits on a computer screen, Macrae, Milne, and Bodenhausen (1994) might have had subjects view videotapes of four different people, each displaying some stereotypically consistent and some stereotypically neutral behaviors. That might, in fact, have been more interesting for the subjects. But the possibilities for confoundings would have skyrocketed. One of the actors might have been especially good at displaying the stereotypically consistent behaviors, but not the neutral behaviors. One might have been especially ugly (or attractive) and, hence, memorable. And, given that we expect behavioral sequences to make at least some sense, it would have been extremely difficult to have the actors display the neutral and consistent behaviors in a random order. In short, the more elaborate the scenario you construct for an experiment, the more likely you are to introduce **confounding variables**. These confounding, extraneous variables are also referred to as **artifacts**, and they can best be avoided by keeping your procedure and your manipulation as simple as possible.

It should be clear by now why you cannot really tell whether an experiment is internally valid until you see both the design *and* the details of the procedure. The point is simply that you have to be very careful in constructing your procedure. It is incredibly easy to introduce confounding variables and things that will serve as a basis for plausible alternative explanations of your results. As Hendrick and Jones (1972) have pointed out, most sources of alternative explanations will be quite specific to some detail of your procedure or setting: The room was too hot, so subjects got drowsy and inattentive and missed the part where you said they had a chance to win a prize, which was supposed to be the independent variable; or, the opinion scale you were using as your dependent measure was ambiguously worded, so many subjects just marked "Not Sure." However, there are a few general sources of alternative explanations—in addition to those in Table 1 of Chapter 7—that you can be prepared for.

Chance and Other Alternative Explanations

It may have occurred to you that you are getting fairly close to the end of the chapter on experimentation and there has still been no mention of statistics. For many people, experimental design and statistics do seem always to be uttered in the same breath, like a compound curse. But they are really separate topics. Experimental design is an exercise in logic or common sense. It is a process in which you lay out the conditions necessary to obtain interpretable information bearing on your hypothesis. Statistical analysis is a process that tells you whether you may discount one specific alternative explanation for the results of your experiment: that is, that the results you obtained were due to chance.

There are many excellent statistics texts that will show you how to do the necessary analyses. Here, I just want to make sure you understand why chance has to be ruled out as an explanation for the results of an experiment. Earlier it was mentioned that most data of interest in the social and behavioral sciences have a great deal of built-in variability. You might anticipate, for example, that most of your friends would be in favor of tighter gun control laws. But if you were to ask them to respond to an attitude scale on the topic, you surely would not expect them all to check exactly the same point on the scale. Some would be more extreme than others, and some, unless you have an unusually homogeneous group of friends, would even be opposed to such laws. Similarly, the people assigned to the various conditions in an experiment can usually be expected to vary in how they respond to the dependent measure, even in the absence of a manipulation or independent variable. Further, there is no particular reason to expect that the average response of subjects in the control condition, say, would be exactly the same as the average response of subjects in the experimental condition. If you were to randomly divide your friends into two groups and calculate the average attitude toward gun control in each group, you would expect the two averages to differ slightly. Similarly, in an experiment, just on the basis of the chance assignment of different people to different conditions, you would expect the average response to the dependent measure in one condition to be a little more or a little less than the average in any other condition. Thus, in order to claim that your independent variable has had any effect on your dependent variable, you have to know whether the difference between conditions is greater than this variability due to chance. Basically, that is what statistical analysis will tell you: whether the difference between conditions is sufficiently large that you can rule out chance as a plausible explanation for that difference.

After chance, the things most likely to give you trouble in your efforts to establish the internal validity of an experiment have to do with the peculiar role that many people assume when they become subjects in an experiment. For most people, even most college students, it is a very unusual experience, and you should not be surprised to find that people behave in unusual ways when they are in unusual settings. Experimenters, of course, want to obtain responses to independent variables that are natural or representative. In fact, many people justify the use of deception in research with precisely this argument, that is, that it is necessary to disguise the true purpose of the research so that people can respond to the independent variable in as unselfconscious or natural a manner as possible. Subjects, on the other hand, seem to approach the experimental situation with an attitude that is something like, "Tell me what you want me to do and I'll do it and we can get this over with as quickly as possible."

The sources of this compliance on the part of subjects are, no doubt, complex. There is an element of respect for science and the attempt to learn about why people behave as they do. There is an element of simple courtesy toward the, usually, older and higher-status experimenter. But, whatever its sources, the results are usually distortions of behavior. It is as if most subjects assume that the experimenter is trying to prove something and view their task as helping him or her to do so. Thus, any cue given by the setting or the experimenter about what the hypothesis is, what the study is attempting to demonstrate, or how the subject is expected to behave is likely to be seized on by the subject, who is often all too ready to behave accordingly. Such cues are referred to as the **demand characteristics** of the experimental situation; they suggest to the subject what the situation demands (Wagstaff, 1991). One of the major purposes of an experimental cover story, of course, is to keep demand characteristics to a minimum. If the true purpose of the experiment is hidden in the folds of the cover story, then it is less likely that subjects will be able to pick up cues that tell them how to respond. As you have seen, however, cover stories can introduce confounding variables.

Even with a good clean cover story, you may have problems. Rosenthal (1966, 1976) and his colleagues have found that even in apparently well-controlled laboratory settings, experimenters who expect their subjects to respond in certain ways are more likely to obtain those responses than are experimenters with no such prior expectations. For example, in a number of studies, experimenters were asked to administer a person-perception task to subjects. The experimenters were to show a series of photos to each subject and ask the subject to rate each photo in terms of whether the person pictured had been experiencing success or failure. The ratings were to be made on a scale from –10 (extreme failure) to +10 (extreme success). The photos had all actually been previously determined to be neutral on this scale. However, some experimenters were led to believe that the subjects' ratings would average about +5, whereas others were led to believe they would average about –5. In study after study, it was found that experimenters with the former expectation obtained significantly more positive ratings from their subjects than experimenters with the latter expectation. Note that this happened even though the experimenters all read precisely the same instructions to their subjects, a feature of the procedure that Rosenthal took pains to confirm by recording the experimenter–subject interactions. However the experimenters were conveying their expectations, it was apparently being done by some very subtle cues.

As you might expect, advocates of laboratory experimentation as the method of choice for the social and behavioral sciences were not too pleased with the implications of Rosenthal's data, and critics were quick to point out flaws in the research (e.g., Chow, 1992). However, the evidence that such experimenter expectancy effects are real and can indeed bias experimental results has become so overwhelming that even Rosenthal's erstwhile critics now concede that they can be a problem (Barber, 1976). The problem is, in fact, quite serious, because research has demonstrated that there are not just one or two aspects of the experimenter's behavior that convey cues to subjects. Rather, it seems to be the case that almost everything the experimenter does may unintentionally convey what he or she expects—tone of voice, relative emphasis on certain words, leaning forward or backward at certain points in the procedure, looking at subjects, nodding, frowning, smiling (e.g., Freidman, 1967; Duncan and Rosenthal, 1968; Jones and Cooper, 1971). Hazelrigg, Cooper, and Strathman (1991) have found that experimenters with a high need for control are particularly susceptible to the bias, as are subjects with a strong need for social approval.

What all this means for you is that any experiment you design must include some way of avoiding such effects, and there are several ways of doing that. The first, which is not recommended, is to automate everything. Greet the subjects, put them in a booth with a computer terminal, and turn it on. Your manipulation(s) can be delivered via the screen, and subjects can type out their responses to your dependent measure on the keyboard. Many experiments on social judgment are now conducted in this manner. Stimuli such as traits and other descriptive material are presented on a computer screen, and subjects respond by punching in numbers or typing out answers. The virtue of this approach, of course, is standardization. Everything that each subject in a given condition sees is exactly the same. Its drawback, which I believe outweighs that virtue in some circumstances, is that it lacks what Aronson, Brewer, and Carlsmith (1985) have called **experimental realism**. It is not very involving, and it seems to have no effect on subjects. In fact, from the subjects' point of view, it is likely to be downright boring.

Another way of avoiding experimenter expectancy effects is to retain a live experimenter for interacting with and directing subjects, but devise ways to keep the experimenter from knowing which condition any given subject has been assigned to. If the experimenter does not know how the subject is expected to respond, the likelihood of his or her influencing that response is reduced. The term used to describe this situation is **blind**: The experimenter is kept blind as to the condition to which the subject has been assigned. Exactly how you do that depends on your procedure, but it can usually be done without too much trouble. You might, for example, have the manipulation and the dependent measure administered by different experimenters.

In addition to the overly compliant, helpful attitude that seems to characterize many subjects in laboratory experiments, there is another factor that plays a part in their eager search for cues about what is expected of them. Many subjects appear to suffer from **evaluation apprehension** (Geen, 1991). That is, they seem to be anxious not only about getting through the experiment as smoothly and quickly as possible, but also about winning a positive evaluation from the experimenter. They want the experimenter to approve of them, to like them, to believe they have a good personality. Therefore, they may be particularly attentive to cues about how the experimenter expects them to behave.

When people first began to use experimentation as a tool to investigate social and behavioral processes, it was used rather naively. It was assumed that because the experiment had proved so successful in physics and chemistry—and even with animal behavior—it could be employed with humans as subjects. There was little effort to control for or to assess the sorts of contaminating influences we have been discussing. However, when critics began to point out that experiments on human behavior and social processes might be a little more complicated than had been thought, that there were certain problems that needed looking into, you would have thought they had called for a return to the Dark Ages. Researchers were vying to outdo each other in denouncing the critics as backsliders and turncoats.

Critics of experimentation in the social sciences usually emphasize one or the other of two major points, both of which seem reasonable. The first is that experiments need to be done more carefully than they have been in the past. The purpose of the last few pages, of course, has been to alert you to some of the more pervasive difficulties that have been encountered and to suggest a few ways in which you can avoid them. Suls and Gastorf (1980) reported that in terms of controlling for experimenter effects, for example, there has indeed been an improvement in the quality of published research since 1960. But all too many experiments still yield ambiguous results because of the failure to include adequate controls. The second major point emphasized by critics of experimentation is that experiments need to be more selectively employed than they have been in the past. There is an old quote from Abraham Maslow that runs, "If the only tool you have is a hammer, it is tempting to treat everything as if it were a nail." As you have seen from the preceding chapters, experimentation is certainly not the only tool available. The question is: When is experimentation appropriate?

What Experiments Can and Cannot Do for You

It has already been pointed out that, of all the research methods discussed, an experiment can provide you with the clearest evidence of a cause-and-effect relationship. It achieves that distinction, of course, by allowing you to manipulate one variable and observe what happens to another, under conditions that (you hope) enable you to rule out all other plausible reasons for changes in the latter variable. Experimentation is usually considered vastly superior to correlational research in this respect, and rightly so. Naturally occurring events are often a complicated mesh of several variables, and it is impossible to tell which are essential to producing the effect in question. Experimentation enables you to systematically untie such knots, manipulate the variables one at a time, and separate the essential from the nonessential.

For example, in the mid-1960s there was a murder on the streets of New York that caused a wave of national indignation. It was not the murder per se that was so unusual. What aroused the national conscience was that it later came to light that a number of people had heard the victim's cries, and some had even witnessed the crime from their apartment windows, but none had done anything to help. None had even bothered to call the police. Newspapers and magazines picked up the story and proclaimed it to be yet another horrible example of urban apathy, of not wanting to be involved, and, generally, of the impending disintegration of civilized society. If you think about it for a moment, you can probably come up with several reasons why someone might not have helped the woman in distress. Maybe the newspapers were right: The witnesses just did not care. Maybe they were afraid for their own safety should they try to intervene. Maybe they were reluctant to get caught up in the identification, prosecution, and trial of the criminal. Maybe they thought someone else had already notified the police. Using this actual event as a stimulus to their thinking, Latane and Darley (1970) designed and carried out a series of laboratory experiments on the last possibility, which they conceptualized as diffusion of responsibility. They were able to show that when a person believes that a number of others are aware of an emergency situation, that person is much less likely to help than when he or she believes no one else knows that help is needed. In other words, what Latane and Darley did was to single out one component of a complex stimulus situation. They then designed an experiment in which they could manipulate that one component to see what effect it (alone) had on the dependent variable of interest (helping behavior in emergency situations). Such analysis of complex variables is one of the most appropriate uses of experimentation.

In addition to this analytic use of experiments, Gergen (1978) has suggested another role that might be referred to as the **sensitizing function**. As he put it, occasionally an experimental demonstration can unsettle the way we look at things. Here the task of the experiment is really to bring to our awareness certain aspects of our behavior that need to be dealt with, to sensitize us to the consequences of some facets of social life. According to Gergen, Asch's research on conformity really served this consciousness-raising function. It sensitized people to the tremendous power of groups to producing conformity to norms. Thus, this research did more than merely reproduce in the laboratory behavior already known to exist; it created a new self-consciousness.

There is no guarantee, of course, that just because you can produce a finding in the laboratory, it has anything at all to do with how people behave outside of the experimental situation. A great deal of the criticism of experiments on social and behavioral processes has focused on this point. Experiments are often said to be artificial and to lack **external validity**. Experiments are said to have external validity when the obtained results hold true in different settings, with different subjects, and under different conditions. In addition, it is sometimes pointed out that the ability to demonstrate that A causes B under one set of conditions does not preclude the possibility that B causes A under a different set of conditions. Even though it may be true that any particular experiment may be artificial and leave specific questions (such as whether B can cause A) unanswered, blanket criticisms of experimentation such as these strike me as silly. Artificiality may be a desirable characteristic in many instances. Henshel (1980) has pointed out, for example, that much of what is now known about biofeedback and our ability to control bodily functions previously thought to be beyond the realm of voluntary control was learned under extremely artificial experimental conditions. Similarly, Campbell and Stanley (1966) have noted that artificiality is essential to the analytic separation of variables discussed earlier, and that such analytic separation has been fundamental to advancing our understanding in many fields. Campbell and Stanley have also noted that those who complain of the low external validity of experiments may be expecting too much from any given experiment. They suggest that such critics need to adopt a somewhat longer time perspective, and that experimenters can explore the generality of findings by means of conceptual replications.

Summary

The advantages of experimentation as a research method can be illustrated with some old research on competition. By taking a phenomenon that he had observed among bicycle racers—that competition leads to improved performance—into the laboratory, Triplett was able to manipulate the variable of interest, avoid self-selection of subjects to conditions, and control a number of extraneous variables. Thus, he could rule out a number of alternative explanations for his observation.

In several ways, an experiment is simply an extension of the other research methods already discussed. Experimentation is a technique that helps you to be very precise and explicit about the conditions under which your observations take place. It is based on the assumption that all knowledge involves comparison. Experimentation goes beyond the other methods by introducing the notion of manipulation, of changing something to see what will happen. That aspect of the environment that is manipulated is the independent variable, and that aspect which you examine to see whether your manipulation has had any effect is the dependent variable.

One of the key choices facing a would-be experimenter is how to manipulate the independent variable: by instructions to the subjects or by an event that happens to the subjects. The latter is more likely to get and hold the subjects' attention, but the former is less likely to introduce extraneous, confounding variables. Because the purpose of an experiment is to see whether changes in the independent variable produce changes in the dependent variable, other things that might plausibly be expected to have an effect on the dependent variable must be controlled. In a typical experiment, then, you must be able to rule out the possibility of preexisting differences among the subjects assigned to the different conditions. Two techniques for doing this are matching and random assignment. Generally, random assignment is preferable, but it may not work well when you have only a small number of subjects. Using a table of random numbers can allow you to assign subjects to conditions randomly.

An experiment on stereotypes by Macrae, Milne, and Bodenhausen was used to illustrate the detailed planning that often goes into a well-designed experiment and also to introduce some additional concepts. Experimenters often design their research so that they can investigate the effects of more than one independent variable on the dependent variable. Such designs typically take the form of a factorial experiment, which has the advantage of letting the experimenter explore interactions among the variables. Some standard designs mentioned were the posttest-only control group design, the pretest-posttest control group design, and the Solomon four-group design. However, it was pointed out that the most common practice is to add as many or as few conditions as are necessary to test the hypothesis of interest to you.

Once you have decided how many conditions you need, the real work (and art) of experimentation begins. You have to lay out a detailed procedure, making sure that you do not introduce confounding variables in the process. At some point in the procedure, deception may be necessary, but it should be avoided if possible. Next, several general alternative explanations that are the bane of most experimenters were discussed: chance, demand characteristics, experimenter expectancy effects, and evaluation apprehension. Those do not exhaust the list, of course.

By far the most common use of experimentation is the dissection of complex variables, a use referred to as its analytic function. It is also possible to employ experimentation as a technique for sensitizing people to certain consequences of normal behavior. Early research on conformity served such a function by alerting people to the power of groups to induce conformity.

Recommended Readings

Aronson, E. (Ed.) (1992). *Readings about the social animal* (6th ed.). New York: W. H. Freeman.

Although I have summarized a few experimental procedures for you in this chapter, if you really wish to gain an understanding of the care and attention to detail that go into designing a good experiment, there is no substitute for reading the original reports. Sometimes that can be a little difficult, especially if your library does not have journal issues that go way back—where some of the classics are to be found. Fortunately, Elliot Aronson has put together a paperback book that reprints reports of several dozen important experiments from a variety of areas. Included are Asch's experiments on conformity, which first appeared in the 1950s, and Milgram's famous research on obedience. More recent examples of experiments on such topics as aggression, persuasion, group conflict, and social cognition are also included. Thus, in addition to providing a detailed tutorial on experimental methodology, the book will also serve to introduce you to some important substantive areas of research.

Aronson, E., Brewer, M., and Carlsmith, J. M. (1985). Experimentation in social psychology. In G. Lindzey and E. Aronson (Eds.), *Handbook of social psychology* (3rd ed.), vol. 2, pp. 1–79. New York: Random House.

The original version of this chapter appeared in 1968 in an earlier edition of the *Handbook*. The current version has been expanded to address criticisms of classical experimentation that emerged in the 1960s and 1970s and to incorporate greater discussion of field experiments. It remains, arguably, the single best source for a discussion of the art of experimentation on social behavior. The authors bring their considerable experience as innovative experimenters to bear on the nitty-gritty problems of staging an experiment in such a manner that subjects will respond naturally. With the help of numerous examples and illustrations, they discuss such issues as building a plausible cover story, delivering the independent variable by instructions versus an event that happens to the subject, the use of deception, and the advantages of a live experimenter. Criticisms of the experimental method are given thoughtful and balanced consideration, as are the ethical problems raised by deception. As with most research methods, the best way to learn how to experiment is to try it—but read this chapter before you do.

Overman, E. S. (Ed.) (1988). *Methodology and epistemology for social science: Selected papers of Donald T. Campbell*. Chicago: University of Chicago Press.

Donald Campbell is one of the most important figures in the methodology of social science. In a career spanning almost 50 years, he has produced hundreds of thought-provoking and informative articles on topics ranging from the indirect measurement of attitudes to quasi-experimental designs. Overman has assembled 19 of the most important of those articles in this collection, and they are all worth reading. Many deal explicitly with topics that we have covered in the last eight chapters, including internal and external validity, artifacts and controls, and reforms as experiments. In fact, many of them are the *original* article on the topic. And you need not be put off by the fact that many of them first appeared in academic journals. Campbell's writing is clear and jargon-free. When he introduces new terms, they are well defined and, typically, profusely illustrated. Also included are an introductory commentary by Overman, an autobiographical perspective on his scholarly interests by Campbell himself, and a full bibliography of Campbell's writings. If you are really interested in learning how to be a better methodologist, the latter will provide you with an excellent, ready-made reading list.

Petroski, H. (1992). *To engineer is human: The role of failure in successful design.* New York: Vintage Books.

The author of this book is a professor of civil engineering at Duke University, and the essays collected here first appeared in journals such as *Technology Review* and *American Scientist.* The essays themselves are delightful, nontechnical discussions of some basic principles of engineering design—principles that apply in fields other than engineering as well. As Petroski notes, "Engineering design shares certain characteristics with the positing of scientific theories, but instead of hypothesizing about the behavior of a given universe, whether of atoms, honeybees, or planets, engineers hypothesize about assemblages of concrete and steel that they arrange into a world of their own making." Using real-life examples—from buses that bend in the middle to bridges that undulate in the wind—he talks about testing hypotheses and learning from failures. The concept of failure is, in fact, central to progress, and Petroski makes a convincing case to that effect. He also includes a quote from Barry LePatner that summarizes the point nicely: "Good judgment is usually the result of experience. And experience is frequently the result of bad judgment."

9

Evaluation Research

To evaluate something means to ascertain its value or worth, to examine and judge it, to determine its merit (Scriven, 1991). Evaluation is something you do all the time. You evaluate people, places, courses, restaurants, almost everything you come in contact with, and it is done so quickly and automatically sometimes that you are not even conscious of its occurrence. In fact, it seems to be unusual for people to withhold judgment about anything (e.g., Gilbert, 1991). And once you have formed an opinion about something, of course, you are likely to act on that opinion as if it were the truth. You have a bad meal in a restaurant and never go back. You meet someone who seems unpleasant and abrasive and you make it a point to avoid them in the future.

The danger, of course, is that your initial evaluations may not be based on good evidence. You might have visited the restaurant on the chief cook's night off. The person who seemed abrasive might have been under a lot of stress that particular day. The consequences of these faulty judgments are usually benign. There are many other restaurants and people around, and the absence of the ones that were misjudged is unlikely to create a great deficit in your life. Usually, you are even protected from regretting their absence, because you never find out that you misjudged them. But if you could afford to eat out only once in a great while, you might be a little more careful. You might call the restaurant and find out ahead of time what night the chef was off. You might ask around to see whether anyone else had eaten there and what their opinion was of the place. The point is that when your resources are scarce, you have to be more careful about how you use them.

On a societal level, resources usually are scarce, so society does indeed have to be careful about how they are allocated. Support of a program like Medicare may mean that there are other worthy programs that cannot be funded. Providing free school lunches for poor children sounds like a great idea, but what will that mean about the availability of funds for Aid to Families with Dependent Children? The law requires that any new government spending be financed either by cuts in existing programs or through new taxes. And there is always opposition to new taxes. Even when funds for a particular program are available, we want to know whether or not they are being used properly. If those free school lunches are being served, are they going to the neediest kids? Are they nutritious? Are the supplies for them being purchased at economical prices?

Because funds are limited, people are particularly sensitive about waste and inefficiency in government. In May of 1994, for example, a White House aide used a presidential helicopter to ferry himself and a few friends to suburban Maryland for an afternoon of golf. Public outcry over the tab—about $13,000—cost him his job. When things like that occur, taxpayers feel that they are the ones being taken for a ride, and rightly so. With increasing government expenditures on social, educational, and medical programs, there has been increasing pressure from the taxpayers—via Congress—to see that the money is being well spent, to see that the public at large is getting its money's worth.

What Is Evaluation Research?

The growth and spread of evaluation research is the direct result of this mounting pressure for accountability and sanity in the allocation of the nation's resources (Weiss, 1987). As research methods go, however, evaluation research is still relatively young. And, like many adolescents, its identity is somewhat diffuse (Sechrest and Figueredo, 1993). **Evaluation research** can best be characterized as a heterogeneous assortment of techniques, procedures, and methods for systematically "assessing the conceptualization, design, implementation, and utility of social intervention programs" (Rossi and Freeman, 1993). That definition takes in a lot of ground. Translated, what it means for you is that all of the methods discussed in the preceding chapters are relevant to evaluation research: participant observation, archival research, interviewing, quasi-experimentation, experimentation, the whole kit and caboodle.

But there is more. There is an element in evaluation research that is largely absent from any of those methods taken individually, although it was briefly touched on in the discussion of participant observation: Evaluation research is often, even usually, a political undertaking (Cook, Leviton, and Shadish, 1985; Chelimsky, 1987). Programs compete for funds and attention. They have constituencies, people who profit from their continuation and suffer when they are terminated. There are conflicts of interest that have to be negotiated. The people in charge of running a program may see it in a completely different light from those charged with evaluating it. There is institutional inertia to be overcome, both to get new programs started and to end programs that are ineffective, or too costly for the benefits derived. All of this makes evaluation research tremendously exciting, of course, but it can also make it tremendously frustrating (see Box 1). To top it all off, the evaluation researcher is usually attempting to get some evidence about a program that he or she had no part in setting in motion. But let us take these things one at a time.

Policies, Programs, and the Need for Evaluation

It is important to note at the outset that policy and program are not the same thing. A **policy** is a general, usually somewhat abstract, statement of princi-

---

Box 1

A Metaphor for Evaluation Research?

According to Webster's (1991) dictionary, a metaphor is a figure of speech in which a word or phrase denoting one kind of object or idea is used in place of another to suggest a likeness, or analogy, between them. The metaphors we adopt to describe or think about things do make a difference. If we try to analyze the human mind as if it were a computer, for example, there are many aspects of experience—such as the influence of emotions on thought—that we might miss altogether. If we think of human memory as some sort of internal file cabinet where things are simply sorted and stored, then some of the more interesting memory-related phenomena—such as false and constructed memories—will escape us.

Similarly, Sechrest and Figueredo (1993) note that early enthusiasts of evaluation research failed to anticipate the social and political complexities they faced because, in part, they were operating under the implicit influence of an inappropriate metaphor. They went into the field with a pure science image of a mechanical universe, governed by fixed laws and made up of identical units. All that had to be done was to implement the program (manipulate) and assess the results (measure), with appropriate controls, of course. But what looked clean and simple on the drawing board was often a mess in the streets. Had they not been so bound by the "dominant Newtonian paradigm of social science," they might have been ready for a few of the problems that they eventually had to face. Specifically, Sechrest and Figueredo suggest that it might have helped had they thought of evaluation research as the tropical nightmare of a Darwinian jungle:

> A steaming green Hell, where everything is alive and keenly aware of you, most things are venomous or poisonous or otherwise dangerous, and nothing waits passively to be acted upon by an external force. This complex world is viciously competitive and strategically unpredictable because information is power, and power confers competitive advantage. The Darwinian jungle manipulates and deceives the unwary wanderer into serving myriads of contrary and conflicting ends. (p. 648)

And watch out for tiger pits in the underbrush!

---

ple. It is designed to influence decisions and determine actions by pointing out a desired end result. As Unrau (1993, p. 654) puts it: "Policy serves to provide the conceptual and principal means for thinking about a social problem." And, typically, policy implies that certain lines of attack on the problem are preferable to others. Congress, for example, might decide that it is bad for the nation for small businesses to be driven out of business. Its reasoning might be that with fewer small businesses, there would be a growth of monopolies, a decrease in competition, gradually rising prices, and lessened pressure for innovation. Thus, the Small Business Administration (SBA) might be charged by Congress with finding ways to encourage and sustain small businesses. One thing the SBA might do is loan money at low interest rates to people with an idea for starting a new business. This money-lending scheme would be a program by which the SBA hoped to realize the congressional policy of encouraging small-scale entrepreneurship. Note that the SBA could have come up with other programs to achieve the same aim. They might have started a series of workshops on management techniques designed to help those already in business to run their establishments more efficiently and more profitably. A **program**, then, is simply a specific procedure, or plan, for attempting to reach the goal spelled out in a policy. A given policy might be realized by any of several different programs (Cook, Leviton, and Shadish, 1985).

Congress, of course, is not the only source of policy. It depends on what the problem is that needs to be addressed. At the national level, the administrative branch of government can, and often does, set policy by calling attention to particular social problems—such as substance abuse—and encouraging funding to attack those problems to the exclusion of others—such as mental illness and homelessness (e.g., Humphreys and Rappaport, 1993). At the local level, city council members might become concerned about the number of injuries and deaths due to drunk driving and charge the police department with finding ways—that is, programs—for getting drunk drivers off the highways and streets.

But—and this is one of the reasons why some people have shied away from evaluation research—policy is often set without the advice and consent of those who are later asked to evaluate the programs intended to implement the policy. In the preceding chapters, it has been assumed that you have complete control over your research, all the way from problem definition to the final report. Evaluation research involves relinquishing some of that autonomy and, quite often, working on problems that others have defined for you. The trade-off is that your research may have more of an impact on the real world, but there is no guarantee of this. As Weiss (1987), Sechrest and Figueredo (1993), and others have pointed out, it is not at all clear how much the results of evaluation research actually influence decision making. Policy making and policy revision are, and are likely to remain, political processes, at least for the foreseeable future. Well-conducted program evaluations, however, can and do help to shape the evolution of policy by producing pertinent and important information about which programs are worthy of continued support and which are not. In the words of Cronbach et al. (1981):

> The proper mission of evaluation is not to eliminate the fallibility of authority or to bolster its credibility. Rather, its mission is to facilitate a democratic, pluralistic process by enlightening all the participants.

The key word here is "enlighten," which simply means "to furnish knowledge to." And that knowledge is indeed important, because it appears that many programs that may have looked great on the drawing board turn out not to accomplish what they were intended to accomplish. They just do not fly. For example, Mosteller (1981) and his colleagues collected a number of reports on social, sociomedical, and medical innovations that had been subjected to careful evaluations. The programs were quite diverse, ranging from an attempt to reduce delinquency among girls to a treatment for cancer of the bronchus. Mosteller and his colleagues studied the evaluation reports and scored each innovation on a 5-point scale, from +2 to –2. If the evidence indicated that the program (or treatment) appeared to work very well, it was given a +2. If it had no effect, it was given a 0. If it was much worse than the treatment it replaced, it was assigned a –2. Unfortunately, of 28 different innovations reported upon in the literature, fewer than half were beneficial. Fifteen of the 28 received a score of 0 or less. That is cause for concern, and it is also an excellent justification for evaluation research. As Mosteller (1981) has noted, if we are going to enjoy the benefits of social, educational, medical, and technological innovations, we need to weed out the bad from the good. If we do not, we end up paying double for programs that do not work, because these programs will cost us both in dollars and by blocking the introduction of more effective programs. The way to begin the sorting process is by being very clear about exactly what the program is supposed to do.

What Is Supposed to Be Accomplished?

From a practical point of view, the major problem with policy is that it is abstract. "To do the greatest good for the greatest number" may be an admirable goal, but how would you know when it was being done? Statements of policy are usually not quite that lofty, but they are often close. Pearsol and Gabel (1992), for example, noted that one of the goals of the AIDS Education and Training Centers Program set up by the federal government was to enhance health care provider sensitivity to those with AIDS by improved understanding. That seems to be a worthwhile goal, but how would one know when it had been reached? What, exactly, does "enhanced sensitivity" mean? The point, of course, is that policy has to be translated into clearly stated, measurable objectives before evaluation proper can even begin. As Rossi and Freeman (1993) put it, the distinction between the goals envisaged in policy and the actual, operational objectives to be achieved by a program is vital. Program objectives must be specified in clear, precise, and measurable terms. In other words, if you do not know where it is you are trying to go, you will not know when you get there. You also will not know if you do not get there.

Specifying those objectives is the first stage of the evaluation process. If you are in on the setting of policy, that is clearly an advantage, because then you are likely to have a firmer grasp of the intentions behind the policy. But even if you are called in after the policy has been chiseled in stone, your first task as an evaluation researcher is to see that clear objectives are spelled out, and that may not be as easy as it sounds. Most programs originate in response to a perceived social problem. If poor children are not receiving proper nutrition (the problem), then perhaps a National School Lunch Program (the program) is needed. But, as Rossi and Freeman (1993) point out, social problems are to some extent *social constructions* that emerge from the varied interests of different groups of stakeholders. In other words, defining social problems and setting objectives for specific programs are *political processes*. You may put in a lot of time and effort only to find out that half of the people concerned think you measured the wrong things. They were hoping that summer program for teenagers would reduce the rate of high school dropouts; they did not really care about increases in average reading scores. Lack of prior agreement about objectives will give everybody ammunition to shoot the program down, and your efforts along with it. Of course, if they do not like what you find, they will manufacture some ammunition of their own. But more about that later.

Given the importance of clearly stated objectives, how do you go about writing them? Shortell and Richardson (1978) have made some suggestions that may help. First, they pointed out that there are a number of issues relevant to the program that you should think about. These are:

1. *Content:* Is the program intended to change behavior? Or is it intended to change more subjective things, such as knowledge, opinions, or attitudes?

2. *Level of abstraction:* Are there objectives that differ in their concreteness and order of hoped-for achievement? For example, a program might plan to provide educational outings and trips for underprivileged children (a concrete objective) so that their interest in school will be maintained (a more abstract objective that may be realized later). Beware of objectives that are too abstract, however.

3. *Target:* For whom, precisely, is the program intended?

4. *Short-term or long-term effects:* Will the effects of the program show up immediately, or will you have to wait until next year to see whether it made any difference?

5. *Magnitude of effect:* How big a change do you expect?

6. *Stability of effect:* How long is the effect supposed to last?

7. *Conflicting effects:* If there is more than one objective (which there usually is), do any of them conflict with one another?

8. *Similarity of objectives:* If there is more than one objective, are they basically similar, or will you be looking for effects in different domains?

9. *Importance:* If there is more than one objective, which are the most important?

10. *Second-order consequences:* Are there likely to be any unintended side effects of the program?

That is quite a list, but if you go through it systematically, you will find that you have sharpened your thinking about what the program is supposed to accomplish. That, in turn, will help you to communicate the objectives to others and may possibly make agreement, or at least negotiation, easier.

Mohr (1992) suggests a somewhat different approach for specifying objectives. He suggests drawing an outcome line such as that depicted in Figure 1. An outcome line is actually an initial "theory" of the planned program and its effects. It is the result of thinking through the activities that will be carried

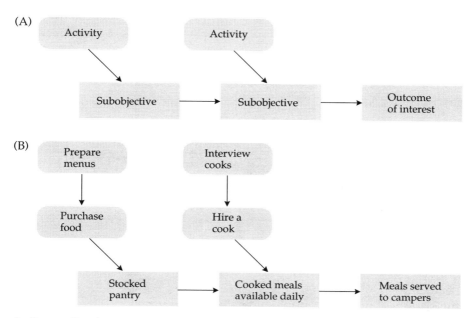

1 Outcome lines force you to be specific about the steps involved in reaching an outcome of interest. (A) A generic outcome line in which the activities of program personnel are linked via subobjectives to the outcome of interest. (B) A portion of an outcome line in which the outcome of interest is serving cooked meals to summer campers. Note that there would need to be an outcome line for each objective.

out by program personnel and sequentially linking each of those activities with its result. Specific program activities may produce the outcome of interest directly, or they may produce subobjectives that lead to the outcome of interest. In thinking about program activities and objectives, it is best to use strong verbs, verbs that are action-oriented and describe an observable behavior. To increase, to write, and to go are examples of strong verbs. To encourage, to promote, and to understand are considerably weaker. They do not imply a specific action that you can see with the naked eye.

Once the objectives have been clearly stated, the next step is to decide what will serve as an index, or indicator, of each. This, of course, is the key step in operationalizing the objectives, a process you should be familiar with by now. At first glance, however, it might seem that if you have followed all of the above suggestions in writing your objectives, they would already be, ipso facto, operationalized. Not so! Consider the following example to see why. Suppose that you are asked to conduct an evaluation of a psychiatric inpatient clinic, and that one of its objectives is to provide frequent feedback to treatment staff about each patient. That is a reasonable objective, but it can be operationalized in many different ways. For example, there could be weekly staff meetings at which each patient's behavior during the last week is discussed. Or, you could arrange for the ward nurse to call each member of the treatment staff daily and report on their patients. Clearly stated, measurable objectives have to be operationalized, and usually, there are several ways in which that can be done. And remember, even if you could get all stakeholders to agree on the objectives—which is unlikely in itself—they might still disagree about the best way to operationalize each.

Once you have the objectives and they have been operationalized to your, if not everyone's, satisfaction, there are still several steps to the overall evaluation process: (1) implementing the program; (2) checking to see whether the implementation is actually carried out as planned and making adjustments where necessary; (3) assessing the overall impact of the program; and (4) analyzing the costs of the program relative to its benefits and effectiveness. For example, years ago the National Institute of Mental Health decided to establish Community Mental Health Centers around the nation. After that decision was made and the objectives of the program were established (vague though they may have been), there remained the tasks of: (1) funding, staffing, and building (or renting) Community Mental Health Centers (implementation); (2) checking to see whether the Community Mental Health Centers were doing what they were supposed to be doing (formative evaluation); (3) finding ways to determine whether their presence made any difference (impact assessment); and (4) calculating the costs of the program relative to benefits and effectiveness. But, let's take these one at a time, beginning with implementation.

Implementation in Complex Environments

With the objectives in place, the program activities planned out in detail, enough money to get the job done, and good relations with the program personnel, what could go wrong? Well, just about everything. The typical social or educational innovation is part of an open system, and that means there are all sorts of uncontrollable external forces pushing and pulling on the components of the program. As Weiss (1972) once put it, just as you get everything under way and the data collection is running smoothly, the program will slither off in a completely new direction. It will not happen overnight. In many respects it would be better if it did, because that would get your attention. It is more likely that the program will evolve gradually, that slight changes will be introduced from time to time as the program personnel find better ways to do things and as the internal and external political climates change. This evolutionary process seems to be the rule, not the exception. The actual results of new programs often bear little likeness to the original intent. They are usually much more modest than it was anticipated they would be, and, in spite of that, they take longer to accomplish. For example, Piper, King, and Moberg (1993) were involved in a study in which an adolescent health promotion curriculum was to be tried out in a number of middle schools in Wisconsin. It took them 9 months to secure the cooperation of just 22 schools. During that 9 months two staff members spent over half of their time just on recruitment—writing to hundreds of schools, talking to school officials over the telephone, and traveling to schools to make presentations on the planned program.

Unfortunately, the setting of the typical program is extremely complex, and that complexity is often not taken into account in planning. In many instances it may be impossible to take it into account for the simple reason that it is not sufficiently well understood. Even when the complexity of the environment is appreciated, it may not be predictable. For example, in the 1970s the federal government set up a large-scale field experiment in New Jersey to evaluate a technique for supporting needy families. This technique is referred to as a negative income tax, and works as follows: Payments are made to families when their income is below a certain level. But, unlike some welfare programs, payments do not completely stop when family income rises above that level. Rather, as income rises, payments gradually decrease. The question of interest was whether this type of sliding scale would provide more incentive for people on welfare to work. Under the old system, there was little incentive to work because the family was likely to experience a drop in income—their welfare payments would be cut off completely—when someone got a job outside the home.

To the chagrin of everyone, while the experiment was under way, there was a shift in the welfare policy of the state of New Jersey. New Jersey had been chosen as the site of the experiment partly because its state welfare laws covered only households headed by females. Suddenly, New Jersey extended its coverage to households headed by unemployed males. Some of those households were, in fact, part of the negative income tax experiment. Not only did this change complicate the comparisons that had been planned for the experiment, it also got local officials upset about the possibility that some people were double-dipping, that is, accepting both state and federal payments. In an effort to get at the guilty parties, state officials obtained a court order for the records of the experiment (which families were receiving payments and how much). The order was not enforced, but the program was required to reimburse local welfare departments for the excess amounts they had given to families receiving both forms of payment (Kershaw and Fair, 1976). The point is that when the negative income tax experiment was being planned at the federal level, there was no way of anticipating what the government of New Jersey was going to do 4 or 5 years down the road. That was simply an unknown in the equation.

But even when you know the specific obstacles that must be overcome in order to operate a program smoothly, there is often a tendency to overestimate the ease of doing so. Part of that problem may be the understandable optimism of those starting out on a new endeavor. But part of it may be a failure to appreciate a very simple statistical fact. For example, suppose you have designed a remedial reading program and plan to evaluate it by using the following experiment. Four schools in your community in which first-graders scored below the national average on reading comprehension tests will be used. Two of the schools will be randomly selected to serve as controls and will continue their usual reading instruction for first-graders when school opens in the fall. First-graders at two other randomly selected schools will be exposed to the new reading program. You have all your materials ready to go, some money from the Board of Education to carry out the study, and the approval of the local school superintendent. There is just one catch. The superintendent says she does not like to make the teachers in her schools participate in research. She leaves it completely up to each teacher and principal whether or not they take part in projects such as yours. That means you have to get the approval of 4 principals and, assuming 3 first-grade classes in each school, 12 teachers—16 people altogether. But, says the superintendent, they are generally a cooperative lot, and she is about 90% sure that they will agree to help you out. Suppose that her estimate is correct, that is, that the chances are 90 out of 100 that each of the 4 principals and 12 teachers will say yes. What is the probability of getting them all to agree? Ready for this? The probability that all sixteen will agree is 0.185, and that is pretty low. It means that you probably are not going to be able to implement the program as planned. A smaller sample of schools may be necessary—maybe only one control school and one in which the first-graders are exposed to the remedial reading program.

But whatever circumstances you have to settle for, it is usually a good idea to conduct what is referred to as a **formative evaluation**, an early examination of how the program is working—or whether it is working at all—so that you can improve its operation and make any necessary adjustments. As Scriven (1991) notes, you can think of formative evaluation as an early warning device. It lets you know if changes need to be made while there is still time to make them. It does not have to be a full-blown assessment of the entire program. Rossi and Freeman (1993) note that even though "formative studies vary in their rigor and in the sophistication of their data collection and analysis, in many cases even simple formative studies provide insight into the problems an intervention may face and ways to overcome them" (p. 137).

Not only may you need to tinker with the program as it actually gets under way, but from time to time you will also need to see whether it is still similar to the way it was the last time you looked. All too often, it will not be. Halfway through the fall, one of those nice teachers who agreed to help you out may inform you that he does not like your remedial reading program after all. Furthermore, a couple of weeks ago he discovered a way of doing it better and has been trying that out on his first-graders.

What do you do in a situation like this? The first rule is simple: *Stay calm!* You may still be able to salvage some useful information. You may be able to rethink your model of the program itself. That is, instead of considering the program as a static entity that is put in place and evaluated, you may be able to develop a more dynamic conception of the program. For example, if the teacher mentioned above were sufficiently clear about how he had changed your remedial reading instruction, you might be able to consider his change as part of a new, two-stage version of your treatment. If so, you would be able to compare his students with the controls (no remedial reading) and with those first-graders exposed only to the remedial reading program as you designed it. You never know, his idea might be better than yours.

The key to being able to take advantage of such shifts in programs is staying flexible, and Cronbach et al. (1981) have offered a few suggestions about how you can do that. One thing to avoid is committing every dollar you have to spend and every hour you have available to obtaining the data described in the initial evaluation plan. You will need a little slack to regroup when something unexpected occurs. In other words, you should expect the unexpected—and be prepared to take advantage of it. Another thing that may help is to think of the overall evaluation as taking place in stages, with some analysis and rethinking occurring in the gaps between stages. Surprise results and program changes that are identified in the early stages may help to sharpen your thinking about exactly what kinds of data you should be collecting, and you can make it a point to get those data in the later stages. But if the program is completely overwhelmed by internal and external changes, your best bet may be to forget the evaluation altogether and prepare a careful, well-documented treatise on why and how things went wrong, as Piper, King, and Moberg (1993) did for the study mentioned earlier. That, in fact, might be just as useful to interested parties as your evaluation would have been.

Using All the Tools You Have

But how, exactly, does one go about conducting a formative evaluation? Or, for that matter, how do you actually conduct an overall evaluation of the program that captured your interest in the first place? An overall evaluation of the processes and outcomes of a program, by the way, is referred to as summative evaluation. If this were a typical evaluation research textbook, you would be in for some heavy methodological discussions at this point. But, lucky for you, most of the methods used in evaluation research have already been covered in the preceding chapters. Participant observation, qualitative interviewing, standardized interviewing, archival research, content analysis, quasi-experimentation, experimentation—everything that we have covered can be and has been tailored for use in specific evaluation projects. The key to carrying out high-quality evaluation research is to choose the best single method, or blend of methods, for the research that you want to do. It is a task that deserves some thought and planning after you have developed a thorough familiarity with the policy that is to be implemented by the program and the resources available for doing so. What is being advocated, of course, is the same general research strategy spelled out in Chapter 1, that is, an open-minded exploration of the best method(s) available for finding out what you want to know about the program of interest.

Lest I be accused of avoiding an issue, however, I must point out that there is a controversy among evaluation pundits about the relative merits of quantitative versus qualitative research. There are some who say that all the problems of evaluation research can be traced to a lack of "rigor." (For a possible contributor to this perception, see Box 2). But I do not believe it. It seems to me that Posavac's (1992) position is the most reasonable one. He has noted

---

Box 2

The Oversight Bias

It is easy to understand why people who have a stake in a particular program might be biased in their interpretations of the quality of research attempting to assess that program. If the research indicates that the program is not accomplishing its goals, for example, they might lose their jobs, or be assigned additional duties, or have to start all over. But what about people who do not have a stake in the program? Is there any reason to believe that their assessments of the research evaluating the program might be biased? Unfortunately, there is. Wilson et al. (1993) suggest that the more important the topic of research, the more likely people are to overlook methodological flaws in their assessment of the research—a tendency they refer to as the oversight bias.

To see if this really occurs, Wilson et al. wrote out descriptions of several research projects, all of which were methodologically flawed. They were missing needed control groups, or used correlational data to infer causation, or did not randomly assign subjects to conditions. But there were two versions of each description. In one the topic of the study was important—women who had been assaulted by their husbands—and in the other the topic was considerably less important—women who were concerned about eating alone in restaurants. The two versions of a particular description were identical in all other respects. Subjects were then asked to read six different descriptions of research projects—three addressing important topics and three addressing unimportant topics—and to make a series of judgments about each: How sound is the study in terms of its methodology? How appropriate are the conclusions of the study? How important is the topic of the study? The subjects, by the way, were people who should be able to make these judgments—they were all faculty members in psychology and medicine.

The results indicate that, indeed, subjects rated the versions describing studies of important topics as significantly more rigorous than the methodologically identical versions describing studies of unimportant topics. Exactly why this occurs is not clear, but it is cause for concern. You would expect that as the importance of the topic of research increased, the standard we would use in evaluating the evidence would also be raised. Alas, that appears not to be the case. It is almost as if we give in to wishful thinking: "It really is an important topic and we really do need to know more about it, so maybe this study isn't totally worthless." But if the methodology is flawed, it may indeed be worthless—regardless of how important the topic is.

that the primary concern should be with the utility of the data obtained, not with the method by which they are obtained. If you can find out something useful about a program by talking to a few disgruntled employees, then talk to them. If the only way you can get the data you need is by participant observation, then participate and observe (and do not forget to take good notes). If you need a time series design with switching replications, then set it up and switch when the time comes. If you need archival data, then locate the necessary records and extract whatever you require. Use whatever you have in your toolbox that will get the job done, that is, whatever you have that will help you determine whether the program's objectives are being achieved. Having said that, you should be forewarned that the more powerful your methodology, the more likely your results are to be accepted. As Chelimsky (1987) has put it: "It is rarely prudent to enter a burning political debate armed only with a case study, *even if that case study were the most rational approach to the original policy question*" (p. 27, emphasis added).

Actually, you are already familiar with the essential components of the most useful, and most rigorous, evaluation designs that you could employ, although you may not have put the pieces together yet. These designs are referred to, generally, as **randomized trials** and involve experimental designs that combine some of the quasi-experimental designs from Chapter 7 with random assignment of subjects to treatment and no-treatment groups. We discussed random assignment in Chapter 8, but let's just take a moment to refresh your memory by pointing out what's involved in a slightly different way. Think back to the chapter on survey research for a moment. There, random selection of subjects to be interviewed was discussed, and several ways in which it could be done were highlighted. The point, of course, was to obtain a representative, unbiased sample, one whose characteristics were similar to those of the population as a whole. If you selected such a sample, you could feel fairly confident about inferring that what they had to say in answer to your questions was representative of the attitudes and opinions of the population. With random assignment of subjects to treatment and no-treatment groups, the goal is essentially the same. You want the subjects in each group (i.e., sample) to be similar to the subjects in each of the other groups (i.e., the other samples).

Random assignment of subjects to conditions is not always feasible. But when it is, you overcome at one fell swoop many of the ambiguities discussed in Chapter 7 that result from the use of nonequivalent groups for the treatment and control conditions. The reason is that randomly assigning subjects to conditions enables you to assume that the groups are equivalent at the outset. Thus, any differences that appear on the posttest cannot be attributed to pre-existing—that is, pretreatment—differences among the groups. Of course, that is assuming that the groups all experience the same nontreatment events between random assignment and posttest. As Cook and Campbell (1979) put it, random assignment "does not guarantee that the initial comparability between groups will be maintained over the course of an experiment." That is up to you—and fate. But random assignment does give you that initial comparability to work with, and that is a genuine advantage (Figure 2).

The internal validity of all of the designs discussed in Chapter 7 (with the exception of the one-group designs, which are hopeless) can be considerably enhanced by randomly assigning subjects to conditions. For example, when we follow the method of Campbell and Stanley (1966), and let R stand for random assignment, the untreated control group design with pretest and posttest becomes:

Group 1	R	O	X	O
Group 2	R	O		O

With that simple addition, it becomes a true experimental design, with nothing "quasi" about it. Mosteller (1981) describes a large-scale evaluation study

"Find out who set up this experiment. It seems that half the patients were given a placebo, and the other half were given a different placebo."

2 A verifiable evaluation of a new treatment always includes a group of subjects who are given a placebo treatment. In medical research the placebo would be a pill, for example, that looked and tasted like the real drug but which had no pharmacological effect. In education research the placebo group would be treated like the treatment group except that the placebo group would not be exposed to the treatment itself. (Cartoon © Sidney Harris, from *Scientific American.*)

that used this design. It was carried out by the Blue Cross insurance company in Kansas, and its purpose was to determine whether or not the apparently excessive use of hospitalization, which is extremely costly, would decrease if the company started paying for more outpatient care. Five thousand people were randomly assigned to an added-benefits group, free of charge. What that meant was that for one year, the company would pay for much of their outpatient care—that is, things that were not covered under the regular plan unless the patient was hospitalized. These 5000 people constituted the treatment group and were compared with a randomly selected group of 10,000 who continued on the old system (coverage of hospital costs only) for a year.

Random assignment was very important in this study because it gave the researchers some confidence that the two groups could be considered initially comparable in terms of their year-to-year medical problems and costs. The results, by the way, were surprising and contrary to expectation. The amount of hospitalization for the group with the added outpatient benefits went up 16%, whereas for the control (regular plan) group it went up only 3%. It may be that the added outpatient benefits, which were free, induced people to consult their physicians more often, and hence, more problems were found that required treatment. However, the fact that the results were in the direction opposite to what was expected again underscores the need to evaluate new programs.

Note that an even better design for this study would have been a time series with long-term follow-up, like this:

				YEARS AFTER INTERVENTION			
				1	4	7	10
Group 1	R	O	X	O	O	O	O
Group 2	R	O		O	O	O	O

Why? Because it might have turned out that finding more problems early in that first year resulted in fewer costly hospitalizations and lessened mortality in subsequent years for the treatment group. The point here is that each of the quasi-experimental designs described in Chapter 7 can be converted into true experiments by randomly assigning subjects to conditions. But if random assignment is not possible, a time series with switching replications, or any one of the other quasi-experimental designs, may still be your best bet in trying to assess a particular program.

Is It Really Worth It?

Here it is necessary to mention one additional type of data that is becoming increasingly important in the evaluation process. As Rossi and Freeman (1993) note, one of the most important considerations in deciding whether to expand, continue, or terminate a program—regardless of whether it meets its stated objectives—is whether or not the program is an efficient way to implement the desired policy. Efficient is usually defined in terms of economics: Is the program a good use of scarce economic resources? If the program of interest is one of several alternative programs that could achieve the same objectives, a **cost–benefit analysis** may be required. That means that all the costs and benefits of the program have to be converted to monetary values. That, in turn, enables you to see whether the program is worth what it is costing—that is, whether the benefits exceed the costs.

Converting everything to a dollar value, however, may force you to make some very arbitrary judgments. Suppose, for example, that one of the innovations of interest is a new treatment for patients dying of cancer, and that, on average, it seems to prolong the life of those treated by 6 months to a year. How much, precisely, is 6 more months of life worth? And how do you figure quality of life into the equation? As Rossi and Freeman (1993) point out, because the outcomes of social programs are often difficult to translate into monetary values, there is considerable controversy surrounding cost–benefit analyses. At a minimum, anyone doing such an analysis must be very precise about their assumptions and how their figures were arrived at. Reducing the high school dropout rate by 3% is worth exactly how much in dollars? Decreasing the average patient stay in the hospital after major surgery by half a day is worth what? Actually, half a day less in the hospital is worth quite a bit, and you could easily place a monetary value on it. The point is simply that you would need to be very clear about how you arrived at that value.

Cost-effectiveness analysis, in contrast, does not convert everything to dollars. Rather, it uses whatever units you focused on in operationalizing a given program's objectives and tells you what it has cost to achieve those effects. Comparison with different, or alternative, programs is usually not the object here. The results of a cost-effectiveness analysis of a preschool flu vaccination program, for example, might be phrased in terms of the cost to reduce the incidence of flu by 500 cases. Or it might be phrased in terms of the cost of reducing school absenteeism by 100% over the previous year. With cost-effectiveness analysis, there is no need to convert one day's absence by one child to a dollar value, as there would be with a cost–benefit analysis of the same program.

Both cost–benefit and cost-effectiveness analyses, however, are affected by an important complication that has to do with the question of perspective: that is, from whose point of view are the costs, benefits, and effects of the program to be calculated? That perspective can make a tremendous difference.

Politics in Real-World Settings

Abt (1979) has related that he once heard a surgeon say that if he had a female patient whose mother and sister both had breast cancer, he would recommend an immediate bilateral radical mastectomy as a prophylactic measure. That is a rather drastic preventive step to take. It is not like being told that you should brush your teeth three times a day. From the surgeon's point of view, however, it would maximize the cost-effectiveness ratio for the patient, because the only benefit he was focusing on was pure duration of life. Without breasts, the patient's chances of living longer would be increased, because even relatively frequent screening is likely to miss some of the most deadly forms of breast cancer, which do seem to have a hereditary component. Needless to say, from the patient's point of view, there would be other considerations than pure duration of life. She would want to think about how the operation would influence the quality of her life as well. Besides, in 1979, only about 16 out of every 100,000 women died of breast cancer. That is an item of information that the patient would undoubtedly want to take into account in deciding whether or not to follow the surgeon's recommendation. With odds that slim, and in her favor, she might well decide to take her chances and stay out of the operating room.

Multiple Constituencies

The conflicting perspectives of an individual patient and his or her physician on the relative benefits to be derived from a given course of action illustrate only a small part of the more general problem, however. Evaluation is, as was stated earlier, a political undertaking. If political influence and intrigue stopped once policy had been set and the objectives of a program agreed upon, evaluation of the program might proceed in a relatively straightforward manner. But it does not work that way. For example, in 1981, the nation's air traffic controllers went out on strike for more pay. There were at the time several studies in the literature that purported to demonstrate how stressful the job was (e.g., Rose, Jenkins, and Hurst, 1978). Air traffic controllers were said to experience disorders such as ulcers and depression much more frequently than did members of the general population. The reason, or so the research seemed to indicate, was the nature of their high-pressure job, a job that required constant alertness and in which a mistake could cost hundreds of lives. Those studies had been in the literature for years and were generally considered noncontroversial. At the time of the strike, however, they were dug out and held up to ridicule, and their results were called into question. It was claimed by those who wanted to end the strike that the studies had been poorly designed and sloppily done. Now, it appeared, air traffic controllers really had one of the poshest jobs around—short hours, high pay, and only a 2-year training period. You did not even have to go to college to qualify.

The point, of course, is that when the stakes are high—as they usually are in evaluation research—different, and more powerful, motives come into play. (See Box 3 for another implication.) It is all well and good to think of evaluation research as just another scientific endeavor, but it is not. Evaluation research, more than any other form of research in the preceding chapters, directly touches people's lives and well-being. Thus, high-quality evaluation research requires that you take into account the multiple perspectives that can be brought to bear on the program of interest. Failure to do so can have serious consequences.

One of the things that evaluation research has in common with participant observation is that they both take place in real-life, action settings. Both are carried out where something else is going on, something other than pure research. And that something else takes priority. As Piper, King, and Moberg (1993) found in the course of their efforts to gain entry to middle schools in Wisconsin, there is little or no commitment in such settings to scientific research or to program evaluation. Research is simply seen as unimportant. Even if you do gain entry to the setting, you are there to evaluate what is going on, and that means,

---

Box 3

Methodology as an Ethical Issue

As usually understood, ethics is the study of what is good and what is bad, of what is morally appropriate behavior. We have discussed a number of ethical issues in the preceding chapters, including the use of deception in research, informed consent, and invasion of privacy. Rosenthal (1994) has recently argued, however, that ethical issues impinge on the research process in a much more pervasive manner than most people think. He suggests that ethics and methodological quality are intimately related, and that a poor design is ipso facto unethical. To use one of his examples, suppose you were interested in whether private schools enhance the intellectual abilities of their students more than public schools. To address the issue, you might administer achievement and IQ tests to children from randomly selected private and public schools. If you did this, then regardless of what you concluded, according to Rosenthal, you would have engaged in unethical behavior. Why? Because the design could not possibly provide an answer to the original research question—remember selection and history as threats to internal validity? Students', teachers', and administrators' time and effort would have been wasted, as would the money spent in conducting the study, money that might have been spent on better-quality research.

Rosenthal extends this broader view of research ethics to additional components of the process, including data analysis and reviewing the literature. Contrary to received wisdom, for example, he suggests that it is unethical not to probe any data we collect from every conceivable point of view. As he puts it: "If the research was worth doing, the data are worth a thorough analysis, being held up to the light in many different ways so that our research participants, our funding agencies, our science, and society will all get their time and their money's worth" (p. 130). As implied by the quote, his argument is based on cost-benefit analysis. In evaluating the ethical appropriateness of research, the costs—time, money, effort, danger to subjects—must be weighed against the potential benefits—new knowledge that might help people, advance science, or provide needed information for decision making. Thus, poorly designed research that produces ambiguous results is unethical—it has costs, but no benefits. It also follows from Rosenthal's view of ethics that not doing potentially beneficial research that could easily be done at low cost is unethical. Think about that. You may be behaving unethically at this very moment.

---

of course, that it has to continue to go on in order for the evaluation to take place. Thus, like a good participant observer, the evaluation researcher must be as unobtrusive as possible and not disrupt the normal course of events. The extent to which you are able to do that depends very heavily on your relationships with the people running the program.

There are many potential sources of friction between program personnel and someone who has been called in to evaluate "their" program. Because of the nature of most social and educational programs, program personnel are likely to be service oriented. They are teachers, social workers, therapists, probation officers, health professionals—people whose job it is to deliver services to others. They are oriented toward helping others, toward doing whatever is necessary to see that those in their charge learn, or get a job, or stay out of trouble. Thus, program personnel and evaluators are likely to have completely different orientations at the outset. To the program personnel, it does not matter what it is about the program that makes it work, just so it works. To the evaluators, it is important to document everything; gut feelings and testimonials are not considered high-quality evidence. The difficulty of documenting exactly what program personnel do is a recurring problem in evaluation research (Greene, Dumont, and Doughty, 1992). They are often just too busy doing whatever it is they do to help you.

Program personnel are likely to be irritated by the skeptical attitude of those evaluating their work and may believe that "outsiders" do not really understand the constraints they must work under (Pearsol, 1992). Program personnel have to believe in what they are doing in order to be effective, and they are likely to see the researcher's questioning and nitpicking as a depressing and unnecessary intrusion. The effects of these different orientations toward the program are likely to be magnified by personality differences between program personnel and researchers. The program personnel are more likely to be action oriented, concerned about people, and interested in dealing with specific, individual cases. Researchers, in general, are likely to be somewhat more detached, concerned about theoretical and methodological issues, and to have little or no loyalty to the particular program being evaluated.

On the basis of these different orientations, Weiss (1972) has called attention to several specific issues that are likely to provoke conflict between program personnel and evaluation researchers. The first has to do with selection of program participants and assignment of some participants to control groups. Program personnel are likely to have a number of implicit criteria for selecting participants. They usually want persons they believe they can help or those who are most in need (Loseke, 1992). Thus, they are likely to get agitated when evaluation researchers start talking about random selection of clients and random assignment of some clients to a no-treatment control condition. They may view the latter as unethical because it means withholding services from people who need them. Evaluation, of course, requires data, and often that means new questionnaires that the program's clients must fill out and records that program personnel have to maintain. Program personnel view such tasks as intrusions, paper-shuffling exercises that keep them from doing what they do best. There is also an element of rivalry between evaluation researchers and program personnel, compounded by the sense of threat that program personnel may feel at being evaluated in the first place. Program personnel are likely to see themselves as doing the real work of the agency, often on a tight budget and under less than optimal conditions. They may see evaluation researchers, with their clipboards and their questionnaires and their turned-up noses, as just another hassle they have to put up with. But those clipboard carriers seem to have the boss's attention, and what they tell him or her about the program may well have serious implications.

Many of these potential sources of conflict can be short-circuited with a little common sense. Involving program personnel in the evaluation from the outset will help. Making them a part of the process can lessen the likelihood of an "Us versus Them" relationship developing. It also helps to make clear that the evaluation is focusing on the program and not on how well or how poorly individual program personnel are doing their jobs. Weiss (1972) has noted that management incentives for program personnel to facilitate, rather than hinder, the evaluation process can be a real boon. And, as always, a little simple, straightforward communication about what is going on at each step of the process is a big help. There is a danger here, however. If the feedback given to program personnel indicates that some parts of the program are working better than others, or that certain things are simply not working at all, they may try to change the program in midstream. After all, they see their job as doing the most they can for each individual client that the agency is supposed to serve. If you tell them that something they have been doing is a waste of time—assuming you can convince them of that fact—they will try something new tomorrow. If they do, then you may have a different program on your hands.

Mixed Motives

Although the potential for conflict does seem to be greatest with those actually doing the day-to-day work of implementing the program of interest, there are other vested interests in any program that can make life difficult for the evaluator. Shortell and Richardson (1978) have said that there are at least five different groups that have a stake in the typical evaluation: (1) the organization that is being evaluated; (2) the individual program administrator(s); (3) the agency that is funding the organization and the evaluation; (4) the public and consumer groups; and (5) the program evaluators themselves. Be sure to note that this is an underestimate of the concerned parties in most instances. For example, the program administrators in many service agencies are different from those who actually deliver services, and it is the latter, as you have just seen, for whom there is the greatest potential for conflict with evaluation researchers. But even if you take Shortell and Richardson's list as a minimum, look at the variety of different motives that may be seeking a way to express themselves in one lowly little evaluation project:

1. The organization may hope to
   a. show other groups that it is effective
   b. justify past expenditures
   c. justify future requests for more money
   d. determine what should be done next
   e. justify firing program personnel

2. Individual program administrators may hope to
   a. gain a pat on the back or a promotion
   b. gain greater control over subordinates
   c. learn how to serve clients better
   d. show that the program should be redirected
   e. be able to avoid evaluations in the future

3. The funding agency may hope to
   a. spend unspent money so that their allocations will not be decreased in the future
   b. find out whether services are being efficiently delivered
   c. obtain evidence necessary for policy alteration

d. make themselves look good to Congress

e. justify terminating the program

4. The public and consumer groups may hope to

a. find out how tax dollars are being spent

b. gain more control over the program

c. obtain the evidence necessary to oust program administrators

d. redirect the program to other target groups

e. get the program moved to another neighborhood

5. Program evaluators may hope to

a. contribute to knowledge

b. make a name for themselves

c. see the program improved

d. see the program terminated

e. none of the above

It is not just a problem of multiple interest groups, then, each with a different perspective. Rather, as Cochran (1980) has said, each party has multiple motives, and it is important to remember that survival is likely to top each person's list. Evaluation is not just an academic exercise. Members of the groups mentioned above may feel quite strongly about what they want a particular evaluation to accomplish. Their very livelihood can depend on the outcome. That means they may do whatever they can to see that the desired result is obtained. And doing whatever they can includes everything from foot-dragging and throwing monkey wrenches to facilitating your every move and telling you more than you really wanted to know.

Given this crossfire of motives, there is likely to be constant pressure on the program to change, to do more of this and less of that, and even to stop doing some things altogether. From the point of view of someone trying to evaluate what is going on, these pressures can present real problems. On the other hand, the fact that a program does change, or is implemented differently at different sites, does not necessarily mean that it is a failure. Consider this example.

An Illustration: Respite for Caregivers

In recent years, it has been recognized that the stress involved in caring for an aging member of one's family can be quite severe. The problems can, indeed, be overwhelming, particularly when the aging relative is afflicted with Alzheimer's disease. In many cases such individuals are not only unable to perform the tasks of daily life, but are also unaware of the efforts of others to care for them and are thus unappreciative. In spite of the burden, however, many people are extremely reluctant to institutionalize an elderly person, regardless of whether the person is a parent, a spouse, or a companion. The reasons for this reluctance are varied. Some people are concerned about the quality of care the elderly will receive in an institution; some cannot afford the cost of a nursing home; and some simply do not want to part with the loved one. From society's point of view, there are also reasons for attempting to keep the elderly at home as long as possible. The longer the elderly can be maintained in their own homes by a friend or relative, the longer the delay in the need for more costly kinds of care.

In recognition of the potential value to society of maintaining the elderly in their own homes for as long as possible, several states have experimented with respite programs for those who care for the elderly. A *respite* is simply a brief period of rest, or relief. The idea behind these programs is that if the caregivers are freed from their 24-hours-a-day, 7-days-a-week burden even for short periods of time, they will be better able to maintain their own equilibrium and better able to help the person they are caring for in the long run. If they know, for example, that every Tuesday and Thursday they can take their loved one to an adult day care center where he or she will be well cared for—while they go shopping, or read a book, or do whatever else they might want to—then they can get through the rest of the week on their own. And, again from society's point of view, providing the facilities for two 8-hour days of care in a day care center is a whole lot less expensive than continuous around-the-clock care in a nursing home.

While this all sounds very reasonable, there was until recently very little evidence that it worked. In the late 1980s, however, the Michigan Department of Mental Health funded a program called the Michigan Model Projects Specialized Respite Care Program (Kosloski and Montgomery, 1993). The legislation that had set aside the funds mandated that the program be evaluated in terms of its effectiveness in relieving the burden of caregiving. The program was implemented at seven sites around the state of Michigan. At two of the sites, adult day care was provided between the hours of 8 A.M. and 5 P.M., 5 days a week. At two other sites, in-home care was provided during the day and/or evening throughout the week; that is, someone would come to the caregiver's home on request and stay with the elderly person while the caregiver went out and did whatever he or she wanted. At the other three sites, both adult day care centers and in-home care were available. Families could use the respite care program as much or as little as they wanted, and the care was free to those making less than $9000 a year. A minimal fee was charged those in higher income brackets.

Kosloski and Montgomery set out to assess the effectiveness of the respite care program on the basis of three outcomes for the caregivers: subjective burden, objective burden, and morale. To do so, they employed a quasi-experimental design, the untreated control group with pretest and posttest. In case you've forgotten, that's this:

	PRETEST	RESPITE	POSTTEST
Group 1 (treatment group)	O	X	O
Group 2 (control group)	O		O

Initially, the treatment group consisted of 76 caregivers who used one of the seven sites, and the control group consisted of 40 caregivers taken from the waiting lists for the sites. Both of these groups suffered attrition during the 6 months between pretest and posttest. In the treatment group, 20 care recipients were institutionalized and 9 died during the 6 months, leaving 47. In the control group, 9 were institutionalized and 6 died, leaving 25. The characteristics of the two groups of care recipients are given in Table 1.

Given that caregivers (and recipients) were not randomly assigned to conditions, and given the attrition in both groups, Kosloski and Montgomery had to examine a number of variables to see whether the final groups differed in any way that might reasonably be expected to influence the dependent vari-

Table 1 Characteristics of Care Recipients

	FREQUENCIES	
	RESPITE USERS (N = 47)	CONTROLS (N = 25)
Age		
40–49	1	0
50–59	1	1
60–69	8	7
70–79	24	7
80–89	10	9
90–99	3	1
Total	47	25
Gender		
Male	23	11
Female	24	14
Total	47	25
Alzheimer's Diagnosis		
Yes	21	18
No	11	6
Missing	15	1
Total	47	25
Mean global health rating (1 = perfect, 5 = not good)	3.2	3.5
Number of hospital days (past year)	2.6	4.6
Personal care activities of daily living (0–15)	10.2	9.3
Household task activities of daily living (0–15)	11.7	11.2

Source: Kosloski and Montgomery, 1993.

ables of subjective and objective burden and morale. As may be seen in Table 1, the two groups of care recipients were indeed quite similar in a number of relevant ways. Among the caregivers in the two groups, they found no significant differences in age, gender, marital status, or use of outside support services, nor in initial levels of subjective burden, objective burden, or morale. They did find a slightly greater representation of minority members in the control group (30% vs. 10%), and that the average income of members of the control group was somewhat less than that of the treatment group. However, using a statistical adjustment, they were able to show that these differences did not influence the results. Similarly, they found no significant differences between the initial treatment and control groups in the proportions of care recipients who were institutionalized or died. So, in spite of the nonrandom assignment and the attrition, it appears that the final treatment and control groups were indeed roughly equivalent at the beginning of the evaluation.

The major outcome variables were assessed in interviews with the caregivers at the time of their entry into the respite care program and again 6 months later. For those on the waiting lists, the investigators simply waited 6 months between the first and second interviews. Subjective burden was measured by questions that addressed stress in the relationship with the care recipient, feelings of being manipulated, nervousness, and perceptions of excessive demands being made by the care recipient. Objective burden was measured by six items on which the caregivers were asked to report how much time they had for themselves, for recreation, for vacations, for other friends and relatives, and for their own work. Morale was assessed by a series of items on which the caregivers were asked how often they felt lonely, anxious, optimistic, in good spirits, and so on.

The results indicated that with respect to objective burden, the respite care program appeared to have no effect whatsoever. The caregivers who actually made use of the program did not differ from those still on the waiting list in terms of reported demands on their time. However, in terms of subjective burden and morale, the program was indeed effective. At the initial interviews, caregivers beginning the program and those on the waiting lists did not differ in either morale or subjective burden. But, as you can see in Figure 3, 6 months after entering the program, caregivers in the treatment group reported feeling significantly less stressed and having significantly higher morale.

There was one other finding of interest. Among caregivers in the treatment group, actual use of the respite care program varied considerably. Over the 6-month period, the mean amount of time that respite care was employed was 220 hours, or about five and a half 40-hour weeks. But use varied from a total of 4 hours to 1137 hours. The interesting thing was that the *amount* of use was not related to the outcome variables; that is, caregivers who used the respite care program experienced reductions in subjective stress and increases in morale, but those caregivers who used respite care a lot did not experience more of these changes than those who used it only a little. As Kosloski and Montgomery (1993, p. 14) put it, "perhaps there is an optimal amount of use for an individual caregiver and that more use is not necessarily better." Or,

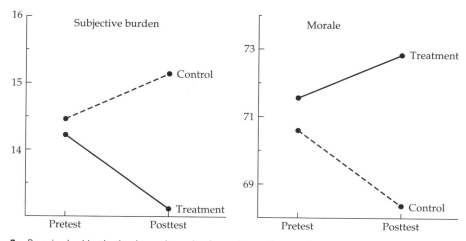

3   Perceived subjective burden and morale of caregivers prior to and 6 months after beginning participation in the Michigan Model Projects Specialized Respite Care Program. (From Kosloski and Montgomery, 1993.)

perhaps, it is just the knowledge that respite care is available should you need it that makes the difference.

Note that the Michigan Model Projects Specialized Respite Care Program was implemented in different ways at different sites. You will recall that at two of the sites, only day care was available and only during weekdays between 8:00 A.M. and 5:00 P.M. At two other sites, only in-home care was available, but it was available during the day or in the evening. Cook, Leviton, and Shadish (1985) point out that this type of variation in the ways programs are implemented at different sites is not at all unusual and that it can, in many instances, create problems for evaluators. In the report by Kosloski and Montgomery (1993), for example, there is no information about whether or not the effects they found were greater at one site than at another. The differential implementation might also account for why some caregivers used the respite care program more than others. It may be that those who used the program the most were the ones for whom it was most convenient, that is, those who could use in-home care in the day or evening.

This lack of detail in reports of evaluation research appears to be a common problem (Greene, Dumont, and Doughty, 1992; Moskowitz, 1993). That does not necessarily mean that the research itself is flawed, it just means that sometimes it is difficult to know exactly what was done. And if you do not know what was done, you may not really know what produced the effects of interest, and you surely will not be able to replicate the results.

Summary

Evaluation research is different from the other research methods that have been discussed in the preceding chapters. It is an assortment of techniques, procedures, and methods for analyzing the implementation and impact of social, educational, and medical innovations. It is also a fairly recent development, traceable directly to increased government expenditures on such innovations and the accompanying pressure for accountability and sanity in allocating the nation's scarce economic resources. For the practitioner, evaluation research is likely to differ in another way from other methods. It involves relinquishing some autonomy in picking and choosing the problems to be pursued and working on research problems that have been defined by those who have established policy, or set programs in motion, or both. The quid pro quo for this, however, is that the work of evaluation researchers has a chance of having a greater impact on society.

The evaluator's first step is to translate the organization's policy into clearly stated, measurable objectives. You need to ask yourself a series of questions about what the program you are evaluating is really intended to do. Once you have the objectives clearly in mind, you have to operationalize each: What, precisely, are you going to use as an indicator that each objective has been achieved? But even then, you have only just begun. Next, you have to get as many of the interested parties as possible to agree that your version of the objectives is really what the program is all about and that the measures you propose are valid indicators of those objectives. That, of course, is likely to require some diplomatic skill, not to mention extended negotiations.

Once you have the objectives operationalized to at least your satisfaction, the next step is the implementation of the program. Some of the objectives should be concerned with assessing implementation in its early stages; this process is referred to as formative evaluation. It gives you information needed for fine-tuning the program and making any needed changes before it is too late. If you neglect it, you may find that the program you had in mind never made the transition from the drawing board to reality. But, assuming you get the program in place and running, you then have to evaluate its impact, a process referred to as summative evaluation. To do it well, you should not be shy about using every tool you have, from participant observation to randomized control trials. The primary concern is with the utility of the information you obtain, not the method by which you obtain it.

Evaluation often takes place in a turbulent setting. More than any of the other research methods, evaluation research is likely to have a direct effect on people's lives, and they are not likely to behave as disinterested scientific observers while you calmly go about your business. If they have a stake in the outcome of the research, they are likely to let you know about it forcefully. And, for the typical program that is subjected to evaluation, there are likely to be multiple interested parties. The greatest potential for conflict seems to be between the people charged with the day-to-day operation of the program and those charged with evaluating it. Making it clear that the evaluation is focused on the program and not on how well, or how poorly, individuals are doing their jobs may help tone down some of the conflict. A little common sense and being as unobtrusive as possible will also help. The tendency of programs to evolve and change while the evaluation is in process can also present problems for the evaluator. A program, quite often, just will not stand still long enough for you to get a reading on how things are working out. This problem is inherent in the nature of evaluation research because you are not likely to have the necessary authority and control to keep the program from shifting, or being implemented in different ways. The best thing to do is to anticipate that the program will indeed shift and plan your evaluation in stages. Flexibility and keeping some resources in reserve will also help.

An evaluation of the Michigan Model Projects Specialized Respite Care Program was used to illustrate some of the features confronted in field settings. The inability to assign caregivers to treatment versus control groups necessitated the use of a quasi-experimental design, the untreated control group with pretest and posttest. To establish the initial equivalency of groups in the face of nonrandom assignment and attrition, it was necessary to collect a fair amount of demographic data for purposes of comparing the caregivers and care recipients in the two groups. The program itself appears to have been effective in reducing the subjective burden of caregivers and increasing their morale. However, the program was implemented in different ways at different sites, and that may or may not have affected the outcome.

Recommended Readings

Cook, T. D., Leviton, L. C., and Shadish, W. R., Jr. (1985). Program evaluation. In G. Lindzey and E. Aronson (Eds.), *The Handbook of Social Psychology* (3rd ed.). New York: Random House.

It is indicative of the relatively recent emergence of evaluation research that in the first and second editions of this handbook, published in 1954 and 1968 respectively, there were no chapters on program evaluation. That changed with the third edition, and in it, Cook, Leviton, and Shadish have provided a thoughtful overview of the field. They are particularly good at describing the political context of evaluation and how it impinges on each and every component of the process—from problem definition to the criteria to be employed in evaluating programs to how the results of evaluations are used. They also discuss at length the similarities between the evaluation of social programs and the evaluation of specific products—such as that done by *Consumer Reports*. But they are careful to note the differences in the two types of evaluation. For example, in the evaluation of social programs, it is typically not just performance that must be assessed, but *changes* in performance. Also, social programs are usually focused on people, not objects, and people are active, reactive, questioning agents—and sometimes they are just plain ornery. Cook et al. also develop the idea of "leverage" and discuss ways in which the impact of evaluations can be enhanced.

Rossi, P. H., and Freeman, H. E. (1993). *Evaluation: A systematic approach* (5th ed.). Newbury Park, CA: Sage.

Since the first edition of this text appeared in 1979, it has become a standard for the field of evaluation research. It has sold thousands upon thousands of copies and has been adopted at dozens upon dozens of universities and colleges. The coverage is comprehensive. Included are chapters on diagnostic procedures, tailoring evaluations, program monitoring, impact assessment, and several chapters on experimental and quasi-experimental designs for evaluation—all laced with numerous examples and illustrations. In addition, there is an excellent chapter on the social context of evaluations, in which the authors make a strong case that good evaluation research and clear-eyed evaluators will continue to be in demand for the foreseeable future. As they put it, our society has come to believe "that communal and personal problems are not fixed features of the human condition but can be ameliorated through the reconstruction of social institutions. ... It is clear that sensible, orderly procedures are required in order to choose which problems to confront first, and which programs to implement in order to deal with them. Our position is clear: systematic evaluations are invaluable to current and future efforts to improve the lot of humankind" (pp. 453–454). Unfortunately, this may be the last edition of *Evaluation* that we see, since one of the authors died while this fifth edition was in press.

Scriven, M. (1991). *Evaluation thesaurus* (4th ed.). Newbury Park, CA: Sage.

This is an unusual and—not "but"—valuable book. Following an introductory essay of 43 pages on the transdisciplinary nature of evaluation, the bulk of the book (about 350 pages) is devoted to an alphabetized list of extended critical and often sardonic definitions and discussions of key concepts in the field of evaluation. Scriven defines evaluation as the process of determining the merit, worth, and value of things and points out that it is a dangerous subject—one that was actively suppressed for many years. Why? "It is the investigative journalism of commerce, social services, and the academy; it is the auditor's voice; it is the threat of judgment bruising to one's self-concept; the threat of an outsider treading one's own turf, a threat of loss of power" (p. 41). The definitions and discussions that constitute the *Thesaurus* proper are thoughtful and provocative. This is the beginning of the entry for *Enemies List:* "Worst enemies make best critics. They have three advantages over friends, in that they are more motivated to prove you wrong, are less concerned about the effect on you, and are more experienced with a radically different viewpoint. ... But who enjoys working with, thanking, and paying an enemy? The answer is: a good evaluator" (p. 131). The book is a delight and well worth reading. It is also available in paperback.

Cook, T. D., and Shadish, W. R. (1994). Social experiments: Some developments over the past fifteen years. *Annual Review of Psychology*, 45, 545–580.

The *Annual Review of Psychology* publishes in-depth reviews of current research in all areas of psychology. The reviews of a particular topic area are scheduled on a rotating basis, usually every 3 or 4 years. Cook and Shadish—who are two of the leading methodologists in the field—point out that, surprisingly, theirs is the first chapter in the series to focus specifically on causal inference and social experimentation. As they use the term, "social experiments" are those that take place outside of laboratory settings and that tend to have less physical isolation of materials, less control over extraneous variables, and longer-lasting treatments. They are also usually designed to test an intervention that might best be described as a "global package of many components." The chapter itself focuses on four key topics: (1) changes in the theory of social experimentation (including ideas about establishing causation and suggested new names for internal and external validity); (2) the use of randomized experiments in field settings; (3) quasi-experimental designs; and (4) generalizing causal relationships. The authors note that current practice favors the use of randomized experiments whenever possible. But progress has been made in enhancing the power of quasi-experimental designs by the use of additional and better-matched controls, more pretest observations, and repeated application/removal of the treatment.

Valenstein, E. S. (1986). *Great and desperate cures: The rise and decline of psychosurgery and other radical treatments for mental illness*. New York: Basic Books.

Valenstein has written a chilling history of what can happen when the effects of new and drastic medical procedures are not properly evaluated. He focuses on treatments for mental illness, primarily lobotomy—a procedure in which holes are drilled in a patient's skull and parts of the brain are destroyed. The operation was first performed in November of 1935 by a Portuguese neurosurgeon named Egas Moniz, who later collected a Nobel Prize for this so-called "breakthrough." Within no time at all, the operation was being performed on mental patients far and wide—in spite of the fact that it was based on "the flimsiest of theories and on completely inadequate evidence" (p. 62). How could this have happened? Valenstein provides a timely and disturbing chronicle of the personal, social, and professional forces that can result in such dangerous and harmful procedures becoming widely accepted and used even in the absence of good evidence for their effectiveness. And, unfortunately, many of those forces are still with us: desperately ill people; premature reports of spectacular cures based on one or two case studies; uncritical media promotion of innovative therapies; professional jealousies and conflicts; and zealous self-promoters. Read the book. It is, indeed, a cautionary tale about the importance of proper evaluation.

10

Simulation

One of the thoughts that may have occurred to you by now is that the individual research methods in this book could be arrayed along a continuum. Disregarding evaluation research for the moment, which as you now know employs a variety of methods, we began in Chapter 2 with that most open and unstructured of procedures, participant observation. We then worked our way along to the controlled environment of the laboratory experiment, described in Chapter 8. With each new method, techniques for refining and structuring your observations of behavior were introduced. The purpose of each new methodological nicety, of course, was to help you keep from kidding yourself, to help you keep from falling into the trap of concluding more than you should from your research. Each method has built on and extended those that preceded it. In doing so, each has opened up new opportunities for learning about people and behavior, but each has also brought new restrictions on which behaviors can be studied and a gradual shift away from the study of ongoing real-life activities. The price of increased methodological rigor seems to have been an increased remoteness from everyday life.

Another, somewhat more subtle, shift occurred in moving from participant observation to experimentation. The examples cited, and they are reasonably representative, seem to have conveyed a waning interest in discovering what the social world is like and a growing focus on what was described in Chapter 1 as verification: the testing of specific hypotheses.

Of course, you might say that these two shifts in emphasis underscore the point that has been made repeatedly in the preceding pages. There is no one superior method, no single avenue to truth. The method of choice depends on the question of interest. However, advocates of the research techniques to be discussed in this final chapter claim that a compromise choice is possible. Their argument is that simulations take advantage of the rigor and precision of the experimental approach while at the same time allowing you to investigate some of the more complex, dynamic processes usually thought of as the province of some of the less-structured methods. Let us see.

Scientific Metaphors

Webster's (1991) Ninth New Collegiate Dictionary defines the verb *simulate* in these terms: "to assume the outward quality or appearance of, often with the intent to deceive." The noun *simulation* is defined as "the act or process of simulating; feigning; a sham object; counterfeit; the imitative representation of the functioning of one system or process by means of the functioning of another." As Abelson (1968) noted many years ago, such definitions are a potential source of embarrassment to those who would like to use simulations in research. The cliché is that scientific research is a quest for truth. How can you arrive at the truth via a method the very name of which has such a strong connotation of phoniness? Needless to say, critics of the various simulation techniques find the dictionary definitions of "simulate" and "simulation" to be a source of wry amusement. Those definitions are precisely the point, they say: **Simulations** are imitations.

Why not study the real thing? Why bother with an imitation when you know ahead of time that it is only an imitation—and probably an imperfect one at that? One answer, of course, is that sometimes it is just completely impractical to study the real thing directly. For example, suppose you were interested in the sorts of errors made by pilot trainees in their first attempts to fly a plane. Putting trainees into a multimillion-dollar aircraft for their first attempts would not be a sound economic policy, although it would probably ensure that the more uncoordinated trainees would quickly be eliminated from the program. Rather, it would be a better idea to use a flight simulator, which is a detailed physical model of the cockpit of an airplane. Such simulations are useful for both training and research. Would-be pilots can practice reading the instruments and manipulating the controls until they have the entire arrangement of dials, meters, knobs, and switches so well in mind that they do not waste precious seconds trying to decide whether that little green dial with the red letters is their altitude or their airspeed. As for the research aspect, such simulators have proved invaluable in human factors engineering (the designing of those very dials, meters, knobs, and switches so as to minimize misreading and mishandling and maximize comfort for the human operator).

As Gauch (1993) has pointed out, one of the major purposes of science, generally, is to describe reality through models. The notion of modeling, of constructing an analogue of some system, is the key to simulation. But most of the simulations of interest in the social and behavioral sciences do not involve physical models. They involve models that are looser, more abstract, models that do not attempt to duplicate every single detail of the real thing, as the flight simulator does. The models of interest in the social and behavioral sciences, then, are like scientific metaphors, analogues that attempt to capture and represent in a different form the basic characteristics of the thing modeled (e.g., Locke, 1986). The hope, of course, is that the model will be easier to study than the real thing, and that by learning how the model works, you will, in fact, be learning about the real McCoy.*

A simulation, then, is an imitation of the processes and products of a system, an imitation that is intended to expose the basic operating characteristics of the system being simulated. Note that there are two central features here. First, there is a focus on processes. Something dynamic is modeled, something that changes over time. Second, there is a focus on discovery. The purpose of a simulation is to uncover the essence of the phenomenon being modeled, to see how it works. There is no point in going to all the time and effort required to conduct a simulation when you know ahead of time how the thing is going to turn out. As Abelson (1968) put it, a simulation is most worthwhile when it produces unanticipated results.

As you might guess, there are several general categories of simulations. We shall discuss three basic types in this chapter: role-playing, analogue experiments, and games as research settings. I have omitted computer simulations, that is, simulations in which a computer is programmed to manipulate the data of interest in ways suggested by the model you have constructed. Such simulations can indeed be informative (Ostrom, 1988; Stasser, 1990), especially when the model is a complex one. However, they have been omitted here because a usable understanding of computer simulations requires a degree of sophistication about programming that is beyond the scope of an introduction to research methods. So, let's consider the other three types one by one.

Role-Playing

As you are no doubt aware, the importance of the concepts of role and norm in the study of social behavior can hardly be exaggerated. Norms, of course, are rules about what constitutes appropriate behavior in particular situations, and they are based on agreement or consensus. They change over time, just as do other aspects of society. In that connection, it is both instructive and amusing to read through an old book of etiquette in which the norms of some bygone era have been cast into sets of dos and don'ts for the socially anxious. There are norms about nearly every aspect of social behavior, from the type of clothes we wear to the side of the street we drive on—that last one is an official norm in that we have made it into a law. People who are categorized by having the same subset of norms applied to them are said to occupy the same role. And once a person has been categorized as occupying a certain role— automobile driver, father, student, raconteur—certain definite behaviors are expected of them. The concept of role calls attention to the normative nature of our expectations about the behaviors of someone occupying a particular role—whether that someone is oneself or another person.

---

*The real McCoy, by the way, was a rumrunner during the Prohibition era. He was known for the high quality of his products, in contrast to the bathtub gin of his competitors.

Much of our social behavior, then, is governed by the norms, or rules, that define what is appropriate for someone acting out a particular role. We are rule-following agents. As Harre and Van Langenhove (1991) put it, we "position" ourselves with respect to those with whom we are interacting by making use of a variety of implicit and explicit understandings. The intriguing thing about this is that in many situations we may behave appropriately without knowing precisely which rule we are following, or why we are doing what we are doing. There are many ways in which this state of affairs could come about. We may, for example, have learned what to do in a particular situation by simply watching what everybody else does and imitating them. Or there may be nonverbal cues from others in some situations to guide our actions, cues so subtle that we never consciously recognize their power. In much of our interpersonal behavior, it appears that we never take that step back that would give us the perspective necessary to analyze what we are doing. We muddle through, however, doing what appears to come naturally.

According to Greenberg and Eskew (1993), under certain circumstances role-playing can give us that necessary perspective. **Role-playing** research is research in which subjects are asked how they would feel or behave—or how another person would feel or behave—in a given situation. In other words, subjects are asked to behave "as if" the situation were real and indicate how they would respond. A key aspect of such research, and one that has resulted in much criticism of role-playing, is that subjects are clearly aware that their responses have no "real" consequences. Hence, critics say that there may be no correspondence between what they say they would do and what they would actually do if they were really in the situation (e.g., Aronson et al., 1990). But role-playing should not be used to find out what subjects would do in real situations. As Greenberg and Eskew (1993) point out, that would be a completely inappropriate use of role-playing as a research tool. As they put it:

> It need not be argued that there exists any correspondence between what people say they would do and what they actually do for there to be any value to role-playing data. The value of role-playing studies lies not in assuming that people really would do what they say, but in learning what they say they would do. The mere expression of intended behavior can reveal a great deal about people's beliefs regarding the norms that regulate behavior. (p. 225)

The purpose of role-playing, then, is to uncover the implicit understandings and situational features that guide behavior, including the implicit rules governing behavior and social discourse. (For an example of research using trained actors to play the role of patients in simulated medical interviews, see Box 1.)

Given that general purpose, role-playing studies vary in at least three ways (Greenberg and Eskew, 1993). First, they differ in the subjects' degree of involvement. At the low end of this dimension, subjects may simply be asked to read a brief paragraph describing a situation and answer a few questions about their responses to the paragraph. For example, Occhipinti and Siegal (1994) asked subjects to read a story about a shopkeeper at a bar

---

Box 1

Role-Playing and the Medical Interview

Using what they referred to as high-fidelity simulations, Elstein, Shulman, and Sprafka (1978, 1990) studied the diagnostic problem-solving behavior of experienced physicians. They were particularly interested in finding out whether physicians reputed to be good diagnosticians went about diagnosing a case differently from physicians without such reputations. To make the necessary comparisons, it was deemed essential to have members of the two groups diagnose the same cases. This was done by training actors to play the roles of patients. Scripts for the actors were developed from actual cases, and the actors memorized the medical histories of the patients involved. The research consisted of having physicians interview the actors and make a diagnosis. It was completely up to the physicians to decide which questions to ask, how many to ask, and in what order. If laboratory tests were requested by the physicians, the results of those tests were provided without comment. The interviews were recorded on videotape so that they could be analyzed at leisure—and repeatedly. As you will recall from Chapter 3, one of the great advantages of recordings is that you can go back to them to check the reliability of coding, or with a different coding scheme, should you get a new idea about what to look for.

The results of the simulations suggested that successful diagnosticians generate hypotheses about possible problems or diseases quite early in an encounter with a patient. They then progressively home in on the most likely diagnosis by selectively seeking certain types of information. The point here, however, is to note that this research probably could not have been done using real patients, even though the presenting complaints and medical histories that the actors learned were from such patients. The use of trained actors and memorized case material was, of course, a substitute, but it was an excellent way of simulating physician–patient interviews. It allowed the investigators to learn something about the diagnostic process under controlled conditions that seemed to capture the essential pattern of the real-life situation.

---

in a French village who was selling croquettes to tourists. The croquettes were labeled "poison" (a possible misspelling of the French "poisson," meaning fish), "not poison," or not labeled. Some subjects were led to believe the mislabeling was a simple mistake, while others were told that the shopkeeper happened to be very hostile toward tourists. The purpose of the research was to examine the circumstances under which subjects would, or would not, discount what the label actually said. But the point here is that after reading a version of the story, subjects were simply asked, "Which croquettes would you prefer, given that you ordinarily preferred fish?" Since the subjects, of course, were not tourists, not in France, not buying croquettes, and would not really have to take a chance on being poisoned, this study would qualify as not very involving. In contrast, at the high end of the involvement dimension is a famous role-playing study carried out in the basement of the Stanford University psychology department some years ago by Zimbardo and his colleagues (Haney, Banks, and Zimbardo, 1973; Zimbardo et al., 1982). Student volunteers were assigned roles as prisoners or guards and actually acted out these roles for several days and nights. The study turned out to be more involving than anyone expected. It began on a

Sunday and was scheduled to run for 2 weeks. Six days later the study was terminated because of the unusual reactions that had begun to emerge among both the prisoners and the guards. Five prisoners had to be released even prior to that because of extreme depression, crying, and acute anxiety. In contrast, the guards wanted to continue; in fact, several had already become so involved in their roles that they would stay around after their official shifts were over, apparently because they enjoyed the power and control associated with their roles.

The second way in which role-playing studies vary has to do with the nature of the role that subjects are asked to play. There are four possibilities: Subjects can be asked to play either themselves or someone else, in either a familiar or an unfamiliar role. For example, in both of the studies just mentioned, subjects were asked to play themselves in unfamiliar roles—as a tourist about to buy mislabeled croquettes in a foreign country, or as a guard (or inmate) in a prison. There are studies in which subjects have been asked to take the role of others in unfamiliar settings (e.g., Neale, Huber, and Northcraft, 1987), but it is unclear what the results mean. If the role a person is asked to play is indeed completely unfamiliar to them, then, by definition, they have no expectations, or implicit understandings, of how a person in that role would behave.

The third type of variation typically found in role-playing research has to do with specificity of response. In some studies, subjects are simply asked to provide one or two very specific responses. They may, for example, be asked to take the role of a juror in a criminal trial and, after hearing the case, make a few simple judgments, such as Guilty versus Not Guilty and length of sentence to be imposed (e.g., Dexter, Cutler, and Moran, 1992). In contrast, other studies require subjects to act out a role, to improvise and really put themselves into it—with no clear directions about exactly what they are to do or say. In the latter case, uncovering the dimensions of the implicit **role/rule framework** guiding their performance may be more difficult. You may have to focus all the analytic devices at your command on those performances: videotape, audiotape, coding, content analysis, and, yes, questioning the role-players about the details of their performances. Why did you do that? What did you mean when you said this place reminds you of Ohio?

Given the possible variations, what's the best approach? As with so many questions about methodology, the only complete answer to that question is: Well, it all depends on what you are interested in. However, if your purpose is the general one of finding out what people believe to be appropriate behavior in certain contexts, then Greenberg and Eskew (1993, p. 232) offer this advice: The most informative data are likely to be generated when role-playing subjects are highly involved, playing themselves in familiar roles, and responding in an unrestricted manner. I agree.

Analogue Experiments

Probably the most common type of simulation is a variation of the experiment, a variation introduced into research by Kurt Lewin in the 1930s. Experimentation per se was, of course, already familiar by then. What was new was Lewin's insistence that entire social constellations could profitably be studied via the experimental approach. The key to his method is what he referred to as transposition, the carrying over of the essential structural characteristics of some real-world phenomenon into the experimental setting. Thus, the basic overall pattern, not simply one or two of its elements, must be abstracted and recaptured by the experimenter on a smaller scale and in a relatively well-controlled environment (Figure 1). Lewin (1951) felt that experiments become artificial and unlifelike when only one or two aspects of a phenomenon are realized in the research and not the essential pattern.

There is a relatively subtle distinction between the experiment, as described in Chapter 8 and as usually practiced, and the sort of experimental

*"Sure, we're dealing with tiny particles, but your formula is just a **symbolic** representation."*

1 Like mathematical equations, simulations are representations of the essential features of the things being modeled. Simulations do not attempt to duplicate all features of the things modeled. If they did, they would simply be copies—and, thus, pointless. (From *All ends up: Cartoons by Sidney Harris*, Los Altos, CA: William Kaufman.)

simulation we are discussing here. As described earlier, an experiment is usually focused on establishing cause-and-effect relationships between variables or testing specific hypotheses: If A, then B. Analogue experiments usually allow subjects greater freedom of behavior. The focus is on observing what will happen when the social phenomenon is transposed (with all essential characteristics intact) to the controlled setting and set in motion. How will the processes work themselves out? If A, then what? To help make this distinction clearer, consider the following example.

In recent years, one of the most active areas of social research has been on various aspects of the legal system (e.g., Foley, 1993). This research has been motivated, at least in part, by an understandable, even laudable, desire among psychologists and sociologists for their research to have some immediate, real-world impact. By simulating components of the legal system—such as trials or police lineups—in the laboratory, researchers can analyze those components under controlled conditions not attainable in actual trials or police lineups. One of the major areas of interest has been an examination of the factors influencing decision making by jurors, an area referred to as mock jury research.

In a typical mock jury study, subjects are asked to read the evidence for and against a defendant, or they may be asked to view a videotaped presentation of the evidence. After being exposed to the evidence, they are, again typically, asked to make a judgment about guilt or innocence and, possibly, recommend a sentence. Within such a generic framework, there are, of course, literally dozens of variables that you might want to examine. You could, for example, manipulate the attractiveness of the defendant to see whether it makes a difference in the likelihood of the jurors' reaching a guilty verdict—it does, by the way, and if the defendant committed a crime that had a victim, the attractiveness of the victim also makes a difference.

But if the interest is really in how the legal system works, what about actual procedural aspects of trials? Are there things about the ways in which actual trials are conducted that influence the outcome? One aspect that has received some attention is judges' instructions to jurors. As Kerwin and Shaffer (1994) point out, one of the major functions of such instructions is to ensure that members of juries know they are to base their decisions only on legally admissible evidence, and that things they read in the newspaper or saw on television or heard their neighbors say are not legally admissible. Even in the courtroom, of course, jurors are sometimes exposed to evidence that is not legally admissible. When that occurs, or when there is a lot of damaging pretrial publicity, the judge simply instructs the members of the jury to *disregard* it: Forget it, pretend you didn't hear it, don't let it influence your decision!

As you might expect, several mock jury studies in which "jurors" were exposed to damaging evidence that they were later told to disregard found that they do not—or cannot—disregard it (Dexter, Cutler, and Moran, 1992). That is, it does indeed influence their decisions, as shown by comparing those decisions with the decisions of other "jurors" who were not exposed to the damaging evidence. However, Kerwin and Shaffer (1994) point out that these studies failed to capture an essential component of real-life jury trials and that, therefore, they are of questionable relevance to what happens with real juries. The studies that found jurors unable to disregard evidence when so instructed exposed mock jurors to evidence and asked them for *individual decisions*—that is, without deliberation or discussing the trial with other jurors. They were, in effect, studies of mock jurors, but not of mock juries.

To see whether deliberation really makes a difference, Kerwin and Shaffer (1994) designed an experiment in which some subjects were asked to make individual decisions about guilt or innocence after reading the transcript of a court case. Other subjects read the same case, but were asked to discuss it with a small group of other "jurors" and reach a unanimous verdict. The transcript described the trial of a 27-year-old male accused of armed robbery. The prosecution's case was based on the "rather weak testimony" of an eyewitness who was in the store that was robbed, but who had hidden during the robbery itself. In the transcript, the defense attorney strongly challenged this eyewitness as unreliable. The critical evidence in the transcript was supplied by the testimony of a police officer who said that a red bag, matching one used by the robber, was found in the accused's apartment. The bag also contained an amount of money close to the amount that had been stolen. The defense attorney immediately responded that the bag and money had been obtained during an illegal search of the apartment and should not be admitted as evidence. In the transcript read by some subjects, the judge ruled that the testimony about the bag and money was indeed inadmissible and was not to be considered in reaching a verdict. In contrast, in the transcript read by the remaining subjects, the judge ruled that the testimony about the bag and money was admissible.

To summarize the design, all subjects read precisely the same evidence. However, half were instructed to disregard the damaging information about the bag and the money in reaching their verdict, and half were not. In addition, some subjects in each of these conditions were asked for their individual opinions about the guilt or innocence of the accused, while others were asked to discuss the case with their peers (who had also read it) and reach a group decision, as real juries must do. Kerwin and Shaffer (1994) anticipated that the latter subjects would be less likely to disregard the judge's instructions. While they might, personally, still believe that the accused was guilty, they would also anticipate pressure from other "jurors" to adhere to proper legal procedure. The results are depicted in Figure 2. There it may be seen that when the damaging evidence was admissible, juries and individual jurors reached essentially the same verdicts. But when the damaging evidence was inadmissible, juries were significantly less likely to convict the defendant than were individual jurors. Deliberation really does make a difference.

It is important to be clear about exactly what Kerwin and Shaffer did. Their reading of the mock jury literature on the effect of instructions to disregard suggested to them that some of the earlier research had omitted an *es-*

2 Mean verdict recommendations as a function of simulation method and judge's ruling on the admissibility of incriminating evidence. Higher means indicate greater likelihood of conviction. (Data from Kerwin and Shaffer, 1994.)

sential theoretically relevant element. One of the defining characteristics of a jury, after all, is that members of a jury are expected to deliberate. Thus, an experimental analogue of a jury that leaves out deliberation might better be termed a mockery than a mock jury. As Brewer (1985) put it:

> Designing an experiment as an analogue involves a two-stage process: (1) the abstraction of essential elements in a complex social situation, and (2) their reconstruction in a different, scaled-down setting in such a way that an isomorphism is preserved between the original and the analogue situation. For every feature of the external situation considered theoretically relevant, there is a corresponding feature contained in the laboratory situation. (p. 163)

Mock jury research has, in fact, received a fair amount of criticism on just this point: the failure to include essential theoretically relevant variables. But it is important to note that the objections to mock jury research are not blanket objections to analogues and simulations in research. The objections are to poor analogues, analogues that are not based on a careful diagnosis of the social and psychological processes operating in the domain of interest.

One way to think of simulations is as theory-building devices, techniques that help you to get a grasp on what may be involved in a social system. In the end, of course, you will have to deal with that "may." How can you establish that the processes, or features, identified in a simulation really correspond to those operating in the system simulated? Locke (1986) argues that you do that through a process of approximation. With a careful analysis of the complex social system to be simulated and, perhaps, a plausible hypothesis or two about what is involved, you select what you believe to be its "essential features" and try to simulate the system. Then, guided by the results of the initial attempts and a close inspection of the actual procedures of the analogue experiment, you may find that you need to incorporate new variables—as Kerwin and Shaffer (1994) did by giving some subjects the opportunity to discuss the case and requiring them to render a group verdict. As Locke (1986) put it, "Just what is essential cannot necessarily be known in advance; discovering these essentials is an inductive procedure."

Be sure to note that in selecting what you believe to be the essential features of a social system, you will by definition be leaving out everything that you believe to be nonessential. The fact that models and simulations require you to do that, to dispense with variables you think may be extraneous and "see what happens if ...", is one of their greatest appeals and sources of usefulness. It allows you to get to the heart of the matter, to see what really makes things work the way they do. The problem is to avoid introducing new variables into the simulation, variables that have no counterpart in the reality being simulated. Such variables, of course, raise questions about the validity of the simulation. But before taking up the question of validity, let us describe one more variety of simulation.

Games as Research Settings

War games, which have been used as training exercises for hundreds of years, seem to have been among the first full-blown simulations. These large-scale tactical operations, complete with umpires and scorekeepers, provide an opportunity for armed forces personnel to try out equipment and maneuvers under combat-like conditions. They are, of course, a form of role-playing. In the tradition of war games, but on a smaller scale, there are now a variety of simulation games available, games primarily intended as learning devices for the people involved. There are dozens of marketing games for business students (Wolfe, 1993), simulation games for family therapy (Finger, Elliott, and Remer, 1993), games for teaching persistence (Whitehill and McDonald, 1993), and literally scores of others. Often the intention of the inventors of such games is to provide the players with some holistic insights into the issues and forces involved in the topic of concern. Rather than simply being told about legitimate conflicts of interest in society, for example, the game player might be put in the position of having to deal with diametrically opposed demands from other players representing those interests.

The simulation games most useful for research are somewhat different from those used for teaching. They are actual contests between two (or more) people who are not asked to role-play anyone or anything. They are simply asked to play the game according to the rules. The outcome is usually not known in advance; it depends upon the actions of the participants. The usual focus of research using such games is on the social interactions that occur between players. The hope is that the game will provide a structured, well-defined task by means of which the dynamics of interaction may be studied.

A great deal of the research employing games has used some variation of an interpersonal situation termed the prisoner's dilemma (Komorita and Parks, 1994). The name stems from the following setting: Suppose that two people are arrested on suspicion of committing a crime—say, armed robbery. They are taken to the police station and put in separate rooms for questioning. Suppose, further, that they are guilty, and that each is sincerely interested in putting in as little time as possible behind bars. The problem is that neither can be sure of what the other is going to do. If neither confesses, both are likely to be charged with a lesser offense, such as illegal possession of weapons, because the evidence on the armed robbery charge is only circumstantial. Thus, both will get off with minimum sentences. If both confess, both are likely to get a long jail term. However, if one confesses and the other does not, the one who confesses will get a light sentence in return for providing evidence against his or her (former) colleague, whereas the latter will be penalized much more severely. Each prisoner's dilemma, then, is whether to trust the partner not to confess and refuse to confess oneself (that is, to cooperate with the partner) or to confess and save oneself before the partner confesses (that is, to compete with the partner). The situation is called a mixed motive situation because it pits the motivation to cooperate against the motivation to compete. The basic structure of the prisoner's dilemma is depicted in Figure 3A.

The rewards involved in simulation games modeled after the prisoner's dilemma are not jail terms, of course, but prizes of various sorts—usually points or money. Such games are usually played by two people for a series of trials. On a given trial, each player is confronted with a choice between a

(A)

	Prisoner A can:	
	Refuse to confess	Confess
Refuse to confess (cooperative)	A gets 6 months B gets 6 months	A gets 90 days B gets 10 years
Confess (competitive)	A gets 10 years B gets 90 days	A gets 5 years B gets 5 years

Prisoner B can:

(B)

	Response of player A	
	Cooperative	Competitive
Cooperative	+5 / +5	+10 / −20
Competitive	−20 / +10	−5 / −5

Response of player B

3 The prisoner's dilemma in real life and as a game for studying social interaction. (A) The basic structure of the prisoner's dilemma. Each prisoner must decide whether to act competitively (confess) or cooperatively (refuse to confess), but the outcome is also affected by what the other prisoner decides to do. (B) Possible combinations of responses and rewards in a game modeled after the prisoner's dilemma. Player B's payoff is shown to the left of the slash in each box; player A's is on the right.

cooperative and a competitive response and is also faced with the puzzle of what the other player will choose on that trial. The reason that puzzle is so important is that the outcome of a given trial is determined by what both players choose. This can be seen in Figure 3B, which depicts the general pattern of the various possible combinations of responses and rewards. If both players choose cooperation on a given trial, both players win a moderate amount (+5); if both players choose competition, both players lose (–5). The opportunity also exists for one player to exploit a cooperative opponent by making a competitive choice when the opponent makes a cooperative choice. In the latter case, the person making the competitive choice comes out way ahead (+10) and the person making the cooperative choice loses badly (–20).

One of the things that has been examined using the prisoner's dilemma game is how one can induce cooperation on the part of the other player. For example, suppose the game is to be played for a number of trials, with the two players making their choices simultaneously on each trial and no opportunity to communicate. What must be relied on then is the pattern of cooperative and competitive choices. There are several possibilities. You can simply elect the cooperative choice on every trial in the hope that the other person will see what a nice person you are and begin making the cooperative choice in turn. The analogy here in terms of international affairs is with unilateral disarmament. Unfortunately, it doesn't work in the prisoner's dilemma game. Neither does continuous choice of the competitive response. What appears to work is a "tit-for-tat" strategy, in which you choose what the other player chose on the previous trial (Patchen, 1987). If they chose competition on trial 83, you choose it on trial 84. If they cooperated on 85, you do likewise on 86. The other player soon gets the message and, usually, you end up with continuous mutually rewarding choices.

There are a variety of other variables that can be examined within the framework of the prisoner's dilemma game, including such things as the personalities of the players, their expectations about each other, the effects of being able to communicate about choices, and the magnitude of the rewards and costs associated with cooperative and competitive choices. As Komorita and Parks (1994) point out, research using the prisoner's dilemma game may have important implications for our understanding of how cooperation evolves and may help to explain cooperation in a variety of settings. Researchers in many disciplines—including psychology, ecology, economics, and biology—are finding the basic prisoner's dilemma model to be useful in exploring the parameters of cooperation and competition.

Another game format that has proved useful in studying some aspects of social interaction has its origins in a phenomenon called "the tragedy of the commons" (Hardin, 1968). The name comes from jointly held lands (commons) in old New England on which all villagers could allow their cattle to graze, free of charge. The potential tragedy was that if individual villagers got greedy and increased the size of their herds, they might profit more—so long as nobody else got the same idea. If everyone increased the size of their herd, the land would quickly be overgrazed, and everyone's cows would get thinner, not fatter. The dilemma, then, pits short-term profit for the individual against long-term profit for the community. As Komorita and Parks (1994) point out, this is an example of a **social trap**, and it involves a basic dilemma that we face in many areas of life, from disposal of toxic wastes and control of exhaust emissions to overpopulation. It is easiest (i.e., most profitable) for a manufacturer to dump wastes in the nearest river, but we all suffer when such dumping is allowed. Many people believe that everyone should be free to have as many children as they like, but if that practice continues much longer, the world will run out of food.

Edney (1979) has designed a game called the "nuts game" that he claims captures the essential characteristics of the tragedy of the commons. It is a simple game in which a small number of people are seated around a bowl containing marbles. The game is so constructed that the marbles have some real value—say, each can be exchanged for 10 cents at the end of the game. The aim of the game is simple: Each person is to get as many marbles as possible. This is done by just reaching in and grabbing a handful whenever the spirit moves you. Every 10 seconds, the number of marbles in the bowl is doubled (by the game's equivalent of God); but if the bowl is ever completely emptied by the players, the game is over. One other detail: The players may not talk to each other during the game.

Think about that for a moment. The rational thing to do, of course, is for all the players to exercise a little restraint and let the number of marbles double a few times. Suppose, for example, that there were 10 marbles (worth a total of $1) at the outset. Care to take a guess how much there would be in the pot if everyone could wait just 4 minutes before grabbing some marbles? Over $8,000,000—yes, that's 8 million dollars. So four players could each get $2,000,000 just by waiting 4 minutes—but nobody ever does. I have tried this game as a demonstration in classes, and usually people start getting excessively greedy when there is about $16 in the bowl—excessive greed here means that they take so many marbles that on subsequent trials the number of marbles in the bowl begins to decrease.

There are several variations of this particular game (Komorita and Parks, 1994). In one, for example, the pot is not doubled on each trial, but is increased by a certain percentage of what remains. That, in fact, may be a better approximation to the original tragedy of the commons, since the grass on the commons would not double instantaneously, but would grow incrementally. The point here, however, is that the game is an attempt to capture and represent in a different form the basic dilemma involved in the tragedy of the commons. To the extent that it does, it is an apt scientific metaphor. It is a model that is useful in understanding the dynamics of reactions to the dilemma (e.g., Dawes, 1990; Kerr, 1990).

The prisoner's dilemma and the nuts game are just two examples drawn from a variety of games that can be useful in research. (For an example that makes use of a computer video game, see Box 2.) They are all models, analogues. Each is structured so as to capture what the investigator believes to be

---

Box 2

Coordinating the Flight Team

A flight simulator is a detailed, full-size working model of the pilot's compartment of an airplane. Such working models have become essential training tools for both military and commercial pilots. Many modern aircraft, however, have a flight crew—not just one pilot—and there is evidence that over 50% of modern aircraft accidents are due to communication and coordination failures among crew members. In order to prevent such failures, we need to know more about how groups of people can work together most efficiently in complex, high-pressure settings such as the multiperson airplane cockpit.

Why not study crew coordination in those fancy flight training simulators? Unfortunately, they cost millions of dollars and are simply not available to most people interested in doing research on group processes. As a substitute, Bowers et al. (1992) have constructed what they refer to as a low-fidelity simulation that can be used to study team coordination and performance. They use a commercially available video game to simulate the flight of a helicopter gunship. The game is played via a computer through a video splitter, which sends the image that would normally be depicted on the computer screen to two monitors in separate cubicles. The "pilot" is seated in one cubicle and makes input to the computer via a joystick. The second team member is seated in the other cubicle and uses the computer keyboard for input. The joystick controls such things as the heading of the aircraft, and the keyboard controls the view displayed on the screen (front, back, left, right) as well as weapon selection. The two team members can communicate only via an intercom. And, as Bowers et al. note, communication is indeed required for successful performance of the task.

The point here is that with a little ingenuity and a minimum of equipment, Bowers et al. were able to construct a setting that allows them to examine some of the processes involved in communication and coordination of team members. The equipment needed was, basically, an intercom, a computer with an extra monitor, and a joystick. Be sure to note, however, that in constructing this "low-fidelity" simulation, Bowers et al. did not need to duplicate everything about aircraft crews. They were careful to preserve only what they believe to be the essential characteristics necessary for team research: two or more interdependent subjects who must coordinate their efforts to succeed. Preserving those "essential characteristics" is the key to simulation.

---

the essence of some real-life situation. And, once the rules of the game are clearly specified, the manner in which interaction proceeds can be studied—usually much more easily than in the real-life setting. The influence of different types of participants, different payoffs, and different rules can be examined. The latter is particularly important and is one of the genuine advantages of simulations: You can see what happens when you change the rules, something that is difficult to do in most natural settings. Of course, there are problems with the use of games, but those problems are common to nearly all types of simulations in research.

Evaluating Simulations

The use of simulation in research has been the target of much criticism over the years. Part of the reason for this is that there are so many varieties of simulations—different types of role-playing, for example, and scores of different experimental games. Critics addressing themselves to one particular type of simulation, or one particular use of simulation, have sometimes not been sufficiently cautious in making clear the boundaries of their critiques. They often seem to imply that because one particular simulation was flawed, or inappropriately used, all simulations must be useless. Aronson et al. (1990), for example, pointed out that role-playing research in which people are simply asked to imagine themselves in a particular role and report how they would behave is not useful *if it is intended as a substitute for observing how they really behave in that role.* Few would disagree with that. There is a vast literature demonstrating that what people say they will do and what they actually do are often quite different. But, as you have seen, there are other varieties of role-playing that evoke greater involvement and spontaneity and that can be more informative. Similarly, some years ago Nemeth (1972) argued that the prisoner's dilemma game is not a good vehicle for studying bargaining, which many of its promoters believed it would be. Nemeth's point is that the game is too abstract and ambiguous. By eliminating the possibility of direct communication, aspects essential to bargaining as a process are also eliminated. You cannot make clear to your opponent in the game your plans, your goals, the reasons behind your choices. But, again, as we have seen, the game can be useful in understanding other phenomena. The key to assessing any particular simulation, then, is to ask yourself two questions: (1) Was simulation called for in this instance? (2) If so, was it done well enough for the results to have some bearing on the phenomenon of interest? A few comments on each of these issues may help you answer these questions.

When to Simulate

It is important to remember that simulations may be used for a variety of purposes. They can be quite useful as teaching tools, especially when those participating are induced to behave in self-surprising ways. In the Nuts Game, for example, subjects are sometimes quite annoyed with themselves when they find that they and their competitors have foolishly brought the game to a premature end by being overly greedy. Similarly, simulations such as war games can yield valuable insights into the dynamics (and problems) of moving large bodies of troops—insights that can be obtained in no other way, short of war itself. When simulations are used for teaching, the important considerations in evaluating them are, of course, what and how much was learned by whom. Another use of simulations is as a vehicle for testing specific hypotheses. Many of the simulation games, such as the prisoner's dilemma game, are used in this way. Does physiological arousal increase the frequency of competitive choices? Does the reward structure (i.e., how much players can win by exploiting their opponents) make a difference? Does cooperation fade as the stakes go up? When simulations are used in this way, the important considerations in evaluating them are generally the same as those discussed in connection with experimentation (Chapter 8).

The most important use of simulation methods, and the one most difficult to evaluate, is one that simulations share with participant observation: They are both great goads to theory development. They get your mind churning about what is really involved in rumor transmission, or social interaction, or whatever it is that interests you. Of course, with participant observation you are supposedly focused on taking in what is going on in the situation, and with simulation development you are focused on explaining it (via building a model). Most people, however, find these two activities difficult to separate. As soon as they see something interesting, they begin reaching for an explanation.

As noted earlier, a simulation is a scientific metaphor, an analogue. But, as Kaplan (1964) has said, the key question is whether there is something to be learned from an analogy if you choose to draw it. To suggest that getting married is like buying a car on time is pointless, unless it leads you to consider aspects of the marriage situation that you might not have thought of otherwise. That analogy could, in fact, be a worthwhile one to pursue because marriage has one of the features that Abelson (1968) says is essential among candidates for simulation: It involves a variety of forces interacting in complex ways that make the outcomes difficult to predict. The hope in such situations is that an analogue, a model of the processes that might be involved, will both strip away most of the irrelevancies and reveal something of the essential underlying character of the phenomenon. Note that the model will, almost by definition, be an oversimplification. But don't let that scare you.

Try another example. Take some complex aspect of individual behavior, or some complicated social situation, and develop a model for it. Ask yourself if the analogy leads you to any new implications, any unanticipated aspects of the situation, any previously unconsidered dimensions. If it does not, it is useless. But don't give up too quickly. Mull it over, twist it around, pursue it. If the model does suggest something new, you are well on your way to simulation. Thus, a partial answer to the question of when simulation is an appropriate strategy is this: when something new can be learned from the model you develop. Further, that is most likely to occur when the situation being modeled is a complex one, involving a variety of forces. Another way of saying this is that simulations should be evaluated in terms of their **heuristic fertility**—that is, the extent to which they suggest new observations, research, and ideas. If nothing new is suggested by the model you develop, then you have wasted your time. That is why a model of a situation involving no more than one or two variables is not likely to be useful.

It follows that much of the value of developing a simulation is realized before the simulation is ever actually carried out, during what Palys (1978) referred to as the confrontation and explication process. That occurs when you sit down, pen in hand, all ready to whip out a model, and you realize how much you do not know about the phenomenon that has piqued your interest. You are confronted by your own ignorance. Painful though it is, that is really a crucial first step. It is there that the processes of model building and simulation begin. What, after all, is really involved in dating choices, or white flight to the suburbs, or the bandwagon effect in national elections? You will find that you have to get your assumptions out on the table, define your terms, fill in gaps, resolve inconsistencies. In other words, the most important part of simulation is the formulation of detailed ideas about the processes involved. So, when evaluation time rolls around, forget all the stage settings, the fancy mathematics, and the magnificent machines. Ask yourself, What were the ideas behind this simulation? What social and behavioral processes have been clarified?

There are a couple of other things you might want to think about in assessing a simulation, or in developing your own. The first is related to the fact that models are simplifications of some more complex reality. Because of that, when you get to the explication phase of the confrontation-explication process, you probably will have to go a lot further than you would like in specifying your assumptions. Everything must be made precise for the model; no ambiguities are allowed. There is good reason for that, of course. As Kaplan (1964) put it, the precision demanded in models keeps you from fooling yourself about what you know. You must be able to trace every process, every transition, from start to finish. If you cannot, if you reach a point at which it is not clear how you got there, something is wrong, something has been left out. In Kerwin and Shaffer's (1994) mock jury study, for example, jurors were asked to give their opinions about a verdict both before and after deliberating the case, and there was a change that could be accounted for only by deliberation. The other point is that all of this takes time—all of the attention to detail, specifying assumptions, coming to grips with what is really involved. It is usually time well spent, but it can be frustrating. You can end up after a day of staring at blank pieces of paper and crumpling up false starts with the feeling that nothing has been accomplished. But don't give up. Keep thinking about it. Tomorrow you may have that Aha! experience.

Validity

Years ago, Abelson (1968) coined the term *simulation gap*. It refers to the frequently large differences between the nature of simulations and the nature of the systems they are supposedly imitating. Computers, for example, can be programmed to do some things that give them the appearance of having human intelligence, such as playing chess. But the way in which the computer decides on its next move at any particular juncture in the game may bear no resemblance to the way a human player would decide. Although such a chess-playing computer could be lots of fun to have around, it would have little value as a model of human chess playing.

The problem of bridging the simulation gap is, of course, a problem of validity, and it is the most serious difficulty associated with simulations. Once you have developed a model of some system, how can you be sure that what happens in the model is really the same as what happens in the system itself?

Strictly speaking, you cannot. There will always be an element of uncertainty, a leap of faith required to get from the model back to the system modeled. But what you can do is be aware of some of the ways in which models and simulations are likely to fool you. Then your judgment about the validity of a particular simulation will, at least, be well-informed.

It has already been noted that a model is, by definition, a simplification. Kaplan (1964) has suggested that, rather than thinking of a model as an *over*-simplification, it might be more useful in assessing validity to think of the model as an *under*complication. Such a twist calls attention not only to the fact that some variables have been left out, but also to the fact—if you will pardon the pun—that when included, those variables may complicate things. For example, in an early attempt to model the propagation of rumors, Allport and Postman (1947) set up a serial reproduction simulation in which college students were asked to pass along a story that they had been told. They found that the stories became increasingly distorted as they were passed from person to person. But, as Rosnow (1991) has noted, Allport and Postman left out several potentially important variables, variables that they themselves had identified as crucial in the transmission of wartime rumors. One was that the rumors always had a great deal of significance for the lives of those who transmitted them. People did not seem to pass on rumors about things that did not concern them. Thus, there is a possibility that their subjects would have been much more accurate if they had been dealing with materials of some personal significance to them.

Several years ago, Dillehay and Nietzel (1980) introduced a concept of importance in this connection, the notion of **applied explanatory power.** Their idea is that a simulation may be perfectly valid, in the sense that the processes involved correspond to processes operating in the system modeled, and yet knowledge of those processes may not be very useful because of other, more powerful factors that dominate the actual system. The distinction, of course, is between theoretical and practical significance. If your intention is merely to develop an understanding of the system, then you may not be too concerned with applied explanatory power. But if you want to use your theoretical system as a guide for social action, then the applied explanatory power of your concepts becomes a key to their validity. As Dillehay and Nietzel (1980) put it, "What is statistically significant and theoretically valid for a given situation may yet be of little or no practical value because the relationship described accounts for so little of the variance in the focal outcome variable . . . what is of importance to a practitioner is the amount of variation in the behavior he/she confronts that is accounted for by the relationship specified in the proposition."

One final thing to remember in evaluating simulations is that any particular model is only one way of representing something. There may be many other ways of doing precisely the same thing. Thus, even though you may have a completely appropriate model of some large system, it is not necessarily the case that all of the model's properties correspond to aspects of that larger system. The fallacy that may tempt you here is what Kaplan (1964) referred to as "map reading." Just because Texas appears in green on your map of the United States, do not expect it to be covered with grass. The map, as a representation of reality, has properties that do not correspond to reality.

Summary

Simulations and models are imitations of convenience, scaled-down versions of social and behavioral systems. They can be useful for a variety of purposes, including teaching and research. When used in research, the purpose of a simulation is, typically, to help you understand how the system being modeled operates. Simulations are most useful when they lead to unanticipated consequences. They are most likely to do that when the system being simulated is a complex one, involving a variety of competing forces.

There are several varieties of simulations, and we focused on three: role-playing, analogue experiments, and games as research settings. In general, role-playing is most useful in helping you to uncover the implicit understandings that guide social interaction in specific situations—what is referred to as the role/rule framework. The roles that people are asked to play in such research can differ in at least three ways: (1) degree of involvement; (2) required response specificity; and (3) whether people are asked to play themselves or someone else. Such research appears to be most informative when subjects are highly involved, playing themselves, and free to behave as they deem appropriate.

The second type of simulation discussed, the analogue experiment, may be thought of as an extension of the laboratory experiment. In contrast to the typical hypothesis-testing experiment, laboratory simulation involves greater freedom for the participants. The focus is on observing what will happen when some social phenomenon is transposed to the relatively well-controlled laboratory environment and set in motion. Some mock jury research was used to illustrate the importance of capturing *all* of the essential characteristics of the system being simulated in such research. Instructions to disregard evidence were more likely to be heeded by jurors required to deliberate than by jurors allowed to make individual decisions. The ability to manipulate some aspects of the system being modeled is one of the prime advantages of simulations. You can see "what would happen if..." Such manipulations are often not possible in the world outside the laboratory.

A third type of simulation involves the use of games, that is, structured tasks over which participants interact according to sets of rules. The rules are constructed to capture the essence of some real-life situation, and the game provides a vehicle for studying the dynamics of social interaction via a simulation of that situation. The best-known of these games is the prisoner's dilemma, a game designed to put each player in a bind between cooperation and competition. Other games, such as the Nuts Game, have different structures, of course, and are intended to model different types of interactions. The attempt in each is to define the rules so as to capture the essential dynamics of the interaction of interest.

Some problems are associated with the evaluation of simulations. It is important to keep in mind that simulations are partial; they are not intended to duplicate everything about the system being modeled. Some aspects of the system will, of necessity, have been left out. Thus, it will always be necessary to ask how the results of the simulation would be influenced by those other processes and pieces that help make up the larger system. Investigators also need to be clear about what they hope to achieve via simulation. Do they just want to understand what is going on? Or do they want to use that understanding to change the world?

Recommended Readings

Hardin, G. (1985). *Filters against folly: How to survive despite economists, ecologists, and the merely eloquent.* New York: Viking.

Garrett Hardin is an ecologist who is widely known for an article he published in *Science* many years ago entitled "The Tragedy of the Commons." In this book, he provides some sage advice about clear thinking and how to separate fact from fancy. As he puts it, "We all have to learn to filter the essential meaning out of the too verbose, too aggressively technical statements of the experts." The "experts" can, and often do, hide behind extravagant language and impressive arrays of numbers. Hardin points out that while language, numbers, and fluency with both—literacy and numeracy—are essential for communication, they can just as easily be used for obfuscation as for illumination. He suggests some ways we can get more of the latter while keeping the former to a minimum. He also introduces the concept of "ecolacy" to suggest that in our attempts to understand the world around us, we need to pay special attention to the time dimension: that is, "what further changes occur when the treatment or experience is repeated time after time?" While we may not be able to foresee all the changes that will occur as the result of an intervention, we will at least be ahead of the game if we take Hardin's revision of the First Law of Ecology seriously: We can never do merely one thing.

Komorita, S. S., and Parks, C. D. (1994). *Social dilemmas.* Madison, WI: Brown and Benchmark.

As you know by now, social dilemmas are situations in which one must choose between maximizing one's own selfish interest or maximizing collective interests. Komorita and Parks provide a detailed, up-to-date summary of what is known about such dilemmas. They focus primarily on three prototypes: (1) the prisoner's dilemma (both the 2-person and *N*-person varieties); (2) social traps; and (3) the public goods paradigm. They also cover a number of important topics that we only mentioned in passing, such as the role of personality in responding to social dilemmas. Social dilemmas appear with surprising frequency in everyday life and, perhaps because of that, they are of interest to workers in a variety of disciplines. Thus, in addition to work in psychology, Komorita and Parks discuss political science, economic, and biological approaches to social dilemmas. Political scientists, for example, have constructed a game called "Chicken," which they believe models some features of the nuclear arms race, by a simple rearrangement of the payoffs in the prisoner's dilemma game. In biology, game theory has been used to model the way that seemingly incompatible species come to coexist. From the depletion of food fish in the Atlantic to the use of geothermal energy, Komorita and Parks point out other intriguing applications of the work on social dilemmas. It is well worth reading.

McGrath, J. E. (Ed.) (1981). Judgment calls: An unorthodox view of the research process. *American Behavioral Scientist*, *25*, 123–232.

Methodology textbooks and journal articles always seems to make research appear to be such a rational process, so clean-cut, and, well, *scientific*. Appearances are often deceiving, as the authors of this special issue of *ABS* point out. They argue that research does not get carried out in the way it is later described as having been carried out. It is greatly affected by all sorts of extraneous factors and, typically, involves a series of compromises between the ideal and the possible. Available resources, for example, are supposed to facilitate research, but they do much more. They constrain both the choice of problems to be investigated and how the research will be carried out. How likely is it that someone who has spent several years equipping a nice experimental laboratory is going to select a method other than experimentation for research? Not very. McGrath and his colleagues forcefully present the case for triangulation of measurement that has been advocated since Chapter 1. Their view is that not only are all methods flawed, but each is so seriously flawed as to be almost worthless *when used alone*. Salvation lies in a plurality of methods. The continued use of a particular instrument or method simply because other researchers in the area have used it is the most heinous of sins. Build a new instrument, try a new approach. *Do something different!*

Whicker, M. L., and Sigelman, L. (1991). *Computer simulation applications: An introduction*. Newbury Park, CA: Sage.

A computer simulation is basically one in which a computer is programmed to manipulate the data of interest in ways suggested by a model, or theory, you have constructed. In the preceding chapter, we mentioned such simulations only in passing. As noted in the text, the major reason for this omission is that a usable understanding of computer simulations requires a degree of programming skill that is beyond the scope of an introduction to research methods. However, if you have, or are planning on developing, that skill, you may want to look at this brief text by Whicker and Sigelman. They offer a readable introduction to the many steps involved in computer simulation—from deciding what to model to the more technical aspects of programming languages. Along the way, they make numerous practical suggestions that you are sure to find helpful. For example, "Beginners would be well advised not to commit themselves to a special simulation language until it becomes apparent that their interest in modeling will be long-lasting and that a particular language is best suited to their interest" (p. 58). Yes, indeed. For basics, they suggest just sticking with BASIC. The book also has an annotated bibliography on computer simulation that you may find useful as a starting point for exploring the field.

Appendix: Table of Random Numbers

On the following pages are 5632 numbers between zero and nine. They are grouped into sets of four merely to help you keep your place and to make the table somewhat easier to read. As an example of how you might use the table, consider the following. Suppose you have 30 people, each of whom you want to assign randomly to one of two groups, say, an experimental group and a control group. First, assign each person a number, 01–30. Second, pick an arbitrary starting point in the table, such as the 13th number in the 21st row of the first page (it should be 9 of 9966, unless I miscounted). Third, beginning at that number, look at two-digit numbers (99, 66, 83, 50, 03, 38, ...) and assign the first 15 persons whose numbers you come across in this manner to the experimental group. Those people should be numbers 03, 08, 28, 19, 09, 16, (starting on the next row) 30, 22, 05, 15, 11, 10, 29, (starting on the next row) 27, and 24. The other 15 people would be assigned to the control group.

As another example, suppose you had 100 people you wanted to interview and five interviewers. To randomly assign interviewees to interviewers, you would first assign a number (00–99) to each interviewee. Then, starting at some arbitrary point in the table and reading two-digit numbers, you would assign the first 20 people whose numbers you come across to interviewer 1, the second 20 whose numbers you find to interviewer 2, and so on.

8915 7829 5908 2605 8614 9658 9162 8096 3221 5131 3062 0649 2029 2018 4122 4473
2105 1170 1800 8165 7671 9233 0009 4817 8072 2905 1277 5801 6116 8276 8821 8712
5054 6239 5249 2123 5688 2978 1469 4973 6891 5688 7193 6112 4611 6150 1519 7640
8303 9793 0554 1603 3281 1499 9082 9902 5809 0760 0849 0149 4944 3460 0297 9294

2216 0982 3201 8329 7989 7583 0992 7920 2019 9110 9843 8989 0209 1462 8268 1352
9404 1244 4847 6660 2249 3364 4758 9388 3568 3813 3235 0327 7367 1627 0481 0162
6577 8819 0569 8569 3649 1162 2539 6588 0364 3994 6351 1846 0241 3944 2449 4708
2248 9282 9113 6833 6073 3597 7829 8104 7041 6935 2263 3250 6133 4935 4133 8516

1663 5576 3803 8878 4893 5002 2926 2098 5244 7962 8242 2814 2182 5476 8656 8174
8312 3201 9580 4528 2422 9507 1511 5044 7531 9737 2860 4524 5248 5301 3665 2503
3630 1852 3385 8452 3412 2024 5393 4576 1347 4232 7502 8109 6645 6952 4318 0708
3946 6852 0371 0355 1916 1110 9342 7518 3729 9754 0377 2284 1780 5341 4061 5866

2588 0245 3261 4267 9646 6666 8676 8051 4196 4019 1668 6790 8290 4686 2799 8744
7837 1831 8353 4959 3673 3931 0037 7944 0947 0392 8885 8950 1596 3594 7194 4619
2345 7493 4809 2431 0514 5612 7024 3951 9128 2420 7503 2529 7363 8545 3230 9517
0192 9321 7591 3371 9320 6693 0948 3203 5361 8664 5179 6731 4577 6528 6301 0632

7774 5110 9871 8258 1483 1028 8543 7393 9190 3272 2290 5010 0824 4520 3758 8019
4384 7106 7389 2738 7773 3669 9659 4923 1720 1621 8955 8103 1708 1334 7387 8729
4783 5058 8854 4001 4553 8517 1277 7818 7254 4471 1379 5086 6328 0688 6233 7338
7201 2579 7839 8585 3214 8403 3381 6207 6799 0706 9727 0812 2941 6374 3484 4422

8374 5137 1591 9966 8350 0338 4570 0887 9648 8092 2819 7431 0957 3169 8132 8216
5092 7630 5296 2216 3370 0373 0528 0515 1111 0098 4310 9019 2954 5150 0859 6946
3671 1116 5333 1940 2762 7827 2265 4924 3812 9943 7253 0439 3082 9895 7284 3932
0988 2936 2350 7979 4755 2602 3990 6520 8043 7572 6177 5401 9781 6547 6288 5193

2007 8566 5202 6359 9404 9731 4344 3318 4414 0795 6538 3683 2561 5868 2378 8108
1961 6059 9390 3460 0467 0454 3676 8873 8224 7238 7938 2550 1087 4360 4076 3289
6897 0150 1509 6409 9831 3897 5532 2435 3558 4954 9217 6719 1570 2365 7766 7695
0655 2019 0574 5284 7999 3931 5545 7836 5969 6505 7511 3907 9951 3862 5910 6863

2388 2668 9163 4880 4846 9195 8282 9927 3258 8617 7617 2313 5676 6293 2210 7405
2869 5749 7337 7533 2397 3640 8844 2309 1674 0038 1928 0500 2991 0483 0795 5241
9282 3180 8625 3479 3852 5832 4289 0053 2545 0673 6880 7987 7595 9172 2084 6877
6119 2933 6812 5025 4490 9370 5289 4295 3115 6160 9606 3596 9601 3093 7923 5763

7024 0463 8889 2412 7401 9781 6411 1215 5850 1080 4170 1847 3143 3805 8653 1105
2875 3775 1988 7073 3982 9691 0143 0979 2011 3443 6045 4025 7198 4782 6611 5525
5419 1638 2581 1028 4488 5806 2462 6024 9058 0531 1099 0798 9663 7890 4922 5519
7612 9196 5836 8061 8597 4566 6481 8035 6470 0301 6501 6386 5774 8684 5904 4348

6545 0532 5524 3247 9367 2851 6202 2819 3484 9375 6297 3260 8973 7320 7625 9809
6650 1763 5204 7818 1537 5719 0382 0818 8399 3619 3844 4794 4593 3577 1936 1561
7891 2170 0255 4366 1647 9503 5036 4076 7289 0535 2208 7486 4967 2740 4763 1236
0821 0518 8280 3439 8234 4412 1122 3378 8184 5755 8820 4148 7743 5960 5853 4510

6384 1575 4974 4807 9354 7243 2049 5103 8661 1010 6344 7753 1966 0018 5969 6509
4477 4908 8421 3109 6790 8855 1421 6543 5533 2240 8751 5071 7307 6391 1253 8574
6005 7290 4890 1234 8334 6070 0255 1126 9758 8607 5832 1587 8739 6605 7310 0847
1033 2827 1671 9637 6867 5856 5992 2027 7132 4539 8266 0047 4297 7982 4529 4480

```
7537 9411 3187 2807 1514 6346 0935 1642 8074 6420 8922 4764 4242 2673 2769 0640
7932 4739 0271 2888 1003 4397 6375 8768 3940 5729 4240 9273 4371 9712 9572 8743
7009 8784 8199 1586 5979 3749 0443 3734 4893 9291 9186 8304 2683 8961 2230 7046
3468 5007 4391 3033 0013 7463 5803 0636 5514 0724 4870 5742 5764 0200 7839 4405

5311 1902 8291 7051 6746 5657 9475 2359 6205 0886 5936 1020 0064 3303 0766 3927
8681 5263 9716 5500 3867 7368 1118 0845 2523 5585 7536 4971 7583 1181 1795 8010
2300 0300 4984 5229 2049 5418 7055 9112 8773 1215 3964 8424 0075 6166 7572 9589
5109 6534 0210 7810 5195 9331 3636 7438 6988 0647 1269 3817 3414 6309 0690 7985

4983 9859 8102 2787 5725 0818 7359 1140 8908 7571 3149 9692 9196 7783 5066 7590
3953 1599 4789 9602 4360 2560 1071 4242 4164 6797 3563 6203 0212 9132 7144 2274
1731 3387 4968 7213 8336 8037 7634 5781 7350 5762 9168 1134 4449 9130 1503 6454
3311 3719 6241 0975 9308 7640 4673 6446 0296 7053 1905 1498 0074 5000 6898 5476

9514 0767 8975 9216 6882 2223 4315 2222 5103 9683 9643 9266 0543 3703 5049 8667
8797 2706 9011 2967 3346 0057 6600 9343 0325 4857 0673 8558 1763 0811 4701 2548
1768 5723 1776 2576 2266 4498 6697 9406 5364 4250 9267 9235 9307 7480 1054 4828
4228 6263 2045 2360 0509 2364 6340 7014 1609 7712 9265 0388 6970 8603 5553 1290

6551 1515 7999 7531 4452 8806 4104 1252 4113 1306 2320 5324 4945 9385 5195 2008
4732 6399 6623 8811 6707 6661 7462 3981 0161 1902 2951 8780 7613 9103 8828 7199
1258 0570 2893 5368 2469 0924 5455 0489 1985 1612 2824 4897 6759 9575 4032 2115
7940 8497 3205 5971 3896 5343 3099 3338 3578 5419 4848 9747 3007 0587 8666 5939

4868 3491 2967 5297 4576 9792 5316 1741 4019 3263 3653 8739 4191 4081 6235 7517
2338 8562 9203 8438 5026 4353 4430 7901 6035 4539 8382 6661 5100 9679 5037 5877
4294 1847 2865 5411 0779 0357 3898 6022 8239 2459 0843 5296 4992 7456 9116 6573
6062 1705 1853 5549 5104 2500 5184 7037 6756 5851 7662 6316 2622 6648 3664 3767

2885 9734 3182 7811 0088 0764 1981 5379 4295 5674 6052 4364 8289 6148 6003 8828
9198 6904 9248 4319 1037 1841 1945 6361 4735 2911 8431 4390 4196 0692 9302 8841
8116 8035 7690 8337 9091 5111 6098 3509 4384 4009 2432 1264 3167 6507 5921 1375
9380 3072 7111 1506 2177 7512 6636 7300 6376 8923 5434 3167 1878 2342 2352 5714

1433 1489 6308 8673 9910 3268 7462 3457 7462 5297 8417 0379 7031 1474 2028 7735
6925 3927 7124 9584 9320 0543 8254 3062 2915 0600 2932 9609 9500 4493 3838 4577
1825 6093 4496 2558 4446 6250 3732 3283 8729 1399 7216 6359 4003 7725 6620 2681
7244 7044 2720 4556 3766 6382 4346 2467 9839 0660 7590 1533 1485 7991 2336 9549

9355 0103 0123 8586 8300 5742 5497 6006 4208 3424 2810 6796 8899 7990 8359 6106
2748 7511 9242 2655 0401 7082 9791 6949 2985 3503 1084 8787 3910 7619 1294 6750
2773 9051 9524 8478 6115 4466 7362 4363 5526 0447 8788 8339 2615 6226 4237 9916
4126 8830 6934 2605 7480 3283 3271 0871 3419 5194 2980 8332 9342 8944 1216 3440

6780 2061 1138 9155 0608 4680 7945 9709 3231 6813 6055 4552 4284 0440 9041 5225
4785 2441 4977 5112 5971 0883 1766 1977 1539 0321 5456 2921 2294 6733 9699 3843
8725 8566 7481 9260 3812 7053 2088 8202 7078 6132 0506 8278 6937 2943 2759 8953
5449 4252 8083 9451 3481 3403 1593 4396 1346 3579 4402 9619 1996 9210 8597 3290

9528 1517 0047 5774 4616 1248 0391 2244 1550 3812 6602 1681 6254 9514 5668 8176
7008 4741 5559 6020 1958 0240 6311 4136 1283 3948 4546 3322 0938 2028 8099 6574
1560 9850 2023 4256 4013 8331 8845 2018 5392 6078 4757 9545 7830 0641 5604 7860
1966 8976 8770 5215 1158 6216 3128 9413 7935 2154 6437 0252 3473 0217 6958 9189
```

Glossary

Analytic files: Used for sorting and storing portions of field notes taken by participant observers. As ideas occur about the processes being observed, these files are created to store examples from the field notes of those processes in operation. (Compare *mundane files*.)

Aphorism: A concise statement usually though of as expressing an important principle, such as "Nothing ventured, nothing gained."

Applied explanatory power: A concept having to do with the practical significance of research findings. A theoretically important relationship may be valid in a particular setting, but not explain much of the variation in behavior that occurs in that setting; in that case, its applied explanatory power would be low.

Applied research: Research intended to obtain information that will help you to make an intelligent decision in a specific situation. (Compare *basic research*.)

Archival research: An investigation that makes use of public or private documents pertaining to the past.

Archives: Public or private documents recording any aspect of an organization's, institution's, or individual's actions.

Artifact: An extraneous variable produced unintentionally by some aspect of a research design that generates effects that become confounded with the effects of the variable of interest.

Attention: The focusing of your consciousness on some person, event, or object. In participant observation, there is a danger of paying too much attention to the most salient aspects of a setting.

Attention-feedback-regulation cycle: One possible mechanism that may help to explain the fact that observing someone's behavior causes that behavior to change. By observing someone's behavior, you call their attention to what they are doing, and that, in turn, may cause them to change, that is, regulate their behavior.

Attrition: In longitudinal research, the loss of some respondents from the study between contacts with the researcher. Some may die, some may move away and leave no forwarding address, and some may just change their minds about continuing to participate in the research. Attrition may introduce a bias into your data; those people who tolerate three or four interviews, for example, may be quite different from those who do not.

Balanced replication: An experimental design that can be used when you believe the results of some experiment were produced by a flaw in the procedure. You redo the experiment precisely, flaw and all, and you also add a condition that has everything the first experiment had except the flaw. With the flawed condition, you should obtain the same results as in the original experiment. With the new, unflawed condition, you should not (you hope.)

Basic research: Research that is intended to test or refine some theoretical proposition. (Compare *applied research*.)

Behavior code: The descriptions and definitions of the behaviors you intend to observe, with rules that tell you how to apply the definitions and with examples of the behaviors that represent each category to be noted.

Blind: The state of an experimenter who does not know to which condition of an experiment a given subject has been assigned. It prevents the experimenter's expectations from influencing the results.

Blind scoring: The process of scoring (or coding) material while remaining unaware of its sources. In content analysis, for example, you may want some verbal material coded to see whether certain categories or types of information are present. However, you do not want the persons doing the coding to know the source of the material because it might bias their interpretations of what they are reading.

Blocking: The division of a sample of subjects that differ in identifiable ways into subsamples based on those identifiable characteristics.. By then allotting equal numbers from each subsample to each of the experimental conditions, you reduce the possibility of having different types of subjects in different conditions.

Category construction: The process of deciding which particular behaviors or concepts you are going to observe and defining precisely what you mean by each. No ambiguities are allowed. Each concept or type of behavior will form a category.

Category system: A carefully constructed set of interrelated concepts for use in recording what is observed. In content analysis, the material of interest is read and scored for the presence or absence of certain concepts according to such a system. In observational studies, the category system consists of a set of interrelated behaviors.

Closed question: See *closed-ended question*.

Closed-ended question: A question that requires the respondent to select one of a small number of previously set answer options, such as Yes or No or Strongly Agree, Agree, Disagree, Strongly Disagree.

Coding: The process of observing behavior or reading material of interest, noting the presence or absence of certain behaviors or concepts specified by the coding scheme or category system, and assigning a score to the behavior or material.

Cohort study: A type of survey that allows you to examine longitudinal changes. Different samples are selected from the same (it is hoped) population such that some have and some have not experienced certain events. For example, tenth- and twelfth-graders from the same school system might be selected to examine the effects of high school education on prejudice. The danger is that the tenth-graders of 2 years ago (i.e., today's twelfth-graders) might not really represent the same population as today's tenth-graders.

Concealed identity: A strategy for participant observation in which you do not tell the people in the setting that you are actually doing research. Rather, you simply move into the setting and pass yourself off as a regular member.

Conceptual replication: The process whereby an experiment on a particular topic is redone, but the way in which the independent and/or dependent variables are operationalized is changed.

Confounding variable: An extraneous variable that is inadvertently included along with the variable you are attempting to manipulate or measure.

Construct validity: A measure has construct validity if it measures what it is supposed to measure, nothing more and nothing less. The Scholastic Aptitude Test, for example, would have construct validity if it really assesses aptitude for learning.

Content analysis: A research method in which texts—such as books, diaries, speeches, newspaper and magazine articles, television and movie scripts, or descriptions generated by subjects for the purpose of the study—are examined for the presence or absence of certain specified types of information or concepts.

Contingency questions: Those questions in survey research that are to be answered only by subjects who answer a previous question in a certain way. Thus, whether or not a respondent is asked the second question depends on, or is contingent upon, how he or she answered the first.

Control: To regulate something, to have power over it. In an experiment, to control a certain variable means to keep it from influencing the results. This can be done in several ways: random assignment of subjects to conditions, for example, is intended to control for individual differences among subjects in the various conditions.

Convenience sample: In survey research, those respondents who are easiest for you to contact; that is, the most convenient ones. When you limit your sample to these people, it is likely to be biased.

Cost–benefit analysis: A procedure for measuring the effectiveness or efficiency of a program. The final value is obtained by calculating the cost required to produce a given benefit. In cost-benefit analysis the effects of a program must be converted to a dollar value, which often requires making some very arbitrary assumptions.

Cost-effectiveness analysis: A technique for assessing the efficiency of a program. It is carried out by calculating the cost of the program per unit of change produced. For example, you might determine how much it costs to raise the average reading scores of first graders by ten points.

Cover story: A plausible, but false, explanation to a subject of the purpose of the experiment. Its point is to keep the subject unaware of the true purpose of the experiment in cases in which awareness of its true purpose would influence the subject's response to the independent variable.

Coverage error: A problem in survey research that stems from the fact that some members of a population of interest may not be included in the sampling frame and thus cannot be included in any sample that is drawn from the population.

Criticism: The art of making discriminating judgments, of finding the faults and merits of an idea or a research report.

Cross-sectional survey: A survey in which members of the sample are interviewed or administered a questionnaire one time only. (Compare *longitudinal study*.)

Curiosity: The desire to find out how things work, why they are as they are. Curiosity is one of the prime motive forces behind research.

Debriefing: Explanation of an experiment and the answering of any questions that subjects have after the experiment. At the end of an experiment, particularly if deception was involved, it is essential to explain everything to the subjects—including the reasons for the deception.

Deduction: The act of inferring how a given general principle would apply in a specific situation.

Demand characteristics: Those cues that tell a subject how he or she is expected to respond in an experimental or interview situation. Care should be taken to eliminate all such cues from the situation; otherwise, you will not know whether your result is evidence of the variable of interest or simply evidence that the subjects did what they thought you wanted.

Dependent variable: The effect; the variable in which change is determined by changes in one or more independent variables. (Compare *independent variable*.)

Description: The act of attending to and recording the details of situations, events, and people. One of the most difficult things about learning how to describe well is learning to pay attention not only to what is present in a situation you are trying to describe, but also to what is absent. Description is also one of the objectives of survey research. When used for this purpose, surveys attempt to ascertain the distribution of attitudes, beliefs, and other characteristics of a population or sample.

Differentiation: The ability to see different aspects of a problem and to take those various factors into account in making a decision. (Compare *integration.*)

Disciplined abstractions: Analytic concepts grounded in your own observations of a particular setting. When developing disciplined abstractions, you ask yourself what general concept a particular behavior is an example of. For example, banging one's fist on the table at a meeting may be related to "commitment to an ideal"; it may also be an example of rudeness.

Double-barreled question: A question that is really two or more questions combined.

Elements: The individual units that make up a population. In sampling, a typical goal is to select elements from the population in such a way that the sample is representative of the population.

Emergent context: The events that follow a given social act and help you to interpret what the act really meant.

Empirical approach: The gathering of information about the way the world is; that is, relying on experience and observation. (Compare *rational approach.*)

Ethics: The study of the values that guide our actions and influence our choices. In research on human subjects, there is often an ethical dilemma produced by the conflict between the fact that we value obtaining new knowledge and the fact that we value the individual's right to privacy.

Ethnography: A detailed descriptive account of life in a particular cultural setting. Usually an ethnography is written by someone who has employed participant observation and has lived in the particular setting for some period of time.

Ethology: A field of study concerned with the behavior of animals in their natural settings.

Evaluation apprehension: A concern of many subjects participating in experiments or interviews. Wanting to make a good impression, they may be worried about how you—as the experimenter or interviewer—are going to evaluate them. As a result, their behavior may not be natural.

Evaluation research: Any of a variety of techniques, methods, and procedures used to assess the effects of social, educational, and medical innovations. Usually, evaluation research is focused on a particular program and is designed to find out whether the program is producing the effects anticipated.

Exact replication: Repeating a piece of research precisely, with all the details the same as the first time.

Expectations: Our anticipations of relationships among things. They are likely to get us into trouble because they may induce us to read things into what we are observing that are not really there.

Experiment: A form of research in which you manipulate one variable to see whether changes in it have any effect on another variable. The variable you manipulate is the *independent variable,* the one you observe (or measure) for changes is the *dependent variable.*

Experimental realism: The extent to which the activity a subject is asked to do in an experiment is involving and captures his or her attention.

Experimenter expectancy effects: The influence of the experimenter's expectations about how the subject will respond. Because of his or her expectations, the experimenter may unintentionally influence the subject's response. Ideally, of course, only the independent variable should influence the subject's response.

Explanation: The process of making something understandable. Explanation in research is the process of clarifying the relationships among variables, thereby showing how one influences another.

External validity: The generalizability of research findings to other settings or populations. Research findings that completely lack external validity would not hold up in any other situation or among any other group of subjects. Variables that interfere with your ability to generalize to another setting or subject population are referred to as threats to external validity.

Extralinguistic behaviors: Behaviors accompanying speech other than the substantive or content aspects of speech itself. Some examples of extralinguistic behavior that may tell you things about the speaker are pauses, tone of voice, and accent.

Factorial design: An experimental design in which more than one independent variable is manipulated. Conditions are constructed such that a given level of each independent variable occurs in conjunction once (and only once) with each level of the other independent variables.

Field experiment: Research conducted in field or naturalistic settings in which one or more variables (the independent variable) are manipulated in order to see what effect that will have.

Field notes: The copious descriptive notes taken by participant observers of the things they observe. The taking of good, complete field notes is an essential component of participant observation.

Field research: A research method in which one immerses oneself in the ongoing social life of a setting and systematically records (see *field notes*) all that is seen and heard. The point is to reach an understanding of the "how" of social life in the setting and to develop a set of disciplined abstractions (analytic concepts that can account for what has been observed).

Fixed-response question: See *Closed-ended question.*

Focus group: A small group of people similar to the intended survey respondents who are convened in the initial stages of survey design to discuss the concepts and issues to be addressed in the research. The hope is that they will help to clarify any ambiguities and point out any related issues that you missed.

Formative evaluation: The initial assessment of a social, educational, or medical program that serves to establish whether the program has actually been put into place and is operating as planned.

Funnel sequence: In interviewing, an ordering of the set of questions such that the interview begins with the broadest, most general, question and progresses to questions about the most minute details.

Hawthorne effect: The tendency of subjects who believe that you have taken an interest in them and their well-being to exert more effort than normal to try to do whatever it is they think you want them to do. This effect was first documented in the 1920s at the Hawthorne plant of the Western Electric Company.

Heuristic fertility: The extent to which something suggests new ways of doing things, new ideas for research, or new theoretical developments.

Illusion of control: The belief that you can exercise control over certain events when, in reality, you cannot. Some research by Langer has demonstrated that we often act as if we are able to influence events that are really determined by chance.

Independent variable: The cause; in an experiment, the variable you manipulate or change in order to see what will happen. (Compare *dependent variable.*)

Index: An indicator of the concept of interest. In archival research you must decide what items of information you are going to use as an index, or marker, of the thing you are interested in. For example, allotments to police budgets might be used as an index of authoritarian attitudes in a community. In survey research, *index* has a different meaning. There an index is the combination of answers to two or more questions assessing the same thing. Such combinations are useful because they help to create response variability and because it is sometimes difficult to measure concepts with a single question.

Induction: The act of inferring a general principle from isolated observations of examples of that principle in action.

Informed consent: A procedure in which potential research participants are told what the research will involve and any harm it might do them, and are then given a free choice about whether or not they want to take part.

Integration: The perception of links or connections among the differentiated aspects of a problem. (Compare *differentiation*.)

Interaction: A statistical term used to refer to the joint effect of two or more independent variables on the dependent variable in an experiment. The presence of an interaction means, for example, that independent variable 1 has a different effect on the dependent variable at different levels of independent variable 2.

Internal validity: The question of whether or not the independent variable in an experiment is what really made a difference in the dependent variable. Did you manipulate what you thought you did? Did you measure what you thought you were measuring? Artifacts and other variables that interfere with your ability to show that the independent variable was what really produced the change in the dependent variable are referred to as *threats to internal validity*.

Interobserver agreement: The degree of similarity of the codings or measurements of different observers. When an observer watches and codes a set of events into categories, it is important to know how much of what he or she says occurred really occurred. One way to check this is to have two or more observers watch and code the same events. If their codings are similar, you can be more certain that the codings reflect reality and not some figment of the observers' imaginations.

Interrupted time series: A type of design in which observations are made at several intervals before and after an intervention or manipulation. The manipulation constitutes the interruption in the series of observations.

Interrupted time series with switching replications: A time series design in which repeated observations are made on two or more groups and the manipulation is introduced to each of the groups at a different time.

Interview guide: A list of topics to be covered in a qualitative interview.

Interview schedule: The list of questions, probes, response alternatives, and directions to the interviewer for a standardized interview.

Inverted funnel sequence: An ordering of the set of questions in an interview that starts with very narrow, circumscribed topics and gradually broadens out to more general topics.

Leading question: A question asked in a manner calculated to encourage the respondent to give a particular answer.

Levels: See *Treatments*.

Longitudinal study: Research in which data are collected over a period of time in order to examine changes that occur in the intervening periods.

Main effect: A statistical term referring to a situation in which one independent variable has the same effect on the dependent variable regardless of the level of the other independent variable(s) present.

Manipulation: In an experiment, a change made to the independent variable to see what effect that change has on the dependent variable.

Matching: A type of assignment of subjects to conditions in which information about the subjects' standing on some variable is used to equate the subjects in the various conditions with respect to that variable.

Method of multiple working hypotheses: An approach to research in which you generate several possible explanations for the phenomenon of interest and gather evidence bearing on them all. The idea is that if you are entertaining several hypotheses, you will not become so fond of any particular one that you ignore contrary evidence.

Multiple operationism: The devising of several ways to measure the thing of interest. As a measure of interpersonal attraction, for example, you might use self-reports, heart rate increases, and eye contact.

Multistage cluster sample: A sampling technique that can be used when it is difficult to list or to construct a sampling frame for all of the elements in a population. For example, you might divide the population into groups, or clusters, of elements, then select a sample of those clusters. Next, you would select a sample of the elements within each of the clusters that you selected in the first stage. You would then have a two-stage cluster sample.

Mundane files: A set of files used by fieldworkers for keeping track of all the information they have about specific people, organizations, or events in the setting they are observing. A mundane file might be set up for a specific person, for example, and each time that person appeared in a day's field notes, a copy of that day's notes would be put in the file.

No-treatment control subjects: In experimental and quasi-experimental designs, subjects that are not exposed to the manipulation or intervention. These subjects give you something to which you can compare the results from those exposed to the manipulation.

Nonequivalent groups: Groups that are different at the outset of a study. In designing certain quasi-experiments, it is often necessary to use nonequivalent, intact groups for the treatment and control conditions. The problem is that when the treatment and control groups differ *after* your intervention, you may not know whether it was the intervention or that initial nonequivalence that caused the difference.

Nonparticipant observation: A variation of observational research in which an observer is present in a setting and may code observed behaviors into a category system, or simply make notes about what is occurring, but does not take part in the ongoing activities of the setting.

Nonreactive: Neither creating in subjects an awareness that they are taking part in research nor doing anything that would alter their natural responses. Nonreactive research does not create a reaction in subjects. (Compare *reactive*.)

Nonresponse error: In survey research, a distortion created when some members of a sample choose not to respond to the survey. The people who choose not to respond may differ in some systematic way from who people who do respond; thus, absence of data from the nonresponders makes the results unrepresentative of the population.

Nonverbal behavior: Any behavior other than vocalization; that is, all of the gestures, manners of dress, posture, tics, facial expressions, ways of walking, and so forth that may tell you something about the person in question.

Observer drift: The tendency of two or more observers who are watching and coding the same sequences of behaviors to increasingly come to agree with one another and gradually move away from the strict definitions and rules specified in the behavior code; that is, to drift away from the code. One way to solve this problem is to have frequent reviews of and drills on the behavior code. Observer drift can, of course, occur even when there is only one observer.

Obtrusive: In research, this is something that you do not want to be. Webster defines *obtrusive* as "calling attention to oneself." For an investigator, this is undesirable because it may change the behavior of the people being observed. Making them too aware of the fact that they are being observed (or tested, or listened to, or experimented upon) is likely to decrease the spontaneity of their behavior.

One-group pretest-posttest design: A quasi-experimental design in which observations are made on one group of subjects before and after some intervention or manipulation. This design is not as good as the untreated control group design with pretest and posttest for inferring whether or not the intervention really made a difference.

One-shot case study: A form of research in which you make some observations, or measurements, or both, on the members of a group after an event has occurred. The problem is that you have nothing with which to compare your observations. The group might have been precisely the same before the event occurred, but you have no way of knowing.

Open-ended question: A question that cannot be answered with a simple "yes" or "no." The point of open-ended questions is to encourage subjects to elaborate, to give fuller information. An example: "How do you feel about the president's economic program?"

Operationalization: Choosing a measure or index that you are willing to accept as an indicator of the concept you are interested in. For example, you might select grade point average as your way of measuring intelligence. (If you did, many people would argue with you, because GPA reflects many things in addition to intelligence, such as effort and the difficulty of the courses you take.)

Outcropping: A geological term referring to projections of underlying rock strata that break through the topsoil at various points. In connection with archival research, the term refers to the fact that many social phenomena are manifest in a variety of ways. Hence, quite different indices might plausibly be used to measure the same underlying phenomenon. Increased authoritarianism during a certain period, for example, might be reflected in police budgets (going up) or library withdrawals of books on psychology (going down). Both of these would be outcroppings of the same phenomenon.

Panel study: A type of survey in which members of a sample are interviewed repeatedly, with the purpose of tracing changes over time in the variables of interest.

Participant observation: A general research method, most often used by anthropologists, in which the researcher immerses himself or herself in the day-to-day activities of the people he or she wishes to study. Margaret Mead, for example, lived among the natives of Samoa while doing the research that served as the basis of her book *Coming of Age in Samoa*.

Patched-up design: The basic all-purpose design for the versatile experimenter. A patched-up design is constructed by adding the conditions and measures that are required in the particular circumstances confronting you. You add whatever is needed to make the comparisons that need to be made and to rule out any and all plausible alternative explanations.

Perception: The process of taking in information. Perception includes a variety of subprocesses such as attention, short-term memory, and rehearsal of short-term memory.

Plausible alternative explanation: A reason other than the intervention or manipulation of interest that can rationally be argued to have produced the change observed in the dependent variable.

Population of interest: The complete collection of elements constituting a group about which we wish to learn something: all people in the United States; all left-handed biology majors at Slippery Rock College.

Posttest-only design with nonequivalent groups: A quasi-experimental design in which members of an intact group are exposed to an intervention or manipulation. Subsequent observations of that group are then compared with observations of another group that was not exposed to the intervention. The basic problem with this design is that you have no way of knowing whether the two groups were really equivalent before the intervention occurred.

Predictive validity: The ability of a measure to predict the results of another. A test has predictive validity, for example, if scores on that test enable you to predict scores, or performance, on some subsequent task. If people who scored high on the Scholastic Aptitude Test earned higher GPAs in college, the Scholastic Aptitude would have predictive validity with respect to college grades.

Preexisting conceptual scheme: The beliefs that we all carry around in our heads about what is likely to be related to what. Such beliefs can fog our perceptions by making it easier for us to think that we have observed something when, in fact, we have not. Expectations and stereotypes are closely related to this concept and exert similar biasing influences.

Pretesting: The relatively informal trying out of a set of questions (say, for an interview schedule) to see whether they are eliciting the type of information you are after or to make sure they are understandable, or, in an experiment, the trying out of a manipulation on a few people to see whether or not it is perceived as intended. The word *pretest* is also used to refer to the initial measurement that takes place before the manipulation in research in which the design is pretest-manipulation-posttest. The point, of course, is to see whether the manipulation makes a difference in whatever it is you are measuring on the pretest and posttest.

Primacy effect: The tendency of the first information we obtain about a person or event to be given undue weight; the reason so many people think it is important to make a good first impression on others.

Proactive records: Records biased by their keepers for any of a variety of reasons. Whether the motive is simply to make themselves look good or to protect their jobs, you need to be aware that records do serve the purposes of their keepers and, hence, may be biased.

Probe: A follow-up question or comment used to try to get a respondent to elaborate on answers given in an interview. Two examples: "Could you tell me a little more about that?" "And what did you do then?"

Proxemics: A word popularized by the anthropologist Edward Hall that refers to the study of interaction distance and the variables that affect it. It comes from the word *proximity,* which Webster defines as the state or quality of being near or close. As a little exercise in proxemics, you might try standing about 6 inches away from your course instructor when you tell him or her what you thought of this course.

Qualitative interview: A type of interview in which the interviewer has some freedom to ask different questions or the same questions in different orders for different respondents as long as certain predetermined topics are covered. The predetermined topics and possible questions constitute an *interview guide.*

Quantification: The process of transforming concepts and ideas into measurable entities.

Quasi-experiment: A research design that only approximates being truly experimental. For example, in some situations, you may not be able to randomly assign subjects to conditions. Or, you may not be able to manipulate the independent variable, but may be forced to rely on some naturally occurring change.

Quota matrix: An array used to classify subjects according to several different variables, such as age and sex. A quota matrix is useful in assigning subjects to conditions of an experiment by *matching.*

Random sample: A sample selected in such a way that every element in the population of interest has an equal chance of being included in the sample.

Randomization: The process of assigning subjects to conditions in such a way that each subject has an equal chance of being assigned to each condition. Also referred to as random assignment.

Randomized trials: A phrase used in medical and epidemiological research to refer to experiments in which subjects are randomly assigned to conditions. Usually such research is intended as a trial of a new drug or treatment or lifestyle change. Randomized trials are vastly superior to clinical impressions in establishing that the new drug or procedure is effective.

Rational approach: An approach to research in which you decide ahead of time exactly which behaviors you are going to observe in order to obtain evidence on a particular question of interest to you. (Compare *empirical approach.*)

Reactive: Producing a change in a subject or process that would not have occurred otherwise. In general, experimentation is much more reactive than archival research. (Compare *nonreactive.*)

Reliability: The extent to which observations and other measures are repeatable. A measure is said to be reliable if it gives the same result when used again under the same conditions.

Replication: The production of the same results; repeatability. One of the requirements of good science is that the observations and experiments that form its foundation be repeatable, or replicable. If Newton were the only person who had ever seen apples fall to earth, physics would be in trouble.

Representative sample: A sample whose nature and distribution of attributes correspond to the nature and distribution of those same attributes in the population.

Research design: The process of deciding what procedures, measures, subjects, and paraphernalia you will need to test your hypotheses; often the most creative, exciting part of the entire research process.

Research interview: A social interaction between two people in which the interviewer initiates and varyingly controls the exchange with the respondent for the purpose of obtaining information bearing on a predetermined objective.

Retrospective context: The events preceding a given behavior from which that behavior emerged.

Return rate: In survey research, the percentage of the entire sample who actually fill out and return the questionnaires mailed to them. If 100 questionnaires were sent out and 69 came back, the return rate would be 69 percent.

Role-playing: Research in which subjects are asked to imagine themselves in a certain situation and tell you how they would respond. If you decide to use this approach, be very careful about what you conclude. Remember, you will have no evidence about how subjects *actually* respond in those situations. What people say and what they do are often quite different.

Role/rule framework: The norms and implicit rules that govern behavior in a specific situation.

Sample: A subset of the elements of a population, chosen for study with the hope that what is found to be true of the sample will be true of the population.

Sampling: The process of selecting a sample of the units of interest. In content analysis, for example, you must select the text materials to be analyzed. In survey research, you must select respondents to be interviewed. There are a variety of different techniques for sampling and a variety of different types of samples.

Sampling error: Discrepancies introduced by the fact that when one or more samples are drawn from a population, the characteristics of the samples may differ from each other and from the characteristics of the population.

Sampling frame: A list of all the elements in a population; used as a basis for selecting a sample.

Sampling interval: The interval chosen for use in systematic random sampling.

Selective deposit: The fact that some of the things of interest to archival researchers may never have been recorded on paper; that only certain parts of the past make their way into records.

Selective survival: The fact that many records of the past simply do not survive very long, and that therefore, the records available in archives are not necessarily all that were once available.

Sensitizing function: The function that research or theory can serve by heightening people's awareness about what is possible. Asch's research, for example, in which implicit group pressure was sufficient to induce normal people to deny the evidence of their own perceptions, served such a function.

Simple random sample: A sample selected from a population without the use of a sampling interval, but in which every member of the population has an equal chance of appearing in the sample. One way to select such a sample would be to number all the members of the population, put the numbers on slips of paper in a hat, and draw out as many slips as you want members in your sample. The members of the population whose numbers you draw out would make up your simple random sample.

Simulation: A model that attempts to capture and represent, in a different, usually smaller and simpler, form, the essential characteristics of the thing modeled.

Single-factor design: An experimental design in which there is only one independent variable.

Snowball sampling: A procedure in which you identify one or more members of the population of interest to include in your sample and then ask them to identify other members of the population to include in the sample. It typically does not result in a representative sample.

Social desirability bias: Bias introduced by the tendency of people to want the approval of others. In survey research, for example, respondents may be reluctant to tell you anything negative about themselves because they fear you might disapprove. Thus, they may give you a socially desirable answer that differs from the truth.

Social trap: A situation that provides incentives for individuals to perform behaviors that will have detrimental effects for society at large if many individuals actually perform those behaviors.

Socially desirable behaviors: Those behaviors that are approved and accepted by the society around you: making good grades, being polite, dressing neatly.

Solomon four-group design: An experimental design in which two groups are pretested and two are not, then one pretested and one non-pretested group are exposed to the intervention or manipulation. Subsequently, all four groups are tested.

Spatial behavior: Behavior that has to do with the way in which people structure and use the space around them. Such behaviors can often be used as the focus of observations, or as the dependent variable in experimental research.

Standardized interview: An interview in which the interviewer uses a fixed set of questions and asks them in the same order of all respondents.

Static group comparison: See *Posttest-only design with nonequivalent groups.*

Stereotype: The sum of the characteristics attributed to objects, people, and events on the basis of your beliefs about what they are usually like.

Stratified sample: A sample selected from a population containing two or more distinct subgroups in a manner designed to ensure that the members of the subgroups are represented in the sample in proportion to their presence in the population.

Summative evaluation: The determination of the effectiveness of a social, educational, or medical program. Also referred to as impact assessment.

Survey research: The best-known of the methodologies of social science. It involves interviewing, or administering a questionnaire, to a sample of respondents chosen to represent a population of interest.

Systematic random sample: In survey research, a sample taken by selecting every nth element in the sampling frame.

Table of random numbers: An array of numbers in which each digit has an equal chance of being followed by each of the digits 0 through 9. Such tables are useful in the process of *randomization*. For instructions on how to use a table of random numbers, see the Appendix.

Tailored design: See *Patched-up design.*

Theoretical elaboration: The process of proposing and testing explanations and formulating those that are verified into ever more comprehensive theories. Theories help us to make sense of facts and guide us in our search for more.

Theory: A proposed explanation for some empirical (observed) phenomenon. A theory is usually thought of as being a little more elaborate than a hypothesis. One way to think of it might be that one proposed explanation constitutes a hypothesis; two or more related hypotheses constitute a theory.

Threats to internal validity: Sources of bias that would prevent you from claiming that your independent variable really made a difference in your dependent variable. Specific threats to internal validity are enumerated in Table 1 in chapter 7.

Treatments: A statistical term referring to the different degrees or stages of the independent variable present in an experiment. If the independent variable is simply present or absent, there are two treatments. If there are low, medium, and high amounts of the independent variable in different conditions, you have three treatments, and so on. Synonymous with *levels.*

Triangulation of measurement: Very similar to multiple operationism. The principle that the things of interest should be measured in more than one way—just in case one of your measuring sticks is warped. If you are interested in loyalty within groups, for example, you should think of several different ways of assessing how loyal group members are: How long do they stay in the group? Do they say bad things about the group to others? How hard do they work on group projects?

Unit of analysis: In survey research, an element of the population of interest. Units of analysis are the entities about which you want to find out something: people, families, cities, countries.

Unrepresentative sample: A sample whose members' attributes do not necessarily correspond to those of the population of interest. The people who are consistently late to a class, for example, are probably an unrepresentative sample of the entire class. Perpetual tardiness may indicate lack of interest or an inability to plan one's time well—qualities that the other members of the class might not share.

Untreated control group design with pretest and posttest: A design in which observations are made on two groups before and after an intervention or manipulation occurs in one of the groups. If subjects can be randomly assigned to the two groups, it will be a true experiment.

Validity: The extent to which a measure really measures what it is supposed to—nothing more and nothing less. A valid indicator of self-esteem, for example, would be a measure on which only those people with high self-esteem scored high and only those with low self-esteem scored low. See also *internal validity, external validity, construct validity,* and *predictive validity.*

Verification: The process of testing proposed explanations and theories to see whether they are, in fact, accurate. Verification is a crucial step in the research process.

References

Abelson, R. P. (1968). Simulation of social behavior. In G. Lindzey and E. Aronson (Eds.), *Handbook of social psychology* (2nd ed.). Reading, MA: Addison-Wesley.

Abelson, R. P., and Miller, J. C. (1967). Negative persuasion via personal insult. *Journal of Experimental Social Psychology, 3*, 321–333.

Abt, C. C. (1979). Government constraints on evaluation quality. In L. E. Datta and R. Perloff (Eds.), *Improving evaluations.* Beverly Hills, CA: Sage.

Adair, J. G., Dushenko, T. W., and Lindsay, R. C. L. (1985). Ethical regulations and their impact on research practice. *American Psychologist, 40*, 59–72.

Adair, J. G., Sharpe, D., and Huynh, C. L. (1989). Hawthorne control procedures in educational experiments: A reconsideration of their use and effectiveness. *Review of Educational Research, 59*, 215–228.

Adams, J. L. (1980). *Conceptual blockbusting: A guide to better ideas* (2nd ed.). New York: Norton.

Adler, P. A. (1985). *Wheeling and dealing: An ethnography of an upper-level drug dealing and smuggling community.* New York: Columbia University Press.

Adler, P. A., and Adler, P. (1987). *Membership roles in field research.* Newbury Park, CA: Sage.

Adorno, T. W., Frenkel-Brunswik, E., Levinson, D., and Sanford, R. N. (1950). *The authoritarian personality.* New York: Harper.

Allport, G. W., and Postman, L. (1947). *The psychology of rumor.* New York: Holt, Rinehart and Winston.

Altman, I. (1975). *The environment and social behavior: Privacy, personal space, territory, crowding.* Monterey, CA: Brooks/Cole.

American Psychological Association (1992). Ethical principles of psychologists and code of conduct. *American Psychologist, 47*, 1597–1611.

Anastasi, A., and Urbina, S. (In press). *Psychological testing* (7th ed.) New York: Macmillan.

Anderson, C. A., and DeNeve, K. M. (1992). Temperature, aggression, and the negative affect escape model. *Psychological Bulletin, 111*, 347–351.

Aronson, E., Brewer, M., and Carlsmith, J. M. (1985). Experimentation in social psychology. In G. Lindzey and E. Aronson (Eds.), *Handbook of social psychology* (3rd ed.). New York: Random House.

Aronson, E., Ellsworth, P. C., Carlsmith, J. M., and Gonzales, M. H. (1990). *Methods of research in social psychology* (2nd ed.). New York: McGraw-Hill.

Asch, S. (1952). *Social psychology.* New York: Prentice-Hall.

Associated Press (1988, February 27). Many question judges' objectivity. *Florida Times Union/Jacksonville Journal*, p. B-4.

Auster, C. J. (1985). Manuals for socialization: Examples from Girl Scout Handbooks 1913–1984. *Qualitative Sociology, 8*(4), 359–367.

Babbie, E. R. (1990). *Survey research methods.* Belmont, CA: Wadsworth.

Bakeman, R., and Gottman, J. M. (1987). Applying observational methods: A systematic view. In J. D. Osofsky (Ed.), *Handbook of infant development* (2nd ed.). New York: Wiley.

Bales, R. F. (1950). *Interaction process analysis*. Cambridge, MA: Addison-Wesley.

Bales, R. F. (1970). *Personality and interpersonal behavior*. New York: Holt, Rinehart and Winston.

Barber, T. X. (1976). *Pitfalls in human research: Ten pivotal points*. New York: Pergamon.

Baron, R. S. (1986). Distraction-conflict theory: Progress and problems. In L. Berkowitz (Ed.), *Advances in experimental social psychology*, vol. 19. New York: Academic Press.

Bartlett, J. (1992). *Bartlett's familiar quotations* (16th ed.) (J. Kaplan, Ed.). Boston: Little, Brown and Company.

Barzun, J., and Graff, H. F. (1992). *The modern researcher* (5th ed.). Fort Worth, TX: Harcourt Brace Jovanovich.

Bass, R. F. (1987). Computer-assisted observer training. *Journal of Applied Behavior Analysis, 201,* 83–88.

Baum, A., Fleming, R., and Singer, J. E. (1982). Stress at Three Mile Island: Applying psychological impact analysis. *Applied Social Psychology Annual, 3,* 217–248.

Baum, W. K., and Hardwick, B. (1988). Oral histories. In J. C. Larsen (Ed.), *Researcher's guide to archives and regional history sources*. Hamden, CT: Library Professional Publications.

Baumrind, D. (1985). Research using intentional deception: Ethical issues revisited. *American Psychologist, 40,* 165–174.

Benney, M., Riesman, D., and Star, S. A. (1956). Age and sex in the interview. *American Journal of Sociology, 62,* 143–152.

Benton, J. E., and Daly, J. L. (1991). A question order effect in a local government survey. *Public Opinion Quarterly, 55,* 640–642.

Berkowitz, L. (1989). Frustration-aggression hypothesis: Examination and reformulation. *Psychological Bulletin, 106,* 59–73.

Berkun, M. M., Bialek, H. M., Kern, R. P., and Yagi, K. (1962). Experimental studies of psychological stress in man. *Psychological Monographs, 76,* 1–39.

Bernardin, H. J., and Pence, E. C. (1980). Effects of rater training: Creating new response sets and decreasing accuracy. *Journal of Applied Psychology, 65,* 60–66.

Beveridge, W. I. B. (1957). *The art of scientific investigation.* (3rd ed.). New York: Vintage Books.

Beveridge, W. I. B. (1980). *Seeds of discovery: The logic, illogic, serendipity, and sheer chance of scientific discovery.* New York: Norton.

Billiet, J., and Loosveldt, G. (1988). Improvement of the quality of responses to factual survey questions by interviewer training. *Public Opinion Quarterly, 52,* 190–211.

Bishop, G. F., Tuchfarber, A. J., and Oldendick, R. W. (1986). Opinions on fictitious issues: The pressure to answer survey questions. *Public Opinion Quarterly, 50,* 240–250.

Biswas, A., Olsen, J. E., and Carlet, V. (1992). A comparison of print advertisements from the United States and France. *Journal of Advertising, 21*(4), 73–81.

Bowers, C., Salas, E., Prince, C., and Brannick, M. (1992). Games teams play: A method for investigating team coordination and performance. *Behavior Research Methods, Instruments, and Computers, 24,* 503–506.

Bowers, K. S. (1973). Situationism in psychology: An analysis and a critique. *Psychological Review, 80,* 307–336.

Box, G. E. P., Hunter, W. G., and Hunter, J. S. (1978). *Statistics for experimenters: An introduction to design, data analysis, and model building.* New York: Wiley.

Boyd, R. S. (1990, June 10). Accessibility of information may make privacy a thing of the past. *Florida Times-Union* (Jacksonville, Florida), p. A-9.

Bradburn, N. M., Rips, L. J., and Shevell, S. K. (1987). Answering autobiographical questions: The impact of memory and inference on surveys. *Science, 236,* 157–161.

Bradburn, N. M., and Sudman, S. (1988). *Polls and surveys: Understanding what they tell us.* San Francisco: Jossey-Bass.

Brecher, E. M., and Brecher, J. (1986). Extracting valid sexological findings from severely flawed and biased population samples. *Journal of Sex Research, 22,* 6–20.

Bretl, D. J., and Cantor, J. (1988). The portrayal of men and women in U.S. television commercials: A recent content analysis and trends over 15 years. *Sex Roles, 18*(9/10), 595–609.

Brewer, M. B. (1985). Experimental research and social policy: Must it be rigor versus relevance? *Journal of Social Issues, 41,* 159–176.

Brush, S. G. (1974). Should the history of science be rated X? *Science, 183,* 1164–1172.

Brush, S. G. (1991). Women in science and engineering. *American Scientist, 79,* 404–419.

Buck, R. (1993). The spontaneous communication of interpersonal expectations. In P. D. Blanck (Ed.), *Interpersonal expectations.* New York: Cambridge University Press.

Buford, B. (1992). *Among the thugs.* New York: Norton.

Burchard, W. (1958). Lawyers, political scientists, sociologists—and concealed microphones. *American Sociological Review, 23,* 686–691.

Burton, S., and Blair, E. (1991). Task conditions, response formulation processes, and response accuracy for behavioral frequency questions. *Public Opinion Quarterly, 53,* 50–79.

Campbell, D. T. (1986). Relabeling internal and external validity for applied social scientists. In W. M. K. Trochim (Ed.), *Advances in quasi-experimental design and analysis.* San Francisco: Jossey-Bass.

Campbell, D. T. (1988). *Methodology and epistemology for social science: Selected papers.* Chicago: University of Chicago Press.

Campbell, D. T., and Stanley, J. C. (1966). *Experimental and quasi-experimental designs for research.* Chicago: Rand-McNally.

Carpenter, E. H. (1988). Software tools for data collection: Microcomputer-assisted interviewing. *Social Science Computer Review, 6,* 353–368.

Cartwright, D. (1953). Analysis of qualitative material. In L. Festinger and D. Katz (Eds.), *Research methods in the behavioral sciences.* New York: Holt, Rinehart and Winston.

Chamberlain, T. C. (1965). The method of multiple working hypotheses. *Science, 148,* 754–759. (Original work published 1890)

Chamblin, M. C. (1993). *Attitudes toward sex education in the public schools.* Unpublished manuscript. University of North Florida, Jacksonville, Florida.

Chelimsky, E. (1987). The politics of program evaluation. *Society, 25*(1), 24–32.

Chow, S. L. (1992). *Research methods in psychology: A primer.* Calgary, Alberta: Detselig.

Christensen, L. (1988). Deception in psychological research: When is it justified? *Personality and Social Psychology Bulletin, 14,* 664–675.

Cialdini, R. B. (1993). *Influence: Science and practice* (3rd ed.). New York: Harper Collins.

Clark, H. H., and Schober, M. F. (1992). Asking questions and influencing answers. In J. M. Tanur (Ed.), *Questions about questions: Inquiries into the cognitive bases of surveys.* New York: Russell Sage Foundation.

Cochran, N. (1980). Society as emergent and more than rational: An essay on the inappropriateness of program evaluation. *Policy Sciences, 12,* 113–129.

Cochran, N., Gordon, A. C., and Krause, M. S. (1980). Proactive records: Reflections on the village watchman. *Knowledge, 2*(1), 5–18.

Cohen, J. (1960). A coefficient of agreement for nominal scales. *Educational and Psychological Measurement, 20,* 37–46.

Colasanto, D., Singer, E., and Rogers, T. F. (1992). Context effects on responses to questions about AIDS. *Public Opinion Quarterly, 56,* 515–518.

Collison, M. N.-K. (1992, February 26). A Berkeley scholar clashes with feminists over validity of their research on date rape. *Chronicle of Higher Education,* pp. A35–A37.

Cone, J. D., and Foster, S. L. (1982). Direct observation in clinical psychology. In P. C. Kendall and J. N. Butcher (Eds.), *Handbook of research methods in clinical psychology*. New York: Wiley.

Cook, T. D., and Campbell, D. T. (1979). *Quasi-experimentation: Design and analysis issues for field settings*. Chicago: Rand McNally.

Cook, T. D., Leviton, L. C., and Shadish, W. R., Jr. (1985). Program evaluation. In G. Lindzey and E. Aronson (Eds.), *The handbook of social psychology* (3rd ed.). New York: Random House.

Cook, T. D., and Shadish, W. R. (1994). Social experiments: Some developments over the past fifteen years. *Annual Review of Psychology, 45,* 545–580.

Copeland, J. T. (1993). Motivational approaches to expectancy confirmation. *Current Directions in Psychological Science, 2,* 117–121.

Cordray, D. S. (1986). Quasi-experimentation in a critical multiplist mode. In W. M. K. Trochim (Ed.), *Advances in quasi-experimental design and analysis*. San Francisco: Jossey-Bass.

Cott, J. (1987). *Visions and voices*. New York: Doubleday.

Courtwright, D. (1989, January 26). *Photographs as historic evidence*. Faculty colloquium presentation, University of North Florida, Jacksonville, Florida.

Cox, E. P. (1980). The optimal number of response alternatives for a scale: A review. *Journal of Marketing Research, 17,* 407–422.

Cronbach, L. J. (1957). The two disciplines of scientific psychology. *American Psychologist, 12,* 671–684.

Cronbach, L. J., Ambron, S. R., Dornbusch, S. M., Hess, R. D., Hornik, R. C., Phillips, D. C., Walker, D. F., and Weiner, S. S. (1981). *Toward reform of program evaluation*. San Francisco: Jossey-Bass.

Csikszentmihalyi, M. (1990). *Flow: The psychology of optimal experience*. New York: Harper Perennial.

Dabbs, J. M., Jr., and Morris, R. (1990). Testosterone, social class, and antisocial behavior in a sample of 4462 men. *Psychological Science, 1,* 209–211.

Dandoy, A. C., and Goldstein, A. G. (1990). The use of cognitive appraisal to reduce stress reactions: A replication. *Journal of Social Behavior and Personality, 5,* 275–285.

Danielson, E. S. (1989). The ethics of access. *American Archivist, 52,* 52–62.

Darwin, C. (1969). *The autobiography of Charles Darwin* (N. Barlow, Ed.). New York: Norton. (Original work published 1887)

Dawes, R. M. (1990). Social dilemmas, economic self-interest, and evolutionary theory. In D. R. Brown and J. E. K. Smith (Eds.), *Frontiers of mathematical psychology*. New York: Springer-Verlag.

Dexter, H. R., Cutler, B. L., and Moran, G. (1992). A test of voir dire as a remedy for the prejudicial effects of pretrial publicity. *Journal of Applied Social Psychology, 22,* 819–832.

Dillehay, R. C., and Nietzel, M. T. (1980). Constructing a science of jury behavior. *Review of Personality and Social Psychology, 1,* 246–264.

Dillman, D. A. (1978). *Mail and telephone surveys: The total design method*. New York: Wiley.

Dillman, D. A., and Tarnai, J. (1988). Administrative issues in mixed mode surveys. In R. M. Groves, P. P. Biemer, L. E. Lyberg, J. T. Massey, W. L. Nicholls, II, and J. Waksberg (Eds.), *Telephone survey methodology*. New York: Wiley.

Dorsey, B. L., Nelson, R. O., and Hayes, S. C. (1986). The effects of code complexity and of behavioral frequency on observer accuracy and interobserver agreement. *Behavioral Assessment, 8,* 349–363.

Doty, R. M., Peterson, B. E., and Winter, D. G. (1991). Threat and authoritarianism in the United States, 1978–1987. *Journal of Personality and Social Psychology, 61,* 629–640.

Dowd, M. (1983, December 4). Work and motherhood tie in survey of women's values. *Lexington Herald-Leader*, p. A-29.

Duncan, S., and Rosenthal, R. (1968). Vocal emphasis in experimenters' instruction reading as unintended determinant of subjects' responses. *Language and Speech, 11*, 20–26.

Durdan, C. A., Reeder, G. D., and Hecht, P. R. (1985). Litter in a university cafeteria: Demographic data and the use of prompts as an intervention strategy. *Environment and Behavior, 17*, 387–404.

Dykman, B. M., and Reis, H. T. (1979). Personality and correlation of classroom seating. *Journal of Educational Psychology, 71*, 346–354.

Eagly, A. H., and Chaiken, S. (1993). *The psychology of attitudes.* Fort Worth, TX: Harcourt Brace Jovanovich.

Eder, D., and Parker, S. (1987). The cultural production and reproduction of gender: The effect of extracurricular activities on peer-group culture. *Sociology of Education, 60*, 200–213.

Edney, J. J. (1979). The nuts game: A concise commons dilemma analog. *Environmental Psychology and Nonverbal Behavior, 3*, 252–254.

Eisenberger, R. (1992). Learned industriousness. *Psychological Review, 99*, 248–267.

Ellis, C. (1986). *Fisher folk: Two communities on Chesapeake Bay.* Lexington, KY: University of Kentucky Press.

Ellsworth, P. C. (1977). From abstract ideas to concrete instances: Some guidelines for choosing natural settings. *American Psychologist, 32*, 604–615.

Elstein, A. S., Shulman, L. S., and Sprafka, S. A. (1978). *Medical problem solving: An analysis of clinical reasoning.* Cambridge, MA: Harvard University Press.

Elstein, A. S., Shulman, L. S., and Sprafka, S. A. (1990). Medical problem solving: A ten-year retrospective. *Evaluation and the Health Professions, 13*, 5–36.

Evans, G. W., and Lepore, S. J. (1993). Household crowding and social support: A quasi-experimental analysis. *Journal of Personality and Social Psychology, 65*, 308–316.

Evans, L. (1988). Older driver involvement in fatal and severe traffic crashes. *Journal of Gerontology: Social Sciences, 43*, S186–S193.

Evans, R. I. (1989). *Albert Bandura, the man and his ideas: A dialogue.* New York: Praeger.

Eysenck, H. J. (1965). *Smoking, health, and personality.* New York: Basic Books.

Eysenck, H. J. (1980). *The causes and effects of smoking.* London: Maurice Temple Smith.

Faludi, S. (1992). *Backlash: The undeclared war against American women.* New York: Doubleday Anchor.

Festinger, L., Riecken, H. W., and Schachter, S. (1956). *When prophecy fails: A social and psychological study of a modern group that predicted the destruction of the world.* New York: Harper and Row.

Fine, G. A. (1990). Organizational time: Temporal demands and the experience of work in restaurant kitchens. *Social Forces, 69*, 95–114.

Finger, S. C., Elliott, J. E., and Remer, R. (1993). Simulation as a tool in family therapy. *Journal of Family Therapy, 15*, 365–379.

Finkel, S. E., Guterbock, T. M., and Borg, M. J. (1991). Race-of-interviewer effects in a preelection poll. *Public Opinion Quarterly, 55*, 313–330.

Fischhoff, B. (1980). For those condemned to study the past: Reflections on historical judgment. In R. A. Shweder (Ed.), *Fallible judgment in behavior research.* (New Directions for Methodology of Social and Behavioral Science, no. 4.) San Francisco: Jossey-Bass.

Fiske, S. T., and Taylor, S. E. (1991). *Social cognition* (2nd ed.). Reading, MA: Addison-Wesley.

Fletcher, G. J. O. (1984). Psychology and common sense. *American Psychologist, 39*, 203–213.

Foley, L. A. (1993). *A psychological view of the legal system.* Madison, WI: Brown & Benchmark.

Folio Weekly (1989, October 17). Before we show you a good time we'd like to get to know you. *Folio Weekly*, p. 27.

Forsyth, B. H., and Lessler, J. T. (1992). Cognitive laboratory methods: A taxonomy. In P. N. Biemer, R. M. Groves, L. E. Lyberg, N. A. Mathiowetz, and S. Sudman (Eds.), *Measurement errors in surveys*. New York: Wiley.

Fossey, D. (1983). *Gorillas in the mist*. Boston: Houghton Mifflin.

Foster, S. L., Bell-Dolan, D. J., and Burge, D. A. (1988). Behavioral observation. In A. S. Bellack and M. Hersen (Eds.), *Behavioral assessment: A practical handbook* (3rd ed.). New York: Pergamon Press.

Fowler, F. J., Jr. (1992). How unclear terms affect survey data. *Public Opinion Quarterly, 56*, 218–231.

Fowler, F. J., Jr. (1993). *Survey research methods* (2nd ed.). Newbury Park, CA: Sage.

Fowler, F. J., Jr., and Mangione, T. W. (1990). *Standardized survey interviewing: Minimizing interviewer-related error*. Newbury Park, CA: Sage.

Freeman, D. (1984). *Margaret Mead and Samoa: The making and unmaking of an anthropological myth*. New York: Viking Penguin.

Freud, S. (1938). *The basic writings of Sigmund Freud* (A. A. Brill, Ed.). New York: Random House.

Frey, J. H. (1989). *Survey research by telephone* (2nd ed.). Newbury Park, CA: Sage.

Friedman, H. S. (1982). Nonverbal communication in medical interaction. In H. S. Friedman and M. R. DiMatteo (Eds.), *Interpersonal issues in health care*. New York: Academic Press.

Friedman, N. (1967). *The social nature of psychological research: The psychological experiment as a social interaction*. New York: Basic Books.

Frost, R. (1949). *The complete poems of Robert Frost*. New York: Henry Holt and Co.

Gabennesch, H. (1988). When promises fail: A theory of temporal fluctuations in suicide. *Social Forces, 67*, 129–145.

Gauch, H. G. (1993). Prediction, parsimony, and noise. *American Scientist, 81*, 468–478.

Geen, R. G. (1991). Social motivation. *Annual Review of Psychology, 42*, 377–399.

Geer, J. G. (1988). What do open-ended questions measure? *Public Opinion Quarterly, 52*, 365–371.

Geer, J. G. (1991). Do open-ended questions measure "salient" issues? *Public Opinion Quarterly, 55*, 360–370.

Geller, E. S., and Kalsher, M. J. (1990). Environmental determinants of party drinking: Bartenders vs. self-service. *Environment and Behavior, 22*, 74–90.

Geller, E. S., Kalsher, M. J., Rudd, J. R., and Lehman, G. R. (1989). Promoting safety belt use on a university campus: An integration of commitment and incentive strategies. *Journal of Applied Social Psychology, 19*, 3–19.

Gergen, K. J. (1978). Experimentation in social psychology: A reappraisal. *European Journal of Social Psychology, 8*, 507–527.

Gergen, K. J. (1980). Toward intellectual audacity in social psychology. In R. Gilmour and S. Duck (Eds.), *The development of social psychology*. London: Academic Press.

Gilbert, D. T. (1991). How mental systems believe. *American Psychologist, 46*, 107–119.

Giles, H. (1990). Social meanings of Welsh English. In N. Coupland (Ed.), *English in Wales*. Philadelphia: Multilingual Matters.

Gilovich, T. (1991). *How we know what isn't so: The fallibility of human reason in everyday life*. New York: The Free Press.

Glass, D., and Singer, J. E. (1972). *Urban stress: Experiments on noise and social stressors*. New York: Academic Press.

Glenn, N. D. (1977). *Cohort analysis*. Newbury Park, CA: Sage.

Goffman, E. (1961). *Asylums*. Garden City, NY: Doubleday Anchor.

Goodall, J. (1989). Interview. *Lear's, 2*(4), 17–20.

Goodall, J. (1990). *Through a window: My thirty years with the chimpanzees of Gombe.* Boston: Houghton Mifflin.

Gordis, L., and Gold, E. (1980). Privacy, confidentiality, and the use of medical records in research. *Science, 207,* 153–156.

Greenberg, J. (1988). Equity and workplace status: A field experiment. *Journal of Applied Psychology, 73,* 606–613.

Greenberg, J., and Eskew, D. E. (1993). The role of role playing in organizational research. *Journal of Management, 19,* 221–241.

Greenberg, J., Solomon, S., Pyszczynski, T., and Steinberg, L. (1988). A reaction to Greenwald, Pratkanis, Leippe, and Baumgardner (1986): Under what conditions does research obstruct theory progress? *Psychological Review, 95,* 566–571.

Greene, J. C., Dumont, J., and Doughty, J. (1992). A formative audit of the ECAETC year 1 evaluation. *Evaluation and Program Planning, 15,* 81–90.

Greene, M. (1986). Qualitative research and the uses of literature. *Journal of Thought, 21*(3), 69–83.

Greenwald, J. (1994, February 21). Famine and feast. *Time,* pp. 42–44.

Griffin, D. R. (1985). Recollections of an experimental naturalist. In D. A. Dewsbury (Ed.), *Leaders in the study of animal behavior.* Lewisberg, PA: Bucknell University Press.

Grotevant, H. D., and Carlson, C. I. (1989). *Family assessment: A guide to methods and measures.* New York: Guilford Press.

Groves, R. M. (1987). Research on survey data quality. *Public Opinion Quarterly, 51,* S156–S172.

Groves, R. M. (1989). *Survey errors and survey costs.* New York: Wiley.

Groves, R. M., Biemer, P. P., Lyberg, L. E., Massey, J. T., Nicholls, W. L., II, and Waksberg, J. (Eds.) (1988). *Telephone survey methodology.* New York: Wiley.

Groves, R. M., Cialdini, R. B., and Couper, M. P. (1992). Understanding the decision to participate in a survey. *Public Opinion Quarterly, 56,* 475–495.

Groves, R. M., and Lyberg, L. E. (1988). An overview of nonresponse issues in telephone surveys. In R. M. Groves, P. P. Biemer, L. E. Lyberg, J. T. Massey, W. L. Nicholls, II, and J. Waksberg (Eds.), *Telephone survey methodology.* New York: Wiley.

Guerin, B. (1993). *Social facilitation.* Cambridge: Cambridge University Press.

Hafferty, F. W. (1991). *Into the valley: Death and the socialization of medical students.* New Haven, CT: Yale University Press.

Hall, E. T. (1966). *The hidden dimension.* Garden City, NY: Doubleday.

Hall, J. A., and Briton, N. J. (1993). Gender, nonverbal behavior, and expectations. In P. D. Blanck (Ed.), *Interpersonal expectations: Theory, research, and applications.* New York: Cambridge University Press.

Haney, C., Banks, C., and Zimbardo, P. (1973). Interpersonal dynamics in a simulated prison. *International Journal of Criminology and Penology, 1,* 69–97.

Hans, V. P., and Slater, D. (1983). John Hinckley, Jr., and the insanity defense: The public's verdict. *Public Opinion Quarterly, 47,* 202–212.

Hardin, G. (1968). The tragedy of the commons. *Science, 166,* 1103–1107.

Harre, R., and Van Langenhove, L. (1991). Varieties of positioning. *Journal for the Theory of Social Behaviour, 21,* 393–407.

Harris, L. (1987). *Inside America.* New York: Vintage.

Harris, M. (1974). *Cows, pigs, wars, and witches: The riddles of culture.* New York: Crowell.

Harris, M. (1985). *The sacred cow and the abominable pig: Riddles of food and culture.* New York: Simon and Schuster.

Harris, M. J. (1993). Issues in studying the mediation of expectancy effects: A taxonomy of expectancy situations. In P. D. Blanck (Ed.), *Interpersonal expectations: Theory, research, and applications.* New York: Cambridge University Press.

Hawkins, J. W., and Aber, C. S. (1993). Women in advertisements in medical journals. *Sex Roles, 28,* 233–242.

Hawkins, R. P. (1982). Developing a behavior code. In D. P. Hartman (Ed.), *Using observers to study behavior.* (New Directions for Methodology of Social and Behavioral Science, no. 14.) San Francisco: Jossey-Bass.

Hazelrigg, P. J., Cooper, H., and Strathman, A. J. (1991). Personality moderators of the experimenter expectancy effect: A reexamination of five hypotheses. *Personality and Social Psychology Bulletin, 17,* 569–579.

Hedrick, T. E. (1988). Justifications for the sharing of social science data. *Law and Human Behavior, 12,* 163–171.

Hendrick, C. (1990). Replications, strict replications, and conceptual replications: Are they important? In J. W. Neuliep (Ed.), Handbook of replication research in the behavioral and social sciences [Special issue]. *Journal of Social Behavior and Personality, 5*(4), 41–49.

Hendrick, C., and Jones, R. A. (1972). *The nature of theory and research in social psychology.* New York: Academic Press.

Henshel, R. L. (1980). The purposes of laboratory experimentation and the virtues of deliberate artificiality. *Journal of Experimental Social Psychology, 16,* 466–478.

Hill, M. R. (1993). *Archival strategies and techniques.* Newbury Park, CA: Sage.

Hite, S. (1987). *Women and love: A cultural revolution in progress.* New York: Knopf.

Holsti, O. R. (1969). *Content analysis for the social sciences and humanities.* Reading, MA: Addison-Wesley.

Hooper, F. H. (1988). The history of child psychology as seen through handbook analysis. *Human Development, 31,* 176–184.

House, C. C., and Nicholls, W. L., II (1988). Questionnaire design for CATI: Design objectives and methods. In R. M. Groves, P. P. Biemer, L. E. Lyberg, J. T. Massey, W. L. Nicholls, II, and J. Waksberg (Eds.), *Telephone survey methodology.* New York: Wiley.

Hovland, C. I. (1959). Reconciling conflicting results derived from experimental and survey studies of attitude change. *American Psychologist, 14,* 8–17.

Humphrey, L. (1975). *Tearoom trade: Impersonal sex in public places* (rev. ed.). Chicago: Aldine.

Humphrey, R. (1985). How work roles influence perception: Structural-cognitive processes and organizational behavior. *American Sociological Review, 50,* 242–252.

Humphreys, K., and Rappaport, J. (1993). From the community mental health movement to the war on drugs. *American Psychologist, 48,* 892–901.

Hyman, H. (1954). *Interviewing in social research.* Chicago: University of Chicago Press.

Inness, J. C. (1992). *Privacy, intimacy, and isolation.* New York: Oxford University Press.

Jacob, H. (1984). *Using published data: Errors and remedies.* Beverly Hills, CA: Sage.

Jones, E. E. (1966, August 1–7). *Conceptual generality and experimental strategy in social psychology.* Paper presented at the International Congress of Psychology, Moscow, USSR.

Jones, F. (1984, August 23). Summer and drink don't mix. *Toronto Star,* p. A-19.

Jones, R. A. (1977). *Self-fulfilling prophecies: Social, psychological, and physiological effects of expectancies.* Hillsdale, NJ: Erlbaum.

Jones, R. A. (1982). Stereotyping as a process of social cognition. In A. R. Miller (Ed.), *In the eye of the beholder: Contemporary issues in stereotyping.* New York: Praeger.

Jones, R. A. (1986). Individual differences in nicotine sensitivity. *Addictive Behaviors, 11,* 435–438.

Jones, R. A. (1987). Psychology, history, and the press: The case of William McDougall and the *New York Times. American Psychologist, 42,* 931–940.

Jones, R. A. (1989). Academic freedom, or constrained academics? *Dialogue,* Fall, 5–6.

Jones, R. A., and Cooper, J. (1971). Mediation of experimenter effects. *Journal of Personality and Social Psychology, 20,* 70–74.

Jones, R. A., Hendrick, C., and Epstein, Y. (1979). *Introduction to social psychology.* Sunderland, MA: Sinauer Associates.

Jones, R. A., Morrow, G. D., Morris, B. R., Ries, J. B., and Wekstein, D. R. (1992). Self-perceived information needs and concerns of elderly persons. *Perceptual and Motor Skills, 74,* 227–238.

Jones, S. R. G. (1992). Was there a Hawthorne effect? *American Journal of Sociology, 98,* 451–468.

Jorgensen, D. L. (1989). *Participant observation: A methodology for human studies.* Newbury Park, CA: Sage.

Judd, C. M., Kidder, L. H., and Smith, E. R. (1991). *Research methods in social relations* (6th ed.). Fort Worth, TX: Holt, Rinehart and Winston.

Jussim, L. (1986). Self-fulfilling prophecies: A theoretical and integrative review. *Psychological Review, 93,* 429–445.

Kaplan, A. (1964). *The conduct of inquiry: Methodology for behavioral science.* San Francisco: Chandler.

Kendrick, D. T., and MacFarlane, S. W. (1986). Ambient temperature and horn honking: A field study of the heat aggression relationship. *Environment and Behavior, 18,* 179–191.

Kerr, N. L. (1990). Applied perspectives on social and temporal dilemmas: An introduction. *Social Behavior, 5,* 201–205.

Kershaw, D., and Fair, J. (1976). *The New Jersey income-maintenance experiment* (Vol. 1). New York: Academic Press.

Kerwin, J., and Shaffer, D. R. (1994). Mock jurors versus mock juries: The role of deliberations in reactions to inadmissible testimony. *Personality and Social Psychology Bulletin, 20,* 153–162.

Kimmel, A. J. (1988). *Ethics and values in applied social research.* Beverly Hills, CA: Sage.

Kirk, J., and Miller, M. L. (1986). *Reliability and validity in qualitative research.* Beverly Hills, CA: Sage.

Komorita, S. S., and Parks, C. D. (1994). *Social dilemmas.* Madison, WI: Brown and Benchmark.

Kosloski, K., and Montgomery, R. J. V. (1993). The effects of respite on caregivers of Alzheimer's patients: One-year evaluation of the Michigan Model Respite Programs. *Journal of Applied Gerontology, 12,* 4–17.

Krippendorff, K. (1980). *Content analysis: An introduction to its methodology.* Beverly Hills, CA: Sage.

Kruskal, W., and Mosteller, F. (1981). Ideas of representative sampling. In D. W. Fiske (Ed.), *Problems with language imprecision.* (New Directions for Methodology of Social and Behavioral Science, no. 9.) San Francisco: Jossey-Bass.

Kunda, G. (1992). *Engineering culture: Control and commitment in a high-tech corporation.* Philadelphia: Temple University Press.

Lam, D. J., and Yang, C. F. (1989). Social behavior in the *real* Hong Kong: Comment on Wheeler. *Personality and Social Psychology Bulletin, 15,* 639–643.

Lana, R. E. (1969). Pretest sensitization. In R. Rosenthal and R. L. Rosnow (Eds.), *Artifact in behavioral research.* New York: Academic Press.

Langer, E. J. (1983). *The psychology of control.* Beverly Hills, CA: Sage.

Langer, E. J. (1989). *Mindfulness.* Reading, MA: Addison-Wesley.

Latane, B., and Darley, J. M. (1970). *The unresponsive bystander: Why doesn't he help?* New York: Appleton-Century-Crofts.

Lavrakas, P. J. (1993). *Telephone survey methods: Sampling, selection, and supervision* (2nd ed.). Newbury Park, CA: Sage.

Lester, D., and Stack, S. (1989). Bias resulting from the choice of sample and results of cross-national analyses of suicide rates. *Quality and Quantity, 23,* 221–223.

Levine, R. J. (1986). *Ethics and regulation of clinical research* (2nd ed.). Baltimore: Urban and Schwarzenberg.

Lewin, K. (1951). Problems of research in social psychology. In D. Cartwright (Ed.), *Field theory in social science.* New York: Harper and Row.

Lewontin, R. (1995, April 20). Sex in America. *New York Review of Books, 42*(7), pp. 24–29.

Lieberman, M. A. (1961). Relationship of mortality rates to entrance to a home for the aged. *Geriatrics, 16,* 515–519.

Lippmann, W. (1922). *Public opinion.* New York: Harcourt Brace.

Locke, E. A. (1986). Generalizing from laboratory to field: Ecological validity or abstraction of essential elements? In E. A. Locke (Ed.), *Generalizing from laboratory to field settings.* Lexington, MA: D. C. Heath.

Lofland, J. (1971). *Analyzing social settings: A guide to qualitative observation and analysis.* Belmont, CA: Wadsworth.

Lofland, J., and Lofland, L. H. (1984). *Analyzing social settings: A guide to qualitative observation and analysis* (2nd ed.). Belmont, CA.: Wadsworth.

Lohr, S. (1994, January 9). For Big Blue, the ones who got away. *New York Times,* section 3, pp. 1, 6.

Loseke, D. R. (1992). *The battered woman and shelters: The social construction of wife abuse.* Albany: State University of New York Press.

Macrae, C. N. (1992). A tale of two curries: Counterfactual thinking and accident-related judgments. *Personality and Social Psychology Bulletin, 18,* 84–87.

Macrae, C. N., Milne, A. B., and Bodenhausen, G. V. (1994). Stereotypes as energy-saving devices: A peek inside the cognitive toolbox. *Journal of Personality and Social Psychology, 66,* 37–47.

Madey, S. F., and Gilovich, T. (1993). Effect of temporal focus on the recall of expectancy-consistent and expectancy-inconsistent information. *Journal of Personality and Social Psychology, 65,* 458–468.

Malcolm, J. (1984). *In the Freud archives.* New York: Knopf.

Marks, J. (1993). Scientific misconduct: Where "just say no" fails. *American Scientist, 81,* 380–382.

MassMutual (1990). *MassMutual American family values study.* Washington, D.C.: Mellman & Lazarus.

Markus, G. B. (1979). *Analyzing panel data.* Newbury Park, CA: Sage.

Marvell, T. B. (1989). Divorce rates and the fault requirement. *Law and Society Review, 23,* 543–567.

Maugh, T. H., II (1989, January 5). Researcher does his best work in bars. *Florida Times-Union* (Jacksonville, Florida), p. D-1.

McClendon, M. J., and O'Brien, D. J. (1988). Question-order effects on the determinants of subjective well-being. *Public Opinion Quarterly, 52,* 351–364.

McCracken, G. (1988). *The long interview.* Newbury Park, CA: Sage.

McGuire, W. J. (1964). Inducing resistance to persuasion: Some contemporary approaches. In L. Berkowitz (Ed.), *Advances in experimental social psychology,* vol. 2. New York: Academic Press.

McGuire, W. J. (1973). The yin and yang of progress in social psychology: Seven koan. *Journal of Personality and Social Psychology, 26,* 446–456.

McKenzie-Mohr, D., and Zanna, M. P. (1990). Treating women as sexual objects: Look to the (gender schematic) male who has viewed pornography. *Personality and Social Psychology Bulletin, 16,* 296–308.

McPhee, J. (1990). *Looking for a ship.* New York: Farrar, Straus, Giroux.

McPhee, J. (1993). *Assembling California.* New York: Farrar, Straus, Giroux.

Mead, M. (1949). Preface to the 1949 edition. In *Coming of age in Samoa: A study of adolescence and sex in primitive society*. New York: Mentor. (Original work published 1928)

Merton, R. K. (1987). Three fragments from a sociologist's notebooks: Establishing the phenomenon, specified ignorance, and strategic research materials. *Annual Review of Sociology, 13*, 1–28.

Mesch, D. J., and Dalton, D. R. (1992). Unexpected consequences of improving workplace justice: A six-year time series assessment. *Academy of Management Journal, 35*, 1099–1114.

Messner, M. A., Duncan, M. C., and Jensen, K. (1993). Separating the men from the girls: The gendered language of televised sports. *Gender and Society, 7*(1), 121–137.

Milgram, S. (1969, June). The lost letter technique. *Psychology Today*, pp. 30–33, 66, 68.

Miller, M. C. (1990). Hollywood: The ad. *Atlantic Monthly, 265*(4), 41–68.

Mishler, E. G. (1986). *Research interviewing: Context and narrative*. Cambridge, MA: Harvard University Press.

Misra, S. (1992). Is conventional debriefing adequate? An ethical issue in consumer research. *Journal of the Academy of Marketing Science, 20*, 269–273.

Mohr, L. B. (1992). *Impact analysis for program evaluation*. Newbury Park, CA: Sage.

Molstad, C. (1986). Choosing and coping with boring work. *Urban Life, 15*, 215–236.

Morris, J. (1992). *Locations*. New York: Oxford University Press.

Moskowitz, J. M. (1993). Why reports of outcome evaluations are often biased or uninterpretable: Examples from evaluations of drug abuse prevention programs. *Evaluation and Program Planning, 16*, 1–9.

Mosteller, F. (1981). Innovation and evaluation. *Science, 211*, 881–886.

Moyers, B. (1990). *A world of ideas, II: Public opinions from private citizens*. New York: Doubleday.

Myers, D. G. (1993). *Social psychology* (4th ed.). New York: McGraw-Hill.

National Archives and Records Administration (1991). *Regulations for the public use of records in the National Archives*. Washington, DC: National Archives and Records Administration.

National Center for Health Statistics (1988). *Vital statistics of the United States, 1986: Vol. 2, Part A*. Pub. No. (PHS) 88-1122. Public Health Service. Washington, DC: U.S. Government Printing Office.

National Center for Health Statistics (1990). *Health promotion and disease prevention: United States*. (Vital and Health Statistics, series 10, no. 185.) Washington, D.C.: U.S. Government Printing Office.

National Park Service (1993). *National park statistical abstract*. Washington, D.C.: U.S. Government Printing Office.

Neale, M. A., Huber, M. A., and Northcraft, G. B. (1987). The framing of negotiations: Contextual versus task frames. *Organizational Behavior and Human Decision Processes, 39*, 228–241.

Neisser, U. (1981). John Dean's memory: A case study. *Cognition, 9*, 1–22.

Nemeth, C. (1972). A critical analysis of research utilizing the prisoner's dilemma paradigm for the study of bargaining. In L. Berkowitz (Ed.), *Advances in experimental social psychology*, vol. 6. New York: Academic Press.

Neuharth, A. (1992). *Confessions of an S.O.B.* New York: Signet.

Newcomb, T. M. (1929). *The consistency of certain extrovert-introvert behavior patterns in 51 problem boys*. (Teachers College contributions to education, no. 382.) New York: Teacher's College.

Nisbett, R. E., and Ross, L. (1980). *Human inference: Strategies and shortcomings of social judgment*. Englewood Cliffs, NJ: Prentice-Hall.

Norins, H. (1990). *The Young and Rubicam traveling creative workshop*. Englewood Cliffs, NJ: Prentice Hall.

Norman, D. A. (1988). *The psychology of everyday things.* New York: Basic Books.

O'Carroll, P. W., Loftin, C., Waller, J, B., Jr., McDowall, D., Bukoff, A., Scott, R. O., Mercy, J. A., and Wiersema, B. (1991). Preventing homicide: An evaluation of the efficacy of a Detroit gun ordinance. *American Journal of Public Health, 81*, 576–581.

Occhipinti, S., and Siegal, M. (1994). Reasoning about food and contamination. *Journal of Personality and Social Psychology, 66*, 243–253.

Office of Technology Assessment (1987). *The electronic supervisor: New technology, new tensions.* (OTA-CIT-333.) Washington, DC: U.S. Government Printing Office.

Oksenberg, L., Cannell, C. F., and Kalton, G. (1991). New strategies of pretesting survey questions. *Journal of Official Statistics, 7*, 349–366.

Oksenberg, L., Coleman, L., and Cannell, C. F. (1986). Interviewers' voices and refusal rates in telephone surveys. *Public Opinion Quarterly, 50*, 97–111.

Olson, P., and Sivak, P. L. (1986). Perception-response time to unexpected roadway hazards. *Human Factors, 28*, 91–96.

Oreskes, M. (1990, August 12). Poll on troop move shows support (and anxiety). *New York Times*, p. 8.

Ostrom, T. M. (1988). Computer simulation: The third symbol system. *Journal of Experimental Social Psychology, 24*, 381–392.

Palinkas, L. A., Russell, J., Downs, M. A., and Petterson, J. S. (1992). Ethnic differences in stress, coping, and depressive symptoms after the *Exxon Valdez* oil spill. *Journal of Nervous and Mental Disease, 180*, 287–295.

Palys, T. S. (1978). Simulation methods and social psychology. *Journal for the Theory of Social Behavior, 8*, 341–368.

Parker, K. (1987, November 29). Conflicting survey results prove that you can't pigeonhole women. *Florida Times-Union/Jacksonville-Journal*, p. G-3.

Patchen, M. (1987). Strategies for eliciting cooperation from an adversary. *Journal of Conflict Resolution, 31*, 164–185.

Pearsol, J. A. (1992). A formative audit of the ECAETC year 1 evaluation: The evaluator's response. *Evaluation and Program Planning, 15*, 91–93.

Pearsol, J. A., and Gabel, L. L. (1992). The ECAETC evaluation study. *Evaluation and Program Planning, 15*, 75–80.

Peshkin, A. (1986). *God's choice: The total world of a fundamentalist Christian school.* Chicago: University of Chicago Press.

Phillips, A. P., and Dipboye, R. L. (1989). Correlational tests of predictions from a process model of the interview. *Journal of Applied Psychology, 74*, 41–52.

Piazza, T. (1993). Meeting the challenge of answering machines. *Public Opinion Quarterly, 57*, 219–231.

Piper, D. L., King, M. J., and Moberg, D. P. (1993). Implementing a middle school health promotion research project: Lessons our textbook didn't teach us. *Evaluation and Program Planning, 16*, 171–180.

Pirsig, R. M. (1974). *Zen and the art of motorcycle maintenance: An inquiry into values.* New York: Morrow.

Pollitt, K. (1993, October 4). Not just bad sex. *New Yorker*, Oct. 4, pp. 220–224.

Posavac, E. J. (1992). Communicating applied social psychology to users: A challenge and an art. In F. B. Bryant, J. Edwards, R. S. Tindale, E. J. Posvac, L. Heath, E. Henderson, and Y. Suarez-Balcazar (Eds.), *Methodological issues in applied social psychology.* New York: Plenum Press.

Pratkanis, A., and Aronson, E. (1992). *Age of propaganda: The everyday use and abuse of persuasion.* New York: W. H. Freeman.

Presser, S., and Zhao, S. (1992). Attributes of questions and interviewers as correlates of interviewing performance. *Public Opinion Quarterly, 56*, 236–240.

Quittner, A. L., Glueckauf, R. L., and Jackson, D. N. (1990). Chronic parenting stress: Moderating versus mediating effect of social support. *Journal of Personality and Social Psychology, 59,* 1266–1278.

Rasinski, K. A. (1989). The effect of question wording on public support for government spending. *Public Opinion Quarterly, 53,* 388–394.

Rathje, W., and Murphy, C. (1992). *Rubbish! The archaeology of garbage.* New York: Harper Collins.

Reed, S. K. (1988). *Cognition: Theory and applications* (2nd ed.). Pacific Grove, CA: Brooks/Cole.

Reid, J. B. (1982). Observer training in naturalistic research. In D. P. Hartman (Ed.), *Using observers to study behavior.* (New Directions for Methodology of Social and Behavioral Science, no. 14.) San Francisco: Jossey-Bass.

Reinfurt, D. W., Campbell, B. J., Stewart, J. R., and Stutts, J. C. (1990). Evaluating the North Carolina safety belt wearing law. *Accident Analysis and Prevention, 22*(3), 197–210.

Repp, A. C., Nieminen, G. S., Olinger, E., and Brusca, R. (1988). Direct observation: Factors affecting the accuracy of observers. *Exceptional Children, 55,* 29–36.

Riessman, C. K. (1987). When gender is not enough: Women interviewing women. *Gender and Society, 1,* 172–207.

Roberts, L. J., Luke, D. A., Rappaport, J., Seidman, E., Toro, P. A., and Reischl, T. M. (1991). Charting uncharted terrain: A behavioral observation system for mutual help groups. *American Journal of Community Psychology, 19,* 715–737.

Roberts, R. R., and Renzaglia, G. A. (1965). The influence of tape recording on counseling. *Journal of Counseling Psychology, 12,* 10–16.

Robinson, D., and Rohde, S. (1946). Two experiments with an anti-Semitism poll. *Journal of Abnormal and Social Psychology, 41,* 136–144.

Roethlisberger, F. F., and Dickson, W. J. (1939). *Management and the worker.* New York: Wiley.

Ronai, C. R. (1992). The reflexive self through narrative: A night in the life of an erotic dancer/researcher. In C. Ellis and M. G. Flaherty (Eds.), *Investigating subjectivity: Research on lived experience.* Newbury Park, CA: Sage.

Rose, R. M., Jenkins, C. D., and Hurst, N. W. (1978). Health change in air traffic controllers: A prospective study. *Psychosomatic Medicine, 40,* 142–165.

Rosenberg, M. J. (1965). When dissonance fails: On eliminating evaluation apprehension from attitude measurement. *Journal of Personality and Social Psychology, 1,* 28–42.

Rosenhan, D. L. (1973). On being sane in insane places. *Science, 179,* 250–258.

Rosenthal, R. (1966). *Experimenter effects in behavioral research.* New York: Appleton-Century-Crofts.

Rosenthal, R. (1976). *Experimenter effects in behavioral research* (Rev. ed.). Hillsdale, NJ: Erlbaum.

Rosenthal, R. (1994). Science and ethics in conducting, analyzing, and reporting psychological research. *Psychological Science, 5,* 127–134.

Rosnow, R. L. (1991). Inside rumor: A personal journey. *American Psychologist, 46,* 484–496.

Ross, L., and Nisbett, R. E. (1991). *The person and the situation: Perspectives of social psychology.* Philadelphia: Temple University Press.

Rossi, P. H., and Freeman, H. E. (1993). *Evaluation: A systematic approach* (5th ed.). Newbury Park, CA: Sage.

Sales, S. M. (1973). Threat as a factor in authoritarianism: An analysis of archival data. *Journal of Personality and Social Psychology, 28,* 44–57.

Samelson, F. (1980). J. B. Watson's Little Albert, Cyril Burt's twins, and the need for a critical science. *American Psychologist, 35,* 619–625.

Sanchez, M. E. (1992). Effects of questionnaire design on the quality of survey data. *Public Opinion Quarterly, 56,* 206–217.

Sato, I. (1991). *Kamikaze biker: Parody and anomy in affluent Japan.* Chicago: University of Chicago Press.

Scarr, S. (1985). Constructing psychology: Making facts and fables for our times. *American Psychologist, 40,* 499–512.

Schachter, S., Redington, K., Grunberg, N., Apple, W., and Schindler, S. (1980). *Springtime, suicide, and wills.* Unpublished manuscript. Columbia University.

Schaeffer, N. C. (1991). Hardly ever or constantly? Group comparisons using vague quantifiers. *Public Opinion Quarterly, 55,* 395–423.

Schaps, E. (1972). Cost, dependency, and helping. *Journal of Personality and Social Psychology, 21,* 74–78.

Scheper-Hughes, N. (1984). The Margaret Mead controversy: Culture, biology, and anthropological inquiry. *Human Organization, 43,* 85–93.

Schroder, H. M., Driver, M. J., and Streufert, S. (1967). *Human information processing.* New York: Holt, Rinehart and Winston.

Schur, E. M. (1984). *Labeling women deviant: Gender, stigma, and social control.* Philadelphia: Temple University Press.

Schwarz, N. (1990). Assessing frequency reports of mundane behaviors: Contributions of cognitive psychology to questionnaire construction. In C. Hendrick and M. S. Clark (Eds.), *Research methods in personality and social psychology.* Newbury Park, CA: Sage.

Schwarz, N., and Bienias, J. (1990). What mediates the impact of response alternatives on frequency reports of mundane behaviors? *Applied Cognitive Psychology, 4,* 61–72.

Schwarz, N., Knauper, B., Hippler, H. J., Noelle-Neumann, E., and Clark, L. (1991). Rating scales: Numeric values may change the meaning of scale labels. *Public Opinion Quarterly, 55,* 570–582.

Schwarz, N., Strack, F., and Mai, H. P. (1991). Assimilation and contrast effects in part-whole question sequences: A conversational logic analysis. *Public Opinion Quarterly, 55,* 3–23.

Scott, G. C. (1980). Playboy interview. *Playboy, 27*(12), 81–138.

Scriven, M. (1991). *Evaluation thesaurus* (4th ed.). Newbury Park, CA: Sage.

Sechrest, L., and Figueredo, A. J. (1993). Program evaluation. *Annual Review of Psychology, 44,* 645–674.

Seidman, I. E. (1991). *Interviewing as qualitative research: A guide for researchers in education and the social sciences.* New York: Teachers College Press.

Shaiken, H. (1987, March 22). When the computer runs the office. *New York Times,* section 3, p. 3.

Sharpe, D., Adair, J. G., and Roese, N. J. (1992). Twenty years of deception research: A decline in subjects' trust. *Personality and Social Psychology Bulletin, 18,* 585–590.

Shortell, S. M., and Richardson, W. C. (1978). *Health program evaluation.* St. Louis: Mosby.

Shuy, R. W. (1986). Ethical issues in analyzing FBI surreptitious tapes. *International Journal of the Sociology of Language, 62,* 119–128.

Shweder, R. A. (1975). How relevant is an individual difference theory of personality? *Journal of Personality, 43,* 455–484.

Simmons, V. M. (1985). Reconstructing an organization's history: Systematic distortion in retrospective data. In D. N. Berg and K. K. Smith (Eds.), *Exploring clinical methods for social research.* Newbury Park, CA: Sage.

Simonton, D. K. (1988a). Age and outstanding achievement: What do we know after a century of research. *Psychological Bulletin, 104,* 251–267.

Simonton, D. K. (1988b). Galtonian genius, Kroeberian configurations, and emulation: A generational time-series analysis of Chinese civilization. *Journal of Personality and Social Psychology, 55,* 230–238.

Smith, T. W. (1987). That which we call welfare by any other name would smell sweeter. *Public Opinion Quarterly, 51,* 75–83.

Snyder, M. (1992). Motivational foundations of behavioral confirmation. In M. P. Zanna (Ed.), *Advances in experimental social psychology,* vol. 25. New York: Academic Press.

Solomon, R. L. (1949). An extension of control group design. *Psychological Bulletin, 46,* 137–150.

Spaeth, M. A. (1987). CATI facilities at survey research organizations. *Survey Research, 18*(3–4), 18–22.

Stasser, G. (1990). Computer simulation of social interaction. In C. Hendrick and M. Clark (Eds.), *Research methods in personality and social psychology.* Newbury Park, CA: Sage.

Stewart, C. J., and Cash, W. B., Jr. (1991). *Interviewing: Principles and practices* (6th ed.). Dubuque, IA: Wm. C. Brown.

Stone, P. J., Dunphy, D. C., Smith, M. S., and Ogilvie, D. M. (1966). *The general inquirer: A computer approach to content analysis.* Cambridge, MA: MIT Press.

Strodtbeck, F. L., James, R. M., and Hawkins, C. (1957). Social status in jury deliberation. *American Sociological Review, 24,* 713–719.

Suchman, L., and Jordan, B. (1992). Validity and the collaborative construction of meaning in face-to-face surveys. In J. Tanur (Ed.), *Questions about questions: Inquiries into the cognitive bases of surveys.* New York: Russell Sage Foundation.

Sudman, S., and Bradburn, N. M. (1982). *Asking questions: A practical guide to questionnaire construction.* San Francisco: Jossey-Bass.

Suedfeld, P., and Bluck, S. (1993). Changes in integrative complexity accompanying significant life events: Historical evidence. *Journal of Personality and Social Psychology, 64,* 124–130.

Suedfeld, P., Corteen, R. S., and McCormick, C. (1986). The role of integrative complexity in military leadership: Robert E. Lee and his opponents. *Journal of Applied Social Psychology, 16,* 498–507.

Suls, J., and Gastorf, J. (1980). Has the social psychology of the experiment influenced how research is conducted? *European Journal of Social Psychology, 10,* 291–294.

Swan, G. E., Carmelli, D., and Rosenman, R. H. (1990). Cook and Medley hostility and the type A behavior pattern: Psychological correlates of two coronary prone behaviors. *Journal of Social Behavior and Personality, 5,* 89–106.

Synnott, A. (1988). The presentation of gender in advertising. In A. A. Berger (Ed.), *Media USA: Process and effect.* New York: Longman.

Tagg, J. (1988). *The burden of representation: Essays on photographies and histories.* Amherst: University of Massachusetts Press.

Taylor, S. E. (1991). *Health psychology* (2nd ed.) New York: McGraw Hill.

Taylor, S. J. (1987). Observing abuse: Professional ethics and personal morality in field research. *Qualitative Sociology, 10,* 288–302.

Temples of thrift. (1989, March 6). *New Yorker,* 27–28.

Tetlock, P. E. (1981). Pre- to postelection shifts in presidential rhetoric: Impression management or cognitive adjustment. *Journal of Personality and Social Psychology, 41,* 207–212.

Teubner, A. L., and Vaske, J. J. (1988). Monitoring computer users' behavior in office environments. *Behaviour and Information Technology, 7,* 67–78.

Thomas, R. D. (1992). *Dave's way.* New York: Berkley.

Tomerlin, J. (1988, February). Solved: The riddle of unintended acceleration: A long look at a growing problem. *Road and Track,* pp. 52–59.

Tonkin, E. (1992). *Narrating our pasts: The social construction of oral history.* New York: Cambridge University Press.

Topf, M. (1988). Interrater reliability decline under covert assessment. *Nursing Research, 37,* 47–49.

Tourangeau, R. (1984). Cognitive science and survey methods. In T. Jabine, M. Straf, J. Tanur, and R. Tourangeau (Eds.), *Cognitive aspects of survey methodology: Building a bridge between disciplines.* Washington, DC: National Academy Press.

Tourangeau, R., and Rasinski, K. A. (1988). Cognitive processes underlying context effects in attitude measurement. *Psychological Bulletin, 103,* 299–314.

Townsend, R. (1984). *Further up the organization: How to stop management from stifling people and strangling productivity.* New York: Knopf.

Triplett, N. (1897–1898). The dynamogenic factors in pacemaking and competition. *American Journal of Psychology, 9,* 507–533.

Trochim, W. M. K. (Ed.) (1986). *Advances in quasi-experimental design and analysis.* San Francisco: Jossey-Bass.

Tuttle, R. H. (1990). Apes of the world. *American Scientist, 78,* 115–125.

Unrau, Y. A. (1993). Expanding the role of program evaluation in social welfare policy analysis. *Evaluation Review, 17,* 653–662.

U.S. Bureau of the Census (1987). *Estimates of the population of the United States by age, sex, and race: 1980 to 1985.* (Series P-25, no. 985). Washington, DC: U.S. Government Printing Office.

U.S. Bureau of the Census (1992). *Statistical abstract of the United States: 1992* (112th edition). Washington, DC: U.S. Government Printing Office.

U.S. Bureau of the Census (1993). *Statistical abstract of the United States: 1993* (113th edition). Washington, DC: U.S. Government Printing Office.

van Driel, B., and Richardson, J. T. (1988). Print media coverage of new religious movements: A longitudinal study. *Journal of Communication, 38*(3), 37–61.

Van Gundy, A. B. (1992). *Idea power: Techniques and resources to unleash creativity in your organization.* New York: AMACON.

Van Maanen, J. (1988). *Tales of the field: On writing ethnography.* Chicago: University of Chicago Press.

Vesperi, M. D. (1985). *City of green benches: Growing old in a new downtown.* Ithaca, NY: Cornell University Press.

von Hoffman, N. (1970). Sociological snoopers. *Transaction, 7,* 4–6.

von Oech, R. (1983). *A whack on the side of the head: How to unlock your mind for innovation.* New York: Warner Books.

Wagstaff, G. F. (1991). Suggestibility: A social psychological approach. In J. F. Schumaker (Ed.), *Human suggestibility: Advances in theory, research, and application.* New York: Routledge.

Walsh, J. P., Kiesler, S., Sproull, L. S., and Hesse, B. W. (1992). Self-selected and randomly selected respondents in a computer network survey. *Public Opinion Quarterly, 56,* 241–244.

Wax, R. H. (1971). *Doing fieldwork: Warnings and advice.* Chicago: University of Chicago Press.

Webb, E. J., Campbell, D. T., Schwartz, R. D., Sechrest, L., and Grove, J. B. (1981). *Nonreactive measures in the social sciences* (2nd ed.). Boston: Houghton Mifflin.

Webster's ninth new collegiate dictionary (1991). Springfield, MA: Merriam-Webster.

Weick, K. E. (1985). Systematic observational methods. In G. Lindzey and E. Aronson (Eds.), *Handbook of social psychology* (3rd ed.). New York: Random House.

Weiss, C. (1972). *Evaluation research: Methods of assessing program effectiveness.* Englewood Cliffs, NJ: Prentice-Hall.

Weiss, C. H. (1987). Evaluating social programs: What have we learned? *Society, 25*(1), 40–45.

Weiss, R. S. (1994). *Learning from strangers: The art and method of qualitative interview studies.* New York: The Free Press.

West, S. G., Newsom, J. T., and Fenaughty, A. M. (1992). Publication trends in *JPSP:* Stability and change in topics, methods, and theories across two decades. *Personality and Social Psychology Bulletin, 18,* 475–484.

Wheeler, L. (1988). My year in Hong Kong: Some observations about social behavior. *Personality and Social Psychology Bulletin, 14,* 410–420.

Whitehill, B. V., and McDonald, B. A. (1993). Improving learning persistence of military personnel by enhancing motivation in a technical training program. *Simulation and Gaming, 24,* 294–313.

Whyte, W. F. (1951). Observational field work methods. In M. Jahoda, M. Deutsch, and S. W. Cook (Eds.), *Research methods in the social sciences.* New York: Dryden Press.

Wilson, D. M., and Donnerstein, E. (1976). Legal and ethical aspects of nonreactive social psychological research: An excursion into the public mind. *American Psychologist, 31,* 765–773.

Wilson, T. D., DePaulo, B. M., Mook, D. G., and Klaaren, K. J. (1993). Scientists' evaluations of research: The biasing effects of the importance of the topic. *Psychological Science, 4,* 322–325.

Wolfe, J. (1993). A history of business teaching games in English-speaking and post-Socialist countries. *Simulation and Gaming, 24,* 446–463.

Wolfe, T. (1974, December). Why they aren't writing the great American novel anymore: A treatise on the varieties of realistic experience. *Esquire, 272,* pp. 152–158.

Wood, J. M., Bootzin, R. R., Rosenhan, D., Nolen-Hoeksema, S., and Jourden, F. (1992). Effects of the 1989 San Francisco earthquake on frequency and content of nightmares. *Journal of Abnormal Psychology, 101,* 219–224.

Worchel, S. (1986). The influence of contextual variables on interpersonal spacing. *Journal of Nonverbal Behavior, 10,* 230–254.

Xu, M., Bates, B. J., and Schweitzer, J. C. (1993). The impact of messages on survey participation in answering machine households. *Public Opinion Quarterly, 57,* 232–237.

Yarnold, P. R., and Grimm, L. G. (1988). Interpersonal dominance of Type As and Bs during involved group discussions. *Journal of Applied Social Psychology, 18,* 787–795.

Zajonc, R. B. (1965). Social facilitation. *Science, 149,* 269–274.

Zajonc, R. B. (1989). Styles of explanation in social psychology. *European Journal of Social Psychology, 19,* 345–368.

Zimbardo, P. G., Haney, C., Banks, W. C., and Jaffe, D. (1982). The psychology of imprisonment: Privation, power, and pathology. In J. C. Brigham and L. S. Wrightsman (Eds.), *Contemporary issues in social psychology* (4th ed.). Monterey, CA: Brooks/Cole.

Zurcher, L. A. (1988). Social roles and interaction. In P. C. Higgins and J. M. Johnson (Eds.), *Personal sociology.* New York: Praeger.

Name Index

Abelson, R. P., 231, 304–305, 319–320
Aber, C. S., 122
Abt, C. C., 288
Adair, J. G., 222, 260–261
Adams, J. L., 10
Adler, P., 44, 65
Adler, P. A., 42, 44, 50, 65–66
Adorno, T. W., 106
Allport, G. W., 321
Altman, I., 79
Anastasi, A., 20
Anderson, C. A., 103
Aronson, E., 101, 122, 231, 241, 266, 270, 299, 306, 318
Asch, S., 259–260, 262, 268, 270
Auster, C. J., 130

Babbie, E. R., 196
Bacon, F., 60
Bakeman, R., 95–96
Bales, R. F., 92–93
Bandura, A., 142
Banks, C., 307
Barber, T. X., 265
Baron, R. S., 8
Bartlett, J., 13
Barzun, J., 134, 136
Bass, R. F., 95–96
Bates, B. J, 193
Baum, A., 225
Baum, W. K., 105
Baumrind, D., 260
Bell-Dolan, D. J., 80, 82, 91
Benney, M., 170
Benton, J. E., 160
Berkowitz, L., 23
Berkun, M. M., 33–35
Bernardin, H. J., 87
Beveridge, W. I. B., 11, 15
Bienias, J., 155
Billiet, J., 169
Bishop, G. F., 151, 156

Biswas, A., 130
Blair, E., 154
Bluck, S., 126, 128, 134
Bodenhausen, G. V., 248–249, 252, 259–260, 262, 269
Boehm, A. E., 99
Boorstin, D. A., 37
Borg, M. J., 170
Bowen, R. W., 234
Bowers, C., 317
Bowers, K. S., 6
Box, G. E. P., 244
Boyd, R. S., 119, 121
Bradburn, N. M., 154–155, 158–159, 175, 185, 190, 201
Brecher, E. M., 183
Brecher, J., 183
Bretl, D. J., 122, 129
Brewer, M. B., 231, 241, 266, 270, 312
Brill, A. A., 12
Brinberg, D., 99–100
Briton, N. J., 128
Brown, C., 163
Brush, S. G., 2, 105
Buck, R., 81
Buford, B., 64, 66, 69
Burchard, W., 84
Burge, D. A., 80, 82, 91
Burnside, A. E., 123
Burton, S., 154
Bush, G., 21
Campbell, D. T., 209–211, 216–217, 225–226, 231, 247, 255, 261, 268, 270–271, 285
Cannell, C. F., 193, 201
Cantor, J., 122, 129
Carlet, V., 130
Carlsmith, J. M., 231, 241, 266, 270
Carlson, C. I., 91
Carmelli, D., 80
Carpenter, E. H., 191

Cartwright, D., 133
Cash, W. B. Jr., 141, 143, 145, 159, 164
Chaiken, S., 208
Chamberlain, T. C., 22
Chamblin, M. C., 190
Chelimsky, E., 274, 284
Chow, S. L., 265
Christensen, L., 260
Cialdini, R. B., 3, 45, 192
Clark, H. H., 146–147, 156, 158, 163, 173
Clinton, W., 176
Cochran, N., 117, 293
Cohen, J., 96
Colasanto, D., 159
Coleman, L., 193
Collison, M. N.-K., 1
Cone, J. D., 80
Cook, T. D., 209–211, 216–217, 225–226, 231, 255, 274, 276, 285, 297, 299–300
Cooper, H., 265
Cooper, J., 265
Copeland, J. T., 10
Cordray, D. S., 215, 226
Corteen, R. S., 91, 123, 125, 127, 130
Cott, J., 142
Couper, M. P., 192
Courtwright, D., 54
Cox, E. P., 157
Cronbach, L. J., 6, 276, 283
Csikszentmihalyi, M., 76
Cutler, B. L., 308, 310

Dabbs, J. M., Jr., 23
Dalton, D. R., 223–225
Daly, J. L., 160
Dandoy, A. C., 256
Danielson, E. S., 118
Darley, J. M., 267–268
Darwin, C., 11, 16
Davidson, J. W., 136
Dawes, R. M., 173, 316

Dean, J., 132–133
DeNeve, K. M., 103
Dexter, H. R., 308, 310
Dickson, W. J., 221–222
Dillehay, R. C., 321
Dillman, D. A., 177, 189, 192, 194–196, 199–200
Dipboye, R. L., 62
Donnerstein, E., 230–231
Dorsey, B. L., 91
Doty, R. M., 108–111
Doughty, J., 291, 297
Dowd, M., 196, 198
Driver, M. J., 123
Dumont, J., 291, 297
Duncan, M. C., 132
Duncan, S., 265
Durdan, C. A., 78
Dushenko, T. W., 261
Dykman, B. M., 83

Eagly, A. H., 208
Eder, D., 56
Edney, J. J., 316
Eisenberger, R., 74
Elliott, J. E., 313
Ellis, C., 29, 68–71
Ellsworth, P. C., 218–219
Elstein, A. S., 307
Epstein, Y., 248
Eskew, D. E., 306, 308
Evans, G. W., 78, 91
Evans, L., 111, 113
Evans, R. I., 142
Eysenck, H. J., 186, 212

Fair, J., 281
Faludi, S., 1
Fenaughty, A. M., 238
Festinger, L., 43, 69
Figueredo, A. J., 274–276
Finger, S. C., 313
Finkel, S. E., 170
Fischhoff, B., 105
Fiske, S. T., 14, 61–62
Fleming, A., 11, 235
Fleming, R., 225
Fletcher, G. J. O., 13
Foley, L. A., 310
Forsyth, B. H., 200
Fossey, D., 73
Foster, S. L., 80, 82, 91
Fowler, F. J., Jr., 145, 150–152, 154, 158, 162–163, 165, 168–169, 170, 172, 177, 184, 187, 200–201
Freeman, D., 58–59, 71
Freeman, H. E., 274, 277, 282, 287–288, 299
Freud, S., 12, 79, 119

Frey, J. H., 168, 188, 190, 203
Friedman, H. S., 79
Friedman, N., 265
Frost, R., 240
Fuller, B., 14

Gabel, L. L., 277
Gabennesch, H., 105
Gallup, G., 203
Gardner, M., 234
Gastorf, J., 267
Gauch, H. G., 304
Geen, R. G., 266
Geer, J. G., 145
Geller, E. S., 78, 96
Gergen, K. J., 5, 268
Gilbert, D. T., 273
Gilbert, N., 1
Giles, H., 77
Gilovich, T., 3, 15–16, 24, 37–38
Glass, D., 258–259
Glenn, N. D., 197
Glueckauf, R. L., 150
Goffman, E., 26, 28, 41
Goldberg, R., 31
Goldstein, A. G., 256
Goodall, J., 73, 100
Gordon, A. C., 117
Gottman, J. M., 95–96
Graff, H. F., 134, 136
Grant, U. S., 123, 126
Greenberg, J., 7, 242–243, 306, 308
Greene, J. C., 291, 297
Greene, M., 121
Greenwald, J., 176
Griffin, D. R., 73–74
Grimm, L. G., 77
Grotevant, H. D., 91
Groves, R. M., 175, 177, 183–184, 192–193, 203
Guerin, B., 82
Guterbock, T. M., 170

Hafferty, F. W., 49
Hall, E. T., 78
Hall, J. A., 128
Haney, C., 307
Hans, V. P., 187, 196
Hardin, G., 315, 323
Hardwick, B., 105
Harre, R., 306
Harris, L., 44
Harris, M. J., 6, 81
Harris, S., 22, 156, 286, 309
Hawkins, C., 84
Hawkins, J. W., 122
Hawkins, R. P., 86, 91
Hayes, S. C., 91
Hazelrigg, P. J., 265

Hecht, P. R., 78
Hedrick, T. E., 120, 248
Hendrick, C., 254, 263
Henshel, R. L., 268
Hill, M. R., 117–118, 133
Hinckley, J., Jr., 196
Hite, S., 1, 20–21
Holmes, S., 5, 18
Holsti, O. R., 128
Hooker, J., 123
Hooper, F. H., 132
House, C. C., 192
Hovland, C. I., 208
Huber, M. A., 308
Humphrey, L., 34–35
Humphrey, R., 27–28
Humphreys, K., 276
Hungerford, M., 14
Hunter, J. S., 244
Hunter, W. G., 244
Hurst, N. W., 289
Huynh, C. L., 222
Hyman, H., 170

Inness, J. C., 85

Jackson, D. N., 150
Jacob, H., 115, 136
Jaffe, A. J., 234
James, R. M., 84
Jenkins, C. D., 289
Jensen, K., 132
Jones, E. E., 25
Jones, F., 230
Jones, R. A., 9, 76, 189, 192, 215, 248, 263, 265
Jones, S. R. G., 222
Jordan, B., 155
Jorgensen, D. L., 44, 50, 52–53, 55, 68, 71
Judd, C. M., 1
Jussim, L., 9

Kalsher, M. J., 78
Kalton, G., 201
Kaplan, A., 239, 319–322
Keech, M., 43
Kendrick, D. T., 78
Kerr, N. L., 316
Kershaw, D., 281
Kerwin, J., 310–313. 320
Kidder, L., 99–100
Kidder, L. H., 1
Kimmel, A. J., 33, 66
King, M. J., 280, 283, 289
Kirk, J., 60, 68
Kohn, A., 235
Komorita, S. S., 313, 315–316, 323–324
Kosloski, K., 295–297
Krause, M. S., 117
Krippendorff, K., 131

Kruskal, W., 184
Kunda, G., 44, 46–48, 56, 60, 70, 83, 141

Lam, D. J., 30
Lana, R. E., 247
Langer, E. J., 28
Latane, B., 267-268
Lavrakas, P. J., 162, 168, 170, 176
Lee, R. E., 91, 123, 125–127
LePatner, B., 271
Lepore, S. J., 78, 91
Lessler, J. T., 200
Lester, D., 116
Levine, R. J., 231
Leviton, L. C., 274, 276, 297, 299
Lewin, K., 76, 309
Lewontin, R., 1
Lieberman, M. A., 232
Lindsay, R. C. L., 261
Lindzey, G., 101, 270, 299
Lippmann, W., 248
Locke, E. A., 304, 312–313
Lofland, J., 43, 52–53, 55, 59
Lofland, L. H., 43, 52–53, 55, 59
Lohr, S., 141
Loosveldt, G., 169
Loseke, D. R., 42, 52, 65, 291
Lyberg, L. E., 192
Lysenko, T., 234
Lytle, M. H., 136

MacFarlane, S. W., 78
Macrae, C. N., 242–243, 248–253, 259–260, 262, 269
Madey, S. F., 15–16
Mai, H. P., 160
Malcolm, J., 119
Mangione, T. W., 145, 163, 165, 169, 172
Marks, J., 2
Markus, G. B., 197
Martin, E., 204
Marvell, T. B., 207, 209, 218, 223, 226
Maugh, T. H., II, 66
McCleary, ___, 117
McClellan, G. B., 123
McClendon, M. J., 159
McCormick, C., 91, 123, 125, 127, 130
McCracken, G., 148
McDonald, B. A., 313
McGrath, J. E., 100, 324
McGuire, W. J., 12–13
McKenzie-Mohr, D., 61

McPhee, J., 29
Mead, M., 58–59, 64, 69, 71
Meade, G. G., 123, 126
Memering, D., 38
Merton, R. K., 30
Mesch, D. J., 223–225
Mesmer, F. A., 19
Messner, M. A., 132
Milgram, S., 231, 270
Mill, J. S., 13
Miller, J. C., 231
Miller, M. C., 122
Miller, M. L., 60, 68
Milne, A. B., 248–249, 252, 259–260, 262, 269
Mishler, E. G., 148, 150
Misra, S., 261
Moberg, D. P., 280, 283, 289
Mohr, L. B., 278
Molstad, C., 49–51, 59
Moniz, E., 301
Montgomery, R. J. V., 295–297
Moore, D. W., 203
Moran, G., 308, 310
Morgan, D. L., 172
Morris, J., 29
Morris, R., 23
Morrison, T., 142
Moskowitz, J. M., 297
Mosteller, F., 184, 276–277, 285
Moyers, B., 142
Murphy, C., 117, 137
Myers, D. G., 65

Neale, M. A., 308
Neisser, U., 132–133
Nelson, R. O., 91
Nemeth, C., 318
Neuharth, A., 4, 32
Newcomb, T. M., 63
Newsom, J. T., 238
Nicholls, W. L., II, 192
Nietzel, M. T., 321
Nisbett, R. E., 2, 5, 14, 38
Nixon, R. M., 132–133
Norins, H., 10
Norman, D. A., 75
Northcraft, G. B., 308

O'Brien, D. J., 159
O'Carroll, P. W., 205–206, 218
Occhipinti, S., 307
Oksenberg, L., 193, 201
Oldendick, R. W., 151, 156
Olsen, J. E., 130
Olson, P., 111
Oreskes, M., 178

Orwell, G., 100
Ostrom, T. M., 305
Overman, E. S., 270–271

Palinkas, L. A., 207
Palys, T. S., 319
Parker, K., 1
Parker, S., 56
Parks, C. D., 313, 315–316, 323–324
Pasteur, L., 235
Patchen, M., 315
Payne, S. L., 172
Pearsol, J. A., 277, 291
Pence, E. C., 87
Peshkin, A., 49, 51
Peterson, B. E., 108, 111
Petroski, H., 271
Phillips, A. P., 62
Piazza, T., 193
Piper, D. L., 280, 283, 289
Pirsig, R. M., 3
Pollitt, K., 1
Posavac, E. J., 283
Postman, L., 321
Pratkanis, A., 122
Presser, S., 154

Quittner, A. L., 150

Rappaport, J., 276
Rasinski, K. A., 151–152, 159–161
Rathje, W., 117, 137
Reagan, R., 196
Reeder, G. D., 78
Reid, J. B., 97
Reinfurt, D. W., 227–229
Reis, H. T., 83
Remer, R., 313
Renzaglia, G. A., 82
Repp, A. C., 80
Richard, M. P., 72
Richardson, J. T., 130
Richardson, W. C., 278, 292
Riecken, H. W., 43, 69
Riesman, D., 170
Riessman, C. K., 147
Rips, L. J., 154–155
Roberts, L. J., 87–90, 92, 94–95, 97–99
Roberts, R. M., 235
Roberts, R. R., 82
Robinson, D., 170
Roese, N. J., 260
Roethlisberger, F. F., 221–222
Rogers, T. F., 159
Rohde, S., 170
Ronai, C. R., 49
Roosevelt, A. E., 14

Rose, R. M., 289
Rosenberg, M. J., 81
Rosenhan, D. L., 65
Rosenman, R. H., 80
Rosenthal, R., 265, 290
Rosnow, R. L., 321
Ross, L., 2, 5, 14, 38, 173
Rossi, P. H., 274, 277, 282, 287–288, 299
Rothfeder, J., 100

Sales, S. M., 106–111, 134–135
Samelson, F., 24
Sanchez, M. E., 168
Sato, I., 69
Scarr, S., 5
Schachter, S., 43, 69, 105
Schaeffer, N. C., 153
Schaps, E., 230
Scheper-Hughes, N., 59
Schober, M. F., 146–147, 156, 158, 163, 173
Schroder, H. M., 123, 125
Schur, E. M., 9
Schwarz, N., 155, 157, 160
Schweitzer, J. C., 193
Scott, G. C., 49
Scriven, M., 273, 282, 300
Sechrest, L., 274–276
Seidman, I. E., 148
Shadish, W. R., Jr., 255, 274, 276, 297, 299–300
Shaffer, D. R., 310–313, 320
Shakespeare, W., 50
Shaiken, H., 83
Sharpe, D., 222, 260
Shepard, S., 142
Shevell, S. K., 154–155
Shortell, S. M., 278, 292
Shulman, L. S., 307
Shuy, R. W., 119
Shweder, R. A., 63
Siegal, M., 307
Sigelman, L., 324
Simmons, V. M., 63
Simonton, D. K., 112–113
Singer, E., 159
Singer, J. E., 225, 258–259
Sivak, P. L., 111

Slater, D., 187, 196
Smith, E. R., 1
Smith, T. W., 152
Snyder, M., 15
Solomon, R. L., 257
Spaeth, M. A., 191
Spirer, H. F., 234
Sprafka, S. A., 307
Stack, S., 116
Stanley, J. C., 209–211, 247, 268, 285
Star, S. A., 170
Stasser, G., 305
Stewart, C. J., 141, 143, 145, 159, 164
Stone, P. J., 122, 133
Strack, F., 160
Strathman, A. J., 265
Streufert, S., 123
Strodtbeck, F. L., 84
Suchman, L., 155
Sudman, S., 158–159, 175, 185, 190, 201
Suedfeld, P., 91, 123, 125–128, 130, 134–135
Suls, J., 267
Swan, G. E., 80
Synnott, A., 122–123, 127, 129–130, 135

Tagg, J., 54
Tanur, J. M., 173
Tarnai, J., 199–200
Taylor, S. E., 14, 33, 61–62, 245
Taylor, S. J., 67
Terkel, S., 173
Tetlock, P. E., 124
Teubner, A. L., 82
Thomas, R. D., 4
Tomerlin, J., 103–104
Tonkin, E., 105
Topf, M., 97
Tourangeau, R., 159–161
Townsend, R., 4
Triplett, N., 237–239, 269
Trochim, M. K., 218
Tuchfarber, A. J., 151, 156
Tufte, E. R., 204
Turner, C. F., 204
Tuttle, R. H., 73

Twain, M., 211

Unrau, Y. A., 275
Urbina, S., 20

Valenstein, E. S., 300–301
van Driel, B., 130
Van Langenhove, L., 306
Van Maanen, J., 41, 172
VanGundy, A. B., 8, 24
Vaske, J. J., 82
Vesperi, M. D., 49
Vicary, J. M., 122
von Hoffman, N., 34
von Oech, R., 10, 38–39

Wagstaff, G. F., 265
Walsh, J. P., 182
Wax, R. H., 51, 64–65
Weick, K. E., 74, 101
Weinberg, R. A., 99
Weiss, C. H., 274, 276, 280, 291–292
Weiss, R. S., 140–141, 144, 147–148
West, S. G., 238
Wheeler, L., 6, 30
Whicker, M. L., 324
Whitehill, B. V., 313
Whyte, W. F., 65
Wilde, O., 13
Wilson, D. M., 230–231
Wilson, T. D., 284
Winter, D. G., 108, 111
Wolfe, J., 313
Wolfe, T., 116
Wood, J. M., 210
Worchel, S., 79
Wren, C., 50

Xu, M., 193

Yang, C. F., 30
Yarnold, P. R., 77

Zajonc, R. B., 7–8, 14
Zanna, M. P., 61
Zhao, S., 154
Zimbardo, P. G., 307–308
Zurcher, L. A., 49

Subject Index

Abortion statistics, 21
Accidental discoveries, see Serendipity
Addiction Research Foundation, 230
Adolescent life in Samoa, 58–59, 64, 69, 71
Advice books, 4
Age, interviewer/interviewee, 170
Aggression, relation to temperature, 78, 103
Air traffic controllers, 189
Alternatives, closed-ended questions and, 155–156
Ambiguity, threat to internal validity, 215
American Library Association, 118
American Society of Archivists, 118
Analogue experiments, 309–313
Analytic files, 56, 148–149
APA, Committee on Ethical Practices in Research, 84, 85
Aphorisms, hypothesis formation and, 13–14
Applied explanatory power, 321
Applied research, 75
  versus basic research, 75–77
Archival research
  choosing denominator, 115
  choosing indices, 111, 113, 115
  defined, 104
  nonreactive nature of, 116
  selective deposit and survival, 116–117
Archives
  access to, 119
  defined, 104
Army recruits and psychological stress, 33–34
Artifacts, see Confounding variables
Artificiality, in experiments, 268
Assessment
  observer reliability and, 95–98
  program evaluation and, 282–283
Attention, observation and, 61
Attention-feedback-regulation cycle, 81–82

Attribution, internal validity and, 211–213
Attrition
  panel studies and, 197
  threat to internal validity, 214
Authoritarianism, 106–110
Autobiographical questions, 154–155
Automobile acceleration, 103–104
Avis, 4

Balanced replication, 254
Base-rate information, 14
Basic research, 74–75
  versus applied research, 75–77
Battered women's shelters, 42–43, 52, 60, 65
Behavior
  coding categories, 90–94
  context of, 5
  of experiment subjects, 264–267
  extralinguistic, 77
  functional significance of, 5
  nonverbal, 77–78
  patterns of, 52–53
  socially desirable, 81
  spatial, 78–79
Behavior coding, 86
  categories for, 90–94
Betrayal funnel, 26
Bias
  interview questions and, 157
  nonresponse, 192–193
  participant observation and, 60–68
  self-selection, 182
  social desirability, 158
Bicycle racers, competition and performance, 237–238
"Blind," 266
Blind scoring, 130
Blocking, 244–245
Blue Cross, 286–287
Boundary drawing, 48
Brewery workers, 49–50, 51, 59
Broad Street pump, 212

Categories
    behavior coding and, 90–94
    guidelines for construction, 128–130
CATI, *see* Computer-assisted telephone
    interviewing
Causality, ambiguity about, 215
Census, 7, 137, 176, 194
Centers for Disease Control, 21
Chance, experiment results and, 263–264
Change, versus progress, 205
Chimpanzee behavior, 100
Class (social), interview and, 170
Closed-ended questions, 151–158
    response alternatives, 155–156
Coding
    behavior, 90
    content analysis, 123–125
Cohen's Kappa, 96
Cohort study, 197
Committee on Cognition and Survey
    Research of the Social Science Re-
    search Council, 173
Committee on Ethical Practices in Re-
    search of the American Psychologi-
    cal Association, 84, 85
Community Mental Health Centers
    program, 280
Compensatory equalization of treat-
    ments, threat to internal validity,
    215
Compensatory rivalry, threat to internal
    validity, 216
Competition, effect on performance,
    237–238
Computer-assisted telephone inter-
    viewing (CATI), 191–192
Computer simulation, 305, 324
Concealed identity, 65
Concealed weapon law, 205–206
Conceptual replication, 25, 254
Conformity, 259–260, 268
Confounding variables, 262–262
Confrontation-explication process, 319–320
Construct validity, 20, 60
Consumer Reports, 14
Content analysis, 121–134
    abuses of, 133–134
    defined, 122,
    nonreactive nature of, 134
    versus systematic observation, 133
Context effects, 159–161
Contingency questions, 189
Control, 216–223, 241
    defined, 216
    illusion of, 28
Control groups
    designing research and, 218–219, 223,
        225
    ethics, 231–232
    interrupted time series and, 223–226
    laboratory experiments and, 241

Convenience sample, 182
Corporate cultures, 44–49
Cost–benefit analysis, 287–288
    ethics and, 290
Cost-effectiveness analysis, 288
Cost-effectiveness ratio, 288
    personal perspective and, 288–289
Coverage error, 181
Cover story, 262
Creativity, 38–39
    inhibitions to, 9–11
Criticism, in evaluating explanatory
    methods, 23
Cross-sectional survey, 196–197
Curiosity, as source of hypotheses,
    11–12

Data graphics, 204, 234
Data sharing, 120
Date rape, 1
Debriefing, 261–262
Deception, 260–262
    see also Ethics
Deduction, 18
Demand characteristics, 265
Dependent variable, 186, 239, 243
Depth interviewing, *see* Qualitative in-
    terview
Description, 29–30
    survey research and, 176
Descriptive reporting, 43–45
Designing research, 207, 270
    factorial, 250–251
    random assignment, 246
Differentiation, content analysis and,
    124–125
Diffusion of responsibility, 268
Diffusion of treatments, threat to inter-
    nal validity, 215
Disciplined abstractions, 44
Divorce laws, no-fault, 207–210, 223,
    226
Dominant responses, 7–8
Doomsday cults, 43, 69
Double-barreled questions, 154
Driver's license exam, 19–20
Drug dealers, 42

Echo, interview technique, 146
Elderly drivers, and safety, 111–113
Element, *see* Unit of analysis
Emergent context, of behavior, 5
Empirical approach, 127
    versus rational approach, 73–74
Employees, motivation of, 44–49
Encoding, 61–62
Epidemiology, 112, 212
Ethics, 32–36
    archival research and, 118–121
    defined, 33
    evaluation research and, 290

field experiments and, 230–232
  observation and, 83–86
  observing illegal/immoral activities,
    67
  participant observation and, 65–68
Ethical misconduct, in research, 235
Ethnographic research, *see* Participant
  observation
Ethnography, 29, 41
Ethology, 73
Evaluation apprehension, 81, 266
Evaluation research
  choosing indices, 279–280
  defined, 274
  implementation, 280–283
  multiple interest groups, 292–293
Exact replication, 25, 254
Expense, survey planning and, 192
Experience sampling method, 76
Experiment
  analytic function, 267–268
  compared to simulation, 310
  defined, 239
  design, 255–259
  sensitizing function, 268
Experimental realism, 266
Experimenter expectancy effects, 265–266
Explanation
  generating, 11–12
  survey research and, 176–177
  theoretical, 7–8
  untested, 31–32
  see also Hypotheses
Explanatory power, simulation and, 321
External validity, 21, 268
  replication and, 254
Extralinguistic behavior, 77
Exxon Valdez, 207

Face-to-face interview, 188–190
Factorial design, 250–251
Fallacies, 38
Family size and intelligence, 14
Feminism, in Hong Kong, 30
Field experiment, versus laboratory re-
  search, 208
Field notes, 53–55
Fieldwork, 41
  see also Participant observation
Fishing communities, 70–71
Fixed-response question, *see* Closed-
  ended questions
Flight simulators, 304, 317
Focus groups, 172, 184–185, 200
Formative evaluation, 282
Freudian slips, 79
Fundamentalist schools, 49, 51
Funnel sequence, 159–160

Games, simulation research and,
  313–317
Gannett Company, 4, 32

Garbage Project, 117, 137
Gender, interviewer/interviewee, 170
Gender representation
  in advertising, 122–123, 127, 129, 130
  in televised sports, 132
Generating explanations, 11–12
Genius, emergence of, 112–113
Graphs, *see* Data graphics

Halo effect, 87
Hawthorne effect, 221–222
Hawthorne Western Electric plant, 222
Heuristic fertility, 319
High Tech Corporation, 46–49, 56, 60, 70
History, threat to internal validity, 212,
  224
HMS Beagle, 11
Home-cruiser program, 23, 113–115
Homing behavior, 73–74
Homosexual behavior, public, 34
Hospital patients, abuse of, 67
Hypotheses
  analogy and, 12–13
  aphorisms and, 13–14
  curiosity and, 11–12
  folk wisdom and, 13–15
  generating, 23–24
  multiple, 21–22
  situational analysis, 12
  see also Theory

Illusion of control, 28
Imitation, of treatment, 215
Independent variable
  defined, 186
  experimentation and, 239, 241–243,
    250–251
Index
  of authoritarianism, 107–110
  selection for archival research, 111,
    113, 115
Induction, 18
Industriousness, and rewards, 75 -76
Inference errors, 16
Informed consent, 35–36, 66, 84, 119,
  159, 230–231
Insanity defense, public reaction to,
  185–188, 195, 198
Institutional Review Board (IRB), 35
Instrumentation, threat to internal va-
  lidity, 213, 224
Integration, content analysis and,
  125–126
Integrative complexity, 125–126, 130
Integrative complexity scale, 124
Intense interviewing, *see* Qualitative in-
  terview
Interaction Process Analysis, 92
Interaction with selection, threat to in-
  ternal validity, 214 - 215
Internal validity
  defined, 211

replication and, 254
threats to, 211–217, 229, 255, 258, 262
Interobserver agreement, 96
Interpreting social exchange/human behavior, 5
Interrupted time series, 223–226
with switching replications, 225–226
Intervention, *see* Treatment
Interview
face-to-face, 188–189, 190
preparation for, 142
probing techniques, 145–146
telephone, 188–189, 190–192
types, 140
Interview guide, 141–144
Interview schedule, 161–165
example, 166–167
Interviewer
effects, 170
error, 172
training, 168–169, 172
Intimate familiarity, 207
Invasion of privacy, 84–86, 119–121, 230
using computer, 100–101
Inverted funnel sequence, *see* Funnel sequence
IRB, *see* Institutional Review Board

Journalists, 43–44
Juries, 310–312

Knowledge, ordinary vs. scientific, 2

Laboratory experiment, defined, 239
Laboratory simulation, 27
Language, interviews and, 147
Laid-off executives, 141, 143–144, 148–149
Leading questions, 155
Legal/ethical boundaries, 84
Loaded questions, 157
Longitudinal survey, 197–198

Magazines, questionnaires in, 178
Main effect, 252
Manipulation, experimental, 239–243
Matching, assigning subjects to conditions, 244–246
Maturation, threat to internal validity, 212–213
MCAT scores, 220–221
Medical interview, and role-playing, 307
Memory distortions
informant, 63 -64
observer, 63
Mental illness, history of treatment for, 300–301
Michigan Model Projects Specialized Respite Care Program, 293–297
Middle-school peer activities, 56–57
Military leadership, 91, 123–126, 130

Mock jury research, 310–312
Modeling, simulation and, 304–305
Mortality, threat to internal validity, 214
Motives for human behavior, 5
Multiple hypotheses, 21–22
Multiple operationism, 25
see also Triangulation of measurement
Multistage cluster sample, 183
Mundane files, 56
Mutual help groups, 86–90

National Archives and Records Services, 104
National Boards, 220–221
National Health Interview Survey, 176
National Park Service, 180–181
Negative income-tax program evaluation, 281
New York Times, 132, 198
New York Times Magazine, 122, 127, 129, 130
Nicotine, physiological reaction to, 258
Noise, relation to stress, 258, 259
Noncoercion, 84
Nonequivalent groups, 207–211
see also Control groups
Nonreactive methods, 116, 134
Nonresponse bias, 192–196
Nonverbal behavior, 77–78
Norms, 305
North Carolina seat belt law, 226–230
Notes, field, 53–55
Nursing homes, 72
mortality rate of applicants, 232
Nuts game, 316

Objectives, for evaluation research, 277–278
Observation
defined, 72–73
errors, 16–17
importance of, 15–18
perceptual biases and, 60–64
see also Participant observation
Observational systems, 86
in early childhood settings, 99
Observer(s)
assessment of, 95–98
training, 88, 94–95
Observer drift, 97
Obtrusive observation, 80–83
Occupational roles, influence of, 27–28
Office assignment, 242, 243
Olympic judging, 87
One-group pretest-posttest design, 209–210
One-shot case study, 208–209
One-sided event, 15–16
Open-ended questions, 145–146
Operationalization
archival research and, 110–116
defined, 24–25

of evaluation objectives, 279–280
question construction and, 151–158
survey research and, 179–180
Optical illusions, 17
Oral history, 105
Outcome line, 278–279
Oversight bias, 284

Panel study, 197
Parole officers, 117–118
Participant observation, 26, 41–44
appropriateness of, 68–69
behaviors and their notation, 53–55
compared to journalism, 43 -44
defined, 41
ethics of, 65–68
Patched-up designs, 218
Penicillin, 11
Perception, observation and, 60
Personnel, evaluation research and, 289–292
Photographs, as field evidence, 54
Pilot test, *see* Pretesting
Planned interventions, 207–226
Plausible alternative explanations, 207
laboratory experiments and, 263–267
ruling out, 216, 218–226
Policy, defined, 274–275
Political candidates, news coverage and, 131–132
Politics, evaluation research and, 274
Polling, political, 203–204
Population of interest, 180
Posttest-only design, 210, 218, 256
Prediction, versus hypothesis, 7
Predictive validity, 20
Pre-existing conceptual scheme, 63
Pre-interview expectations, 62–63
Pretesting
of experiment subjects, 247
of interview questions, 165, 168
of survey questions, 201
Pretest-posttest design, 219, 256–257
Primacy effect, 63
Priming, *see* Encoding
Prisoners and guards, role-playing, 307–308
Prisoner's dilemma, 313–315, 318
Privacy
defined, 84
see also Invasion of privacy
Proactive records, 117
Probability, 282
Probes, interview technique, 145–146, 165
Program
defined, 275
elements for evaluation, 277–279
implementation of, 280–282
Program administrators, evaluation research and, 292

Program personnel, evaluation research and, 289–292
Progress, *see* Change
Prompts, 155
Proxemics, 78
Pseudoscience, 234
Psychiatric patients and self-determination, 26

Qualitative interview
analysis of, 148–150
guide, 141–144
transcripts, 147–148
versus nondirective interview, 141
Quantification, 150–151
Quantitative research versus qualitative, 283–285
Quasi-experiment, 206, 294, 300
Questionnaire, 188–189, 192, 193–194
appearance of, 194–196
economics of, 192
magazine, 178
revising, 200–201
see also Surveys
Questions
closed-ended, 151–158
contingency, 189
open-ended, 145–146
outlining, 184–188
sequence of, 158–160
Quota matrix, 244–245

Race, interviewer/interviewee, 170
Random assignment, 246
Random numbers, 246, 325–327
Random sample, 83
Randomization, 246–247, 300
Randomized trials, 285–287
Rational approach, 127
versus empirical approach, 73–74
Reactivity
archival research and, 116
observation and, 80–83
in assessing observer reliability, 97
Reciprocation, 45
Recording behavior, 80, 82, 88
to assess reliability, 96
Records, *see* Archives
Relative frequency expressions, 153
Reliability, 18–20, 59–60, 95–98, 204
defined, 19
versus validity, 157
Remedial reading program evaluation, 281–282
Repetition, as interview technique, 146
Replication, 25, 253–254
Reporters, *see* Journalists
Representative sample, 181
Research
basic versus applied, 75–77
design, 207, 270

evaluation, 274
nature and component of, 2–5
Research interview, 139
Resentful demoralization, threat to internal validity, 216
Resistance to persuasion, 12–13
Respite care, 293–297
Response alternatives, 155–156
Retrospective context, of behavior, 5
Right not to be harmed by research, 33–34
Right to privacy, 33–34, 68
Right to refuse to participate, 34–35
Role, 305
Role-playing
defined, 306
simulation research and, 305–308
Role–rule framework, 308
Rumors, transmission of, 321

Sacred cows, 6
Samoa, adolescent life in, 58–59, 64, 69, 71
Sampling
content analysis and, 130–133
survey research and, 180–184
Sampling error, 178
Sampling frame, 181
Sampling interval, 183
San Francisco earthquake, 210
SCIENCEnet, 182
Scientific research, defined, 3
Seat-belt use, 78
Selection
self, 182
interation with maturation, 222
threat to internal validity, 214
Selective deposit, 116–117, 133
Selective survival, 117, 133
Self-description, 134
Self-selection, sample bias and, 182
Sensitizing function, 268
Sequence, of questions, 158–160
Serendipity, 235
Silence, as interview technique, 146
Simple random sample, 183
Simulation
compared to experiment, 310
computer, 305, 324
defined, 304, 305
evaluation of, 317–322
Simulation games, 313–317
Simulation gap, 320
Single-factor design, 251
Situationism, 38
Snowball sampling, 144
Social class, interviews and, 170
Social desirability bias, 158
Social dilemmas, 323–324
Social Learning and Imitation, 142
Social norms, 305–306

Social salience, 61–62
Social trap, 316
Socially desirable behaviors, 81
Solomon four-group design, 257–258
Spatial behavior, 78–79
Standardized interview, 140
operationalization, 151 -158
Static group comparison, 210
Statistical analysis, 263–264
Statistical regression, threat to internal validity, 214
Statistics, misuse of, 234
Stereotype
benefits for cognitive resources, 249–253
creativity and, 10–11
word derivation, 248
Stratified sample, 183–184
Stress reduction, 244
Stress, coping response, 256
Subject compliance, 264–266
Subliminal advertising, 122
Summative evaluation, 283
Surgeon General's Report on Smoking, 14
Survey
administration of, 188–196
cross-sectional, 196–197
errors, 177–179, 192–196, 203
functions of, 175–177
insanity defense example, 185–188, 195
longitudinal, 196–198
mixed-mode, 198–200
reliability and, 204
telephone, 188–189, 190–192, 203
Syllogisms, 16
Systematic observational methods, 101
Systematic random sample, 183

Table of random numbers, 246, 325–327
Tailored design, 218
Taped lectures, effect on performance, 219–223
Telepathic communication, 12
Telephone answering machines, effect on nonresponse, 193
Television, sex roles and occupational status, 128
Testing, threat to internal validity, 213
Testing the hypothesis, 255
Theory
building, 29–32
defined, 29
nature of, 7
simulation and, 319
verification, 29, 31–32
see also Hypotheses
Threat
authoritarianism and, 106–110
to internal validity, 210–217, 229, 255, 258, 262

Time, 176
Total Survey Design, 177–201
Tragedy of the commons, 315–316, 232
Training interviewers, 168–169, 172
   case study, 169
Training observers, 88, 94–95
   use of videotape recording in, 95
Transposition, experiments and, 309
Treatment
   compensatory equalization of, 215
   designing research and, 206–211,
     216–226
   diffusion/imitation of, 215
   laboratory experiments and, 242–243
Triangulation of measurement, 25–28,
   110, 324
Two-sided event, 15–16

Unfounded implicit baseline compari-
   son, 240
United States Bureau of the Census, 7,
   137, 176, 194
Unit of analysis, 180
University departmentalization, 10–11
Unrepresentative sample, 183
Unscheduled interview, *see* Qualitative
   interview
Unstructured interview, *see* Qualitative
   interview

Untreated control group design, 210–211
USA Today, 4

Vaccination analogy, 12–13
Validity, 18–21, 99–100
   archival research and, 116–118
   defined, 20
   observation and, 79–80
   simulation and, 320–322
   versus reliability, 157
   see also External validity; Internal va-
     lidity
Variables
   dependent, 186, 239, 243
   independent, 186, 239, 241–243,
     250–251
Verification, 29, 31–32

War games, 313
Watergate hearings, 132–133
Welfare payments, 281
Wendy's Restaurants, 4
Women and Love, 1
Women, attitude toward parenting, 198
Workplace
   computerized observation of, 83
   disputes in, 223, 224–225

Yankelovich Partners, Inc., 176

ABOUT THE BOOK

Editor: Peter Farley

Project Editor: Carol J. Wigg

Copy Editor: Norma Roche

Production Manager: Christopher Small

Book Design: Bessas and Ackerman

Cover Design: Christopher Small and Jefferson Johnson

Book Production in QuarkXpress: Michele Ruschhaupt

Book and Cover Manufacturer: Best Book Manufacturers